GARDENS
ARE FOR EATING

By the same author

GARDENING WITH EASE
GARDENING IN THE EAST
GARDENING FROM THE GROUND UP
AMERICA'S GREAT PRIVATE GARDENS

GARDENS
ARE FOR EATING

Stanley Schuler

THE MACMILLAN COMPANY, NEW YORK, NEW YORK
COLLIER-MACMILLAN LIMITED, LONDON

The Macmillan Company
866 Third Avenue, New York, N.Y. 10022
Collier-Macmillan Canada Ltd., Toronto, Ontario

Library of Congress Catalog Card Number: 74-126511
First Printing
Printed in the United States of America

Contents

Part One
Pleasures and Basics

1

The Joys of a Food Garden

One of my oldest and pleasantest memories is of the vegetable garden behind my grandfather's summer cottage at Mattapoisett, Massachusetts. To a child it looked huge; and in actual fact, I think it was unusually large. It was filled with carrots, beets, turnips, rutabagas, Romaine lettuce, green and wax beans, limas, Country Gentleman and some kind of yellow corn, parsnips, salsify, kohlrabi (Grandfather had a sweet tooth for kohlrabi), and probably lots of other things. It also included a small plot which was mine alone.

I loved the garden for many reasons: Because I put in small seeds which turned into food. Because I adored my grandfather and enjoyed working with him. Because Grandmother turned the produce into simple but tasty dishes which we ate on the verandah overlooking the country road and little Mattapoisett River.

I don't recall that there were any fruit trees that counted for anything on the property. Maybe a Seckel pear, but little else. And except for an old grape vine, there were no small fruits because the fields and woods in the neighborhood abounded in them. We picked raspberries at some forgotten place; blackberries down by the water company's pumping station; blueberries and huckleberries through the open woods across the river. And Grandfather always made a fuss about the Portuguese families that came out from New Bedford and swiped the elderberries which grew in profusion in the narrow strip between road and river.

As I say, it is a pleasant memory. But more to the point, just living with the garden and the wild fruits was an experience which had a life-long effect on me. I like anything to do with gardens, but I am mad about gardens for eating.

During my school years, of course, I was a lot more interested in other things. But since I married, I have had some sort of food garden every summer. At first it was designed to extend our budget. Then came World War II and a bountiful Victory garden. Then, having moved to a place with very little cultivatable land, I was forced to cut back in size; and gradually the pines bordering the patch grew and shaded me down still further in size. Then we built a new house in the middle of a wide-open Greenwich, Connecticut, meadow and suddenly, despite the fact that our family had more or less flown the coop, I was back in big-time gardening with many vegetables and increasing numbers of fruits. And now—again suddenly—having tired of the pressures of the metropolitan area, we are in the beautiful little town of Lyme, Connecticut, and I am savoring plans to turn a small, flat, sunswept pasture into corn, melons, and whatnot.

I know why food gardening appeals to me. And I can make a good guess why it appeals to some other people. Yet I am interested in a rather mystified way that today more and more families seem to be raising fruits and vegetables. In this age of affluence when everyone is boating, golfing, traveling, cocktailing—doing a thousand and one things to amuse themselves—why this trend which can be described only as practical and somewhat arduous? I think there are three reasons, all stemming from the single fact that, despite the undeniable merits of the U.S. food industry, it still fails to satisfy a great many of us.

1. The gourmets, whether they be genuine or simply imitative, cannot always find in the markets the special items they seek. Shallots, fresh marjoram, finger-length carrots, quinces, beach plums, lychees—many things along this line are hard to come by. So the determined gourmet takes things into his own hands and, where possible, raises his own food.

2. Many, many more people are just plain bored with the fare offered by the supermarkets. This is an unkindness to farmers, packers, and retailers, because the quality and variety of fruits and vegetables and nuts available fresh, frozen, canned, or packaged in some other way are, in comparison with the past, outstanding. But they are no longer good enough. Man is easily dissatisfied. Having achieved perfection, we seek superfection. We want still greater variety, less standardized quality. So unless people are lucky enough to have access to really good fresh farm produce, many of them start a garden of their own. In this way they

satisfy their taste for fruits and vegetables at their very best (after all, there is no comparison between store produce and that picked in your own garden at the peak of perfection). And they are limited in their choice of edibles only by their own reluctance to work for them.

3. Finally, despite spiraling incomes, many people are planting gardens for eating in a mild revolt against the spiraling prices of the marketplace. For make no mistake about it, unless you put a high value on your own labor, the food you raise costs very, very little. For instance, last year I spent $6.55 for vegetable seeds. We started harvesting Bibb lettuce in May; and from the middle of June until we moved up-country on Halloween, we did not buy a single vegetable. More than that, we gave away quantities. And we almost completely filled a 14-cu. ft. freezer plus a good many pickle jars.

An even better example of the savings you can make is this: I spent 25 cents for a packet of Delicious 51 muskmelon seeds. During the summer, I gave the spreading vines no more than 75 cents of fertilizer and water. In return I harvested 30 enormous, mouth-watering melons that would have cost from 75 cents to $1.50 in the supermarket; and even more came along after I quit counting.

Comparable savings are possible with fruits and nuts. Of course, the initial cost of the plants is higher and the upkeep is also higher because of the more demanding spray schedules needed to control insects and diseases. But consider the fact that a dwarf apple tree, when mature, yields about two bushels of fruit; a plum tree, one bushel; a single raspberry plant, one quart; a strawberry plant, one pint.

I personally think there is one other reason why food gardening is so satisfying: It's because I still get a little boy's thrill out of watching an insignificant seed turn into an often beautiful delicacy. Why I don't get quite the same thrill out of flowers I do not know. Maybe it is because flower-growing is a pastime almost inherent to home owning whereas I, as a modern man, am not expected to raise my own food; therefore, I instinctively marvel at my ready ability to do so. Whatever the reason, all I know is that food growing is exciting. And fun.

If you have not already discovered this yourself, I hope you will soon.

2

Climate

I don't know that it ever occurs to anyone today to wonder what fruits, nuts, and vegetables grow where. For one thing, geography as I learned it in school is no longer taught; so children are not expected to know the leading crops of the states. In the second place, our supermarkets are filled the year round with such a gorgeous array of produce that it does not inspire wondering comment. The average woman doesn't exclaim: "Figs! Now where in the world could they be coming from this time of year?" On the contrary, she says: "Figs today. That's nice. I haven't seen them since last month. Maybe I should try some."

When you raise your own garden produce, however, the question of what you can grow is of consuming and, of course, paramount interest. The answer depends almost entirely on your climate. You can change the composition of soil, kill bugs, cope with just about all the other variables that affect gardening. But there is nothing you can do about your climate except pray that it will change or hope that some smart hybridizer will come up with new varieties that will thrive in it. The latter event is the more likely.

Over the past 70 years or so, plant scientists have produced countless new varieties of edible plants—many of them able to grow in climates which their ancestors could not withstand. The New Hampshire Midget watermelon is a good example. Until it was developed, watermelons were primarily a Southern crop which you could not count on much farther north than New Jersey. But with the New Hampshire Midget, which matures in about 70 days, you can grow watermelons in every state of the Union.

Such varietal break-throughs to the contrary, a substantial percentage of the different kinds of plants that the home gardener grows for food have a somewhat limited geographical range. Or if you prefer to consider the matter from your own standpoint—regardless of where you live, your food gardening is limited to those species which tolerate your climate.

Exactly what does this tolerance consist of?

The non-gardener and novice gardener and even a good many expert gardeners believe that the key to whether a plant lives or dies in a given climate depends on how cold it gets in winter. For example, orange trees generally die in areas where the temperature drops below 20° F. Similarly, high-bush blueberries generally die in areas where the temperature drops below —20° F.

This, however, does not begin to tell the story of why plants tolerate some climates and not others. For one thing, plants are affected by heat as well as cold. Apples do not grow in southern Florida because the winter temperatures do not reach and stay at a low enough level. Similarly, lettuce plants go to seed and die when summer heat sets in.

Another thing that determines where edible plants are grown is the length of the growing season. This is usually defined as the freeze-free period between the last freeze (killing frost) in spring and the first freeze in fall; but in reality, the growing season for many plants is shorter than this because they make little if any growth until the temperature is well above freezing. Be that as it may, the fact remains that edible plants reach the harvest stage only in areas with a long enough growing season. This is one of the reasons why casaba melons and honeydews, which take almost four months to mature, cannot be grown in the North. It is also the reason why pecan trees live in the North but set fruits only in the South, where the growing season is longer.

Still other climate factors that help to determine where different kinds of food plants grow and why they do better in some areas than others are the following:

Moisture. This actually is a more important climate factor than temperature. Plants cannot grow without water, no matter how favorable the temperature. Today, however, lack of moisture need not keep you from growing food plants in arid areas because you can probably compensate for it by irrigation.

The only natural moisture problems which you can't readily solve and which, therefore, make it difficult or impossible to raise plants in some areas are too much precipitation, too frequent hail storms, and too frequent ice storms (which can raise havoc with dormant fruit and nut trees).

Light. The growth of plants depends not only on the intensity of the light to which they are exposed but also on its duration. This helps to explain—among other things—an Alaskan phenomenon: Along the southern coast, the growing season lasts for roughly 170 days, but because the days during this period are cloudy and rainy, crops are often slow to mature. By contrast, the growing season in the Tanana and Matanuska Valleys lasts for only 100 days, but because the days are very long—up to 21 hours—and sunny, crops mature faster.

Wind. Along the Hawaiian coasts the wind is so strong and steady that the only way farmers can raise mangoes, papayas, and macadamia nuts is to erect large windbreaks between their orchards and the sea. Elsewhere in the United States, the wind rarely interferes with what people plant in their food gardens. But there is no question that, if you live in an area where at least one vicious windstorm is expected every summer, you are not likely to plant corn.

Altitude. This is not a climate factor per se, but I include it here because it helps to make climate and this affects what you can grow in your garden. At high altitudes the temperature is lower (it decreases roughly 1 degree for each 350-ft. rise in elevation above sea level), the light is more intense, and the wind is usually harder and more persistent. In Alaska, the Agricultural Extension Service flatly advises that "land over 2000 ft. elevation is not recommended for farming since freezing can occur any month of the year." An unusual situation, of course; but it illustrates the problem altitude can create for food gardeners.

Now you may wonder why I have belabored the subject of climate vis-à-vis food growing. "Everyone knows you can't raise everything everywhere," you may object. "Take bananas. Who's stupid enough to think that they grow in the North?" But the fact is that, while no one may make such a silly mistake about bananas, a great many people make mistakes about other plants. I don't pretend to have an explanation for this. All I can tell you is that it's true. Throughout this vast country, gardeners are forever trying to grow plants which cannot possibly survive in their particular climates.

In the specific plant-growing material that follows in Part Two, I've done my best to point out in what parts of the country each fruit, nut, herb, and vegetable will grow. But I confess that in most cases I am reduced to the generalities of plant zones. These are derived from "plant hardiness zone" maps like that developed by the Agricultural Research Service of the U.S. Department of Agriculture (page 7). This map divides the continent into ten irregular zones based on their average annual

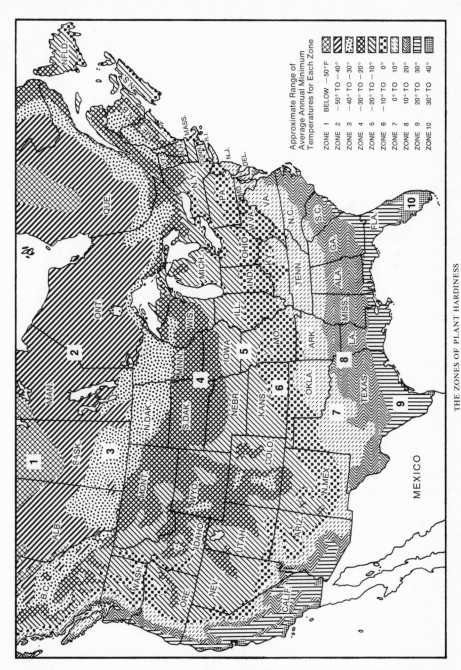

THE ZONES OF PLANT HARDINESS

Plant hardiness zone map developed by the Agricultural Research Service of the U.S. Department of Agriculture. Each zone is split into two approximately equal sub-zones—A and B. A is slightly the colder.

Approximate Range of
Average Annual Minimum
Temperatures for Each Zone

ZONE 1   BELOW −50°F
ZONE 2   −50° TO −40°
ZONE 3   −40° TO −30°
ZONE 4   −30° TO −20°
ZONE 5   −20° TO −10°
ZONE 6   −10° TO   0°
ZONE 7   0° TO 10°
ZONE 8   10° TO 20°
ZONE 9   20° TO 30°
ZONE 10   30° TO 40°

minimum temperatures. In most garden books that refer to plant hardiness zones, it is the practice to say: "Peach. Zone 5. Orange. Zone 9." What this means is that peaches are hardy in areas as far North as Zone 5, where the winter temperature rarely falls below —20°, and that oranges are hardy as far North as Zone 9. Unfortunately, however, such books usually do not tell you how far South peaches, oranges, etc., grow.

In this book, I give both the northernmost zone and the southernmost zone beyond which each plant generally does not grow. In doing this, I am misusing the plant hardiness zone map, because it is patently concerned only with the ability of plants to survive winter cold. But there is no reason, I believe, why the map should not be used—as a convenience—to show each plant's entire range.

A word of caution here, however. While there is a correlation between a community's average minimum temperature and the length of its growing season, it is far from precise. For example, looking at the plant hardiness zone map, you will see that a large U-shaped area in northern New York is in Zone 4. But within that area the mean length of the growing season

Mean date of last 32° temperature in spring (U.S. Weather Bureau).

ranges from 78 days at Indian Lake to 114 days at Stillwater Reservoir to
153 days at Ogdensburg. This means that, while some plants may be listed
as surviving in Zone 4, they may not actually reach harvest stage in all
parts of Zone 4. For this reason, I have also included three Weather
Bureau maps which give the mean dates of the last spring freeze and first
autumn freeze in your area and the mean length of the growing season.
Together with the plant hardiness zone map, these should give you a pretty
good idea whether any given kind of food plant will grow to fruition in your
garden.

When to plant. This question will be discussed at greater length in the
chapters devoted to specific types of food plants. But since we are talking
about climate here, it should at least be noted that climate holds the key
to when you should plant your vegetable and herb garden, berry patch,
or orchard.

The planting of vegetables and herbs, which are for the most part
annuals, depends on the dates of the last spring freeze and first fall freeze.

The planting of perennial plants, including fruit trees and shrubs, can usually be done either in spring or fall; but it is generally safest in spring. This gives the plants plenty of time to become established in their new locations before they are subjected to the rigors of winter.

Where to locate the food garden. There are various factors to consider, but climate plays an especially big role. Here are some good rules to follow, regardless of whether you are raising vegetables, herbs, or fruits:

1. Except in areas that never have frost, do not locate the garden in a valley, at the base of a hill, or at the foot of a sloping field or yard that is surrounded with a stone wall or solid wood fence. Because there is no air drainage, frost settles in such places first. A garden at the top of a slope or part way down is infinitely safer.

This is not to say that it's wrong to put a garden on flat land. On the contrary, this makes for easier gardening in many ways (cultivating, watering, erosion control, etc.). But unless the flat land is open enough

Mean date of first 32° temperature in autumn (U.S. Weather Bureau).

for air currents to move across it and keep frost from settling, it comes in second after a side-of-hill garden.

2. Given a choice of slopes, plant on a southern one. Because it is exposed to the full rays of the sun, the soil warms up earlier in the spring and stays warm later in the fall.

Note, however, that a few very-early-blooming fruit trees, such as apricots, are best planted on a north slope. The idea here is to screen the trees partially from the late winter sun and thus prevent them from blooming before the last spring freeze.

3. Do not locate the garden in the lee of trees, buildings, ridges, or mountains that will block out the sun for several hours of the day. Trees and large shrubs are also a nuisance because they send out roots to rob the smaller garden plants of moisture and nutrients.

4. Avoid windy locations where plants will be battered and soil will be blown away. If this is impossible, plant a windbreak as described on page 15.

5. Be sure the soil is well drained. A moderately light soil is better than an extremely sandy soil, which drains too freely, or a heavy clay soil, which drains sluggishly. But remember that any poorly drained soil can be improved.

The soil that must really be avoided is one which is underlain by rock, hardpan (rock-hard clay), caliche (a rock-hard layer of calcium salts), or permafrost (ground that is frozen the year round). Such soil is almost impossible to drain except by an elaborate network of pipes; and it is frequently too shallow for plants to develop deep root systems, anyway.

6. As a time-saving convenience, locate the garden as close as possible to a water supply (hose bibb, stream, pond, etc.) and to your back door.

How to protect the garden against the elements. Frost. I use the word "frost" even though agricultural scientists are making sturdy efforts to banish it. Their reason—which no one can refute—is that frost is a very inexact term. You might say that frost comes in various grades, not all of which do serious damage. The only frost that is a real menace is the killing frost that comes when the temperature drops to 32° or below. This is why the experts prefer the word "freeze" to frost. When you say your garden was hit by a freeze, there can be little doubt in the listener's mind about what happened.

Anyway—

The first step in protecting your plants against a freeze is, as noted above, to avoid planting them in a low spot where the chill air settles. This increases your chances of escaping damage by the sometimes-border-line freezes that mark the end of winter and the beginning of autumn. In short, you may by this one simple step be able to get your garden off to an earlier start in the spring and to carry it later into the fall.

Other steps to save your plants from frost are of an emergency nature— to be taken when you are pretty sure the temperature is going to drop low enough to give most plants a hard time. The simplest procedure in the vegetable garden and berry patch is to cover your most precious or vulnerable plants with old sheets, mattress pads, tarpaulins, polyethylene film, newspapers, cardboard cartons—anything that will keep the frost from settling directly on the foliage. I use sheet materials for the lower-growing plants such as string beans and cucumbers. Large cartons are dropped down over tomatoes, eggplants, and other individual plants. Newspaper hats or ready-made Hotkaps cover tender seedlings in the spring.

Another interesting way to protect vegetable gardens is to sprinkle them with a fine mist of water continuously throughout the night. This covers the leaves, stems, and fruits with a thin glaze of ice that insulates them against the colder-than-ice air and permits them to thaw out gradually when the sun comes up.

Still another way to protect plants is to ward off frost by heating the air. In tiny gardens, you can burn a charcoal fire in a brazier or string 100-watt

Tree-Heet bricks burning in an orange grove to protect the trees against frost (Mobil Oil Corp.).

incandescent bulbs about a foot above the plants. In large gardens, particularly those with fruit trees, burn petroleum-coke bricks named Tree-Heet. These are inexpensive, flame-free, and almost smoke-free (you can't be accused of polluting the air as you might be if you used conventional orchard heaters). Two bricks burning under the canopy of a tree will raise the air temperature roughly two degrees for a period of about four hours.

Winter. Winter is compounded of several elements that can do great damage in the garden—especially to fruit trees. In mild climates, sudden, occasionally prolonged freezes are the bane of every farmer's and home gardener's existence. The only way to cope with them is either to burn Tree-Heet bricks continuously or, if you are a large-scale orchardist, to stoke up your smudge pots and stir up the air with giant fans.

Two ways to support tree limbs in order to prevent breakage. At left, a tree trunk with a crotch at the upper end is used to keep ice and snow from breaking the limb of an old apple tree. At right, a lightweight, scissors-like tripod supports the fruit-laden branch of a young pear tree.

In cold climates, where heavy snow and ice storms are frequent, large, outspreading branches of old fruit trees should be supported on 2 x 4s with a V-notch in the top or on straight, seasoned tree trunks with a Y-crotch at the top.

Wind. In areas where wind is a problem, your best and least expensive protection is a windbreak of conifers, Siberian elms, Russian olives, honey-locusts, red willows, or amur privet. (A four- or five-foot snowfence is also useful, especially on small properties.) The windbreak trees should be planted far enough from the plants they are protecting not to cut off the sun or to compete for the moisture in the soil. But this need not reduce their effectiveness in breaking up the wind. A good windbreak protects an area that is (depending on the angle of the wind) about ten times as deep as the windbreak is high. In other words, a windbreak 10 ft. high will cut a 30 mph wind to about 15 mph for a distance of 100 ft.

3

Soil

The soil of the United States is as variable as the climate. There are differences not only between regions but also between lots within the same town. If this adds to the confusion of gardening, it also adds to its interest. For instance, the last vegetable garden I had in Greenwich, before I moved to Lyme, was built on clay soil so dense that rainwater ran off it as if it were asphalt. It stayed cold and soggy long after the stony, gravelly soil of my previous Greenwich garden was ready to plant. It was also very acid. When I first turned it over, I rather despaired that it would produce well for me. I totally rejected any ideas of raising melons, strawberries, and other plants that supposedly prefer sandy loam. But the garden turned out to be bountiful beyond any of the fine gardens I had ever had. Everything I planted grew like the proverbial weeds. Admittedly, I had my struggles, especially when heavy rains turned the soil into a quagmire. But it was an unending source of pleasure, even so.

The ideal soil. Of course, if a problem soil can be a pleasure, the ideal soil must be doubly so. It is a loam (a fairly even mixture of sand, clay, and silt) which is rich in organic matter, generally free of stones, lies in a deep layer over a well-drained subsoil, and has a pH of 6 to 7. You may think this a rare commodity, but it is not. I should not go so far as to say, however, that it is the type of soil found widely throughout our land. Most gardeners have to do a certain amount of work to get their soil into productive condition and to keep it there.

Preparing a new garden. This section applies only if you are planting vegetables, herbs, and small fruits. In the great majority of home gardens, fruit and nut trees are handled in a somewhat different way which will be discussed in later chapters.

Ideally, ground for a new garden should be turned over roughly in the fall. This exposes many insects and disease germs to the killing cold, and gives the frost, rain, and snow an opportunity to break down the soil. The garden should then be tilled with a rotary tiller or by hand in the spring, after the soil has dried out sufficiently to make it workable.

The ground for many gardens, however, is not turned over until spring (also after the soil is workable). In this case, the soil is tilled and tilled again until it can be leveled and smoothed with a rake.

No matter when you prepare a new garden, there are a few problems you may run into. These are minimal if the area you are cultivating was formerly a lawn, because lawn grass is easy to turn over and break up into small chunks. In fact, a lawn is just about as easy to turn into a vegetable garden as an old flower garden. But a wooded area and a rough field are something else again.

The former is an honest-to-goodness back-breaker. First you must cut down the trees and shrubs. Then you must pull the stumps, which is more costly but much faster and more thorough than burning or poisoning. Then you must grub out the woody roots that are left, because they interfere with tilling, take a long time to rot, and may send up new growth. Finally you must break up the soil, remove the worst of the stones, and ready the garden for planting.

A rough field is less work to turn into a garden, even if it has a few little shrubs and trees that must be rooted out. Even so, it is no cinch. A good stand of meadow grass is hard to chop up and turn under deeply enough to keep it from growing again. The best solution if you allow enough time, is to mow the grass as close as possible in the fall. (Don't burn it, because that is both dangerous and wasteful of the valuable humus the grass tops will form.) Then cover the entire garden area either with a foot of hay or with a huge sheet of black polyethylene film. This will kill the grass in a couple of months and make it somewhat easier to chop up with a tiller.

Improving soil drainage. If food plants are to thrive, the soil must be well drained. What is good drainage? We can understand it more easily if we consider what it is *not*.

One of the functions of soil is to retain moisture and to release it slowly to plant roots as they need it. If for some reason, soil holds so much moisture that it is often in a soggy condition, the plant roots will drown for lack of oxygen. On the other hand, if moisture drains down through the soil deep into the earth, the plant roots will be unable to reach it and will dry up and die.

Soil that holds too much moisture is poorly drained. Soil that does not hold enough moisture might also be called poorly drained. Good drainage, in other words, is a happy in-between state. The soil retains just enough moisture to meet plant needs.

When soil holds too much moisture—is waterlogged—one of two things is wrong: Either the soil consists of heavy clay or, in rare cases, peat that holds water tenaciously, or it is underlain by a layer of rock, hardpan, caliche, or permafrost.

The only way to improve drainage in a peat bog or in soil underlain by an impervious layer is to put in a system of interconnecting, 4-in., perforated, composition drain pipes. These should be laid at least 1 ft. below the soil surface in a vegetable garden and berry patch; 2 to 3 ft. in an orchard. The pipes should be sloped away from the garden and emptied into a storm sewer, stream, or pond.

Dense clay can usually be drained satisfactorily if you mix into it to a depth of 2 ft. large quantities of coarse sand, small crushed rock, and coarsely chopped pine bark. But you may also need to put in drain pipes if you have heavy rains during the growing season. If by chance you put in or transplant large fruit and nut trees, I'd also recommend that you put in a drain pipe for each planting hole in addition to mixing coarse matter into the clay. In time, such plants become accustomed to a clay soil and do not seem to be affected adversely by it; but before they become established, they may be drowned by the water that settles in a planting hole that lacks a drainage outlet.

To improve drainage in a porous, sandy, or gravelly soil (which really means to improve water-holding capacity), your only course is to mix in large quantities of rather fine humus, such as peat or sawdust, or large quantities of clay, or a mixture of both. The alternative, recommended only for exceptionally porous soil, is to pour a continuous, thin layer of asphalt 2 ft. below the soil surface. A method for doing this was invented several years ago by a couple of Michigan State University agricultural scientists.

Improving soil fertility. No one in this world can look at a sample of unfamiliar soil and tell what plant nutrients it contains. That's why the intelligent gardener who wants bountiful crops but does not want to waste money on unnecessary fertilizers, etc., has a soil test made before he plants anything.

Testing soil is a service offered by all state agricultural extension services either at no charge or the miniscule sum of about a dollar. The best way

to avail yourself of this service is to write to your own extension represen-
tative and ask for instructions and a sampling kit (if they offer one). All
you then have to do is dig up a spadeful of soil from six to ten scattered
locations in your garden area; mix them together; and send a pint back to
the extension service with a brief statement about what you intend to grow,
what you have previously used the ground for, what you have done to it,
and how it is drained. Within a short time, you will get back a neat form
telling what if anything you should do to make the soil more productive.

One thing which very few soils contain in sufficient quantity is humus—
decayed vegetable and animal matter. Nothing is more important. Humus
not only lightens soil and improves its porosity and water-holding capacity,
but also adds nutrients and nourishes micro-organisms which improve
the quality of the soil in various mysterious ways.

Sources of humus are numerous and readily available to all gardeners
at little or no cost. They include well-rotted manure and dehydrated
manure; decayed leaves, grass, and hay; compost; sawdust; and a vast
assortment of commercial products such as peat, chopped tree bark, buckwheat hulls, bagasse, etc. Another excellent source of humus, which is
discussed in Chapter 5, is a winter cover crop—sometimes called green
manure.

The amount of humus which should be added to soil is impossible to
specify. Obviously some soils, such as those composed mainly of sand,
gravel, or clay, need a great deal more than loam soils. But the plain fact
of the matter is that you are hardly likely to add too much humus to any
soil. One reason for this is that the humus already in the soil gradually
disappears as it decomposes. The other reason is that to buy enough humus
to overload your garden you would have to be a plutocrat; and to make
enough, you would have to build a veritable mountain of leaves or hay.

Wonderful as humus is, however, it does not take the place of fertilizer
in the vegetable garden, berry patch, and orchard. In order to give you
bushels of succulent produce, food plants need lots and lots of nourishment—more than flowers, shrubs, and shade trees.

Time was when manure was the standard fertilizer. It is still considered
excellent, not so much because it is inordinately rich in nitrogen, phosphorus, and potassium—it isn't—but because it adds humus to soil as well
as these nutrients. But manure, alas, is not widely available today. So
you might as well scratch it from your mind unless you are close to horse
country.

What most gardeners—and also farmers—use today is dried commercial
fertilizer. The types are legion. Some contain only a single element—
either nitrogen or phosphorus or potassium. Some contain two elements:
Both bone meal and dried sludge, for example, contain nitrogen and
phosphorus. Some are known as balanced fertilizers and contain all three
elements in the percentages shown by the three-digit formula printed on
the bags; for example, 5-10-5, 10-10-10, 10-20-20. Some are balanced
fertilizers which also contain such minor but important nutrients as

magnesium and copper. Some are balanced fertilizers which also contain an insecticide and/or herbicide.

Except for the last type, which is made for lawns, you can use any or all of these fertilizers in your garden and orchard. Each serves a purpose. But unless your soil has a startling deficiency that is most easily and cheaply corrected by a single-element fertilizer, or unless you are dealing with plants which need only a single-element fertilizer, your best bet is to use the balanced fertilizer recommended by your extension service on the basis of a soil test. Lacking such a recommendation, a relatively quick and easy way to determine whether your plants are not getting enough of certain elements is to check the condition of the leaves against Table I.

TABLE I
Plant Nutrient Deficiency Symptoms
(Source: Alabama Agricultural Extension Service and others)

Nitrogen—Small leaves turn light green or yellow; lower leaves lighter color than top; weak plant.

Phosphorus—Plants have dark green leaves; sometimes lower leaves become purplish in color; lower leaves may become yellow between veins.

Potassium—Yellow spots develop between veins on lower leaves; yellowing or even dying of leaf margins on lower or old leaves.

Calcium—Tips of young leaves curl and die.

Magnesium—Leaf margins on lower leaves curl; lower leaves have yellow spots with green veins.

Sulfur—Plants have light green leaves; leaf veins are lighter in color than surrounding area; upper leaves are lighter in color than bottom leaves.

Iron—New upper leaves turn yellow; edges and tips of leaves may die.

Manganese—New upper leaves have yellow or dead spots; veins remain green.

Boron—New tip growth dies; plant becomes brittle.

Copper—Young leaves wilt permanently and wither, but show little if any yellowing.

Zinc—Older or lower leaves yellow, develop dead spots and holes; plant growth is stunted.

Both the timing and method of fertilizer application vary somewhat.

As a general rule, the first and heaviest application is made just before plants start their new season's growth; and one or more additional applications may be made after this at six- to eight-week intervals. On sandy soils, however, large doses of fertilizer are a waste of money because rain leaches out too many of the nutrients; consequently, a series of light, frequent applications is preferred. In either case, once plants begin to set fruit, all feeding may stop. In colder climates, trees and shrubs should definitely not be fertilized after mid-summer, because this is likely to force them to put out new, succulent growth which will be killed by frosts.

One way to fertilize vegetable and herb gardens and berry patches before planting is to spread fertilizer evenly over the soil and work it in well. Another way, called banding, is to make a deep furrow down both sides of the seed or plant row; pour a light strip of fertilizer in each; and then fill in with soil. Growing plants are fertilized by sidedressing—simply scattering fertilizer along both sides of a plant row or in a circle around individual plants, and scratching it in well.

Fruit and nut trees are fertilized by sidedressing, too. Only one tree— the macadamia—is fertilized by punching holes in the ground around the trunk and pouring an equal amount of fertilizer into each (this is the way shade trees are fed). However, if large fruit or nut trees are growing in sod or are surrounded by a ground cover, this is a good way to make sure that they are adequately fed.

No matter how fertilizer is applied, it should be watered in well so that it will start to dissolve at once. Plants cannot absorb dry fertilizer, and may, in fact, be burned by it if it touches their leaves or roots.

Foliar feeding—spraying fertilizer diluted in water on plant leaves—is another application method, but it is used (except by a few enthusiasts) only in fairly isolated cases. It is, for example, a splendid way to feed plants growing in soil that leaches very rapidly. It is also used in warm climates to supply minor nutrients.

In the chapters following, the amounts of fertilizer to use are given in 8-oz. cups. One such cup holds approximately ½ lb. of dry fertilizer.

Changing the pH of soil. The majority of food plants grow best in soil that is neutral or slightly acid. In technical terms, they prefer a pH between 7.0 (neutral) and 6.0 (slightly acid). Fortunately, this is the pH range of most garden soils; but there are many areas where the soil is quite acid and many other areas where it is quite alkaline. New England, for example, has acid soil while the Southwest has alkaline soil.

Changing the pH of a soil is not difficult. To raise it—that is, to make soil less acid—you simply work ground limestone or hydrated lime into the topsoil. Ground limestone lasts longer; hydrated lime works faster. One other difference between the two materials is that limestone can be used at the same time you apply fertilizer; but applications of hydrated lime and fertilizer must be made at least a week apart.

Liming can be done at any time, but is best done in the fall or early winter. The amount of lime required is recommended by your agricultural extension service in its soil test report. If you are silly enough not to have such a test made, use the amounts called for in Table II. One application usually lasts for three or four years.

In addition to lowering soil acidity, lime has several other beneficial effects: It is a source of calcium and magnesium, both of which are essential, though secondary, plant nutrients. It makes the phosphorus and other nutrients in the soil more available to plants. It stimulates the activity of the important micro-organisms in soil. And it helps to improve the structure of soil—especially clay soil—by gluing small particles together into larger particles, and thus improving drainage and aeration.

TABLE II
Pounds of Lime Needed to Raise the pH of 100 sq. ft. of Soil to 6.0

Original pH	In light, sandy soil		In average soil		In clay loam	
	GROUND LIMESTONE	HYDRATED LIME	GROUND LIMESTONE	HYDRATED LIME	GROUND LIMESTONE	HYDRATED LIME
4.0	9	6	17.2	11.5	21.7	14.5
4.5	8.2	5.5	15.7	10.5	20.2	13.5
5.0	6.7	4.5	12.7	8.5	15	10
5.5	5.2	3.5	9.7	6.5	12	8

Note: Do not apply more than 5 lb. of lime per 100 sq. ft. at one time. If soil needs more than this, make several 5-lb. applications at six-week intervals.

To lower the pH of soil—make it less alkaline—is trickier business. Alkaline soils are common to the arid regions of our 17 Western states. The salts build up in the soil because there is not enough rainfall to leach them out and because the water used for irrigation contains large amounts of salts which remain in the soil when the water evaporates at the surface or is taken up by plant roots. In other words, even though it is possible to reduce the alkaline content of soil by applying chemicals, the water that is given to plants by hose, sprinkler, or irrigation ditch tends to raise it again.

This does not mean the situation is hopeless, however. You can ameliorate it to a large extent by proper watering methods, which are discussed a little further on. You should also do the following things: (1) Avoid walking through the garden and tilling the soil any more than necessary. This keeps it from compacting and draining poorly. Adding plenty of humus also helps to maintain drainage. (2) Level the soil very carefully—especially in the vegetable and herb garden—in order to avoid high spots where salts concentrate. (3) Mix gypsum or sulfur into the soil according to the recommendation of your agricultural extension service. These lower the saline content of the soil.

(Elsewhere in the country, if your soil has a high pH which must be reduced somewhat to accommodate a few acid-soil plants such as blueberries and potatoes, apply 1 lb. of finely ground sulfur per 100 sq. ft. This will reduce the pH of loam soil about 1 point; of sandy soil, slightly more. On clay soil, use 2 lb. of sulfur.)

When to water the garden and how much. Obviously you don't need to water your garden at all if you live in a region that has substantial rains regularly throughout the growing season. Few American gardeners are so blessed, however. Most of us have to do a certain amount of watering to keep plants going; and in arid areas we have to do a great deal.

The question you must answer is: When is watering necessary? And how much water should you then apply?

Your soil holds the answer. If it is clay, it holds water better than if it is loam; and if it is loam, it holds water better than if it is sandy or gravelly soil. Or stating the case in another way—sandy soil dries out faster than loam; and loam dries out faster than clay. This is true no matter where you live; and the only way you can change the situation is to load a lot of humus into sandy soil and loam or to add a lot of sand or gravel to clay soil.

But this still does not tell you when you must apply water and how much.

Water is necessary—and you should supply it if the heavens refuse—when the soil around the plant roots begins to dry out. This is the root zone in which the main mass of roots is found. For small plants such as herbs and many of the smaller vegetables, the root zone lies within 12 to 18 in. of the soil surface. For large plants, it goes to a depth of 3 ft. and more.

One way that many gardeners tell when soil within the root zone is too dry is to observe the condition of the plants. When leaves begin to wilt, it's a pretty sure sign the roots are thirsty. But if you always wait for leaves to wilt before you get out your hose, you put an unnecessary burden on the plants—retard their growth. A much better way to judge the situation is to check the actual condition of the soil.

This shows the dramatic effect that water can have on plant growth. For two months there had been almost no rain and my corn grew at a snail's pace. Then, on July 15, we had a good 1-in. soak. On the 16th, in the hot sun, this corn stalk—like the others around it—shot up about 4 in. On the 17th (the day this shot was made) it grew 2 in. more (from the string). On the 18th it grew another inch.

There are two things you can do: (1) Jab a soil probe deep into the ground and withdraw it with a core of soil which you can examine at first hand. (2) Install a couple of Tensiometers which constantly measure the amount of water at different depths in the soil and automatically record the answer on dials mounted on top.

Your plants need to be watered when either of these devices indicates that the soil has dried out to a depth of 12 in.—or less in the case of seedlings and small, shallow-rooted plants.

Neither a Tensiometer nor a soil probe can tell you how much water you should apply *before* you turn on the hose, but they can tell you when you have applied enough. This is when they show that the soil which was dry is once again damp.

Suppose, however, that you don't have a Tensiometer or soil probe. In this case, there is no accurate method for determining whether you have applied enough water to moisten the dry soil in the root zone unless you take the time some day to find out how deeply a measured inch of water penetrates your soil when it is dry. The alternative is to be guided by tests made by experts which show that, *as a general rule,* in order to wet 1 ft. of dry soil, you must apply ¾ in. of water if the soil is sandy; 1½ in. if the soil is loam; and 2½ in. if the soil is clay. In either case, the only way you can actually measure how much water you give your garden is to apply it by a sprinkler under which a rain gauge is set. But this, unfortunately, is something of a nuisance, and it also limits you to watering your garden with a sprinkler—which is not always the best way of doing the job.

You are really much better off using a Tensiometer or soil probe.

When and how much to water the garden if you live in an arid region. We come now to a special problem which was touched on a little earlier: How to satisfy the moisture requirements of plants when your water supply has such a high content of soluble salts that it causes a build-up of salts in soil that is itself too saline.

First, you should understand that when salts are concentrated in soil, they have a harmful effect on many plants—especially deciduous fruits, citrus, avocados, nuts, beans, celery, and radishes. Transplants, particularly of warm-weather crops such as sweet potatoes, are also seriously harmed.

The best way to reduce this danger is to leach salt accumulations down into the soil below the depth to which plant roots grow. This is done by irrigating the soil very heavily at the start of the growing season.

Exactly how heavy is "heavily"? As Leon Bernstein, plant physiologist in the Department of Agriculture's Salinity Laboratory at Riverside, California, points out in a leaflet telling home owners how to protect ornamental shrubs, but which applies equally to food plants: "This depends on the degree to which salinity is to be reduced and the depth of soil to be leached. For each foot of soil to be leached—

—6 in. of irrigation water leaches out one-half of the salt.
—12 in. of irrigation water leaches out four-fifths of the salt.
—24 in. of irrigation water leaches out nine-tenths of the salt."

Bernstein goes on to point out that after salt accumulations have been reduced to a level that the plants can tolerate, you should continue to apply extra water during each irrigation to prevent a new build-up of salts. The saltier the irrigation water and the more salt sensitive the plants, the greater the amount of water needed. For example, during the warmer months in southern California, as much as 3 in. of water may be lost from the soil every ten days to two weeks. This means that simply to satisfy plant needs, you must replace the lost water with an equal amount of fresh water—3 in. But in order to prevent salt accumulation, you must actually apply more than 3 in. of water.

The exact amount required depends on how tolerant or sensitive your food plants are to salt and on how much salt your irrigation water contains.

A vegetable garden mulched with hay. As it decomposes, the hay will add valuable humus and nutrients to the soil. In the meantime it holds in moisture and discourages weeds.

For example, you should apply 5 in. of water if you are growing tomatoes, lettuce, corn, carrots, onions, peas, and squash—all of which have a moderate salt tolerance—and if you have a moderately saline water with an electrical conductivity of 2.0 millimhos per centimeter. On the other hand, you would need only 4 in. of water if you are growing beets, asparagus, and spinach, which have a greater tolerance of salt. Yet again, you would need 9 in. of water if you are growing beans and celery.

How to water the food garden. The best time to water plants is early enough during the day to permit the foliage to dry off before nightfall. This helps to protect them against fungus diseases, which prefer to do their nefarious work at night.

Although farmers have for many years irrigated row crops and orchards by pouring water into furrows between the plants, this is a difficult watering

Black polyethylene film is not an ideal mulch for raspberries and blackberries because it keeps them from spreading. But it was used on this new planting for a special reason: Because he had just bought the property, the gardener did not have time to turn over the meadow and prepare a bed for the berries before they arrived. So he planted them in large holes and then laid the plastic around them to kill the meadow grass.

method for home gardeners because it requires careful leveling of the garden and a sufficiently large flow of water to fill the furrows from end to end. Furthermore, in regions where both soil and water are saline, it has been found that furrow irrigation increases the danger of salt injury to plants. For these reasons, sprinkling of vegetable and herb gardens and berry patches is recommended in the arid West.

Sprinkling is also a perfectly good watering method in other parts of the country, but it is somewhat wasteful of water and can cause some erosion in hillside gardens. I therefore use it only for watering plants that form big mats (melons, cucumbers, strawberries, etc.). All other plants I prefer to water with a canvas soil soaker or a three-tube, perforated plastic hose. Laid alongside a row of plants or in a spiral around trees and other individual plants, these gadgets put the water exactly where it is most needed— around the main root mass. There is no waste, no runoff. And you do not require such a high water pressure as for a sprinkler.

Another excellent way to water fruit and nut trees is to build a low dike around them under the tips of the branches, and to fill the saucer thus formed with a hose.

Using mulches. It seems to me that in recent years there has been a lot more talk about the wisdom of mulching plants than there used to be; yet I have not seen extensive use made of mulches except in shrubbery borders and rose gardens. Please believe me: Mulches are just as valuable around fruit and nut trees and even more valuable in vegetable gardens and berry patches. Why? Because they retard evaporation of moisture from the soil and thus keep plant roots happier and reduce the need for watering. They kill weeds that must be regularly chopped or pulled out if they are not to strangle your food plants. They keep the soil friable and reduce the necessity for cultivating it. They keep vegetables and fruits off the ground —clean and, to some extent, safe from diseases. And the organic mulches also add humus to the soil as they decompose, retard water runoff, and keep plant roots from cooking under the hot sun.

For scattered fruit and nut trees that are grown both for ornament and for the food they produce, the mulch used should be attractive as well as effective. Materials that meet this requirement include chopped tree bark, peat, buckwheat hulls, bagasse, and pebbles.

In a strictly working orchard, vegetable garden, herb garden, and berry patch, however, the beauty of the mulch is of little or no importance. What you want is simply a good mulch at low cost.

My personal favorite is hay. It does everything a good organic mulch is supposed to; decomposes rapidly without turning into the nasty mess that grass clippings and leaves often make; and need not cost you a cent. Yes, that's true even though you don't own a hay field of your own. In suburbia today there is no longer any demand for hay. People with hay fields can't sell the stuff; they can't even find horse owners who will take it from them for nothing. Result: They often have more hay than they can use themselves and they are all too happy to give it to anyone who has the gumption to step forward and ask, "May I have some to put on my garden?"

Other good but not particularly attractive organic mulches include the wood chips and chopped-up branches that utility crews collect when they thin the trees along their lines; sawdust; ground corncobs; and peanut shells. If using the first two, you should make a slight increase in the amount of nitrogen fertilizer you apply to the garden, because the bacteria that decompose the wood mulch tie up the nitrogen in the soil in a form that is unavailable to plants.

Whichever of these mulches you use, apply it in a layer 2 to 5 in. thick. The thicker the layer, the better the job it does in smothering weeds. Remember, however, that the weeds should be chopped to the ground before the mulch is applied.

Of the several inorganic materials used for mulching, the favorite— especially with farmers—is polyethylene film. This is either laid in long strips between the plant rows or laid over the entire garden and then punctured for the plants to come up through. It must be securely weighted down with stones or soil to keep it from billowing in a breeze.

Two types of polyethylene are used. The black is the more common because, in addition to holding in moisture, it kills any weeds that succeed in germinating.

The white film does not kill weeds, but it has an unusual advantage: Unlike the black film, it lets the sun rays through to the soil. This warms the soil much earlier in the spring than is normal. And this, in turn, encourages perennial plants such as strawberries to make growth, flower, and set fruit well ahead of similar plants surrounded with other kinds of mulch.

4

Pests

I am writing this chapter in the middle of January. We have been in our
new house in Lyme for two and a half months. There has been so much
work inside that I have done nothing outside. The very first day we saw
the place I picked the site for my vegetables, herbs, and berries—in a
lovely, flat, little meadow—but I didn't have a chance to turn under the sod
in the fall. I ordered my vegetable seeds last week anyway. Then, on the
weekend, one of our new neighbors commented that vegetable gardening
in Lyme is almost a lost cause because the wildlife runs rampant. I am not
surprised, because this is rough, wild country. Nevertheless, I had not
previously given much thought to the problem. Now I am beginning to
wonder and worry a little. In all my years of gardening I have never had too
much trouble with insects, diseases, or weeds. But on occasion, rabbits,
squirrels, and a sly raccoon have given me fits.

It promises to be an interesting summer unless our two retrievers once
again take up their hunting ways.

Now I don't want to over-emphasize the problem of coping with pests

in the garden. But I don't want to make light of it, either. It's a real problem—worse some years than others; always worse for the food gardener
than the flower gardener. Yet it is nothing to get over-wrought about.
We have at our disposal some pretty good weapons for fighting back.

CONTROLLING INSECTS AND DISEASES

I am not one to decry the use of modern chemicals in the garden.
Admittedly, they have sometimes been used rashly and far too widely.
But if we didn't use them, the United States would not be the greatest
food-producing nation in the world and one of the healthiest.

Modern pesticides are very effective; and they are also safe if you use
the right ones in the way the manufacturers tell you. Suggestions about the
kinds to use to control the various tiny predators you are most likely to
come up against are made in this and the chapters following. The list is
fairly long; but in actual fact, because most chemicals are effective against
several pests, you need only a small arsenal of them.

Generally, the best way to apply insecticides and fungicides is by spraying. In the small garden, a compressed air sprayer with a 2½-gal. capacity
is plenty large enough. But to spray standard-size fruit and nut trees and
even some semi-dwarf varieties, you need something capable of delivering
a spray stream for many feet upwards. The choice lies between an expensive, roll-around sprayer (either motor- or hand-driven) and an inexpensive, less efficient hose sprayer.

The best time to spray plants is right after a rain or after you have irrigated them by sprinkling. Always use a fresh spray mixture; and if it is
made up of a dry chemical diluted in water, pour it into the compressed-
air tank through a fine wire strainer or cloth. This keeps out particles that
will clog the nozzle. After you finish spraying, rinse the sprayer well and
leave it open to dry.

Do not use the same sprayer for applying insecticides or fungicides
and herbicides. If just a trace of herbicide remains in a spray tank, it is
likely to damage or kill plants when you next spray them with insecticide
or fungicide.

Dusting is effective on small plants but troublesome on large. It takes
less preparation and clean-up than spraying, but I have a feeling—unsub-
stantiated—that it uses more chemical and costs more. To cover all plant
surfaces completely with a fine coating of dust, you must have a first-class
duster. I prefer the relatively inexpensive crank-type, which throws out
a fog of powder with each easy turn of the handle. There are also motor-
driven units.

Whichever duster you use, dusting should be done after a rain or after
sprinkling *when the foliage is dry.*

Other ways of controlling insects with chemicals are also employed
in food gardening, but to a limited extent. They include fumigating the

soil, setting out baits, and banding trees with a sticky substance that traps crawling insects. Systemic poisoning, a newly popular method of killing sucking insects by treating the soil with a chemical which plants absorb through their roots, is used in the food garden at this time only for tomatoes.

Still other ways of controlling insects and diseases involve nothing more than sound cultural practices. No chemicals are needed; just good sense.

1. Buy plants from reliable dealers who take pains to raise healthy stock. If you acquire plants from friends or neighbors, inspect them carefully to make sure they are free of insects and diseases. Do not dig up plants in another state or country and bring them home: you may well be violating federal or state quarantines set up to prevent the spread of serious plant pests, such as the gypsy moth, Japanese beetle, European chafer, and white pine blister rust.

2. Plant varieties which have natural resistance to or are tolerant of diseases that are or may be troublesome in your area.

3. Keep your garden as sanitary as possible: Burn diseased plants and plant parts. Eradicate nearby weeds. Pick up garden trash which may harbor insects and fungi.

4. Rotate crops to prevent the excessive build-up of certain pests in one part of the garden. At the same time, you must avoid following one crop with certain others. For example, strawberries should not be planted in soil in which tomatoes, eggplants, peppers, or potatoes grew the preceding year.

5. Turn the soil in the vegetable garden over in the fall so that freezing weather has a chance to work on the pests hiding underground.

SPECIFIC CONTROLS FOR INSECTS
COMMONLY ATTACKING FOOD PLANTS

Aphids. Tiny, soft insects found throughout the country on almost all plants, but especially cabbages, cucumbers, muskmelons, peas, potatoes, tomatoes, apples, grapes, and citrus. By sucking plant juices, the aphids cause stunting of the plants and deforming of buds, flowers, and leaves. Some plants may be covered with a sooty mold; many are blotched with a "honeydew" which is secreted by aphids and which attracts ants. To control spray plants when aphids appear with malathion. Destroy large ant colonies which hoard the aphids. Avoid using multi-purpose sprays that kill ladybugs, which are natural predators of these pests.

Apple curculios. Brown, ¼-in. beetles with long, thin snouts and humped backs. Found east of the Mississippi, they make puncture holes in apples, cherries, pears, and quinces. The fruit becomes misshapen and falls. Control with a general-purpose fruit spray applied according to the schedule in Table X.

Apple maggots. White, wormlike larvae tunnel through apples, cherries, blueberries, and plums in the summer. They are common in the northern half of the country east of the Rockies. Control with a general-purpose fruit spray applied every ten days from July 1 to August 15.

Asparagus beetles. The common beetle is reddish and has blue-black wings with yellow spots. The spotted beetle has orange or light brown wings with black spots. Both feed on the plant stems, which become distorted, and on the ferns in summer. Spray with Sevin.

Blister beetles. Found almost everywhere, these are slender, ½-in. beetles of various colors that blister your skin if you crush them. They feed on leaves and flowers of beans, corn, potatoes, and tomatoes in the summer. Pick off by hand (if you are wearing gloves) or spray with Sevin.

Cabbage worms. Several kinds of green worms that eat holes in cabbages, broccoli, cauliflower, and related plants throughout the U.S. Dust with rotenone as soon as worms appear and repeat treatment weekly as needed.

Cankerworms. These are also known as measuring worms or inchworms because of the way they loop themselves along. But they are most often seen hanging from trees on long threads. A very serious pest in most parts of the country, they can defoliate apples and other deciduous fruits in short order in the spring. Control with a general-purpose fruit spray or with Sevin.

Cherry fruit flies. Found in the North, these are little black or black, white, and yellow flies which eat the leaves of cherry, plum, and pear trees and puncture the young fruits, which are then deformed. Control with general-purpose fruit spray or with methoxychlor applied about June 1. Similar fruit flies attack many other kinds of plants, such as papayas and passion fruit.

Codling moths. Small, gray-brown moths which appear in the spring and produce one generation of worms at that time and a second in mid- to late summer. Prevalent almost everywhere, they attack apples, pears, and English walnuts. The worms tunnel into the centers of the fruits, causing some to fall. Control with a general-purpose fruit spray as in Table X.

Colorado potato beetles. Widespread pests which eat the foliage of potatoes and also of tomatoes, eggplants, and peppers. The beetles are wide and squat; yellow with black stripes and black spots on the head. They lay clusters of orange eggs from which fat, red grubs emerge in the spring. Dust plants with Sevin as soon as you see first signs of trouble, and repeat as necessary.

Corn earworms. Two-inch, striped caterpillars of various colors and with yellow heads. They are a pest wherever corn is grown, and they also make holes in tomatoes and lima bean pods. On corn, they eat the silks and top kernels; leave moist castings behind them as they work. Dust or spray Sevin on the silks when these appear and at ten-day intervals thereafter. Spray tomatoes and beans on the same schedule from the time fruits are set.

Cutworms. Big fat, smooth caterpillars, usually brown, which are found almost everywhere. They cut off the stems of young tomatoes, cabbages, and other transplants; may also feed on the leaves higher up. To control, wrap the stems of newly set plants with aluminum foil or kraft paper. The collars should extend from slightly below the soil surface about 4 in. up.

European corn borers. Found mainly east of the Rockies, these 1 in., whitish caterpillars eat the corn tassels and tunnel down inside the ears. They may also attack beans and other vegetables. To control, spray or dust plants with Sevin as soon as the tassels begin to develop and three or four times thereafter at five-day intervals.

Flea beetles. Tiny, black, hopping beetles found almost everywhere. They make small holes in the leaves of most garden crops. Spray or dust with Sevin or rotenone.

Grape berry moths. Mainly troublesome in the Northwest, these are gray-purple moths which produce green larvae with brown heads. They tie the fruits on grape vines together with webs; the fruits then turn dark purple and fall. Control by spraying with Sevin just before blossoms open and twice afterwards at 15-day intervals.

Grasshoppers. These familiar insects become a real problem only when they are present in vast swarms. Then they feed on almost everything in the vegetable garden. They can, however, be controlled by dusting or spraying plants with Sevin.

Harlequin bugs. A Southern pest, these are black and red bugs which lay black and white, barrel-shaped eggs on the undersides of leaves. The insects suck the plant juices of cabbages and related vegetables. This causes the plants to wilt and turn brown. To control, dust plants regularly from spring on with rotenone.

Hornworms. Huge, green caterpillars—up to 4 in. long—that gorge themselves on tomato fruits and foliage and litter the ground underneath with large droppings. They also devour peppers. eggplants, and potatoes. They are found almost everywhere, but fortunately not in large numbers. Because of their coloring, they are not easy to see during the day; but you can find them after dark with a flashlight. Pick off by hand into a can of kerosene.

Japanese beetles. Handsome, metallic-green beetles with coppery wings which are found east of the Mississippi and north of Georgia. They feast on almost all deciduous fruits and many other things besides. The beetles are easy to pick off by hand into a can of kerosene, and can also be controlled to some extent with Sevin or methoxychlor sprays. If you have a great deal of trouble with them, however, best results are obtained by dusting chlordane on the lawn in the spring to kill the grubs.

Katydids. Familiar insects which eat large, jagged holes out of the leaves of young citrus trees. They are especially active in spring and fall. Spray with malathion.

Leafhoppers. These ubiquitous, streamlined, hopping insects of several colors suck the juices of beans, carrots, cucumbers, melons, and potatoes. Leaves turn brown and curl; plants are stunted. Spray Sevin or methoxychlor on the undersides of leaves when plants are young and three or four times after that at weekly intervals.

Leafrollers. Little caterpillars of assorted colors which roll the leaves of deciduous fruits around them while they eat away. They are found almost everywhere. Applying a dormant oil spray in late winter usually takes care of them.

Leaftiers. These are much like leafrollers, except that they tie leaves around themselves with silky threads. They are fond of celery and strawberries. To control, spray in the spring with methoxychlor.

Mealybugs. Tiny, warm-climate, sucking insects distinguished by the white, mealy wax that covers them. They infest the stems and undersides of leaves of citrus fruits, apples, filberts, grapes, pineapples, etc. Sometimes you can get rid of them with hard streams of water; otherwise, spray with malathion.

Mexican bean beetles. Inhabitants of the East and Southwest, they play havoc with the foliage and fruits of all kinds of beans. The beetles are round, yellow, and have black spots on the wings; lay clusters of yellow eggs from which yellow grubs emerge. Look for them on the undersides of leaves. Control with rotenone or Sevin dust.

Mites. Minute insects that suck sap from leaves, which then turn yellow and fall. The pests can be a problem everywhere and attack many plants, but are primarily interested in eggplants, tomatoes, and beans. Spray with malathion.

Nematodes. These are infinitesimal soil insects operating throughout the United States but particularly troublesome in warmer areas. They attack a host of vegetables, causing stunting, yellowing, warty growths and general malaise. They are also a serious menace to larger plants, especially citrus trees. They are best controlled by regular rotation of vegetable crops. If infestations are severe, fumigate the soil with Chloropicrin, Nemagon, Fumazone, or Vapam.

Orange dogs. Perfect name for 2½-in., brown and yellow caterpillars which resemble a dog at one end and which feed on the foliage of young Southern citrus trees in late summer and early fall. Pick off by hand.

Orange tortrix. This white, brown-headed caterpillar attacks Western citrus. It scars fruits and feasts on leaves, which it rolls and ties around itself. Spray or dust with cryolite.

Oriental fruit moths. Found everywhere peaches are grown, these gray and brown moths produce three or four generations of pink larvae during the growing season. The first larvae attack leaves and tips of twigs; later larvae bore into fruits through the stems. While their principal targets are peach trees, they also attack quinces and other deciduous fruits. Control with a general-purpose fruit spray applied according to the schedule in Table X.

Peach tree borers. Widespread, brown-headed, yellow caterpillars that bore into trunks of peaches, plums, nectarines, cherries, and apricots. Masses of gum ooze from the holes they make. Control by fumigating the soil around the tree trunks with para-dichlorobenzene in the fall. In the spring, when buds are cracking, spray endosulfan on the trunk and branches.

Plum curculios. Similar to apple curculios, these are small beetles found east of the Rockies which make puncture holes in apples, pears, quinces, and the stone fruits. Control with a general-purpose fruit spray as in Table X.

Root maggots. Small, legless, yellowish-white maggots that tunnel in roots and stems of cabbages and related plants. You cannot see them, but you know they are present when plants suddenly start to wilt and then die. To control, work chlordane dust into the soil before planting.

Spotted and striped cucumber beetles. Two beetles, both small and yellow, but one with black spots and the other with black stripes. Nationwide roamers, they eat the foliage of all vegetables in the cucumber family. The grubs burrow in the plant stems. They are particularly troublesome on young plants, but are readily controlled by dusting with rotenone.

Squash bugs. Dark brown bugs with triangular heads are also called stink bugs, because they smell bad when crushed. They suck the sap from squash, pumpkin, and melon plants almost everywhere. Leaves wilt and die. To control, spray plants with Sevin or malathion when the bugs first appear and again when you find brown egg masses on the undersides of leaves. They can also be hand-picked into a can of kerosene or trapped under shingles laid on the ground.

Squash vine borers. The borers, which tunnel through the stems of plants in the cucumber family, causing sudden death, are 1-in. white caterpillars with brown heads. The parents are wasplike, red and orange moths. They are troublesome east of the Rocky Mountains. Dust or spray plants when about 8 in. high with Sevin or methoxychlor, and repeat at weekly intervals for a month. Be sure to treat the runners and crowns of plants.

Strawberry root weevils. A problem for Northern strawberry growers, these white, curved, legless larvae cause stunting of plants by feeding on the small roots. They also tie the leaves together. Control by mixing chlordane into the soil before setting out plants. Spray plants with malathion when the weevils come up out of the ground in the spring.

Tent caterpillars. Several kinds of caterpillars found in most parts of the country; all identifiable by the tent-like webs they build in the crotches of fruit trees, particularly (in the East) apples and cherries. They rip the foliage to pieces. Control by removing the egg clusters in the winter and tearing down the webs, with all the caterpillars inside, in the spring. You can also simply open the webs and spray inside with lead arsenate. But do not burn them, because this does grave damage to the trees.

Thrips. These are tiny, yellow, or brown insects that suck the juices out of various plants ranging from onions to mangoes. They cause white blotches and then withering of leaf tips. Apply malathion.

Whiteflies. Inhabitants of citrus orchards, these small, white, moth-like insects suck the juices of leaves, and leave them speckled and covered with mold. Spray with malathion.

Wireworms. Hard, slender, dark worms, they spend years in the soil feeding on the roots of many plants. Plants may fail to emerge in the spring or may appear thin and patchy. To control, work chlordane dust into the upper 6 in. of soil.

SPECIFIC CONTROLS FOR DISEASES COMMON TO FOOD PLANTS

Unless otherwise noted, these ailments may be encountered almost anywhere in the country.

Anthracnose and other leaf spots. These diseases, which are especially troublesome in wet years, cause spots on leaves and fruits. The spots are of various colors, depending on the disease, and often have pronounced centers. Control by spraying with zineb or maneb at the first sign of trouble. Burn infected leaves and other plant parts.

Bacterial wilt. A disease favored by high temperatures. It attacks tomatoes, eggplants, and peppers, causing sudden wilting and death. There is no cure; but you can control it partially by rotating crops and fumigating the soil with Chloropicrin.

Blackheart. A disease of celery characterized by blackening of the growing tips in the hearts of the plants. To control, spray every week with a solution of ¼ lb. of calcium chloride dissolved in 5 gal. of water. Use a coarse spray and aim it into the hearts of plants.

Black knot. Twigs of plums, cherries, and apricots develop knotty, black excrescences. When this happens, cut the twigs 4 in. below the knots and burn. You should also spray with lime-sulfur when buds begin to open.

Blossom-end rot. Black or brown sunken areas appear at the blossom ends of the fruits of tomatoes, peppers, watermelons, and squash. The disease is thought not to be caused by any kind of organism but by a lack of moisture at the time plants are setting fruits. The obvious way to prevent it, therefore, is to keep the vegetables watered, or mulch the soil around them.

Brown rot. A disease of the stone fruits which causes blossoms to turn brown and fruits to develop brown spots which then spread and become covered with white spores. Gummy cankers may also develop on the trunk and branches. The disease most commonly occurs in warm, humid weather. To control, spray with captan every three days during the bloom period, and every week during the three-week period prior to harvest.

Cane blight. Canes of the bramble fruits develop brown spots; then wilt and die. To control, spray with ferbam at the first sign of trouble. Burn infected canes promptly.

Cedar-apple rust. Leaves of apples, crabapples, pears, and quinces become rusty-looking and distorted. This disease occurs only in areas where red cedars grow. To control it, either chop down all cedars within a mile of your garden or spray fruit trees in mid-spring with ferbam.

Clubroot. A disease of cabbages and all related vegetables, clubroot causes misshapen, swollen roots and yellowed leaves that wilt on hot days. You can prevent it by liming the soil heavily to raise the pH to 7.2 or by pouring a cupful of Terraclor solution around each seedling when it is set in the garden.

Curly top. A disease of tomatoes and beans in irrigated areas of the West. Leaves become thick, brittle, curled, and yellow with purple veins. Growth is stunted. There is no remedy. Destroy plants at once. Plant varieties resistant to the disease.

Damping off. This fungus disease prevents seeds from germinating and causes small seedlings to keel over and die. Prevent it by sowing seeds in a sterile medium; or by fumigating the seed bed; or by dusting the seeds before sowing with Spergon.

Downy mildew. A white or gray, downy mold appears on bean pods and also on the leaves of cucumbers and melons. The disease is worst in wet weather. Spray with zineb.

Early blight. Leaves of tomatoes, potatoes, peppers, and eggplants develop brown spots with concentric lines. The spots grow together, and then the leaves fall off. Control with zineb or maneb sprays applied soon after plants are set in the garden and at weekly intervals thereafter during wet weather (fortnightly intervals during dry weather). You should also make a practice of rotating crops.

Fire blight. A very serious disease of pears, this blight also attacks apples and quinces. It causes bark on twigs to darken; fruits, blossoms, and leaves to blacken and fall. Control is difficult, but you can make some headway by spraying trees several times while they are in bloom with copper fungicides or Bordeaux mixture. Cut out diseased wood at least 6 in. below the diseased area, and burn. Avoid over-feeding trees since this encourages strong growth which, in turn, encourages the disease.

Fusarium wilt. A hot-weather disease of tomatoes, peppers, melons, and peas, fusarium causes wilting, yellowing, and death. There seems to be no cure, but the disease can be prevented by planting resistant varieties and by rotating crops.

Greasy spot. A disease of citrus trees which causes small, oily, brown spots on leaves. Leaves then fall. Control by spraying with copper fungicides in the summer.

Gummosis. This fungus disease attacks citrus trees, beginning on the trunk at ground level. Gum flows from infected areas. Bark near the graft is decayed. The ailment can usually be prevented by proper planting and care, as recommended under Oranges in Chapter 9. If trouble develops anyway, examine the decayed area to see if live bark still extends half way around the trunk. If it doesn't, remove the tree: it's a goner. If it does, re-move the dead bark and a little of the live bark next to it. Disinfect the wound with 1 tsp. potassium permanganate in 1 pt. water. When the wound heals, cover it with tree paint and then replace the soil.

Late blight. A very destructive disease of tomatoes and potatoes which is favored by cool, moist weather in late summer or early fall. It is char-acterized by dark, water-soaked patches on leaves and fruits. The leaf spots usually have a white fungus growth on the under side. Once the dis-ease starts, there is nothing you can do about it except destroy plants and pray that ends matters. However, blight can be prevented by spraying regularly throughout the growing season with zineb or maneb (as for early blight).

Melanose. A fungus disease of citrus trees, melanose produces irregular, rough spots on young leaves, fruits, and shoots. To control, cut off and burn dead twigs and branches that harbor the fungus. Spray trees, one to three weeks after fruits are set, with a neutral copper fungicide and wet-table sulfur.

Mosaic. Another difficult disease of tomatoes, beans, and squash. Leaves become mottled; plants are stunted. The best control is to use resistant varieties. Rogue out infected plants. Kill aphids and leafhoppers that may carry the disease. If you are a smoker, wash your hands thorough-ly before handling susceptible plants and leave your cigarettes, cigars, or pipe in the house.

Powdery mildew. A powder-like growth appears on leaves and some-times on fruits of squash, pumpkins, melons, and watermelons. The ail-ment is most common in humid but not rainy weather. To control, spray with karathane. Plant resistant varieties.

Root knot. A disease caused by nematodes and favored by hot weather. The nematodes work themselves into plant roots, feed on plant juices. Large swellings appear on the roots, and the plants wilt, decay, and eventually die. Plants also become more susceptible to other diseases. Tomatoes, carrots, strawberries, and many other plants, including trees, are attacked by the disease. The best control is to fumigate the soil. See nematodes.

Scab. Dark, scabby lesions develop on leaves, fruits, and twigs of apples, pears, peaches, pecans, and citrus fruits. To control, follow a regular spray schedule as in Table X.

Smut. A disgusting fungus growth that develops in hot weather on ears of corn and sometimes on other parts of the plant. The only control is rotation of crops. Cut off the infected plant part and burn.

2,4-D injury. This occurs when the mist from a 2,4-D spray drifts across the garden. The spray causes leaves to twist and curl. Tomatoes and beans are most susceptible, but all plants may be affected. To avoid the problem, just don't use 2,4-D in the vicinity of your food crops.

Verticillium wilt. This disease, favored by cool weather, attacks tomatoes and peppers. Plants turn yellow, wilt, and die. There is no cure. Plant resistant varieties.

X disease. A difficult Eastern ailment of peaches. Leaves turn yellow about seven weeks after spring growth starts and then become very tattered looking. Trees under three years of age usually die; fruits of older trees are bitter. The disease appears to be caused by a virus transmitted from chokecherries. To control it, cut down all chokecherries within 500 ft. of your peach trees.

CONTROLLING URBAN AND SUBURBAN ANIMAL PESTS

A good many garden experts appear to shrug off animal pests as unimportant. But as I indicated at the start of this chapter, I do not agree. Some animals can do more damage in one hour in a food garden—especially a mature food garden—than most insects do in an entire summer.

Of course, people who live and garden in built-up urban and suburban areas are bothered by fewer animals than those who live in the far-out suburbs and country. Nevertheless, they must contend quite often with the following (which are also troublesome in open areas).

Birds can do serious damage to a stand of corn and small fruits; and every once in a while, they go after other vegetables and large fruits. Blackbirds, cowbirds, crows, grackles, and starlings are the worst offenders; but others may give trouble, too. All are difficult to control.

If you really prize your berries, they are best grown in a high wire enclosure; but you can give them equally good—and much less expensive —protection simply by covering beds, rows, or individual plants with any kind of lightweight, non-metallic netting. This can usually rest directly on the plants. It should pretty well surround them.

Other ways to cope with birds are to scare them off with moving and whirling devices, revolving lights, fireworks, and other sound-makers. These should not be put into use until you actually find the birds at work in your garden. If you anticipate trouble, the birds will become accustomed to the scare-maker you use and return to the garden unless you switch to some other device.

Life-like scarecrows are also useful for a while if employed in the same way. Their value is increased if you also occasionally fire a shotgun into the air from the spot where they stand. Actually trying to shoot birds, however, does little good unless, for some reason, there are only a few that are giving trouble. Large flocks are almost impossible to decimate.

Gophers—properly called pocket gophers—are burrowing rodents that inhabit much of the country. (In the South they are also called salamanders.) They eat roots, tubers, and underground stems; and their burrows may divert irrigation water.

If you have only a few gophers in the garden, catch them with gopher traps; but if you are over-run, use poisoned baits. To use traps, dig a trench at right angles across the gopher's burrow, and place one trap in the burrow on one side of the trench and a second trap on the other side of the trench. The traps must be attached by wires to a stake driven into the ground at the top of the trench, otherwise a gopher that is not instantly killed may drag them off. Do not fill the trench, but cover it with a board. Enough light and air will enter the burrow to bring the gopher hustling to fix his run; and that, hopefully, is the end of the gopher.

If you use baits, cut potatoes, sweet potatoes, beets, carrots, or turnips into ½ x 1 in. pieces and dust them with powdered strychnine alkaloid or thallium sulfate. Dig a trench across the burrow as below, and place a few baits on either side of it in the burrow. Then fill the trench. If the gophers are not quickly eliminated, repeat the baiting process with another vegetable.

Mice are actually more troublesome in large orchards than in small gardens, because they establish vast colonies which amuse themselves by eating the bark on the tree trunks and roots. (When they girdle a tree, it's done for.) Nevertheless, anyone who plants fruit trees should keep an eye out for them.

The easiest way to protect trees is to keep the grass around them cut close so the mice cannot build nests and hide around the trunks. If you mulch trees, pull the mulch away from the trunk about 6 to 12 in. Additional—and more positive—protection is provided by encircling the

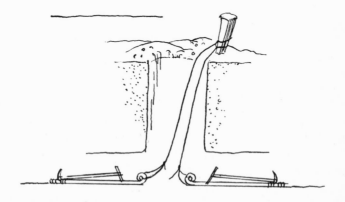

To trap gophers, place two traps in the runway on either side of the trench you dig across it. Tie the traps to a stake above ground.

trunks with ¼-in. wire mesh. This should extend above the ground about 20 in. and be dug in 4.

If you have a big orchard, another way to control mice is to place poison baits in the burrows and/or to broadcast them on the ground under the trees. The poison recommended by the U.S. Fish and Wildlife Service is zinc phosphide rodenticide, which is dusted on cut pieces of apple. Unfortunately, the poison is also deadly to humans, pets, and farm animals.

Moles have no special fondness for vegetable gardens, berry patches, and orchards; but they are as likely to burrow there as anywhere. Since they feed on grubs, the best way to get rid of them is to get rid of the grubs by dusting the soil in the spring with chlordane. Lacking a good food supply, the moles move elsewhere.

You can also trap moles rather easily with steel traps. These should not be allowed to build up a crust of rust, because that slows their action.

Slugs and snails spend their days in comparative hiding. But at night they march forth in armies and chew happily on the leaves of vegetable plants, thus retarding their growth. They also eat sizable holes in edible plant parts, such as your best melons and squashes.

Pick off and crush all you find. The rest should be poisoned with metaldehyde baits scattered through the garden. Cover the baits loosely with boards or stones to keep off dogs and children and also to provide the dark, damp hiding places the mollusks like.

CONTROLLING ADDITIONAL RURAL ANIMAL PESTS

These are often the big troublemakers. They are larger than the urban pests, have larger appetites, and are surprisingly numerous.

The most practical way to keep them under reasonable control is with a gun. But unfortunately many states would rather give pleasure to hunters than food to gardeners; and they prohibit shooting except during hunting season. Some states even go so far as to prohibit the trapping of animals. On the other hand, some enlightened states permit you to shoot marauding animals either on sight or after securing approval of the fish and game authorities.

In other words, before you start gunning for animals that are wrecking your garden, check your state laws. And if and when you do bring out a rifle, be careful about where you aim it.

Deer do extensive damage in summer gardens and also injure fruit trees in winter by rubbing their antlers against the trunks and branches and by nibbling on the tender shoots. If you can't shoot them, you must erect an 8-ft. steel mesh fence or electric fence around your entire garden or orchard. The only practical repellents are nasty-tasting chemicals which are sprayed or brushed on plants that deer like especially. These can be used for winter protection, but should not be applied in summer to plants you are going to eat.

Ground squirrels are occasional Western pests. Handle them like gophers.

Opossums. These ugly, sluggish marsupials sometimes eat berries, other fruits, and vegetables. But they are easily caught in box traps or with No. 2 steel traps baited with fish or dogfood.

Rabbits may be cute, but they are also very destructive in vegetable gardens and in orchards, where they eat the tree bark. Although far more numerous in the country, they are by no means unknown in the built-up suburbs. A hungry cat, fast dog, or well aimed gun are your best means of protection against them.

Scent repellents are useless; but taste repellents similar to those used for deer are fairly effective. They should not be used on edible plants, however; so that really makes them useless, too.

Trapping, where allowed, is uncertain (in fact, when *Sunset* magazine made a survey of its readers some years ago, it found only one person who had ever succeeded in trapping a rabbit—and he used a butterfly net!). Box traps that do not harm the rabbits are used. You are then supposed to release your captives several miles away; and since rabbits do not roam very far, they theoretically will never return. Instead they go to work on someone else's garden.

Happily, there is one non-violent control method that works: Just encircle your garden and the trunks of young fruit trees with 1½-in. wire mesh. This should be sunk 6 in. in the ground and rise about 24 in. above it.

Raccoons are big and wily and have a great fondness for corn and berries. They can make a shambles of a garden in one night.

The fact that everyone has a different idea about how to control coons indicates—not that the animals will fall for anything—but that nothing really works except a gun.

A farmer down the road from me insists that Havahart traps work fine; but exterminators I have consulted just snort at the idea. Another neighbor who lives on the edge of a forested military reservation encircles his garden with dried blood fertilizer but isn't sure it does any good. By contrast, a retired naval officer uses mothballs in the same way and is positive they are wonderful.

I once had the idea—born of desperation—of looping a long string around each row of corn and tieing to it an assortment of bells. I figured that when the coon went after the ears of corn, the bells would set up a clangor and scare him off. For good measure, I floodlighted the garden. The coon came anyway.

So what's the answer? I wish I knew.

Squirrels love nuts, of course. But when they suddenly take it into their heads to eat your corn or tree fruits, they may go on a rampage. They have been known to destroy 500 bushels of fruit in one orchard in a few days.

As with other animal pests, shooting—where it is safe and permitted—is the best method of control. It is also fairly easy to catch squirrels alive in box traps baited with nut meats, pumpkin or sunflower seeds, peanuts, rolled oats, etc.

The animals can be kept out of isolated trees by fastening 24-in.-wide bands of aluminum flashing around the trunks at a height of 6 to 8 ft. All branches hanging to within the same distance of the ground must be cut out.

Woodchucks may eat vegetables and fruits; and their burrows are a menace to garden machinery and the legs of horses and cows. But they are rather easily exterminated by placing special gas cartridges or Cyanogas in the burrows, which are then sealed with sods.

CONTROLLING WEEDS

Many gardeners think of weeds as an unsightly nuisance, but fail completely to appreciate that they also threaten the lives of desirable nearby plants by competing for moisture and nutrients in the soil and, to some extent, by serving as havens for diseases and insects. This is the real reason why weeds must be kept out of the garden.

How do you do this? Largely by the same methods gardeners and farmers have always used:

1. Pull them out by hand; chop them out with a hoe; dig them under with a rotary tiller. It's tedious work, but if you do it regularly, you soon bring the offenders under control.

2. Apply a mulch that will smother them. See Chapter 3.

3. Poison them with an herbicide. In the long run, this control method is almost certain to replace all other methods on the farm; and it may replace them in the home garden. But at the moment, you had better not get too excited about the possibilities.

There are various problems with the herbicides we now have: If mishandled, they can harm the user. They may "drift"—be washed across the garden to desirable plants which they then kill as easily as the weeds they are designed to eradicate. If taken up into food plants, they may be toxic to the consumer.

Finally, herbicides are not effective against all weeds; and they are not harmless to all edible plants. On the contrary, each chemical is effective against a specific (usually short) list of weeds and it is safe to use around only specific edible plants. This presents difficulties if you have a diversified garden that is populated by a diversified collection of weeds.

Herbicides which are at this writing considered safe for the home owner to use around edible plants are the following. All are so-called pre-emergence herbicides which are applied to bare, weed-free soil and which prevent the weed seeds from germinating. Follow the manufacturer's directions very carefully when using them.

Amiben. This is safe to use around asparagus seedlings, lima beans, peppers, pumpkins, squash, and tomatoes.

Dacthal. Safe to use around chestnuts, crabapples, and walnuts.

EPTC. Safe to use around citrus trees.

Trifluralin. Safe to use around apples, chestnuts, pineapple guavas, plums, cherries, apricots, almonds, peaches, and walnuts.

One other way to use modern herbicides is to kill weeds in vegetable gardens and berry patches, coldframes, and hotbeds before they are planted. The chemicals used for this purpose are DMTT and SMDC, more commonly known as Mylone and Vapam. Both are fumigants which kill not only the weed seeds and plant parts in the soil but also fungi and nematodes. To use them, you must first cultivate the soil to a depth of 6 in. and keep it damp for several days to encourage the weed seeds to germinate. Then apply the fumigant, work it in well and water it, and cover the treated area with polyethylene film to keep the poisonous fumes from escaping rapidly. About five days before planting in the soil, remove the film and cultivate the soil shallowly to permit all traces of the chemical to dissipate. The entire treatment process takes two to four weeks, depending on which chemical you use and on the temperature of the soil.

Part Two
Specifics

5

Growing Vegetables

I think the hardest thing about raising vegetables is to figure out how many of this and that to plant. I have never come out right even with the aid of a freezer, canning kettle, and willing friends. So I am quite happy about the figures I came across in an Illinois Agricultural Extension Service bulletin. They certainly do not fit all families and all gardens, but at least they give you a base to build on.

In the first place, the bulletin makes a few suggestions about the quantities of vegetables and fruits (both home-grown and purchased) a family of four consumes in a year.

	DAILY SERVINGS PER PERSON	POUNDS PER YEAR FOR A FAMILY OF FOUR
Potatoes and sweet potatoes	1–2	500
Tomatoes and citrus fruits	1	620
Leafy, green, or yellow vegetables	1–2	660
Other vegetables and fruits	2 or more	640

From here the bulletin goes on to show the yields you can reasonably expect from the most popular vegetables per 100 ft. of row. In Table III I have reduced this to 10 ft. of row because this is a more useful figure for most home gardeners.

TABLE III
Yields of Home-Grown Vegetables

	Approx. yield in pounds per 10 ft. of row	Approx. pounds of fresh vegetable needed for 1 qt.	
		CANNED	FROZEN
Asparagus	5	4	2–3
Beans, lima (pods)	2	4–5	4–5
Bean, snap	6	1½–2	1½–2
Beets	6	2½–3	2½–3
Broccoli	6		2
Cabbage	20		
Carrots	7½	2½–3	2½–3
Corn, early	7½ ears	4–5	4–5
Corn, main crop	8½ ears	4–5	4–5
Cucumbers	10		
Eggplant	6		
Lettuce, head	9 heads		
Lettuce, leaf	5		
Muskmelons	15		
Onions	10		
Parsnips	10		
Peas (pods)	3	4–5	4–5
Peppers	6		1½
Potatoes, early	6		
Potatoes, late	7½		
Pumpkins	30		
Radishes	10 bunches		
Rhubarb	10	1	1½
Spinach	5	2–3	2–3
Squash, summer	16	2½–3	2–3
Squash, winter	40	2	3
Sweet potatoes	8	2½–3	2–3
Swiss chard	5		3
Tomatoes	50	3	
Turnips	5		
Watermelons	2 fruits		

Figuring the garden size. Although this table is an excellent guide to how much you might plant, it obviously does not tell you how much space your garden should occupy. To answer this question, you must consider several things:

1. What space do you have available? Since vegetables should have a full day of sun, the area devoted to the garden must be well away from buildings, trees, and geological features that would shade it.

2. Which vegetables do you want to raise, and how many of them? Here you must determine the length of the plant rows needed to supply you. Then you must determine how wide each row will be and how much additional space is necessary between the rows to allow you to care for your plants.

Average row widths—the space actually occupied by each vegetable— are given in the encyclopedic part of this chapter. The additional space required between rows depends on how you plan to cultivate the garden. Allow 1 ft. if you use a hoe or pronged cultivator or if you apply a mulch. Increase the space to 2 ft. if you use a small rotary tiller. For still bigger mechanical cultivators, the space must be correspondingly wider.

3. How large a garden do you personally feel able to work? This is the hardest question to answer. For one thing, it takes a lot of work to prepare the ground for the garden in the first place. This is true even if you use power equipment. I have known a number of people who started out with big ideas, but who settled for much smaller gardens when they discovered how strenuous digging and tilling are.

In the second place, once a vegetable garden is established, you must keep working it if you expect it to produce the crops you desire. This work is by no means so taxing as the work of preparation; and it can be greatly reduced if you mulch the garden. Nevertheless, the work is demanding simply because it cannot be ignored. And the bigger the garden, the more demanding it is.

4. Will you work the garden to its maximum potential? You should, of course. Garden space is valuable and should be cultivated intensively at all times.

There are two ways you can do this, and both have an effect on the size of the garden. One is called intercropping. This is the practice of planting sma'!, early maturing plants between rows of slower growing plants. Thus you can raise three rows of vegetables in the space normally occupied by the outer two. A few of the best vegetables for intercropping are early peas, radishes, green onions, spinach, beets, and lettuce. These might be planted between tomatoes, eggplants, peppers, etc.

The other way to get the most out of your garden space is by succession cropping. This involves planting several crops one after another in the same row. Thus the soil is never idle. As soon as you have harvested a row of, say, peas, you rip out the plants and put in a row of beans. Or perhaps you follow an early crop of carrots with a second crop of carrots.

This brings us back to the initial question of how large you should make your vegetable garden if you have not had one before. A definite answer is obviously impossible. But here are a few helpful examples of how much space gardens take up:

A. If you raise a 100-ft. row of each of the vegetables listed in Table III, the garden will occupy a space measuring almost exactly 100 x 100 ft. and it should yield 3,000 lb. of produce plus assorted ears, fruits, and heads.

B. If you raise a 100-ft. row of each of the vegetables listed and inter-crop and/or succession-crop to the fullest extent possible, you can reduce the size of the garden to roughly 100 x 80 ft. The yield will remain un-changed.

C. If you limit yourself to those vegetables that make the most efficient use of space—snap beans, beets, broccoli, cabbage, carrots, leaf lettuce, onions, radishes, spinach, swiss chard, tomatoes, and turnips—and if you plant 100 ft. of each of these, your garden will measure only 100 x 20 ft. It should, however, yield 1,250 pounds of vegetables plus 100 bunches of radishes. Intercropping and succession-cropping will either reduce the size of the garden or increase the yield.

Does this still sound like a bigger garden than you want to tackle? If you have never raised vegetables or any other kind of food plants before, it probably does. On the other hand, maybe it doesn't. As I said earlier, many neophyte food gardeners are over-ambitious and put in—or at least try to put in—gardens that are too large and perhaps too diverse to cope with.

This, of course, is something you should not do.

If you're a new gardener, start small. If the garden is something of an experiment ("I don't know whether I'm going to like this, but I want to find out"), keep it down to 50 sq. ft. and plant only a few different things in it. Perhaps it could be a salad garden, with lettuce, scallions, and radishes in the spring followed by beautiful red tomatoes in the summer. Perhaps it could be an herb garden. Or perhaps it could be a strawberry bed (al-though strawberries are classified as a small fruit, they are grown more like vegetables than like other small fruits).

If you look at your first garden, not as an experiment, but as something you really expect to enjoy, you can start somewhat bigger—but even so, I'd recommend that you stay under 200 sq. ft. That would not require too much work, yet it would give you a chance—by succession cropping—to plant and harvest pretty good crops of about ten different vegetables.

After your first year, if you have enjoyed your food-growing experience, you may well want to expand the garden. But here again, think small. Don't jump from 200 to 2,000 sq. ft. If you didn't succeed in killing yourself, you would at least kill your enthusiasm. Expand in easy stages—500, 1,000, 1,500, 2,000. Proceeding in this way, you will never get in too deep.

Laying out the garden. The layout of a vegetable garden depends to considerable extent on its location (discussed in Chapter 2); but it should also be guided by other considerations:

Just because most gardens are laid out in rectangles, you should not arbitrarily select this shape for yours. Other shapes are just as efficient, and are advisable if they make use of space which might otherwise be wasted.

If you plant on a hillside, run the rows across the slope, not up and down. This slows the run-off of water and prevents erosion.

If you use power equipment, make the rows as long as is practicable. This simplifies equipment handling.

Although straight rows may look neater, don't hesitate to make your rows curving or sinuous if this improves land utilization.

Don't waste space on inside garden paths that parallel the plant rows. Paths at right angles to the plant rows, however, tend to simplify some gardening operations (especially watering) and save steps.

Plant perennial crops together along one side of the garden, and group your early annual crops nearby.

Rotate crops every year so that you do not grow the same vegetable or one of its relatives in the same spot more often than once in three years. This helps to prevent a build-up of diseases in the soil. Table IV shows which vegetables are related.

TABLE IV
Related Vegetables

Onions, leeks, shallots, chives, garlic.

Tomatoes, eggplants, peppers, potatoes.

Cucumbers, muskmelons, watermelons, pumpkins, squash.

Cabbage, broccoli, brussels sprouts, cauliflower, kohlrabi, mustard, turnips, ruta-baga, Chinese cabbage, kale, collards, radishes, cress, horseradish.

Beets, swiss chard.

Snap beans, lima beans, shell beans.

Carrots, celery, celeriac, parsnips, dill, caraway, coriander, fennel, parsley, anise.

Improving the garden soil. The main points are covered in Chapter 3. Of these, the most important (because it requires annual attention) is the need for maintaining soil fertility.

Vegetables take enormous quantities of nutrients out of the soil; and while it is possible to replace these simply by making several applications of inorganic fertilizer during the growing season, the ability of the soil to produce fine crops will gradually decline if it is not also enriched every year with humus.

As noted in Chapter 3, innumerable sources of humus are available to the gardener; but one of the best—and cheapest—is the vegetable plants the garden itself produces. These should not be burned or thrown on the garbage truck after you have harvested your crops unless they are diseased or infested with insects. What you should do is to cut off the tops close to the ground with a grass whip, and throw them on a pile somewhere out of sight to decay at their own leisurely pace (building a real compost heap hastens the decay process, but the heap demands too much attention).

In the spring, dig the plant roots left in the garden deeper into the soil. Later, when the plant tops have disintegrated, spread them on the garden and dig them in, too.

Another easy and excellent way to put humus into the soil is to grow a cover crop. Several plants are widely used for this purpose: rye, rye grass, oats, winter vetch, crimson clover, and cowpeas. I prefer rye because it makes substantial growth even when it is sown late in the fall, after most of your vegetables have been harvested. (Early fall sowing is desirable, however.) Sow the seeds across the entire garden or between the vegetable rows at the rate of about 3 lb. per 1000 sq. ft.; rake them lightly into the soil, and water well. If you apply a high-nitrogen fertilizer, such as ammonium nitrate, at the same time, the grass will grow faster and more luxuriantly. Mow the grass in the spring as late as your planting plans permit but before it exceeds 1 ft. in height; and plow it under with a tiller.

Agricultural scientists have proved that if a winter cover crop is grown every year, garden yields are substantially improved. And still higher yields are obtained if a summer cover crop of soybeans, cowpeas, or another legume is planted every fourth year.

Buying vegetable seeds. Although it is tempting to harvest and plant seeds from home-grown vegetables, the amount of money you can thus save is small and the seeds themselves may be of inferior quality. Furthermore, you may wind up with plants that bear little resemblance to those that produced the seed in the first place.

Planting seeds left over from the previous year is also a questionable practice because seeds lose their viability with age. For example, seeds of corn, leeks, onions, parsley, parsnips, rhubarb, and salsify usually will not germinate after they are one or two years old. Similarly, seeds of asparagus, beans, brussels sprouts, cabbage, carrots, cauliflower, celery, kale, lettuce, okra, peas, peppers, radishes, spinach, turnips, and watermelons are usually not good after three to five years.

It is, in short, a better idea to buy fresh seeds each year from reliable seedsmen than to hoard your own.

The varieties you select should be given careful study, although you cannot go very wrong with anything offered by any of the major seed companies. Where you have a choice, however, you should be sure to select varieties which are (1) resistant to disease; (2) suitable for the home garden; (3) recommended for freezing or canning; (4) recommended especially for your climate or not recommended especially for a quite different climate; (5) treated with hot water or bichloride of mercury to prevent seed-borne diseases.

Buying plants. Although it is much more fun to grow your own vegetables from seeds, buying seedlings from garden supply stores saves work. Note, however, that the only vegetables which are commonly sold as seedlings are tomatoes, eggplants, peppers, parsley, rhubarb, asparagus, onions, lettuce, broccoli, and cabbage.

The best plants to buy are those growing in individual pots or bands. These usually are sturdier than plants growing together in a flat; and because the roots are surrounded with a ball of earth, there is relatively little chance of damaging them when you set the plants in the garden. (Plants in individual peat pots are particularly desirable because you do not even have to remove the pots before transplanting: they disintegrate in the ground.)

Even more important than the way seedlings have been grown, however, is their condition at the time you buy them. Make sure they are a rich green (not yellowish); stocky and well branched (not leggy); and growing in moist soil.

How vegetables react to temperature. A few vegetables are perennials; but the great majority are annuals. These are a varied lot.

Some are very hardy plants that need low temperatures to grow well. Examples: peas, onions, lettuce, and broccoli. They should be planted in the garden four to six weeks before the mean date of the last spring freeze. In the southern reaches of the Great Plains and south Texas, in fact, they must be planted in winter if they are to come through at all.

Some vegetables are hardy plants which grow best at low temperatures, but which also do well at fairly high temperatures. Examples: beets, carrots, swiss chard. They are planted in the garden two to four weeks before the mean date of the last spring freeze. Many of them (along with several of the very hardy plants) can also be planted in late summer to give a fall crop.

Some vegetables are tender and should not really be planted outdoors until after the last frost; however, if you want to take a chance, you can plant them on the mean date of the last spring freeze. Repeat sowings of most of these plants can be made well into the summer. Examples: corn, snap beans, and okra.

Some vegetables are very tender and require warm soil and rather high air temperatures. They must not be planted in the garden until all danger of frost is past. Examples: lima beans, sweet potatoes, and muskmelons.

When to start the garden in the spring. Starting the garden always involves a certain amount of risk because you can never be sure on what date in any given year you will have your last spring freeze. That's why you should use the mean date of the last spring freeze as the basis for your calculations. The map on pages 8–9 gives this date for all parts of the country. Note that in the areas east, south, and west of the dotted line that runs more or less from North Carolina across the deep South and up the West coast, there are some years in which no spring freeze occurs at all.

Planting on the mean date of the last spring freeze means that you have a 50–50 chance of escaping a freeze after that. Planting after the mean date improves your chances of escaping a freeze; on the other hand, planting before the mean date reduces your chances of escaping a freeze.

H. C. S. Thom, a senior research fellow with the U.S. Department of

Commerce's Environmental Science Services Administration, has figured out for me the probabilities of having a last spring freeze on a given date before or after the mean dates of the last spring freeze. Here is a summary of what he says:

THE PROBABILITY OF HAVING A FREEZE X DAYS BEFORE OR AFTER THE
MEAN DATE OF LAST SPRING FREEZE   IS

18 days before	95%
14 days before	90%
9 days before	80%
6 days before	70%
3 days before	60%
0 days before	50%
3 days after	40%
6 days after	30%
9 days after	20%
14 days after	10%
18 days after	5%

(The probabilities of having a freeze before or after the mean date of the first fall freeze work out in the same way, but, of course, in reverse. That is, you have a 5 per cent chance of having a freeze 18 days before the mean date of the first fall freeze; a 10 per cent chance of having a freeze 14 days before the mean date; a 95 per cent chance of having a freeze 18 days after the mean date.)

These probabilities apply for Alaska and the entire 48-state area inside the dotted line. If you live in the area outside the dotted line, you should use the following tables:

IF THE MEAN DATE OF LAST SPRING FREEZE IS—	THERE IS A 10% PROBABILITY OF HAVING A FREEZE AFTER—	THERE IS A 5% PROBABILITY OF HAVING A FREEZE AFTER—
Jan. 20	Jan. 9	Jan. 26
Jan. 30	Feb. 10	Feb. 19
Feb. 8	Feb. 28	Mar. 6
Feb. 18	Mar. 10	Mar. 16
Feb. 28	Mar. 23	Mar. 29
Mar. 10	Apr. 2	Apr. 8
Mar. 30	Apr. 22	Apr. 29

IF THE MEAN DATE OF FIRST FALL FREEZE IS—	THERE IS A 10% PROBABILITY OF HAVING A FREEZE BEFORE—	THERE IS A 5% PROBABILITY OF HAVING A FREEZE BEFORE—
Dec. 20	*	Dec. 22
Dec. 15	Dec. 17	Dec. 9
Dec. 10	Dec. 15	Nov. 30
Nov. 30	Nov. 18	Nov. 14
Nov. 20	Nov. 6	Nov. 2
Nov. 15	Nov. 1	Oct. 28
Nov. 10	Oct. 27	Oct. 23

*Probability of freeze is less than 10%.

Freezes occur in Hawaii at high elevations, but statistical information about them does not exist.

What does all this mean? Simply this:

The date on which you sow seeds or set seedling plants in the spring vegetable garden depends on (1) the relative hardiness of the plants as indicated in the encyclopedic section following; (2) the mean date of the last spring freeze in your locality; and (3) how much of a chance you are willing to take that you have already had your last freeze for the season.

Getting a jump on the season. Taking a risk on the weather is one way to get your garden off to an extra early start. And in the case of some plants, such as peas, corn, and beets, it is the only course you can follow. Unfortunately, this does not mean it is a reliable course, for even though you guess right about escaping a freeze, you may run into a long spell of cold, wet, dreary weather that delays seed germination and slows subsequent seedling growth. Two years ago, for example, my hopes for very early crops of several vegetables were dashed—not by a late freeze—but by unseasonably damp, chilly weather throughout the month of April. In retrospect it was obvious that, if I had not rushed the season so much, I would have come out just as well. And yet this year, if I should rush the season again, I might gain my early-crop objectives.

Moral: If you want early crops of some vegetables, you just have to take your chances on the weather.

A more reliable way to get a jump on the season is to start the seeds under glass (indoors or in a coldframe or hotbed) and move the little plants into the garden when the weather permits. Tomatoes, eggplant, peppers, melons, broccoli, cabbage, and lettuce are the vegetables most often handled in this way—especially in areas where the growing season is short.

Here is the procedure.

Indoors. The main problem with starting seeds in the house is lack of sunlight. If you have a really sunny, reasonably warm sunporch, of course, you are in good shape. But an ordinary window—even a large, unobstructed, south window—leaves much to be desired. Oh, yes, it may do; but the plants you grow in it are not much to brag about.

The best way to start vegetables (and flowers) indoors is to ignore the sun entirely. Use fluorescent light instead. All you need is an inexpensive industrial fixture with two or more 48-in. daylight or Grolux tubes. If you hang this 12 to 14 in. above a plant bench in an out-of-the-way corner and keep it burning 18 to 24 hours a day, it will give all the light necessary to produce strong plants.

Sow the seeds in flats filled with one of the new sterile soil mixtures now being sold throughout the country under such names as Jiffy-Mix, Redi-Earth, Cornell Mix, etc. Made of shredded sphagnum peat, vermiculite, and fertilizer, these mixtures—combined with the fluorescent light—produce the best seedlings you or anyone else can grow. One old-time nurseryman commented to me: "It's the only starting mixture I know of that gives two pretty plants for every single seed you sow." A slight exaggeration, of course, but it gives you an idea of how good the mixtures are.

Dampen the soil mixture thoroughly and then squeeze it as dry as possible before sowing seeds. Press the seeds in lightly and cover the larger ones with a little additional mixture. Place the flats directly under the fluorescent light; and except for watering them when the soil surface begins to dry out, there is nothing more you need to do until the seedlings have their first or second set of true leaves and begin to crowd one another.

At that point they should be thinned to no more than 12 plants spaced evenly across a flat measuring approximately 4 x 6 in. If the plants that are thinned out are to be saved, dig them up carefully with a blunt knife and replant them in individual pots or flats filled with dampened soil mixture.

Before moving the little plants into the garden, you must harden them off so that they will not be injured by low outdoor temperatures (and the brilliant rays of the sun if they were grown in a window rather than under fluorescent light). This process should be inaugurated about a week prior to actual transplanting. All you have to do is to set the plants outdoors in a sunny spot sheltered from the wind for an hour or two the first day, a little longer the second day, and so on until, at the end of the week, they are left outdoors for a full 24 hours. Keep the plants on the dry side during this period.

Another way to harden off seedling plants is to move them directly from the house into a coldframe (see below).

Once your plants are accustomed to outdoor living, they should not be brought back indoors even if the weather becomes inclement. Keep them in their flats in the sun and give them reasonable protection against hard winds and biting cold.

An alternative to growing seedlings in flats is to sow two or three seeds in a small peat pot filled with ready-mixed soil, and later to discard all but one plant. The pots add to the cost of the seedlings and take up somewhat more space under your fluorescent light than flats; but they eliminate the necessity of transplanting from one flat to another and then into the garden. This spares the plants the shock which accompanies transplanting operations and thus yields crops a couple of days ahead of normal schedule.

In coldframes. Vegetables started from seeds in coldframes do not attain the same size in the same length of time as those started in ready-mixed soil under fluorescent light. Furthermore, since coldframes are not so warm at night as a house, you cannot start tender plants in them so early in the year.

Soil in coldframes should be enriched with peat and about 2 cups of 5-10-10 fertilizer. It is a good idea to fumigate the soil (before adding peat and plant food) to kill fungi that attack seeds and seedlings. Chloropicrin, Vapam, and Terraclor are several chemicals used for this purpose. If the

Vegetables growing under fluorescent light. The Bibb lettuce formed large enough heads to be eaten before they were moved outdoors.

soil is not fumigated, the vegetable seeds should be dusted with a disinfectant such as Spergon to prevent damping-off.

Sow the seeds in rows about 6 in. apart. Sprinkle with water when the soil begins to dry out. Pull weeds as they appear. Thin the seedlings after they have their first or second sets of true leaves.

Cover the glass top of the coldframe with an old quilt or blanket of straw when the temperature threatens to drop below the freezing mark. Raise the glass an inch or two during daylight hours on mild, sunny days; and as the time approaches to move the plants into the garden, raise the glass higher to harden them off.

In hotbeds. Because the soil in a modern hotbed is heated by a thermostatically controlled electric cable, this kind of propagating unit is considerably warmer than a coldframe and consequently produces stockier plants at a faster pace. Preparation and management, however, are essentially the same as for a coldframe. The only major difference is that you should occasionally adjust the heating cable temperature to suit plant requirements. For tender plants, the soil temperature should start at 70° and then be lowered gradually to about 50°. Hardy plants are held at 50° from start to finish.

(In addition to using a hotbed to raise seedlings for the garden, you can use it in the dead of winter to raise off-season crops of lettuce, carrots, radishes, etc.)

TABLE V
When to Start Seeds Under Glass

	Sow seeds this many weeks before mean date of last spring freeze		
	INDOORS	IN COLDFRAME	IN HOTBED
Very hardy plants	6–8	6–8	6–8
Hardy plants	6–8	5–7	6–8
Tender plants	4–6	1–3	4–6
Very tender plants	3–5	1	3–5

How to get an extra-early start in the garden. If you have an awful urge to have tomatoes, eggplants, melons, and other tender vegetables long before your neighbors, there is one further step you can take to get a jump on the season: Start the plants indoors or in a hotbed two to three weeks ahead of the schedule shown in Table V; move them into the garden two to three weeks before the last frost; and raise them under Hotkaps until the weather is reliably warm.

A Hotkap is a small, circular, waxed-paper tent which is placed over a seedling plant to protect it against frost, wind, and rain. It also serves as a temporary mulch around the plant. (A Hotent is the same as a Hotkap

To facilitate movement of hoses through a vegetable garden, drive a sturdy stake at each end of each row. This will keep you from dragging a hose over the end plants and breaking them.

but larger. It is used for very big, fast-growing seedlings such as musk-melons.) After a Hotkap is dropped over a plant, the edges are weighted down with a little soil and a small hole or slit is cut in the top to provide essential ventilation. When the plant touches the top of the tent, the top is torn out but the sides are left to provide protection against wind. Then, when the weather is warm, the entire tent is removed.

Sowing seeds directly in the garden. Vegetable seeds should never be sown outdoors until the soil is dry enough to be worked without caking. A good test is to squeeze some of the soil in your hand. If it forms a solid ball, it is too wet.

When the soil is suitable for tilling, turn it over to a depth of 8 to 12 in., break up the clods, and then level with a rake. Do not work it so hard that you break it down into a mass of tiny particles. A coarse texture is much better because it is less likely to cake and allows water and oxygen to reach the plant roots more readily.

Mark the plant rows with a length of twine stretched between stakes. Make shallow furrows for small seeds by drawing a hoe or rake handle along the line. Use the corner of a hoe blade to make deep furrows.

Most vegetable seeds are sown by drilling—dropping the seeds into the furrow in a continuous row. The spacing of small seeds is best controlled by tapping the packet very deliberately so that the seeds come out by ones and twos—not in dollops. Do not shake the packet. Large seeds, as of beans, corn, and peas, should be emptied from the packet into your hand and then dropped between your fingers, one by one, exactly where you want them to be. This not only saves seed but also simplifies thinning of plants later on.

Sowing seeds in hills is an alternative to drilling, but is generally used only in the case of cucumbers, melons, pumpkins, winter squash, and some-times corn. A hill is nothing more than a cluster of about six to twelve seeds arranged in a crude circle about 1 ft. across. The spacing between hills depends on the kind of plants you are growing.

The depth at which vegetable seeds are planted ranges from ¼ to ½ in. for very small seeds to 1 to 2 in. for large seeds. The greater depths are used when the soil is sandy or dry.

Seeds should be treated with a fungicide before sowing. Many now on the market are pre-treated by the seed grower. If you buy untreated seeds, drop a pinch of Spergon into each packet and shake well to coat the seeds. This helps to prevent damping-off and decay.

After seeds are sown, rake soil over them to the proper depth and tamp it with a rake or hoe. Then water well—with a fine spray—if the soil is bone dry.

Planting seedlings in the garden. Seedlings that you buy or raise under glass should be transplanted to the garden on a mild, cloudy day or in the late afternoon of a sunny day. This helps to keep them from wilting.

Water the plants well an hour or two before they are moved. Set them in the ground slightly deeper than they previously grew. If they are in peat pots, the tops of the pots must be covered with a little soil to keep the peat from acting as a wick which draws moisture from the plants to the air.

Firm the garden soil around the rootballs so that the plants sit in a slight, saucer-like depression. Then pour a cup of starter solution into each saucer. The solution is made by dissolving in water a concentrated, powdered fertilizer containing a high percentage of phosphorus; for example, a 10-20-10, 10-52-17, or 10-50-10.

Give the plants a little plain water once or twice during the following week.

Dividing perennial plants. Perennial vegetables include asparagus, rhubarb, horse radish, and various herbs. Most of these are propagated by making divisions in the fall or early spring.

In most cases, this is the same easy process used in propagating perennial flowers. All you do is dig up a clump and pull or cut it into smaller clumps or individual rooted plants. If the clump is very large and old, save the young, outer portions and throw away the inner. These are then replanted at the same height they previously grew.

Perennial vegetables can be divided whenever you want new plants; but generally they are allowed to grow for three years or more before divisions are made.

Caring for the garden until harvest. Thin plants which have been seeded directly in the garden as soon as they are well up and you can determine which are the weakest.

Mulch the soil to conserve moisture and keep down weeds. If you don't do this, you must pull or hoe out the weeds regularly. Occasional hoeing is also necessary on unmulched soil to keep it from packing so hard under traffic that air cannot reach plant roots.

Water as necessary to give the plants about 1 in. of water, including rainfall, every week. To make it easier to pull your hose through the garden without knocking down the plants, drive stout, round stakes into the ground at the end of each vegetable row. Special gadgets which have a sleeve that revolves around a central spindle can also be used.

Keep an eye out for insects and diseases.

Harvest vegetables when they are at their peak of goodness.

How long does it take vegetables to mature? This varies between types of vegetable (for example, cress matures in 20 days whereas Casaba melons take 120) and also between varieties of the same vegetable (for example, Oak Leaf lettuce matures in 40 days while Great Lakes takes 90).

In the encyclopedic section, maturity dates are given for each of the varieties listed. These dates are figured in three ways: (1) In the case of vegetables that are started from seed sown in the garden, the maturity dates represent the *average* number of days it takes from time of sowing until the vegetables are ready to be harvested. (2) In the case of vegetables started under glass, maturity dates are figured from the time the seedling plants are set out in the garden until they are ready for use. (3) In the case of most perennial vegetables, maturity dates are for two-year-old plants and represent the number of days it takes from the time the plants come up until they are ready for use.

The stress on the word "average" should be noted. Actually a number of things other than the inherent characteristics of the vegetables themselves affect the speed with which they reach maturity.

One is the weather: Cold, very wet weather retards plant growth whereas warm days with just the right amount of moisture usually hasten it.

Another is the time of sowing seeds: Vegetables sown very early in the spring grow slower than those sown in late spring, when the weather is warm.

A third is the area in which you live: In cold climates with short growing seasons the same vegetable matures faster than it does in a warm climate with a long growing season.

When to plant vegetables for fall harvest. The map on pages 10–11 gives the mean dates for the first autumn freeze in all parts of the country.

To figure out when to plant vegetables for fall use, all you must do is to subtract the maturity dates for the vegetables from the mean freeze date for your locality. In most parts of the country, you should then sow seeds in the garden one to four weeks prior to the date indicated by your calculation. (Example: if the mean date for your first fall freeze is October 30 and if you want to harvest a crop of Detroit Dark Red beets, which mature in 60 days, close to that date, work back 60 days from October 30. This brings you to September 1. Sow the beet seeds in the garden any time from August 1 to about August 21.

On the Pacific Coast, from about San Francisco north, an extended period of very cool fall weather usually precedes the first freeze. Since this is likely to retard the growth of vegetables that grow best when the temperature is high, seed should be sown in the garden a couple of weeks earlier than the formula just given.

In the Southeast, fall crops of vegetables are often difficult to grow because of low rainfall and heavy infestations of insects and diseases.

SOILLESS CULTURE

Growing vegetables and other herbaceous plants in water is not a new idea, and it certainly produces no miracles. Occasional claims to the contrary, vegetables grown in this way are not more productive, bigger, or more nutritious than those grown in fertile soil. There is, therefore, no particular reason to get excited about hydroponics—as this cultural method is known—unless you live in a place where soil is non-existent or unless you are simply looking for some mild amusement. Nevertheless, the idea is sound enough to merit mention.

The simple facts are that you can grow any vegetable in a liquid solution if it receives eight to ten hours of sunlight, or the equivalent artificial light, daily. Tender plants require a daytime temperature of 70° to 80°; a nighttime temperature of 60° to 70°. Hardy plants are grown at 10° lower temperatures.

Plants can be grown without soil in two ways:

1. You can drop the roots through holes in the top of a trough, tank, or other container filled with nutrient solution. Since roots do best in the dark, the tank and its top should not admit very much light. The tops of the plants must be held upright by wires, rods, etc.

Because growing plants remove the oxygen from the water in the tank, arrangements must be made to bubble air constantly into the water. This can be done with a small aquarium pump.

The water level in the tank must be maintained at all times; and since the level of nutrients in the water changes, the tank must be emptied and filled with fresh solution every 10 to 14 days.

2. The other way to raise vegetables without soil is to plant them in containers filled with sand, gravel, vermiculite, or peat. The containers must have drainage holes in the bottom. The nutrient solution is poured into the containers from the top and allowed to trickle through into a catch basin or bucket. This is done two or three times a day—frequently enough to keep the sand moist at all times. The nutrient solution can be used over and over again, but has to be replaced every 10 to 14 days.

The advantages of growing vegetables in sand are that the plants do not need support and you do not have to aerate the solution. On the other hand, you must make some arrangement to fill the containers with solution as it is required.

Whichever way you raise plants, the nutrient solution used is the same. The following suggestions are taken from a booklet published by the Alabama Agricultural Extension Service:

"No one nutrient solution is superior to another for growing plants. The main point is to be sure plant nutrients are available in the right proportions to avoid deficiencies or toxicities, unless such are desired. Either of the solutions (given in Table VI) will do. Amounts suggested for each are based on technical-grade material. You may substitute fertilizer grades if the technical grades cannot be obtained.

"Add minor elements to each solution. Most water—other than distilled water—contains enough molybdenum, zinc, and copper for plant growth if the solution is renewed every 10 to 14 days. For most water, use one of the following minor element solutions, plus an iron solution.

"*Minor Element Solution No. 1.* Mix 7.6 grams (1¼ tsp.) of boric acid and 0.6 grams (approximately ⅒ tsp.) of manganese chloride in 1 liter (quart) of water. Use ½ cup of this solution for 10 gal. of nutrient solution.

"*Minor Element Solution No. 2.* Mix 5.2 grams of boric acid and 0.36 grams of manganese chloride in 1 liter of water. Use 5 milliliters of this solution for each liter of nutrient solution. This rate will supply 5 parts per million boron and 0.5 parts per million manganese.

"*Iron.* Mix 3 grams (½ level tsp.) of chelated iron in 1 liter of water. Use 10 milliliters of the iron solution per liter of nutrient solution or 1⅜ cup per 10 gal. of nutrient solution. If additional iron is needed before the nutrient solution is renewed (indicated by yellowing of young leaves), make an additional application.

"Ferrous sulfate or copperas may be used. Dissolve 5 grams of copperas in 1 liter of water, and use 5 milliliters (1 tsp.) of this solution per liter of nutrient solution.

TABLE VI
Nutrient Solutions for Use in Soilless Culture

Solution No. 1

| CHEMICAL COMPOUND | Amount of chemicals to add per 10 gal. of water | | PARTS PER MILLION IN NUTRIENT SOLUTION |
	GRAMS	LEVEL TSP. (APPROX.)	
Potassium phosphate (KH_2PO_4)	10.1	2	78 K 62 P
Potassium nitrate (KNO_3)	11.5	2½	117 K 42 N
Calcium nitrate ($Ca(NO_3)_2 \cdot 4H_2O$)	22.3	4½	100 Ca 70 N
Magnesium Sulfate (Epsom salts) ($MgSO_4 \cdot 7H_2O$)	18.6	4	48 Mg 64 S

Solution No. 2

| CHEMICAL COMPOUND | Amount of chemicals to add per 10 gal. of water | | PARTS PER MILLION IN NUTRIENT SOLUTION |
	GRAMS	LEVEL TSP. (APPROX.)	
Ammonium phosphate ($NH_4H_2PO_4$)	8.7	2	28 N 62 P
Potassium nitrate	19.0	4	195 K 70 N
Calcium nitrate	22.3	4½	100 Ca 70 N
Magnesium sulfate	18.6	4	48 Mg 64 S

"Solution pH. After mixing nutrient solution, check the pH which tells you whether the solution is acid or alkaline and to what extent. If a pH tester is not available, use indicator (litmus) paper that changes color at different pH levels.

"Most plants grow best in slightly acid solution or soil—a pH 5.5 to 6.5. A pH below 4.0 is too acid for most plants; pH 8.0 or above is usually too alkaline.

"If the solution is too alkaline, add a few drops of diluted sulfuric acid per liter or quart, stir the solution, and check the pH. Continue adding small amounts of the acid until the desired pH level is reached.

"Similarly, you can increase the pH by adding a few drops of sodium hydroxide."

Once the solutions have been mixed and the desired pH obtained, they are ready for use.

ARTICHOKES

Also called globe artichokes. Spreading, thistle-like perennials to 4 ft., producing large, succulent, edible buds from spring on. Grow best in California's four central coastal counties, but also grow in other parts of the country in Zones 8–10. Occasionally productive in Zone 7 if grown as annuals or given careful protection in winter. Grow from divisions of the root. Buds mature in 50 to 100 days.

Varieties

Green Globe. Only variety grown. It has large, usually round buds with green bracts which sometimes have a purplish coloration at the base. Thorns on the bracts are small or non-existent.

Culture

Artichokes can be grown from seeds (germination: 12 days), but do not come true. The plants are therefore propagated by 6-in. lengths of fat rootstalks taken from the base of old stems. These are planted in early spring or fall. Set them 6 in. deep and 4 ft. apart in rows 4 ft. wide. The soil should be deep, fertile, well drained, and moisture-retentive. Hill the soil up slightly or provide drainage ditches between rows so that the plants will not stand in water in wet weather.

Water newly set plants thoroughly. Thereafter, see that the soil does not dry out at any time for very long. Water is needed especially during the bud-formation period.

California farmers who irrigate their artichokes by sprinklers often feed them by injecting soluble nitrogen fertilizer into the water once a month. You can use the same system at home or apply foliar sprays. Or you can sidedress the plants in the spring when growth starts with ½ cup of ammonium nitrate.

Keep plants weeded, or mulch with organic material. The latter treatment is better because it adds nutrients to the soil.

Artichokes are subject to several diseases for which there are no definite controls other than good garden sanitation and planting of disease-free stock. Aphids, slugs, and snails may also be troublesome. But the most serious pest is the artichoke plume moth, the larvae of which bore holes into the buds, stems, and foliage. These are also controlled by good sanitation, including prompt destruction or burial of infested plant parts. You may also spray the plants with malathion about four times at fortnightly intervals before harvest starts.

Artichoke buds can be harvested any time after they are formed. They may be only 1 in. across; but a more popular size is about 4 in. across. Cut the stem 1 to 1½ in. below the base of the bud. Store in the fresh-food section of the refrigerator. The buds deteriorate quickly at temperatures above 50°.

After harvest, cut out the bearing stalks with a knife just below the ground level. New shoots will spring up.

In cold climates, after the plants are nipped by a light frost, cut them to the ground and cover with durable boxes that have tight tops but a few small openings in the sides. Then cover the boxes and ground around them with a heavy mulch of hay, straw, fiberglass insulation, or other light, non-packing material. You should also make sure that the ground slopes away from the plants so that water cannot settle around them.

After four or five years the roots of well grown artichokes in favorable climates become so congested that the plants lose vigor and become less productive. To prevent this, divide the plants every three or four years.

ASPARAGUS

Perennial vegetable with delicate fern-like foliage reaching 3 ft. Grows in Zone 3–8. 1 oz. of seed produces 500 plants. Sow seeds ½ in. deep. Germination: 21 days. Mature plants produce harvestable stalks in 25 days.

Varieties

Faribo Hybrid. Hard to find but produces very large, thick stalks.

Mary Washington. By far the most popular variety. Straight green stalks with a purplish tinge. Excellent for freezing. Has good resistance to asparagus rust.

Waltham Washington. A strain of the above, and also excellent. Lacks the purplish coloring.

Culture

The soil should be a rich, sandy loam with a pH of about 6.5. Very sandy soil and heavy clay are undesirable. Dig to a depth of about 15 in. and mix in large quantities of humus or rotted manure, if available. Preparation of the soil the summer before planting is recommended.

If you grow asparagus from seed, you can sow the seed directly in the garden where the plants are to grow; but it is usually simpler to start them in an out-of-the-way seedbed. Mix in 10-10-10 fertilizer at the rate of 1 cup per 20 sq. ft. Sow seeds on about the mean date of last spring freeze. Because of slow germination, you may want to sow radishes in the rows to mark them. Soaking seeds in warm water for two days helps to speed germination. Weed carefully: young asparagus is so slim that it is difficult to see. Thin out to one plant every 2 or 3 in. Dig up roots early the following spring and transplant to the permanent bed.

Buying roots of one-year-old plants saves time and trouble.

Whatever the source of your plants, they should be set in the garden in the early spring while they are still dormant. First mix 10-10-10 fertilizer thoroughly into the soil at a rate of 10 cups per 100 sq. ft. Open a trench or dig individual planting holes about 6 in. deep and wide enough to receive the roots when they are spread out on the bottom. The roots should be spaced 18 in. apart. If more than one row is planted, space the rows 4 to 5 ft. apart. Cover each root with an inch or two of soil and firm it well. As the plants grow, gradually fill in the rest of the soil until the roots are buried 6 in.

None of the asparagus spears produced in the first year should be harvested. Just keep the beds weeded. Do not cultivate too deeply. Water in dry spells. Let the stalks stand over winter, since they catch and hold snow which helps to maintain a fairly even soil temperature and supplies needed moisture in the spring.

During the second year, cut down the stalks in the early spring. Apply a layer of well-rotted manure, leafmold, or peat, and at the same time apply 6 cups of 5-10-10 or 10-10-10 fertilizer per 100 sq. ft. Work this into the soil to a depth of 3 in. Then, in late June or early July, sidedress each 50-ft. row with 1 cup of muriate of potash. Keep weeds pulled. But once again, do not cut any of the asparagus spears. Leave the tops on over winter.

In the third year, repeat the preceding procedure. Now, however, you can start enjoying the fruits of your labors. Cut all spears from the time they start reaching edible size—6 to 8 in. in length—for the following four weeks, no longer. The cutting is done with a sharp knife 1 or 2 in. below the soil surface. Be careful not to jab other spears which have not yet appeared. If you prefer white asparagus to green, mound soil up around the emerging spears, leaving only the tips exposed.

During succeeding years, your harvest season can be lengthened to six or seven weeks; but do not cut after July 4. Care of the asparagus bed in these years is identical with that in the second year. Keep adding humus to the soil every spring. Apply a balanced fertilizer in early spring and potash after the final cutting. Keep the bed free of weeds. Watch out for asparagus beetles.

Although there is considerable argument as to whether asparagus rows should be kept level or should be ridged, tests by the Delaware Agricultural

Experiment Station indicate that ridging produces larger spears, though it also makes for extra work. A ridge is nothing more than a mound of soil, about 18 in. wide and 4 in. high, which is thrown up over each asparagus row when the first spears have pierced the soil surface in spring.

An asparagus bed that is cared for properly may continue in heavy production for 30 to 40 years.

Special culture

Asparagus may be forced in greenhouses or the basement in much the same way that rhubarb is forced. A simpler way to produce very early asparagus, however, is to place a portable coldframe over some of the plants in the garden. Or you can bury electric heating cable in a circle close around a few garden plants and put a large solid box or barrel over them.

ASPARAGUS PEAS

These are not a true pea, but a relative. Twining, annual plants growing to 1 ft., they have pretty reddish-brown pealike flowers followed by rectangular, flanged, stringy pods which are eaten whole. The flavor resembles both that of asparagus and peas. Grow in Zones 3–10. 1 packet plants 40 ft. of row. Plant seeds ½ in. deep. Germination: 10 days. Plants mature in 90 days.

Culture

Sow seeds outdoors two weeks after mean date of last spring freeze. Sow four or five seeds to a foot and thin to 1 ft. apart in rows 15 in. wide. Grow like peas. Support on brush. Harvest pods when they are 3 in. long or a little less.

BEANS—SNAP

Annual plants to 20 in. Grow in Zones 3–10, and may be successful in 1 and 2 if the soil warms up adequately. ½ lb. plants 75 ft. of row. Sow seeds 1 in. deep in heavy soil; 1½ in. in light soil. Germination: 6 days.

Varieties

Bountiful. 49 days. Broad, flat, stringless green beans to 7 in. Good for French cutting. A favorite.

Brittle wax. 52 days. Round, yellow, stringless beans to 6½ in. Good for freezing and canning.

Contender. 52 days. Stringless, round, green beans to 6½ in. Does well under adverse conditions. Resistant to mosaic and powdery mildew.

Eastern Butterwax. 53 days. Stringless, oval, yellow beans to 7 in. Excellent for freezing.

Executive. 56 days. Round, stringless green beans to 6 in.

Greencrop. 55 days. Broad, flat, stringless green beans to 7½ in.

Improved Tendergreen. 56 days. Stringless, round green beans to 7 in. Mosaic resistant.

Kinghorn Wax. 55 days. Stringless, yellow beans to 6 in. Excellent for freezing and canning.

Pencil Pod Black Wax. 54 days. Round, yellow, stringless beans to 6 in. An old favorite despite its black seeds.

Provider. 50 days. Stringless, round, green beans to 5¼ in. Resists mosaic and tolerates powdery mildew.

Resistant Cherokee Wax. 52 days. Oval, stringless, yellow beans to 6 in. Resists bean mosaic.

Royalty. 51 days. Unusual round, purple, stringless beans turn dark green in boiling water. Grows in colder soils than other varieties and is avoided by Mexican bean beetles.

Rustproof Golden Wax. 50 days. Flat, yellow, stringless pods to 5½ in. Resistant to bean rust.

Spartan Arrow. 51 days. Oval, stringless, very straight green beans to 6½ in.

Stringless Green Pod. 50 days. Stringless, green beans to 6 in. Widely planted.

Stringless wax. 52 days. Flat, yellow beans to 6½ in. Also called Yellow Bountiful.

Tendercrop. 53 days. Round, green, stringless beans to 5½ in. Excellent for freezing. Mosaic resistant. One of the few varieties recommended for Alaska.

Tenderette. 52 days. Round, stringless, green beans to 5½ in. Good for canning and freezing.

Tenderpod. 50 days. Stringless green beans to 5 in. Good for canning and freezing.

Topcrop. 49 days. Round, green pods to 6 in. Mosaic resistant. Recommended for Alaska.

Wade. 56 days. Round, stringless, green beans to 6 in. Resists mosaic and powdery mildew. Still popular after many years in various parts of the country.

White Half Runner. 60 days. Very tasty green beans to 4½ in.; stringless only when young. Good for freezing. Popular in the South. Large plants are bushy at the base and put out 2-ft. tendrils, or runners, at the top.

Culture

Sow seeds outdoors after all danger of frost is past. Repeat sowings at two-week intervals may be made to within two months of first fall frost. Since beans are likely not to set pods in very hot weather, late spring and early to midsummer plantings should not be made in warm climates. Late summer plantings have a good chance of producing a fall crop, however. In extremely cold climates or in areas where the soil may not warm up sufficiently, beans are sometimes planted in hills and covered with Hotents in their early stages.

In drills, sow seeds 2 in. apart in rows 18 to 24 in. wide.

Snap beans are not overly fussy about soil as long as it is well drained and reasonably fertile. Germination is spotty in very heavy soil that is too wet or too hot. One application of balanced fertilizer prior to seed sowing is enough.

Do not cultivate or handle bean plants when they are wet, lest you spread disease organisms. In the Southwest and East, the worst pest is the Mexican bean beetle; but this is readily controlled with rotenone. Aphids are a common pest everywhere. Most diseases that attack beans are avoided by use of disease-resistant varieties.

Harvest beans when young and succulent, before the seeds plump up.

BEANS—LIMA

Annual plants to 20 in. Grow in Zones 4–10. Baby limas are generally reliable in colder zones than the big-seeded types. ½ lb. plants 75 ft. of row. Sow seeds 1 in. deep in heavy soil; 1½ in. in light soil. Germination: 7 days.

Varieties

Burpee's Fordhook. 75 days. A favorite for over 60 years. Large, plump beans.

Dixie Butterpea White. 76 days. A white-seeded baby lima that does well at high temperatures. Popular in the South.

Fordhook U.S. 242. 74 days. Outstanding variety with large, plump beans. Excellent for freezing and canning. Sets beans well when temperatures are high.

Henderson's Bush. 65 days. White baby limas good for freezing and canning.

Jackson Wonder. 65 days. Beans of medium size; speckled. Tolerant of heat and drought. Much planted in the South.

Thaxter. 74 days. A baby lima. Excellent for freezing. Resistant to downy mildew.

Thorogreen. 67 days. Small, light green beans. Good for canning and freezing.

Culture

Lima beans are more sensitive to cold than snap beans and should not be planted until about a week or more after all danger of frost is past and the soil has started to warm up. Sow seeds 2 to 4 in. apart and thin to 8 in. Rows are 24 to 30 in. wide.

Culture is about the same as for snap beans. An additional pest to watch out for is mildew. Harvest beans just before the seeds reach full size.

BEANS—POLE

Annual plants from 6 to 10 ft. Snap beans grow in Zones 3—10; lima beans in Zones 4–10. ½ lb. plants 50 hills. Sow seeds 1 in. deep in heavy soil; 1½ in. in light soil. Germination: 7 days.

Varieties

Burpee's Best. 92 days. Lima. Large pods with big, plump beans. Very tall vines. Excellent for freezing.

Dade. 55 days. Snap bean with large, oval pods. Developed in Florida, it gives good production in hot, humid weather. Resistant to mosaic and rust.

Florida Butter. 85 days. Lima. Small, two-colored beans. Tolerant of hot weather.

Kentucky Wonder. 65 days. Green snap bean with very large pods that are stringless when young. Good for freezing; and the seeds are also excellent for drying and baking. A very popular, old variety.

King of the Garden. 90 days. Lima. Very large pods and beans. Good for freezing. An old favorite.

London Horticultural. 70 days. Also called Cranberry or Wren's Egg. A favorite snap bean which is very good to eat when young. But the variety is most often used as a dry shell bean.

McCaslan. 65 days. A long, flat snap bean, stringless when young. Seeds may be dried.

Romano. 70 days. Snap bean with broad, flat, stringless beans with a unique flavor. Excellent for freezing. Medium-size vines. An old variety sometimes called Italian Pole Beans.

Scarlet Runner. 65 days. Tall-growing vines usually grown in a screen for their ornamental spikes of bright red flowers, but producing 6 in. snap beans of strong but good flavor. The beans should be picked before the seeds make lumps in the shells.

Sieva. 78 days. Lima. Small beans, medium green when fresh, white when dried. Popular in the South. The best variety for dried limas.

Stringless Blue Lake. 62 to 66 days, depending on the strain. A round snap bean of medium size. Popular in the Northwest.

Culture

Grow pole beans like the bush varieties of snap and lima beans. Sow seeds outdoors when all danger of frost is past and soil is warm. To provide support, tie three 7- to 8-ft. poles together in a tripod. Plant the seeds 2 in. apart around each pole and thin to two or three vines per pole in the case of limas; three to five vines in the case of snap beans. Another way to support the beans is to drive two sturdy posts into the ground and stretch two wires between them. One wire should be at a height of about 1 ft.; the other at 6 ft. Tie strong strings between the wires at 9- to 12-in.

intervals. You may have to help the vines get started up whatever support you provide for them.

BEANS—FAVA

Also called broad beans or horse beans. These are an annual shell bean to 21 in. The pods are inedible; the large seeds are somewhat like lima beans and used in the same way. Grow in Zones 3–7. ½ lb. plants 75 ft. of row. Sow seeds 1 in. deep in heavy soil; 1½ in. in light soil. Germination: 7 days.

Variety

Long Pod. 85 days. Large, bushy plants. Broad, thick pods to 10 in. in length and with flat seeds.

Culture

The fava bean is a member of the vetch family, not the bean. It is hardy and grows best in cool weather; therefore, sow seeds in the garden as soon as the ground is workable. Grow like snap beans, otherwise. Watch out for aphids, a major pest. Harvest only when beans are mature.

BEANS—SHELL

Shell, or field, beans are annual bush varieties to 20 in., grown for their seeds. These may be eaten green in some cases, but are usually dried. Some pole beans are also good as shell beans. Grow in Zones 3–10; slower varieties in Zones 4–10. ½ lb. plants 75 ft. of row. Sow seeds 1 in. deep in heavy soil; 1½ in. in light soil. Germination: 7 days.

Varieties

French Horticultural. 68 days. Thick, flat green beans with red coloration. Stringless and semi-edible when young; but grown mainly for the seeds, which are used green or dried. Can be frozen.

Great Northern. 90 days. Small, inedible pods with flattened white beans. Plants are small and hardier than most.

Michelite. 92 days. A Navy bean with inedible pods filled with small, white seeds. Resistant to mosaic.

Pinto. 110 days. Inedible pods with mottled seeds. Grown almost entirely in the Southwest.

Red Kidney. 95 days. Inedible pods with large, kidney-shaped red beans.

White Kidney. 100 days. Similar to the above except for the seed color.

White Marrowfat. 100 days. Inedible flat pods with white seeds.

Culture

Grow like snap beans. Beans to be dried are allowed to ripen on the vine until they are fairly hard. They are then shelled, dried, and placed in a 130° oven for 30 minutes to prevent weevil infestation.

BEETS

Annuals to 18 in. Grow in Zones 1–10, but often do not do well in Alaska because the long days of summer may cause them to blossom and set seed before forming good roots. 1 packet plants 25 ft. of row. Sow seeds ½ to 1 in. deep. Germination: 9 days.

Varieties

Crosby's Egyptian. 56 days. Purplish-red flesh with lighter colored zones.

Detroit Dark Red. 60 days. Very round root with dark, solid-colored flesh. Tops are reddish. Standard strain has medium-size leaves for good greens. There is also a strain with shorter leaves.

Formanova. 46 days. A novelty. Cylindrical beets 6 in. long and 2 in. in diameter. Solid red. They push themselves out of the soil and need to be hilled up.

Green Top. 55 days. Green tops are good as greens. Roots are medium red with lighter zoning.

Long Season. 80 days. Also called Winter Keeper, because it stores well. Roots are large, top-shaped, rough looking but very sweet. Light green leaves are good for greens.

Perfected Detroit. 57 days. Dark red roots a little flat at the bottom.

Red Ball. 38 days. Recommended for Alaska because it does not bolt so rapidly as other varieties.

Ruby Queen. 58 days. Round, deep red flesh. Dark green tops tinged with red.

Culture

Sow seeds outdoors in the spring two to four weeks before mean date of last freeze, and make succession sowings every two or three weeks to within about two months of the first fall freeze. In hot, dry weather, to facilitate germination, sprinkle a little peat or sand over the row to keep the soil from baking; and water regularly until the plants emerge. Sow one or two seeds per inch and thin to 3 in. in rows 9 in. wide. By doing your thinning gradually, you can use some of those you pull out for greens and even for baby beets. (Note that a beet seed is actually a fruit containing several seeds This explains why seedlings come up in clusters, of which you should keep only one.)

Beets should be grown fast to keep them succulent. Mix plenty of humus into the soil; also about 3 cups of 5-10-10 fertilizer per 50 sq. ft. Water in dry weather. Keep the row weeded. Worst pests—and not very bad at that—are blister beetles and beet webworms.

Harvest beets when they are about 1½ in. in diameter. To store, trim off all but ¼ in. of the tops and pack in moist sand in a cool basement. Don't let them freeze.

BROCCOLI

An annual member of the cabbage family to 2 ft. tall. Grows in Zones 1–10. 1 packet produces 200 plants. Sow seeds ¼ to ½ in. deep. Germination: 10 days.

Varieties

DeCicco. 65 days. Similar to Green Sprouting, except that it is much earlier.

Green Comet. 55 days. New, highly touted hybrid variety.

Green Mountain. 60 days. Large heads good for freezing.

Green Sprouting. 80 days. Also called Calabrese. One of several very widely used varieties. First heads as much as 6 in. across.

Spartan Early. 55 days. Ranks with the following in popularity. But recommended for spring and summer crops.

Waltham 29. 80 days. Very popular for late summer and fall crops. Good for freezing.

Culture

Broccoli is a hardy vegetable that does not grow well in very hot summer weather, although it will make a summer crop in more northern areas if kept well watered. For a spring crop, sow seeds under glass and move well-hardened plants outdoors a couple of weeks before the mean date of the last spring freeze. For a somewhat later crop, sow seeds in the garden, where the plants are to grow, about the time of last frost. For a fall crop, make a second sowing in the garden about three to three-and-a-half months before the mean date of the first fall frost.

Space plants 2 ft. apart in rows 2 ft. wide. Soil of average quality and with a pH of about 6.5 is adequate. Mix in 5 cups of 5-10-10 fertilizer per 50 sq. ft. before planting out. Sidedress each plant twice thereafter at three-week intervals with a nitrogen fertilizer such as nitrate of soda or with a balanced fertilizer.

To control root maggots, dust a teaspoonful of 5 per cent chlordane around each seedling plant when it is set out.

To keep green cabbage worms out of the heads, dust the small plants a couple of weeks after they have been set out with rotenone. Spray frequently thereafter with malathion, which also controls aphids. Other pests are similar to those attacking cabbage, but not always troublesome.

Broccoli plants produce a large central head followed by a succession of small side sprouts. All should be harvested with 6-to 8-in. stems when the heads are compact and the buds are tight. When the buds open to show yellow flowers, the heads are over-mature. In cutting the large central head, make the cut on a slant so that water will run off. If the stem is hollow, cap it with a scrap of aluminum foil.

BRUSSELS SPROUTS

Annual to 2 ft. that produces large clusters of tiny, cabbage-like buds. Grows in Zones 1–10. 1 packet produces 250 plants. Sow seeds ¼ in. deep. Germination: 10 days.

Varieties

Jade Cross. 90 days. A fairly new hybrid that is widely grown throughout the country. Sprouts are very uniform in size, and tightly packed.

Long Island Improved. 90 days. Just about as good as the above and almost as widely grown.

Culture

Brussels sprouts are extremely hardy and in milder areas can be left outdoors over winter. For an early crop, start seeds under glass, harden off well, and move outdoors as soon as the soil can be worked in the spring. For a fall crop—which is more reliable—sow the seeds outdoors in a seedbed or where they are to grow about three-and-a-half to four months before the mean date of the first autumn freeze. In the garden, space plants 2 ft. apart in rows 2 ft. wide.

Grow like cabbage and watch out for the same pests.

As the sprouts begin to crowd one another on the stem, remove some of the lower leaves to give them more room. But never remove the top leaves. Harvest the sprouts from the bottom up. The plants can be left in the garden until well after the first frosts because they withstand short periods of cold as low as 10°.

Brussels sprouts freeze very well; but they can also be stored over winter in the North in a cold (but not freezing) basement or garage. Take up the entire plants and stand them close together. Tamp moist earth around the roots.

CABBAGE

Annuals to 15 in. Grow in Zones 1–10. 1 packet produces 250 plants. Sow seeds ¼ to ½ in. deep. Germination: 10 days.

Varieties

Note. Cabbages can be classified in several groups, each with numerous varieties: (1) The domestic group, with early, midseason, and late varieties. Most domestic cabbages, however, are fairly early, tender to eat, and have only moderate wax, or bloom, on the leaves. (2) The Danish group, which matures late, is a little tough and has a heavy bloom which gives the leaves a blue-green color. (3) Red cabbages, with varieties that mature in all seasons. (4) Savoy cabbages, which have very crinkled or blistered leaves in a compact head.

Badger Market. 70 days. Domestic type. Small, round heads with short core. Yellows resistant. Stands in the garden without splitting. Good on muck soils.

Copenhagen Market. 68 days. Domestic type. Small, compact, light green head. Very popular.

Danish Ballhead. 100 days. A small, round, solid Danish type that is good for storage and sauerkraut.

Dwarf Morden. 50 days. Midget variety producing delicious 4 in. round heads.

Early Jersey Wakefield. 62 days. Domestic type with small, pointed heads of excellent flavor. Be sure to get yellows-resistant strain.

Golden Acre Yellows Resistant. 63 days. Domestic type. Deep, small, green heads. Recommended by more state agricultural extension services than any other cabbage. Do not use ordinary Golden Acre, which is susceptible to the yellows.

Greenback. 74 days. Domestic type with medium-size heads. Yellows resistant. May be planted in the fall and overwintered in the South, because it withstands cold.

Harris' Resistant Danish. 95 days. Danish type resistant to yellows. Medium heads.

Marion Market. 75 days. Domestic type with big, round, solid heads. Yellows resistant. Very widely planted.

Penn State Ballhead. 105 days. Danish type with large heads, short cores. Good for sauerkraut and winter storage.

Red Acre. 76 days. Medium-size, globular, deep red heads. Resists splitting. By far the most popular red cabbage.

Red Danish. 97 days. Deep purple red. A fine keeper.

Savoy Chieftain. 88 days. A savoy type. Large heads store well.

Savoy King. 85 days. A hybrid savoy cabbage producing very uniform heads. Fall-sown plants are larger than spring-sown. Has good heat resistance.

Wisconsin All Season. 95 days. Late domestic type. Very large, slightly blue-green heads. Good for sauerkraut and storage. Yellows resistant.

Culture

Cabbages are very hardy and do best in cool, moist climates. In warm climates, therefore, they must be planted very early or very late. In many places, they can be overwintered outdoors.

For a spring crop, start seeds under glass, harden the seedlings off carefully, and move them into the garden any time after the soil can be worked. For a fall crop, sow seeds outdoors in a seedbed four or five weeks before the plants are to be set in the garden, or sow the seeds where the plants are to grow and simply thin them out. Plants to be stored over winter should be started as late as possible so that they are not too mature when you harvest them. In milder parts of Zone 7, it is often possible to sow seeds in a coldframe about the middle of October, carry the seedlings over under the glass cover, and set them out about the first of March for a very early spring crop. In still milder areas, cabbages can be started in the garden in November to produce a mid- to late winter crop.

Set plants 12 to 18 in. apart (depending on the size of the heads) in rows 2 ft. wide. Apply a cup of starter solution per plant. To control root maggots, dust a teaspoonful of 5 per cent chlordane around each seedling.

Cabbages grow in almost any decent soil with a pH of 6.0 to 6.8. Mix in a good supply of humus and about 5 cups of 5-10-10 or 10-10-10 per 50 sq. ft. The latter can be tilled into the soil or applied in bands along the cabbage row. To satisfy the plant's enormous need for nitrogen, sidedress each plant with a tablespoonful of nitrate of soda about three weeks after planting and again three weeks later.

Keep plants well watered at all times. Cultivate shallowly.

The best way to prevent disease in your plants is to start with yellows-resistant varieties (unless you know for a certainty that your soil is not infested with this fungus) and to buy seeds that have been hot-water-treated to control seed-borne diseases. Rotate crops every year. Most common insect pests are root maggots, cabbage worms, and loopers; flea beetles on seedling plants; and aphids in hot weather.

Because cabbage heads tend to split when left in the garden too long, they must be harvested at the right time. Generally they are in prime condition when the heads are firm and glossy green in appearance.

Cabbages should be stored in a humid, dark place with a temperature near but not below freezing. Do not expose them to excessive air movement, but see that they are not so tightly piled that air cannot circulate quietly around them. The heads lose their green color during storage.

CARDOON

A 6-ft. perennial vegetable, closely related to the artichoke, grown for its leafstalks, which are boiled and eaten. Grows in Zones 8–10. 1 packet produces about 50 plants. Plant seeds ¼ in. deep. Germination: 12 days. Matures in 110 days.

Culture

Sow seeds outdoors in a seedbed after last spring freeze and transplant to the garden when well established. Then grow like artichokes. Keep well watered. As the plants mature, draw the leaves together and wrap heavy paper or black plastic film around them. Blanch them for about a month.

CARROTS

Annuals to 20 in. Grow in Zones 1–10. 1 packet plants 30 ft. of row. Sow seeds ¼ to ½ in. deep. Germination: 8 days.

Varieties

Baby-Finger Nantes. 55 days. A novelty. Roots are only 3 in. long, and slender.

Danvers Half-Long. 75 days. Roots about 7 in. long, 2¼ in. wide at the top, and gradually tapering. An old favorite. Good for freezing. Danvers 126 is a good modern strain.

Gold Pak. 77 days. Roots are tapering, up to 10 in. long and only 1¼ in. across at the top. Grown primarily for the market, but interesting in a home garden which has very deep soil.

Red Cored Chantenay. 68 days. Stumpy, 6-in. roots, 2½ in. across at the top.

Royal Chantenay. 68 days. Similar to the preceding, but with slightly longer roots. Chantenay varieties have been popular for years.

Scarlet Nantes. 65 days. Cylindrical roots about 6 in. long and 1½ in. wide. Much grown in many states. Good for freezing.

Tiny Sweet. 65 days. Another 3-in. midget.

Culture

Sow seeds outdoors several weeks before last frost and make succession sowings about every three weeks to within two months of first fall frost. In warm climates, however, midsummer sowings are not likely to do well. Sow two or three seeds to an inch and thin the plants to stand 1 to 3 in. apart (depending on their ultimate diameter) in rows 10 in. wide. Thinning should start when the plants are up a couple of inches, but it is not necessary to do a complete job at that time. If you wait until the roots are about a half inch across before making a final thinning, you can eat those that are then pulled out.

Soil for carrots should be free of stones, deeply dug, and mixed with fertilizer. Use a 5-10-10 at the rate of 2½ cups per 50 sq. ft. Soil should contain humus, but this is best applied at the *end* of the gardening season.

Keep the rows free of weeds and the soil lightly stirred up so that moisture and air can penetrate. Water in dry weather. Hill soil up over roots which become exposed in order to keep the shoulders from greening. Watch out for wireworms, weevils, early and late blights.

Harvest carrots just before they reach maximum size, especially if they are to be eaten raw. Despite the excellence of modern varieties, small carrots are more succulent than mammoths, which become woody. Loosening the soil with a spading fork simplifies harvesting, especially of small varieties with weakly attached tops.

If you do not freeze carrots, they can be stored all winter in a box with an inch of sand in the bottom, Put a layer of carrots on this and cover with more sand; then another layer of carrots; and so on. Keep at a low temperature, but do not freeze.

Special culture

Carrots can be grown in coldframes for an early spring crop and also for a late fall and early winter crop. They are handled in the way described above but need to be covered with glass when the temperature falls below freezing.

CAULIFLOWER

Annual to 30 in. Grows in Zones 3–10. 1 packet produces 150 plants. Sow seeds ¼ to ½ in. deep. Germination: 10 days.

Varieties

Early March. 145 days. A very late-maturing strain of Snowball for mild climates, such as California and Hawaii. It is planted in the fall and harvested in late winter.

Purple Head. 85 days. Heads are purple; turn green when cooked. They are not blanched. Excellent for freezing.

Snowball. 55 to 70 days, depending on the strain. White heads when blanched. Good for freezing. All the strains offered by reliable seed companies are of excellent quality.

Culture

Cauliflower is not so hardy as cabbage but needs cool weather anyway. It does not head up well in warm weather. It also does not grow so well in dry climates as in humid.

For an early crop, start seeds under glass about eight weeks before plants are to be set out, and harden the seedlings off thoroughly before moving them to the garden three to four weeks before the mean date of the last spring freeze. For a fall crop, sow seeds outdoors in a seedbed or where the plants are to grow two-and-a-half to three months (depending on the variety) before the mean date of the first fall freeze. Space the plants 18 to 24 in. apart in rows 2 ft. wide. Give each newly set plant a cupful of starter solution, and dust 5 per cent chlordane on the soil around it to control root maggots.

Cauliflower requires a fertile soil, well drained but retentive of moisture, and with a pH of about 6.5. Mix in plenty of humus. Also mix in 5 cups of 5-10-10 fertilizer per 50 sq. ft. Sidedress each plant with a tablespoonful of nitrate of soda three weeks after planting and twice more at two-week intervals.

Keep weeded, but cultivate shallowly. Water well when the soil begins to dry out.

Pests of cauliflower are similar to those of cabbage.

As noted, purple-headed cauliflower is not blanched. To blanch white varieties, tie the outer leaves up over the head when it is about the size of an egg. Use twine, raffia, or a rubber band, and tie the leaves near the ends so they will not form too tight a covering. Open the leaves occasionally to check the development of the head. This does not take long— usually a week to ten days after the leaves are tied. Harvest the heads as soon as they have attained satisfactory size and are still firm. They get loose and crumbly if allowed to stand too long.

Leaves of cauliflower at right are tied together to blanch the head. Cauliflower at left is still too young for blanching. Endive can be blanched in the same way. Red cabbage and peas are in the background.

CELERIAC

Celeriac is also known as turnip-rooted celery. A 2-ft. annual variety of celery, it is raised for its large, knobby, flavorful root. Grows in Zones 2–10. 1 packet produces 400 plants. Sow seeds ⅛ in. deep. Germination: 21 days.

Varieties

Alabaster. 120 days.
Smooth Prague. 110 days.

Culture

Grow like celery. Keep well watered. Do not blanch the tops, which are discarded. Harvest when roots are 2 in. or more across. To store, cut off tops and cover the roots with sand in a cool (about 35°) place.

CELERY

A rather hard-to-grow annual to 30 in. Grows in Zones 2–10. 1 packet produces 400 plants. Sow seeds ⅛ in. deep. Germination: 21 days.

Varieties

Cornell No. 619. 100 days. Medium-size, green variety.
Giant Pascal. 125 days. Medium-size, green variety. Stores well.

Golden Detroit. 115 days. Dwarf, yellow variety that does well almost everywhere.

Golden Self-Blanching. 105 days. Small plants blanch easily to a clear yellow.

Summer Pascal (Waltham Strain). 120 days. Medium-size. Dark green leaves and stalks are easy to blanch. A favorite in the East.

Tall Utah 52-70. 130 days. Large variety with dark green foliage and medium green stalks. Grown in the West for fall and winter harvest.

Culture

For an early crop, start seeds under glass ten weeks before plants are to be set out. To speed germination, put the tiny seeds in a cloth bag or very fine strainer and soak them overnight in water. Keep the soil in the flats or seedbed moist. Transplant seedlings to the garden when they are 3 or 4 in. tall and when danger of frost is past. You can, however, set them out earlier if you cover them with Hotkaps. Celery is a cool-weather crop, but when exposed to low temperatures the plants tend to bolt and set seeds.

Seeds can also be sown directly in the garden about ten days before the mean date of the last spring freeze; but the plants are not so stocky as those that are transplanted.

For a late crop, sow seeds in an outdoor seedbed about four months before the mean date of the first fall freeze. If nematodes are troublesome, fumigate the soil before seeding. Fumigate the garden area devoted to celery also.

Soil for celery must be well drained but moisture-retentive, very fertile, and with a pH of about 6.5. If you can lay hands on any well-rotted manure, by all means do so. Otherwise, mix in a lot of peat, leafmold, or other organic matter. Also mix in about 3 cups of 5-10-10 or 5-10-20 per 50 sq. ft. If your soil is deficient in boron, apply a scant 1 oz. of borax per 50 sq. ft.

The soil should be deeply dug and well pulverized. Space plants 6 to 8 in. apart in rows 1 ft. wide. Because small celery plants are delicate, be sure to transplant them in cloudy weather and shade them from the sun for the next day or two. You can do this with muslin or small, leafy branches stuck in the soil. Water well.

Sidedress each 50 ft. row of plants with 3 cups of balanced fertilizer one month after planting and again two months after planting. Keep well watered at all times. Cultivate regularly but shallowly—just enough to control weeds and keep the soil loosened. Celery plants are shallow-rooted.

Spray plants every week to control early and late blight and blackheart. Spray with methoxychlor to control tarnished plant bugs and leaftiers.

To blanch celery (it is not necessary that you do so), place two wide boards on either side of the row and hook them together at the top so that as little light as possible reaches the stalks. This should be done when the stalks are about 1 ft. tall. Blanch only a few plants at a time, because the process reduces their keeping quality.

Harvest celery as soon as it reaches maturity; stalks become pithy and hollow when over-aged. Cut the plants with a knife just below the soil line.

To store, dig up the entire celery plant, place it in an upright position in a cool basement, and pack moist sand or soil around the roots. Don't let it freeze. It will keep for several weeks.

CELTUCE

A lettuce relative which resembles lettuce when young and which then develops thick, 18-in.-long seed stalks which are boiled or eaten raw. The young leaves may be used in salads. The stalks are flavored like a blend of celery and lettuce. Grows in Zones 1–10. 1 packet plants 25 ft. of row. Sow seeds ¼ in. deep. Germination: 10 days. Plants mature in 80 days, though the stalks can be used any time after they are 8 in. long.

Culture

Grow like lettuce. Sow seeds as soon as the soil can be worked in the spring and make repeat sowings until mid-spring; then sow seeds in late summer for fall use. Sow seeds thinly and thin to stand 10 in. apart in rows 12 in. wide.

CHAYOTE

A large perennial vine growing to 30 ft. or more in one season, chayote produces a profusion of more or less pear-shaped, small, green or white, squash-like fruits with a single seed. They can be cooked in many ways. The tubers from which the plant grows can also be cooked and eaten, and the leaves can be used as greens. Grows in Zones 8–10.

Culture

Although a perennial, chayote is usually grown as an annual; and if started indoors, it may produce fruits in Zone 7. In the climates where it does best, however, the entire fruits are planted in the garden when frost danger is past. Leave the stem end of the fruits exposed, but cover the rest with soil. At least two plants are needed to ensure setting of fruit. Space them 10 ft. apart. Germination requires 14 days.

The soil should contain a good supply of humus and a handful of balanced fertilizer. Make about two additional applications of fertilizer during the summer. Give the plants full sun and keep watered. A rather sturdy trellis of wood or wire is needed to support the vines.

Allow the fruits to ripen on the vine before picking.

CHICORY

Plants to 1½ ft. which are used in the ways described below. Grow in Zones 3–8. 1 packet plants 25 ft. of row. Sow seeds ½ in. deep.

Varieties

Magdeburgh. 100 days. Plant with dandelion-like foliage which is grown for its long, white roots that are dried, ground, roasted, and used in or instead of coffee. Seeds germinate in 7 days.

Radichetta. 65 days. A fast-growing plant grown for its long, slender leaves, which are used in salads. Seeds germinate in 7 days.

Witloof. 110 days. Also called French endive and Belgian endive. Plant is grown for its roots, which are then forced to produce a slim, pointed sheaf of tightly bunched white leaves used in salads. Seeds germinate in 12 days.

Culture

Radichetta seeds are sown outdoors about the mean date of the last spring freeze. They will perform well if grown in any reasonably good soil mixed with balanced fertilizer.

Witloof and Magdeburgh require a deeply dug soil so they can put down their long roots in a straight line. Mix in a lot of humus and a low-nitrogen balanced fertilizer such as 5-10-10 at the rate of 1 cup per 25 sq. ft. Sow the seeds outdoors three-and-a-half months before the mean date of the first fall freeze. If sown earlier than this, plants may go to seed and not produce good roots.

Sow the seeds two or three to the inch and thin to 4 in. Rows are 1 ft. wide. Water as necessary to maintain the supply. Cultivate lightly. Side-dress with a small amount of balanced fertilizer after two months.

Dig the roots as late in the fall as possible, but before the ground freezes. Roots of Magdeburgh chicory are cleaned, allowed to dry, and then processed. Cut off the tops of Witloof within an inch of the roots. Then grade the roots according to length in three or four groups, and store them in a very cool, humid place. Cover with moist soil or sand.

The roots can be taken out of storage at any time from fall till spring and forced by the half dozen, dozen, or more. Those forced at one time should be of approximately the same length. If not, trim off the bottoms so they are. The best forcing lengths are 8 to 12 in.

Place an inch or two of sand or sandy soil in the bottom of a box. Stand the roots, topside up, on this. They can almost touch. Sift sand in around them and cover the crowns with 6 in. of sand. Water well. Put the box in a room with a temperature of 50° to 60°. Cover with damp burlap to retard evaporation. You may have to sprinkle water on the sand at some later date if it becomes dry below the surface.

After about three weeks, start checking to see whether the leaves put out by the roots are poking through the surface of the sand. As soon as they do, you can start harvesting by cutting them just at the roots. Then replace the 6-in. covering of sand and force the roots a second time. After that, throw them away.

For a more or less constant supply of Witloof, plant a new box every few weeks.

CHINESE CABBAGE

This is not a true cabbage, but resembles a cross between cabbage and celery. It also resembles Cos lettuce. An annual, it reaches 18 in. It is served like lettuce, or shredded into slaw, or boiled. Grows in Zones 1–9. 1 packet plants 40 ft. of row. Sow seeds ½ in. deep. Germination: 9 days.

Varieties

Burpee Hybrid. 75 days. Heads about 13 in. high and 8 in. across.

Crispy Choy. 45 days. More celery-like than other varieties. Can be planted for a spring or fall crop.

Michihli. 70 days. Standard variety producing heads about 18 in. tall and 4 in. in diameter.

Springtime. 60 days. Short, thick heads. Because of its early maturity, you might try it for a spring crop.

Culture

Chinese cabbage is strictly a cool-weather vegetable; hot weather causes it to bolt. It is best started from seeds sown in the garden about two and a half months before the first fall freeze. If you particularly like the vegetable, you may, however, want to take a chance on starting seeds under glass, hardening the plants off, and moving them into the garden about the mean date of the last spring freeze. Only quick-maturing varieties should be handled in this way.

Sow four to six seeds to a foot and thin to stand 1 ft. apart in rows 12 to 18 in. wide. Grow like cabbage, but omit the third application of fertilizer. When watering, be careful not to splash soil up into the head, which is much looser than a cabbage head.

Chinese cabbage has relatively few pests, though aphids and cabbage worms occasionally cause trouble, and flea beetles may attack seedlings. I have had more problems with slugs than anything else.

Start harvesting heads when they approach mature size. They are not damaged by light freezes, especially if banked with straw or hay.

CHIVES

Eight-inch perennial member of the onion family, with mild leaves which are used for seasoning salads, soups, stews, sauces, etc. Grow in Zones 1–10. 1 packet plants 25 ft. of row. Sow seeds ¼ in. deep. Germination: 10 days. Plants mature in 80 days but don't develop into husky specimens until the second summer.

Culture

Growing plants from seed is a tedious business, but not difficult. Sow seeds outdoors in a seedbed any time after soil can be worked in the spring, and thin plants to stand in clumps of six seedlings. In the fall of the following spring, move mature clumps to their permanent place in the garden.

It is much easier to start with large purchased clumps which can be planted outdoors any time after the mean date of the last spring freeze. Space them 9 in. apart in rows 9 in. wide. Soil should contain a goodly amount of humus. Mix in a little balanced fertilizer for each plant. Keep weeded and watered as necessary.

Take clippings of the leaftips regularly to keep plants from putting up flower stalks. If they do flower, cut the stalks to the ground after blossoms begin to wither.

In the fall, pot up some of the clumps and grow them on in a cool, sunny window. If left in the garden, the plants will die down in the winter and then make new growth the next spring.

COLLARDS

Collards are members of the cabbage family and are used in the South as a substitute for cabbage. The plants range from 20 to 36 in. in height and have crumpled leaves that form a cluster or, in some cases, a loose head. Grow in Zones 1–10. 1 packet plants 50 ft. of row. Sow seeds ½ in. deep. Germination: 10 days.

Varieties

Cabbage. 80 days. Medium height. Leaves form a loose head.

Georgia. 80 days. Tallest variety. Non-heading.

Morris Heading. 83 days. Low-growing. Forms a loose head.

Vates. 75 days. Medium height. Non-heading. Hardier than other varieties.

Culture

Grow like cabbage, with both a spring and fall crop in milder areas. Space plants 15 in. apart in rows 2 ft. wide. Leaves may be blanched by tying them together loosely. Harvest while stalks are fairly young and tender and before leaf stems get fibrous and tough.

CORN

Ever-popular annual. Grows in Zones 3–10; but in Alaska it rarely succeeds in Zone 3. 1 packet plants 75 ft. of row. Sow seeds 1 to 1½ in. deep. Germination: 7 days.

Varieties

Aristogold Bantam Evergreen. 89 days. Ears to 9 in. with 16 to 18 rows. 8½ ft. stalks. Recommended primarily by southern agricultural experts.

Barbecue. 74 days. Ears to 9 in. with 10 to 14 rows. Stalks are 5 ft. tall.

Butter and Sugar. 78 days. Mixed white and yellow kernels. This is one of the most popular varieties of this type. Ears to 7½ in. with 12 rows. Stalks to 5 ft.

Golden Beauty. 73 days. Ears to 7½ in. with 12 to 14 rows. Stalks 5½ ft. tall.

Golden Cross Bantam. 85 days. One of the oldest hybrids and still one of the most popular—if not *the* most popular—because of its superb quality. Ears to 8½ in. with 10 to 14 rows. 7-ft. stalks. Excellent for freezing and canning.

Golden Midget. 65 days. A novelty. Slender ears only 4½ in. long with 8 rows. Stalks 3 ft. tall. Good for freezing on cob.

Illinichief Super Sweet. 83 days. Exceptionally sweet corn. Ears to 10 in. with 16 rows. 6-ft. stalks. Plant at least two parallel rows for proper pollinization.

Iochief. 89 days. Resists drought better than most varieties. Ears to 10 in. with 14 to 18 rows. 6½ft. stalks.

Miniature. 66 days. A novelty. Slender 6½in. ears with 8 to 12 rows. Good for freezing on cobs. Stalks 4 ft.

Northern Belle. 74 days. Ears to 8 in. with 14 to 18 rows. 6-ft. stalks. Ears are very uniform.

North Star. 70 days. Grows well in cold weather. 7-in. ears with 12 rows. 5½ft. stalks.

Seneca Chief. 82 days. Very widely planted. Ears to 8½ in. with 12 rows. The quality is hard to beat. Stalks 6 ft. tall.

Silver Queen. 94 days. The white corn most widely recommended by agricultural extension services. Very sweet flavor. Ears to 9 in. with 16 rows. 7-ft. stalks.

Spring Gold. 67 days. 7 in. ears with 12 rows. 5 ft. stalks. Cold-resistant.

Stowell's Evergreen Hybrid. 90 days. A white corn. Ears to 8½ in. with 14 to 18 rows. Stalks 8 to 10 ft. tall. Drought resistant. An improvement on an old favorite.

Culture

Corn needs hot weather to grow well, but it has some resistance to frost; therefore, if you want an extra early crop, you may take a chance on sowing seeds of an early variety in the garden on or even a few days before the mean date of the last spring freeze. If you're not in such a hurry, make your first sowing after all danger of frost is past. Plant an early, midseason, and late variety to give you a succession of crops. Then make repeat sowings of one or more varieties at ten-day intervals to within about two-and-a-half to three months of the mean date of the first fall freeze.

If early-planted corn is nipped by frost, wait several days before ripping out the plants, because it may be that the growing point was not killed—only some of the leaves. In that event, the plants will revive and produce as well as ever.

Sow seeds 4 to 6 in. apart and thin to 1 ft. Rows are 2 ft. wide. Plant at least three rows side by side to ensure pollination.

If you plant corn in hills—though there is no particular value in doing so—sow five or six seeds to a hill and thin to three plants. Space hills 2½ ft. apart.

Corn grows in a variety of soils, but the better it is, the better the results. Mix in plenty of humus and 6 cups of 5-10-10 or 10-10-10 fertilizer per 100 sq. ft. Later, when the corn is 18 in. tall, sidedress each plant with a heaping teaspoonful of balanced fertilizer or nitrate of soda.

Water in dry weather, especially when silks and ears are developing. Keep weeded. Do not remove the suckers from the stalks. Watch out for flea beetles, corn borers, earworms, and smut.

The virulent fungus, *Helminthosporium maydis,* which wiped out much of the field corn crop in 1970, may also attack and ruin your sweet corn. There is no preventive or cure you can effect. The only thing you can do is burn the diseased plants and hope that you won't have trouble again. In several years blight-resistant seed should be available.

If you plant one row of corn at one time to a single hybrid variety, you will find that the ears on all the plants ripen within about five to seven days of one another. Ears should be picked, if possible, just before you are going to cook them. They are ready for harvest when the silks turn brown but before they become completely dry. The ears feel firm; the tip kernels, full. To confirm whether the ears are ready, peel back the husk slightly; note whether the kernels have colored properly; and press one of them with your thumbnail. If the kernel bursts and spatters, it is in the "milk" stage which most people consider ideal. Kernels on over-mature ears do not burst; they just ooze reluctantly.

If an ear you open is not ready to be picked, simply close the husk. No damage will be done.

CORN SALAD

Also known as lamb's lettuce and fetticus. Annual plants produce rosettes of gray-green leaves that can be used for salads or cooked like spinach. Grows in Zones 3–10. 1 packet plants 20 ft. of row. Sow seeds ½ in. deep. Germination: 10 days.

Variety

Large Round Leaved. 60 days.

Culture

Sow seeds outdoors as soon as soil can be worked in the spring and make one or two repeat sowings at two-week intervals. For an extra-early spring crop, sow seeds outdoors the preceding fall two to four weeks before the mean date of the first fall frost, and cover the plants lightly with salt hay or evergreen branches to carry them over the winter. In warm climates, this covering is not necessary.

Space plants 1 ft. apart in rows 1 ft. wide. Grow like lettuce.

CRESS

This is a small (to 8 in.), pungent, annual salad vegetable. Do not confuse with water cress. Grows in Zones 1–10. 1 packet plants 30 ft. of row. Sow seeds ¼ in. deep. Germination: 7 days.

Varieties

Curled. 25 days. Often called Peppergrass. Leaves finely cut and curled, much like parsley.

Upland. 25 days. Half as high as the above. Resembles water cress.

Culture

Sow seeds outdoors a couple of weeks before mean date of last spring freeze. Make repeat sowings every two to three weeks throughout the spring and summer and into the fall (however, cress does a little better in cool weather than hot). Sow a couple of seeds to an inch and thin to 1 or 2 in. in rows 6 in. wide. The plants need little attention, but appreciate a smidgen of fertilizer when seeds are sown.

Cress can also be grown in pots in a cool, sunny window in winter.

CUCUMBERS

Sprawling annuals that put out long branches every which way. Grow in Zones 3–10. 1 packet plants 15 hills. Sow seeds ½ in. deep. Germination: 7 days.

Varieties

Note 1. The best cucumbers for the average home garden are the so-called slicing varieties. These are long and thin, good to eat fresh, and also perfectly satisfactory for preserving. Pickling cucumbers are rather short and blocky and more productive—made for picklepackers. You can eat them, but they are not quite so good as slicing varieties.

Note 2. A new development in the cucumber world is the gynoecious hybrids. These differ from standard cucumbers in that the great majority of their flowers are female, and these appear in almost every node. As a result, each plant yields an enormous number of fruits. Which is great if you are simply wild about cucumbers; but if not, you'd better stick to any equally good but less productive variety. (To ensure germination of the all-female hybrids, seed growers toss a few seeds of standard cucumbers into each package.)

Ashley. 65 days. One of the most popular varieties, especially in the East. Fruits 8 to 9 in. long. Resistant to downy mildew.

Burpee Hybrid. 60 days. Very productive and popular. 8-in. fruits. Resistant to mosaic and downy mildew.

China. 75 days. A novelty but good anyway. Fruits up to 18 in. long and only 2 in. thick.

Gemini. 61 days. Gynoecious hybrid. Fruits 7 to 8 in. long. Tolerant of scab, mosaic, anthracnose, and mildews.

Lemon. 64 days. A novelty. Fruits are about the size and color of a large lemon, and very sweet.

Marketer. 65 days. Another enormously popular cucumber. Fruits 8 in. long.

Mincu. 45 days. One of the few varieties that stands a chance in Alaska. Can be grown wherever an extra-early crop is desired. Fruits 4½ by 2 in. Vines take less space in garden.

Ohio MR 17. 57 days. One of the most widely planted pickling cucumbers, producing 7-in. fruits. Mosaic resistant.

Poinsett. 70 days. Like Ashley, a South Carolina development and rated even better. 8½ in. fruits. Highly resistant to downy and powdery mildew and moderately resistant to anthracnose and leaf spot.

Saticoy Hybrid. 60 days. Tapering, 8-in. fruit. Productive plants. Resistant to mosaic and downy mildew.

West Indian Gherkin. 60 days. A pickling type. Oval fruits are only 1½ in. long and almost as wide; covered with sharp, little spines.

Culture

In most parts of the country, cucumbers are a summer crop, but in very warm climates, they should be grown as a spring crop and also as a fall crop (which is started in August). For an extra-early start in the spring, sow seeds under glass three or four weeks before transplanting to the garden. This transplanting should be done when the seedlings have two true leaves; bigger plants do not withstand moving so well. If soil is not warm enough at time of transplanting or if the weather is unreliable, cover the seedlings with Hotkaps.

The alternative to starting seeds under glass is to sow them outdoors where the plants are to grow after all danger of frost is past and the soil has warmed up. This is the easier procedure and in the long run it produces cucumbers almost as fast. Sow seeds in hills each of which is centered in a growing space measuring about 5 x 5 ft. (In other words, if you plant ten hills in a straight row, the cucumbers produced will cover an area 50 ft. long by 5 ft. wide.) Sow eight to ten seeds per hill and thin to three or four plants.

Another way to plant cucumbers is to sow the seeds in rows at the base of a wire-mesh fence. In this case, the plants should be 2 ft. apart. They will enjoy climbing the fence.

In areas where nematodes abound, the soil for cucumbers should be fumigated about two weeks before planting. Throughout the country, the soil should be mixed with a lot of humus and—a week before planting— with ½ cup of 5-10-10 fertilizer per hill. When the seedlings are thinned,

By growing cucumbers on a wire fence, you save garden space, discourage insects and diseases to a certain extent, and keep the fruits clean. The plants can climb by themselves.

or a week or two later, sidedress each hill with a handful of balanced fertilizer or nitrate of soda.

Keep plants watered and weeded while they are growing and producing; and when they start to bear, pick the fruits every day in order to keep the vines going. Cucumbers can be harvested and used when very small, but are best just as they reach maturity. Overgrown fruits are of poor quality, and if accidentally or purposely left on the vine, they stunt plant growth and reduce the quality and size of the yield.

Insects you may have to contend with are striped and spotted cucumber beetles, aphids, and mites. The beetles are usually the worst, because they ruin seedling plants; but you can control them by dusting or spraying the plants with Sevin or rotenone as soon as the pests appear. If mosaic or mildew are troublesome where you live, grow cucumber varieties that are resistant to those diseases.

DANDELIONS

Ubiquitous perennial weeds that are used in spring salads. Grow in Zones 3–10. 1 packet plants 25 ft. of row. Sow seeds ¼ in. deep. Germination: 14 days. Plants mature in 60 days.

Culture

You will save yourself trouble if, instead of planting dandelions, you simply harvest those growing in your lawn and driveway. However, it is only fair to note that dandelions produced by the seeds offered in catalogs are somewhat larger and more succulent than those growing wild.

Sow seeds in a sunny spot any time in spring or early summer. Thin plants to 9 in. in rows 9 in. wide. They will take care of themselves thereafter. Flavor is improved if you tie the leaves together to blanch the hearts or make a tent of boards over them. Harvest before flowers open. Keep flowers picked off plants you don't harvest.

DASHEEN

A relative of the elephant ear, dasheen is a 3-ft. or larger plant grown for its sweet potatolike tubers. Grows in Zones 7–10. Matures in about 200 days.

Culture

Tubers can be started indoors in pots and moved outdoors after frost, or can be planted directly in the garden on the mean date of the last spring freeze. Plant tubers just below the soil surface, 2 ft. apart in rows 3 ft. wide. Soil must be rich and well drained. Mix in large quantities of humus and about 2 cups of balanced fertilizer per 25 sq. ft.

Plants require partial shade and plenty of moisture. Sidedress each plant with a handful of fertilizer when it is six weeks old and twice again at six-week intervals.

Tubers are ready to be harvested after about six months. Dig them carefully—before the first fall frost—when the soil is dry and will not stick to them. Handle carefully. Store in a cool (about 50°), airy basement.

EGGPLANT

An annual, 30-in. relative of the tomato, with the same requirements. Grows in Zones 4–10. 1 packet produces about 50 plants. Sow seeds ¼ in. deep. Germination: 10 days.

Varieties

Black Beauty. 75 days. Large, dark purple fruits are oval with a blunt end. Standard variety, widely grown.

Black Magic. 72 days. A hybrid. Medium-size, blunt-oval, dark purple fruits.

Burpee Hybrid. 70 days. Another excellent hybrid similar to the above.

Florida Market. 80 days. Large, long, oval, dark purple fruits. Grown in the deep South.

Jersey King. 76 days. A productive hybrid with long, tapering, dark purple fruits.

Mission Bell. 70 days. A hybrid producing lots of long, oval fruits.

White Beauty. 72 days. Just because the medium-size fruits are white, don't let this variety scare you. Very productive.

Culture

Eggplants are sensitive to cold. In warm climates they are started in midsummer for a fall crop and in early winter for a spring crop. Elsewhere they are started in late spring for a summer crop.

Sow seeds under glass (except in the South, when starting a fall crop) eight to ten weeks before plants are moved into the garden. Transplanting to the outdoors must be delayed until all danger of frost is past and the soil is warm. Set plants 2 ft. apart in rows 2 ft. wide. Give each plant ½ cup of starter solution.

The soil should be well drained, rich in humus, and have a pH of about 6.5. Mix in 3 cups of 5-10-10 or 10-10-10 fertilizer per 50 sq. ft. Sidedress plants with a little additional fertilizer when they are half grown.

Keep watered and weeded. Pests to be alert for are similar to those attacking tomatoes; but eggplants seem to be less troubled by all except the Colorado potato beetle.

Fruits are edible from the time they are about one-third full size. But they are at their best from the time they reach two-thirds full size until they are fully grown. Keep fruits picked as they mature. In harvesting, cut the fruits with a short length of stem.

ENDIVE

Also called escarole. Not to be confused with French endive, although the two are related. This is a curled, fringed, leafy, annual vegetable about 9 in. tall. It resembles lettuce and is used the same way. It may also be cooked. Grows in Zones 1–10. 1 packet plants 25 ft. of row. Sow seeds ¼ in. deep. Germination: 10 days.

Varieties

Deep Heart. 85 days. Dark-green, broad leaves only slightly curled. Plants more upright than in most varieties.

Full Heart Batavian. 85 days. Deep green, slightly crumpled leaves.

Green Curled. 95 days. Leaves very finely cut and curled. Leaf ribs are pale green. Another Green Curled strain has pink ribs.

Salad King. 98 days. A large variety that withstands heat better than others, but does not blanch so deeply.

Culture

Endive seeds can be sown outdoors in the spring a couple of weeks before the mean date of the last freeze; but although it is more resistant to heat than lettuce, it may still bolt and go to seed if you get a hot spell before it matures. The leaves are also likely to be bitter. For these reasons, it is safer to sow seeds in the summer in time to make a crop before fall frost.

Grow like lettuce. Sow a couple of seeds to the inch and thin to 1 ft. wide.

Endive should be blanched to make it sweeter and more tender. Various methods are used, but the easiest is to center a 6-in. board over the plants in a row. This should almost touch the tops of the plants. By keeping out the sun, it forces the leaves in the hearts to turn creamy white. However, if moisture gets into the hearts, the leaves may rot. You should, therefore, examine the plants after a rain or heavy fog, and if you find any moisture, remove the board and let the leaves dry before continuing with the blanching.

Harvest as the plants reach maturity and while the leaves are still sweet and tender. The plants will withstand some frost, especially if they are mulched with hay or straw.

You can enjoy your crop late into the fall by lifting the plants with plenty of soil around the roots and putting them in a bright basement or coldframe where they will not freeze. Blanch the hearts by drawing the outer leaves up over them and tying them loosely with string.

FLORENCE FENNEL

Also called fennel or finocchio. A 2½-ft. annual, with spreading feathery foliage, which produces an enlarged, bulb-like, anise-flavored stem that is boiled and used in salads. The leaves may also be used as an herb. Grows in Zones 3–10. 1 packet plants 20 ft. of row. Sow seeds ⅛ in. deep. Germination: 12 days. Plants mature in 90 days.

Culture

Sow seeds outdoors in the spring on or after the mean date of the last freeze. In warm climates, seeds can also be sown in late summer for a fall crop. Thin plants to 6 in. in rows 18 in. wide. Plants do best in a fairly rich soil. Apply a little balanced fertilizer before seed sowing and again about two months later. When the stems are about the thickness of a rake handle, hill soil up around them slightly to blanch them. Harvesting can start a

week or two later. Do not allow stems to become too large, because they
are tough and stringy.

GARLIC

Bulbous plant to 15 in. Grows in Zones 1–10. 1 lb. of cloves plants 20 ft.
of row. "Germination": 7 days. Plants mature in 100 days.

Culture

Separate the bulbs into cloves and plant them 2 in. deep and 4 in. apart
in rows 6 in. wide. In Zones 8 to 10, planting is done in late summer or fall.
In colder climates, plant in the spring as soon as the soil can be worked.

Grow like onions. Do not over-fertilize, lest tops grow at the expense of
the bulbs. Harvest when the tops fall over, and dry the bulbs in a cool,
shady spot.

GOOD KING HENRY

Also called mercury. Hardy perennial, 30 in. tall, grown for its triangular
leaves, which are eaten like spinach. Grows in Zones 3–8. 1 packet plants
20 ft. of row. Sow seeds ¼ in. deep. Germination: 14 days. Plants reach
harvestable size in 60 days.

Culture

Sow seeds outdoors as early in the spring as the soil can be worked. Thin
plants to 6 in. in rows 1 ft. wide. Soil can be of average quality with a little
balanced fertilizer added before sowing and every spring after that.
Harvest leaves when they are young and tender, before plants flower.
Do not strip the plants. In the fall, after killing frost, cut off the dead stalks.
Since this plant makes rather rank growth, divide it every couple of years
to keep it within bounds.

HORSE RADISH

A perennial growing to 30 in. and putting down long, thick, white roots
which are grated to make a fiery sauce. Grows in Zones 3–7. Raise from
root cuttings. Roots mature in 150 days.

Culture

You can buy root cuttings or make your own by cutting an old root into
pencil-size strips about 6 in. long. Plant the strips 1 ft. apart in rows 1 ft.
wide. Be sure that what had been the top of the root is still at the top. Cover
with 3 in. of soil.

The soil should be deeply dug and rich in humus. Horse radish does not
do well in light soils. If you can get hold of some well-rotted manure, mix

it in. Otherwise, scratch a little balanced fertilizer into the soil above the roots.

Cuttings can be planted in spring or fall. During the growing season, keep plants watered and lightly cultivated. Dig roots in the fall and grate them immediately if you want horse radish at its best. Roots can also be left in the ground over winter and dug as needed.

Although horse radish grows on from year to year if not disturbed, the plants deteriorate to some extent and produce tough, inferior roots. It is advisable, therefore, to plant new cuttings annually.

JERUSALEM ARTICHOKE

This is an 8-ft. or taller perennial sunflower *(Helianthus tuberosus)* with warty tubers which may be eaten raw but which are usually boiled or steamed. Grows from tubers in Zones 3–8. Plants mature in 150 days.

Culture

Grow from tubers purchased in the market or collected from friends. Cut the tubers into pieces each containing one or more eyes, and plant them 6 in. deep on or close to the mean date of the last spring freeze. Space the tubers 2 ft. apart in rows 2 ft. wide. Any kind of soil will do, but ideally it should be rather poor; otherwise the exuberant plants will make too much top growth. Water in dry weather and feed sparingly.

Plants can be allowed to grow until hit by frost, or can be cut to within a foot of the ground about the first day of autumn. Dig the tubers, which lie just beneath the soil surface in a 12-in. circle around the stems, any time after the first frost. If you want to harvest all the tubers at this time, they can be stored in sand in a cool basement or in an outdoor trench 24 in. deep. In the latter position, cover the tubers with a little soil or sand and then fill the trench the rest of the way with salt hay or leaves. The tubers can also be left in the garden and dug as needed throughout the winter.

To keep the plants from becoming crowded and taking over the entire garden, be sure to dig up *all* tubers every year.

KALE

Also called borecole. A 30-in. annual member of the cabbage family, with spreading, crinkled leaves which are cooked and served as greens. Grows in Zones 1–10. 1 packet plants 25 ft. of row. Sow seeds ½ in. deep. Germination: 10 days.

Varieties

Dwarf Green Curled. 55 days. Finely curled, bright green leaves.

Vates. 55 days. Most popular variety. Finely curled, dark blue-green leaves. Also called Vates Dwarf Blue Curled Scotch.

Culture

This is a hardy vegetable— in fact, it can be left in the garden all winter in Zone 8 and even in Zone 7 if mulched with straw. You can sow seeds outdoors where plants are to grow about four weeks before the mean date of the last spring freeze; but most gardeners, especially in the South, prefer to grow kale as a fall crop. In this case, seed is sown outdoors six to eight weeks before the mean date of the first fall freeze. It is an excellent succession crop to follow snap beans, beets, carrots, etc.

Sow about one seed to an inch and thin to 8 to 12 in. in rows 1 ft. wide. Soil can be of average quality, but kale grows better if its roots have humus and fertilizer to feed on.

Pests are rarely serious if you are careful to rotate crops, but may include downy mildew and flea beetles.

Harvest the greens when young, either by taking the entire plant or just the outer leaves. Refrigerate promptly; otherwise the greens will wither.

KOHLRABI

An annual to 1 ft., kohlrabi produces a turnip-like and turnip-flavored bulb just above ground on a slender stem. This may be eaten raw, but is usually cooked. Grows in Zones 1-10. 1 packet plants 30 ft. of row. Sow seeds ¼ in. deep. Germination: 12 days.

Varieties

Early Purple Vienna. 60 days. Bulbs are a bit larger than those of White Vienna and have purple skin and white flesh.

Early White Vienna. 55 days. Bulbs have pale green skin and white flesh.

Culture

Seeds are sometimes sown under glass, but the usual practice is to sow them directly in the garden. For a spring crop, make the sowing three to four weeks before the mean date of the last spring freeze. For a fall crop, sow two to two-and-a-half months before the mean date of the first fall freeze. Intermediate sowings can be made, but kohlrabi does best in cool weather.

Sow one or two seeds to the inch and thin to 6 in. Rows are 9 in. wide. Soil should contain humus and about 1 cup of 5-10-10 fertilizer per 20 ft. of row. Water in dry spells. Pests are the same as those of the cabbage.

Harvest bulbs while young and tender.

LEEKS

Leeks are a mild-flavored member of the onion family. Instead of forming bulbs, they form long, cylindrical stalks to 18 in. Grow in Zones 1-10. 1 packet plants 25 ft. of row. Sow seeds ¼ in. deep. Germination: 10 days.

Varieties

American Flag. 130 days. Most widely grown variety. Also called Large American Flag and Broad London.
Swiss Special. 120 days.

Culture

For a very early crop, sow seeds under glass about eight weeks before the mean date of the last spring freeze, harden off well, and plant outdoors on the mean date. Or you can sow seeds directly in the garden about two weeks before the mean date of the last spring freeze.

I have grown excellent leeks in miserable soil, but they do better in well-drained soil that contains a goodly amount of humus and about 1½ cups of balanced fertilizer per 25 ft. of row. Scoop out a trench 4 to 6 in. deep and sow seeds or set seedlings in the bottom. As the plants grow, fill the trench in gradually until it is full and then continue gradually to hill soil up 2 to 3 in. around the stalks. This blanches the stalks. In carrying out this operation, try not to mound the soil up higher than the tight stalk, because if it gets into the base of the outspread leaves while a plant is young, it will form a gritty, hard-to-clean-out layer in the white stalk you harvest.

Sow two or three seeds to the inch and thin to 3 in. in a row 9 in. wide. Keep weeded and, in dry weather, watered. Sidedress with balanced fertilizer when plants are half grown.

Harvest the leeks any time after the stalks are about ¾ in. in diameter. They can be harvested before this; but the larger stalks—up to 1½ in. and more—are better.

The plants will withstand considerable frost and in mild climates can be left in the ground through the winter. But in colder areas they should be lifted and stored upright in a cool (not freezing) basement. Pack soil around the roots and white portions of the stalks. Leeks can also be blanched and put into the home freezer.

LENTILS

Annual vegetable to 18 in. bearing flat pods containing two small, convex-lens-shaped seeds which are used for soup. Grow in Zones 5–10. 1 lb. plants 100 ft. of row. Sow seeds ½ in. deep. Germination: 5 days. Pods mature in 70 days.

Varieties: There are several varieties, but the lentil is not commonly grown in the United States and I have yet to find it offered in catalogs. Buy whatever you can find in the supermarket on the shelf with dried peas and beans.

Culture

Sow seeds 1 to 2 in. apart about the mean date of the last spring freeze.

Rows are 18 in. wide. The soil should be very well drained. Mix 2 to 3 cups of balanced fertilizer into every 50 sq. ft.

If the spring is extremely dry, water the plants occasionally. Otherwise they need no special care other than cultivating or mulching to keep down weeds.

Allow pods and seeds to dry on the plants before harvesting them.

LETTUCE

Annuals to 10 in. Grow in Zones 1–10. 1 packet plants 50 ft. of row. Sow seeds ¼ in. deep. Germination: 7 days.

Varieties

Note. There are four types of lettuce: Crisphead forms a tight, firm ball with rather brittle leaves. It is the kind sold in stores as Iceberg. Butterhead lettuces form a distinct head, but it is somewhat open. The leaves are crisp but fleshy and very delicate. Cos, or Romaine, lettuces form tall, rather slender, upright heads that are not quite so tight as crispheads. Leaf lettuces produce a round, loose bunch of leaves.

Bibb. 58 days. A butterhead lettuce that has been around a long time, but has only recently been "discovered." Heads are small and, to my way of thinking, of unparalleled quality. This variety also grows well in greenhouses and hotbeds.

Black Seeded Simpson. 45 days. A leaf lettuce forming a large bunch of light green, crumpled leaves.

Buttercrunch. 64 days. A delicious butterhead lettuce very similar to Bibb, but heads are heavy and compact. Resists heat better than Bibb.

Dark Green Boston. 75 days. A butterhead type of first-rate quality. Reliable. An old favorite.

Grand Rapids. 45 days. A leaf lettuce that stays popular after years and years of use. Leaves are very frilled and curled.

Great Lakes 659. 84 days. A crisphead type of medium size. Medium green.

Oak Leaf. 45 days. An old favorite of the leaf type. Dark green leaves look very much like twisted oak leaves. More heat-resistant than most lettuces.

Parris Island Cos. 70 days. Firm heads roughly 10 in. tall. Leaves are slightly crinkled and dark green; the hearts are nearly white. Tolerant of mosaic.

Premier Great Lakes. 75 days. A big, deep green crisphead lettuce that is popular in the East.

Prizehead. 45 days. A leaf lettuce despite its name. Crumpled leaves are tinged with red.

Ruby. 45 days. A leaf lettuce popular for the deep reddish color of its frilled leaves.

Salad Bowl. 48 days. Outstanding leaf lettuce. Leaves are numerous, short, wavy, and notched. They form an attractive salad-bowl-size rosette. Resists heat well.

Summer Bibb. 62 days. A butterhead type almost exactly like Bibb but more resistant to heat and, therefore, can be grown well into the summer.

Waldmann's Green. 50 days. A lettuce of the Grand Rapids strain. Leaves finely fringed and ruffled. Widely grown in greenhouses and hotbeds; also does well in the garden.

White Boston. 75 days. A light green butterhead lettuce with a solid, cream-colored heart.

Culture

The easiest lettuces to grow are of the leaf type and the butterheads. Cos is harder and crispheads are much harder. The reason for this is that lettuce does not grow well in heat; therefore, the fast-maturing leaf and butterhead varieties require less attention.

Except in warm climates, where crisphead lettuce is grown as a winter crop, it must be grown in the spring. To get off to a good start, sow the seeds under glass about ten weeks before the mean date of the last spring freeze, harden the seedlings off carefully, and plant outdoors six to eight weeks later.

Butterhead and cos lettuce can be handled in the same way, or the seeds can be sown outdoors as soon as the soil can be worked. Leaf lettuce is almost always seeded outdoors as soon as the soil can be worked. Make one or two repeat sowings at two- or three-week intervals.

For a fall crop of butterhead, cos, or leaf lettuce, sow the seeds outdoors in time for the plants to mature just before the first fall freeze.

Seeds sown directly in the garden should be spaced about two to the inch. Thin or plant crispheads and cos to 1 ft; butterheads to 8 in.; leaf lettuce to 6 in. Rows are 1 ft. wide. If you allow leaf lettuce to grow fairly large before thinning, you can use the thinned plants in salads.

For lettuce to taste its best, it must be grown rapidly. This means, for one thing, that the soil must be of good quality, containing plenty of humus and about 1½ cups of 10-10-10 fertilizer per 50 ft. of row. Sidedress crisphead plants with a little more fertilizer when they are half grown. Keep weeded and well watered in dry weather. Be on the alert for leafhoppers and slugs.

Start harvesting leaf lettuce when the leaves are of usable size. You can pull off a few outer leaves of each plant and let the rest continue to grow; or you can take the entire plant. Head lettuce, particularly of the butterhead type, can also be harvested long before the heads reach full size. If you cut the Bibb plants off close to the ground and sprinkle a little fertilizer around the stalk that remains, it will make new growth which, although it does not form a perfect head, is just as delectable.

Once lettuce starts to bolt upward, it becomes tough and bitter.

Special culture No. 1

Lettuce can be started from seed and grown to maturity in coldframes during the winter in areas where the temperature does not normally drop too far below freezing for any length of time. (Lettuce can withstand temperatures to 28° if they are of short duration; but such a temperature is not likely to damage plants in a coldframe unless of sustained duration.)

In colder areas, such as Zone 7, lettuce can be grown safely in winter in hotbeds.

In both cases, proper attention must be given to ventilation of the frames on mild days and to covering of the glass on very cold days.

Special culture No. 2

Excellent Bibb and leaf lettuce can be grown in glass and plastic greenhouses throughout the winter. Usual practice is to start the seeds in flats and transplant to the soil on which the greenhouse is built. The schedule suggested to commercial growers by the Indiana Agricultural Extension Service is equally applicable to home gardeners. It is shown in Table VII.

Night temperatures of 45° to 50° and day temperatures of 60° to 65° are satisfactory during the winter. Top vents should never be closed tight except during very cold or stormy weather. Too much humidity and too little air movement contribute to the development of some diseases of greenhouse lettuce.

TABLE VII
Suggested Schedule for Raising Lettuce in Greenhouses

CROP	SEED SOWN	PLANTS TRANSPLANTED	CROP HARVESTED
Plan 1			
Lettuce	Aug. 15–31	Sept. 15–30	Nov. 15–30
Lettuce	Oct. 15–31	Nov. 15–30	Feb. 1–15
Lettuce	Dec. 1–15	Feb. 1–15	Apr. 1–15
Lettuce	Feb. 15–28	Apr. 1–15	May 1–15
Plan 2			
Lettuce			
Lettuce	Same as Plan 1, but omit fourth lettuce planting and interplant tomatoes with third lettuce crop.		
Lettuce			
Tomatoes	Jan. 1–15	Mar. 1–15	May 15–July 30

Special culture No. 3

I have grown small but succulent heads of Bibb and Buttercrunch under fluorescent light. They were planted in 2-in.-deep trays of Jiffy Mix. Once thinned, they required no attention except watering.

MALABAR SPINACH

This is not a true spinach, but a hot-weather substitute for it. The annual plants are decorative vines to 4 ft. which are covered with an abundance of large, green leaves. Grow in Zones 3–10. 1 packet produces 50 plants. Sow seeds ½ in. deep. Germination: 10 days. Plants mature in 70 days.

Culture

Sow seeds under glass and move seedlings outside after all danger of frost is past, or sow seeds in the garden after last frost. Sow three or four seeds to a foot and thin to stand 1 ft. apart. Since the vines are best trained on a fence or trellis, rows are only 12 to 18 in. wide.

Malabar spinach grows in almost any soil containing humus and fertilizer. Sidedress in midsummer with a little additional balanced fertilizer or nitrate of soda. Keep watered. Pests are of no consequence.

Vines need to be tied to their supports.

As leaves are harvested, they are quickly replaced by new ones. Vines are generally killed to the ground by the first autumn freeze.

MELONS

Sprawling annuals with branches 6 ft. long. Grow in Zones 3–10, but

Although muskmelons, cucumbers, winter squash, and pumpkins grow together here in a small space, one will not affect the flavor of the other. But if you saved their seeds and planted them next year, you would find that the plants had crossed and become something entirely new.

not all varieties are suited to the colder zones by any means. 1 packet produces 50 plants. Sow seeds ½ in. deep. Germination: 7 days.

Varieties

Note. Two types of melon are grown in the United States: Muskmelons, which are fairly short-season vegetables that can be grown in all areas, and winter melons, which are long-season vegetables including casaba, honeydew, crenshaw, and Persian melons. Cantaloupes are rarely grown in the United States, although many people call muskmelons cantaloupes. The true cantaloupe is generally grown only in Europe, and only one variety of this species is included in the following list.

Banana. 94 days. Popular in the South. A light-yellow melon about 16 in. long and 4 in. in diameter. Flesh is salmon-pink.

Burpee Hybrid. 82 days. Highly recommended by many agricultural extension services. Large melons of excellent quality.

Casaba Golden Beauty. 120 days. A large winter melon with yellow skin and thick, white flesh of unusual flavor.

Charentais Improved. 74 days. A true cantaloupe. Fairly small fruits with ridged but smooth skins and thick, dark orange, sweet flesh. Tolerant of mosaic and several forms of wilt.

Crenshaw. 110 days. Very large winter melon with superb thick, salmon-pink flesh. An excellent early hybrid Crenshaw that matures in 90 days is newly available.

Delicious 51. 85 days. Old favorite. Soft but very sweet and juicy fruits. Resistant to fusarium, but tends to crack at the ends when ripening.

Edisto 47. 90 days. Another favorite. Salmon flesh is very thick and sweet. Resistant to powdery mildew and tolerant of downy mildew.

Gold Star. 87 days. Medium-size, oval fruits with deep orange, juicy flesh. A hybrid. Resistant to fusarium.

Hale's Best Jumbo. 86 days. Similar to the following, but the fruits are slightly larger.

Hale's Best 36. 86 days. One of the most famous melons grown. Still good and still popular.

Harper Hybrid. 86 days. Fruits have an unusual tang, are extremely thick fleshed. Medium-size fruits are not ribbed. Widely planted. Resistant to fusarium.

Harvest Queen. 82 days. Highly recommended by many extension services. Large melons of excellent quality.

Heart of Gold. 86 days. Medium-size, somewhat elongated melons with orange flesh.

Honeydew. 110 days. A winter melon with green flesh. Needs no introduction.

Mainerock. 75 days. A hybrid originated in Maine and particularly suited to areas with short growing seasons. Delicious salmon-orange flesh.

Minnesota Midget. 60 days. A novelty. Vines only 3 ft. long produce excellent 4-in. melons. Fine in small gardens and especially in cold climates.

Persian. 115 days. A globular, ribless winter melon with bright orange flesh.

Saticoy. 90 days. Very thick, orange flesh with superb sweet flavor. Resistant to fusarium·and tolerant of mildew.

Sungold Casaba. 85 days. A muskmelon developed in New Hampshire and excellent for growing in the North.

Supermarket. 88 days. A hybrid. Fruits have prominent ribs, thick orange flesh of somewhat musky flavor. Resistant to fusarium and downy mildew.

Culture

At the start, let me dispel two myths: (1) Melons—at least muskmelons—are much easier to grow than people seem to imagine. (2) If you buy fresh seed every year, you can plant melons next to or right in among cucumbers, squashes, or other cucurbits without any danger of changing the flavor of the melons or of the other plants. If you save and plant seeds from your own garden, *watch out.*

Melons are very tender and must have warm weather to survive and grow. To get an extra-early start on the season, sow seeds indoors or in a hotbed three weeks before the mean date of the last spring freeze; and move the plants into the garden under Hotkaps or Hotents one week after the mean date. The seedlings should have two or three true leaves by this time. For a somewhat later early start, sow seeds indoors or in a hotbed on the mean date of the last spring freeze and transplant to the garden four weeks later, by which time all danger of frost should be past and the soil should be warming up. These plants ordinarily should not require covering, although you may find it advisable if the spring is cool and damp.

Seeds can also be sown directly in the garden just as soon as all frost danger is past, but about a week before the soil has begun to warm up. (In other words, you can sow seeds outdoors about a week before seedlings can be safely set out.) Direct seeding can also be done for some weeks thereafter except in areas with very short growing seasons.

Whether you direct-seed melons or start with seedlings, you will usually get a larger and earlier yield if you mulch the soil around them with black plastic. This is especially beneficial when the spring is cool and dry. The film helps to warm the soil and also to eliminate weeds and to maintain a more constant water supply around the roots.

You can plant melons 2 ft. apart in rows 5 ft. wide or in hills centered in a 5-ft. row. In the latter case, put two or three plants together in each hill and space the hills 4 ft. apart. Give each seedling about a half cup of starter solution. If grown in a windy location, erect some sort of low windbreak on the windward side until the plants are well established.

The ideal soil is well drained and moisture retentive. It must have a pH of between 6.5 and 7, because melons do badly in acid soil. Mix in a good amount of humus and about 3 cups of 5-10-10 fertilizer per 50 sq. ft. If nematodes are prevalent, the soil should first be fumigated.

As the melons grow, cultivate around them very lightly—just enough to keep down weeds. Water regularly and deeply: Like all cucurbits, melons need an ample supply of moisture. Sidedress each plant with about a tea-spoonful of nitrate of soda or balanced fertilizer when the vines begin to run. In areas such as Oregon, where soil lacks boron and magnesium, spray the plants with 1 tablespoon of Epsom salts and 1 teaspoon of borax in 1 gal. of water when the vines begin to run and again when the first fruits are 1 to 2 in. across. Tests indicate that this helps to increase the fruits' sugar content substantially.

Fusarium wilt and powdery mildew are the most common diseases of melons. The only real protection against them is to start with resistant varieties. Other diseases that may be troublesome are anthracnose and alternaria. The worst of the insect pests are striped and spotted cucumber beetles and aphids. Slugs may also be injurious.

Muskmelons give due warning that they are ripening. First the netting on the skin expands and fills in. Then the color between the netting turns from green to tan or yellow, and a small circular crack develops around the stem where it is attached to the fruit. When the melon pulls away easily from the stem, it is said to be at "full slip" and is in prime eating condition. It stays prime for only about three days, so you should make a habit of harvesting the fruit every day or two. Melons on dead or dying vines are no good.

Crenshaw, Casaba, and honeydew melons have no netting. The dark green skin of the crenshaw turns yellowish green when ripe. The fruit should be eaten fairly soon. Casabas are very late to ripen and are im-proved if left on the vine until they are soft. The skin of honeydews turns from white to ivory, and the blossom end softens. Both casabas and honey-dews can be stored in a cool place for several weeks.

MUSHROOMS

Grow indoors in basements, special houses, caves, etc., in Zones 1–10; grow outdoors in Zones 4–8. Grown from spawn. ½ lb. plants 35 sq. ft. Plant spawn 1 to 2 in. deep. Mushrooms mature in 60 days.

Varieties

Meadow mushrooms are most commonly grown. They are properly identified as *Psalliota campestris,* but are commonly identified as *Agaricus campestris.*

Culture

You can grow a few mushrooms under your bed with the special kit sold by some garden supply dealers. The standard method of growing mushrooms is much more complicated, because the temperature must be controlled very exactly.

If grown under controlled conditions, you can plant mushrooms the year round; but it is generally best to start them in the fall, when high summer temperatures have abated.

The mushroom bed is made in a dark place with a fairly high humidity and a temperature between 50° to 60°—preferably 55°. The room should have some ventilation but no noticeable air movement.

The bed itself may be built on the floor or on a raised bench. In commercial mushroom houses, the beds are arranged in tiers.

The "soil" consists of fresh horse manure mixed with straw. Manure mixed with sawdust, shavings, peat, etc., is usable but undesirable; and that coming from a stable in which disinfectants or insecticides have been used must be avoided.

To prepare the manure for use, build it up in a compact pile 4 to 5 ft. high. This can be outdoors, but should be under a roof. Wet it thoroughly. Then in four or five days turn it over. Continue in this way, turning over the pile and dampening it every four or five days for about four weeks. During this period the high heat of the pile should gradually diminish. When the temperature at the center of the pile reaches 70°–75°, the manure is about ready for use. At this point, it should be of a deep brown coloration and not offensively odorous. Pressed in the hand, it holds together but does not form a soggy ball.

Spread the manure in the mushroom bed to a depth of 6 to 8 in. Firm it lightly, but do not pack it down. Allow it to cool further until it reaches 60° or a little less. Sprinkle lightly with water as necessary to keep it moist but not wet.

Mushroom spawn is mixed with dry manure and comes to you in a solid, cake-like form which is broken into pieces about the size of an egg and planted in the bed 10 to 12 in. apart in both directions. Do not water unless the manure begins to dry out, in which case sprinkle with tepid (never cold) water.

In about two weeks, each piece of spawn should send out small, white threads in all directions. You should then cover the bed with ½ to 1 in. of good, damp loam that is free of rubble, weeds, and fertilizer. In the following weeks, sprinkle with water as little as possible but whenever the bed shows signs of becoming dry.

Mushrooms should start to appear in about six weeks. The first will grow in clusters above the pieces of spawn; but later they will pop up throughout the bed. If the temperature is right and the bed is kept damp, you should be able to harvest mushrooms for two to three months. The manure should then be discarded (although it is still good for use in the outdoor garden).

The first clusters of mushrooms are harvested by cutting out the entire clusters very carefully. Cut at the base of the stems, but avoid damaging the spawn underneath. Individual mushrooms appearing from then on are pulled out with a twisting motion. You must get the entire stem, since pieces that are left in the bed will decay and bring the harvest to an end.

Special culture

An easier but much less reliable way to grow mushrooms in milder climates is to plant the pieces of spawn 2 in. deep in your lawn. If you do this in the spring, you should—if the weather is right—be able to harvest them in late summer. The mushrooms may continue to come up for several years.

MUSTARD

A 10-in. annual member of the cabbage family grown for its tasty leaves. Grows in Zones 1–10. 1 packet plants 50 ft. of row. Sow seeds ¼ in. deep. Germination: 9 days.

Varieties

Florida Broad Leaf. 43 days. Leaves large, wide, and with sizable, white midribs.

Fordhook Fancy. 40 days. Leaves so curled they resemble ostrich plumes.

Green Wave. 45 days. Leaves strongly curled. Plants slow to bolt.

Large Smooth Leaf. 45 days. Very large leaves.

Southern Giant Curled. 40 days. Large leaves with fringed edges.

Tendergreen. 35 days. Also called Mustard Spinach because of its spinach-like flavor. Leaves medium large and thick.

Culture

Sow seeds outdoors in the spring two to four weeks before mean date of the last freeze, and make a second sowing several weeks later. For a fall crop, sow seeds four to eight weeks before mean date of the first freeze. Sow a couple of seeds to the inch and thin to 6 to 10 in. Rows are 1 ft. wide.

Soil can be of average quality. Mix in 3 cups of 5-10-10 or 10-10-10 fertilizer per 50 ft. of row. Harvest when leaves are young and tender. Avoid letting plants go to seed because the seeds will be scattered all over the garden and are likely to come up the following spring.

NEW ZEALAND SPINACH

Not a true spinach, but used as a hot-weather substitute for it. Annual plant to 3 ft.; branching and spreading. Grows in Zones 1–10. Especially desirable in Alaska, where spinach is very difficult to grow. 1 packet plants 25 ft. of row. Sow seeds 1 in. deep. Germination: 8 days. Plants mature in 70 days.

Culture

Unlike true spinach, New Zealand spinach is killed by hard frost and thrives in warm weather. Sow seeds outdoors when danger of frost is past.

Because seeds germinate slowly, soak them in 120° water for two hours or soak them in cold water for 24 hours. Sow about 1 seed to an inch and thin to 18 in. Rows are 4 ft. wide.

Grow in average good soil which has been enriched with 5-10-10 fertilizer. Sidedress the plants in mid-summer with additional balanced fertilizer or with nitrate of soda. Keep watered.

To harvest, simply pick off the tender new leaves at the tips of the branches. If you do this regularly, plants will produce a steady crop for you from summer till frost. Be careful not to remove too much of a plant at one time, however.

OKRA

Also called gumbo. A big (to as much as 8 ft.), annual vegetable producing long, pointed, green pods used mainly in soups and stews. Okra is considered a southern vegetable, though it grows in Zones 3–10. 1 packet plants 25 ft. of row. Sow seeds ½ in. deep. Germination: 10 days.

Varieties

Clemson Spineless. 56 days. Plants to 6 ft. Pods straight and ridged. Excellent for freezing.

Dwarf Green Long Pod. 52 days. Plants only 3 ft. tall. Pods spineless and ridged. Good for freezing.

Emerald. 58 days. Developed by a large soup company. Plants to 4 ft. with smooth, slender pods.

Louisiana Green Velvet. 60 days. Very tall plants producing smooth, round pods to 8 in. in length. Especially good for canning and freezing.

Culture

Okra is a very tender plant; so do not sow seeds outdoors until all danger of frost is past and soil has begun to warm up. In warmest climates, repeat sowings can be made at four- to six-week intervals until about the middle of June. To hasten and improve germination, soak seeds for 24 hours in water. Sow at the rate of one to an inch. Common recommended spacing of growing plants is 12 to 18 in., but tests in Arkansas have shown that a spacing of 8 in. increases yields 25 to 35 per cent provided you fertilize and water the plants adequately. Rows are 24 to 30 in. wide, depending on the size of the variety planted.

The soil must have a pH of 6.0 or a little higher. Mix in a good supply of humus along with 2 cups of 6-12-6, 4-12-8, or 10-20-10 fertilizer per 50 sq. ft. Sidedress plants with a little nitrate of soda or balanced fertilizer when they start to set fruit and once again when growth begins to decelerate.

Okra does well in hot, dry weather, but does even better if you keep it well watered. Cultivate lightly. After initial fruiting, some gardeners pinch out the terminal bud in order to force the growth of new side shoots and fruiting stems. When plants get too tall for easy harvesting, commercial growers even cut the plants back to within about 18 in. of the ground in midsummer.

Insects present few problems although corn earworms sometimes attack the plants. A brown leaf beetle also eats the foliage, but does no real damage to the production of pods. Fusarium and nematodes are soil-borne pests that may be troublesome. The best way to protect against them is to rotate crops annually.

Harvest pods when they are 3 in. long. At this tender stage they snap when bent between the fingers. When allowed to reach maturity, they bend without breaking and are too tough to eat.

By harvesting the pods every day or two, you will keep plants in production until they are killed by fall frost. Pods left on the plant decrease yields.

ONIONS

Bulbous plants to 20 in. Grow in Zones 1–10. 1 packet plants 20 ft. of row. Sow seeds ½ in. deep. Germination: 10 days.

Varieties

Note. Maturity dates given are from time of seed sowing until bulbs have reached full size. If you start with sets or plants, you will reduce the time considerably.

Crystal White Wax. 95 days. Medium-size, flat, white onions. Best adapted to the deep South, where this variety is planted in the fall for spring harvest.

Downing's Yellow Globe. 105 days. Medium-size, amber-skinned variety of very good quality. Keeps well.

Early Yellow Globe. 98 days. Mild, medium-size bulbs with deep yellow skin. Good keeper.

Ebenezer. 105 days. Very popular. Bulbs to 3 in. across with yellow-brown skin and slightly yellow-white flesh. An excellent keeper.

Evergreen Long White Bunching. 120 days. Grown for green scallions in milder areas, where they can be wintered over. Can also be grown for fall scallions in colder areas. Does not form bulbs.

Granex. 165 days. Both white- and yellow-skinned strains are available. Bulbs are large and very mild. Grown in very warm climates, where they are planted in the fall for spring harvest.

Red Wethersfield. 105 days. Large, purple-red bulbs with white flesh tinged with pink near the skin. Strong flavor but delicious. Stores very well.

Southport White Globe. 110 days. Medium-size, white bulbs. Keeps better in storage than most other white varieties.

White Portugal. 100 days. Also called White Silverskin. Large, flat, white, mild bulbs that store well. Also used as scallions.

White Sweet Spanish. 110 days. Like Yellow Sweet Spanish except for its white skin.

Yellow Globe Danvers. 105 days. Strong-flavored, medium-size bulbs with yellow-brown skin and yellowish flesh. Good keeper.

Yellow Sweet Spanish. 110 days. This is the variety recommended by the greatest number of agricultural extension services. Bulbs to 6 in. in diameter, with light yellow skin and white flesh. Very sweet and mild. Keeps better than Bermuda onions but not so well as some other varieties listed here.

Culture

Growing onions from seeds is a slow process. In the North seeds are sown outdoors about a month before mean date of the last spring freeze. In warm climates they are sown in October. Scatter three or four seeds to the inch. Rows are 9 in. wide.

Growing onions from sets (small bulbs grown for replanting) produces usable onions earlier in the year than seeds. Their only disadvantage is that you cannot always get the named varieties you favor. The sets, which must not be more than 3/4 in. in diameter, are planted as soon as the soil can be worked in the spring. Plant 1 in. deep and 1 to 4 in. apart, depending on the size of the onions and whether you intend to pick them or let them mature.

Another good way to grow onions is to set out seedling plants as soon as the soil can be worked. Planting depth and spacing are the same as for sets. Seedlings are commonly raised in the South for sale through garden stores and seed dealers everywhere. The bunches should be opened as soon as they are delivered; and if you cannot plant them at once, spread them out to dry. Do not water or heel in. The roots may die, but the little bulbs will produce new roots in short order when they are in the ground.

You can also raise your own seedling onions by sowing seeds indoors under glass about eight to ten weeks before they are to be planted out. The plants should be transplanted before the bulbs start to form, because if these are allowed to develop, the plants will go to seed. The tops of the seedlings are cut back to 4 to 6 in. and the roots trimmed to 1 in. before they are planted out.

Onions grow in a variety of soils provided they are well pulverized and free of stones, contain plenty of humus, have a pH of 6.0 to 6.5, and are enriched with about 4 cups of 5-10-10 or 10-10-10 fertilizer per 50 sq. ft. Sprinkling chlordane in the furrow before seeds, sets, or seedlings are planted controls onion maggots.

While onions are growing, cultivate lightly—just enough to eliminate weeds. Water regularly, since the plants require plenty of moisture. Spray or dust every two weeks with malathion to control thrips.

Harvest scallions when the bulbs are about an inch across or a little less. Shortly before large, dry onions are ready for harvesting, the tops begin to tip over. When about half the tops have done this, turn the rest of them down by hand and allow the bulbs to ripen for a couple of days. Then pull them, cut off the tops 1 in. above the bulbs and continue to dry in a shady, airy place until the necks are completely dry. Onions with necks that are damaged or slow to dry should not be stored. To store, place in a slatted crate or a mesh bag and keep in a cool, dry, well-ventilated place where the temperature does not go below freezing. Do not use the basement unless it is unusually dry and airy.

PARSNIPS

Parsnips are annuals which form big, foot-long, carrot-like, white roots with a distinctive, sweet flavor. Tops are thick and grow to 18 in. Grow in Zones 1–10. 1 packet plants 25 ft. of row. Sow seeds ¼ to ½ in. deep. Germination: 18 days.

Varieties

All American. 95 days. Roots are a little shorter than on most varieties.

Harris' Model. 110 days. Medium-length roots are unusually white and smooth.

Hollow Crown. 105 days. Roots to 15 in. in length.

Large onions ripening in the sun. The tops are turned down when about half of them begin to tip over naturally.

Culture

Parsnips are a better crop in cold climates than in warm, because the roots are improved by frost and freezing. In these areas, seeds are sown in the garden approximately three to three and a half months (depending on the variety) before mean date of the first fall freeze. This gives them just enough time to mature before cold weather sets in. If planted earlier, they will become over-size and stringy.

In warm climates, parsnips are almost always sown outdoors four to six weeks before mean date of the last spring freeze, and they are harvested in late spring. Thus they miss the beneficial effects of cold weather. But what must be must be, because this vegetable does not take kindly to long, hot summers.

Soil should be well drained, light, and improved with humus and 1 cup of 5-10-10 fertilizer per 20 sq. ft. It must also be very deeply dug and picked clean of stone and rubble. Sow two or three seeds to the inch and thin to 3 in. Rows are 18 in. wide. Because of comparatively slow germination, many gardeners sow radishes in the same row to mark the row and also to break up the soil crust.

Sidedress the plants with a little additional balanced fertilizer when they are half grown. Keep weeded and watered.

In warm climates, dig up the plants as soon as the roots mature. Be careful not to cut or break the roots. In cold climates, dig the roots any time after frost and store them in soil in a cold basement, garage, or outdoor pit. Roots can also be left in the ground through the winter and dug as needed. These are improved by being frozen.

PEAS

Annuals to 5 ft. but usually much lower. Grow in Zones 1–10. ½ lb. plants 50 ft. of row. Sow seeds 1 to 2 in. deep. Germination: 7 days.

Varieties

Alaska. 55 days. Of value only because it is very early and hardy. Peas are smooth and round, not wrinkled as in other varieties listed, and are not so sweet or tender. 2½-in. pods. Fusarium resistant.

Alderman. 74 days. Plants to 5 ft. 5-in. pods filled with very sweet peas. Favorite tall variety.

Dwarf Gray Sugar. 65 days. Most widely recommended of the edible-podded varieties. 2½-ft. plants. 3-in. pods. Tolerant of fusarium wilt.

Freezonian. 63 days. Plants 2½ ft. tall. Peas in 3½-in. pods are especially good for freezing since the skin does not peel during the process. Widely grown. Fusarium resistant.

Frosty. 64 days. 28-in. plants. 3½-in. pods. Good quality and freezes well.

Laxton's Progress. 63 days. Plants 16 in. tall. Pods, 4½ in. Prolific. Good freezing variety.

Lincoln. 66 days. 2½-ft. plants with 3½-in. pods. Tastes as fresh peas should taste—delicious. Freezes well. An old favorite.

Little Marvel. 63 days. Probably the most popular variety grown in home gardens. 18-in. plants are covered with 3-in., tightly packed pods. Not equal in quality to some other varieties, but very good anyway.

Progress No. 9. 60 days. Pods to 4½ in. Plants 20 in. tall. Resistant to wilt.

Thomas Laxton. 65 days. 3-ft. plants. 3½-in. pods. Very productive and popular.

Wando. 68 days. 2½-ft. plants are more tolerant of heat than other varieties. Can be planted in summer for a fall crop. 3½-in. pods. Good for freezing.

Culture

Peas are easy to grow, but it takes an awful lot of them to give you very many meals.

In areas with cool summers, such as Alaska, peas can be grown throughout the growing season. In warm climates, they are grown in winter, early spring, and fall. Elsewhere they are best treated as a spring crop, although you may occasionally succeed with them as a fall crop (this is difficult, however, because while the vines are hardy, the blossoms and pods are very tender).

Sow seeds as early in the spring as the soil can be worked. Plant early, midseason, and late varieties at the same time if you want a long harvest. A second sowing of an early or mid-season variety can be made two or three weeks later. Sow the seeds one to an inch and do not thin. Rows of dwarf varieties are 18 to 24 in. wide; of tall varieties, 30 in. wide.

Mix 4 to 6 cups of balanced fertilizer into every 100 sq. ft. of soil. No further feeding is necessary except in cool climates, where one or two sidedressings at monthly intervals will help to maintain production through the summer till frost.

Water in dry weather and keep out weeds. Supporting of dwarf varieties is unnecessary, and of medium-size varieties is usually optional. In the latter case, supports make picking easier and conserve garden space. In areas where damp weather is usually expected at about the time peas are ready for harvest, supports for medium-size varieties are also recommended to keep the pods off the ground, where they might rot. Tall varieties must be supported, of course.

About the simplest way to support the vines is to stretch three or four horizontal rows of string between stakes. A slightly more troublesome way is to stick twiggy branches upright into the soil along the row. A fence of chicken wire can also be used as support, but it is a nuisance to clean free of vines at the end of the season.

Aphids are the most troublesome insect pest. Fusarium wilt is a difficult disease, but does not affect resistant varieties. Rotting of seeds sown in very cold, wet soils can be minimized by treating seeds with Spergon.

Pick peas when the pods are well filled and before the seeds become hard and wrinkled. Pick just before cooking or freezing to enjoy the best flavor and quality. If peas must be picked hours before they are to be used, leave them in their pods and keep in a very cool place.

If you miss any pods, they can be left on the vine to dry. The seeds can then be used in soups.

Edible-podded peas, also called sugar peas, must be picked when they are young, succulent, and free of fiber. If left on the vine, the pods will fill out and the peas can then be shelled and eaten like other peas.

PEPPERS

Peppers are very ornamental, annual plants to 30 in. Grow in Zones 3–10. 1 packet produces 60 plants. Sow seeds ⅛ in. deep. Germination: 10 days.

Varieties

Bell Boy. 70 days. Top-notch hybrid produces large quantities of big, sweet peppers that turn from green to red. 2-ft. plants. Resistant to tobacco mosaic.

Fordhook. 66 days. Sweet and large, fruits are as big around as they are high. Dark green skin turns bright red. Productive.

Hungarian Wax. 65 days. Waxy, yellow fruits 6 in. long and 1½ in. thick. They turn red. They are hot; but there is also a Hungarian Wax that is sweet. Plants under 2 ft.

Long Red Cayenne. 70 days. Hot fruits are 5 in. long and slim; turn from green to red. They are often curled and twisted. Large plants. A very popular hot variety.

Oshkosh. 70 days. A large sweet pepper which is unusual because the green fruits turn yellow when ripe.

Peter Piper. 62 days. A very productive hybrid out of South Dakota. The 3 x 3-in. fruits are sweet, turn green to red.

Red Cherry. 80 days. Small plants produce quantities of round, 1-in.-diameter, green fruits that turn dark red. On the usual Red Cherry variety, these are very hot; but there is also an almost identical Red Cherry variety that has sweet fruits.

Sweet Banana. 70 days. Sweet fruits 6 in. long and pointed. Light yellow skin turns red. Used for pickling.

Yolo Wonder. 78 days. 2-ft. plant with large, sweet green peppers that turn red. Resistant to tobacco mosaic.

Culture

Peppers are grown almost exactly like tomatoes. Seed should be started under glass. Move little plants into the garden about two weeks after last spring frost. Peppers like heat better than tomatoes do; but they should be given somewhat less fertilizer. One light application at planting and another about six weeks later are enough. No staking is necessary. Space plants 20 in. apart in rows 2 ft. wide. Pick fruits when they reach full size and feel firm. They may be picked when the skin is green or when it turns red.

Special culture

The small, hot peppers can be grown indoors in winter from seeds sown in late spring or early summer. Pot up in 4 to 6-in. pots containing a humusy soil; water regularly; fertilize lightly once every six weeks; and keep in full sun. Move indoors before frost, and grow on in the same way in a sunny window at 60°.

PHYSALIS

Also called groundcherry, husk tomato, and in Hawaii, poka. An annual to 24 in. Physalis is a close relative of the tomato, produces cherry-size, yellow, seedy fruits which are enclosed in a paperlike husk. The sweet fruits are used in preserves and pies. Grows in Zones 3–10. 1 packet produces 50 plants. Sow seeds ⅛ in. deep. Germination: 12 days. Fruits mature in 90 days.

Culture

Grow like tomatoes. Space plants 3 ft. apart and don't bother to stake them. Harvest fruits when they fall to the ground. They will keep for several weeks in the refrigerator.

Plants self-seed freely.

POKE

A weedy perennial which grows wild in the East and produces slender, asparagus-like shoots in the spring. Grows in Zones 3–8. Propagated from divisions. Shoots of established plants mature in 20 days.

Culture

If there is a commercial source of poke, I am unfamiliar with it. Perhaps you can persuade one of the Pennsylvania Dutch farmers, who offer poke in their spring markets, to sell you several of the roots. Or perhaps you can find some growing wild.

In any event, although you can propagate plants from seeds of the dark red berries, you will be better off to start with some of the rooted crowns. Plant and grow like asparagus, although you do not have to delay harvesting more than one year. To keep plants from spreading out of hand, cut the roots back occasionally.

Two important points to note about this vegetable are: (1) Since it is a carrier of mosaic, it should never be grown anywhere near plants susceptible to that disease. (2) The roots are very poisonous—perhaps deadly.

To harvest poke, cut the shoots that come up early in the spring. The shoots should be tender and white. Mulching the bed with straw, hay, or leaves helps to keep them this way. Cut the shoots as soon as they are 6 to 8 in. out of the ground by slicing them off just below the soil surface. Be extremely careful not to take any part of the poisonous root.

POPCORN

Grows in Zones 3–10. 1 packet plants 75 ft. of row. Sow seeds 1 to 1½ in. deep. Germination: 10 days.

Varieties

Japanese Hulless. 90 days. 4-in. ears with irregular rows of slender, white kernels. Stalks 5 ft. tall.

South American Hybrid. 105 days. 8-in. ears with up to 16 rows of yellow kernels. Stalks to 7 ft.

Strawberry. 105 days. A novelty. Tiny, 1½in. ears with crimson kernels look like big strawberries. Stalks to 5 ft.

White Cloud. 95 days. Excellent new hybrid does especially well in colder areas. 6-in. ears with pointed white kernels. 5-ft. stalks.

Culture

Grow like corn. Note that if yellow popcorn is planted near white sweet corn, ears of the latter may have some yellow kernels.

In the fall, leave ears of popcorn on the stalks until the kernels are dry. Then pick, shuck, and store in a dry place until the kernels fall off the cob under very little pressure. They are then ready for popping or can be bagged and held for later use.

POTATOES

Annuals to 30 in. Grow in Zones 1–10. Grow from small potatoes or, more commonly, from large potatoes cut into pieces. 5 to 6 lb. of seed potatoes plant about 50 ft. of row. "Germination": 18 days.

Varieties

Irish Cobbler. 90 days. An old variety of good quality, but has deep eyes which some homemakers object to. Susceptible to hollow heart and scab.

Katahdin. 115 days. Leading potato in Maine. Round. Fine quality. Plants give high yields. Resistant to drought and several diseases.

Kennebec. 105 days. Very popular potato, good for baking and frying. Should be planted 8 in. apart. Potatoes develop near surface of soil and are subject to sunburn. Resistant to late blight and several other diseases.

Norgold Russet. 90 days. A smooth, medium-long potato that is unusually white and mealy when cooked. Good resistance to scab.

Norland. 85 days. A smooth, shallow-eyed, oblong, red-skinned potato developed in North Dakota, where it is recommended especially for home gardens. Good table quality. Moderately resistant to scab.

Ona. 110 days. A rather dry, mealy potato but good. Has unusually high resistance to scab and a number of other diseases.

Red Pontiac. 100 days. A high-yielding red variety much grown in Minnesota and North Dakota and recommended for states as far away as Arizona and Georgia.

Russet Burbank. 130 days. This is the potato that Idaho boasts about; but it also does well elsewhere. Long narrow tubers excellent for baking. Resistant to scab. Plants should be spaced 16 in. apart.

Culture

Soil for potatoes can be variable, but should always be well drained, high in humus, and with a pH of 5.5 to discourage scab. Dig it deeply. If you are turning over an area that has been in sod, apply 4 oz. of 5 per cent chlordane dust per 100 sq. ft. after digging and work it in well. This should control wireworms and grubs that may attack the plants.

Fertilizer should be applied at time of planting at the rate of 6 cups per 50 ft. of row. Place it in furrows 2 to 3 in. to each side of the seed drill and slightly below the bottom of the drill.

Use seed potatoes that are certified free of disease. Unless you know the seed has been out of cold storage for some time, keep it for about a week at 60° to 70° to encourage sprout development. If you want an extra-early crop, hold the potatoes for a week or so longer in subdued light until tough, thick, green sprouts are actually formed.

Seed pieces are usually cut from large potatoes. The pieces should be rather blocky, weigh 1½ to 2 oz., and contain at least one eye. Whole potatoes of 1 to 2 in. diameter can also be used. Though they cost more, they are less likely to rot and give a somewhat higher yield than cut pieces of the same weight.

Cut seed pieces should be planted immediately after they are cut if the soil is moist but not if the soil is dry. If pieces must be held for some time before planting, keep them in slatted crates in a humid location at about 60°.

Plant potatoes early in the spring as soon as the soil is dry enough to be worked properly but late enough for the plants to escape a freeze after they emerge. Plant the seed pieces 2 in. deep in moist soil; 3 in. deep in dry soil. Space the pieces 1 ft. apart unless a wider or closer spacing is recommended for the variety you plant. Rows are 2 ft. wide.

Cultivate shallowly to control weeds. Then, when the plants are 6 in. high, pull a little soil up to them on both sides to form a low hill. Later, when the plants are 18 in. high, hill them up a bit more. The hill—actually a ridge—should be about 18 to 24 in. wide. Its purpose is to prevent sunburning (greening) of the tubers. This happens when they are exposed to light, and it may happen even when they are covered with a half inch of soil. So make the hill wide enough and high enough to protect all the potatoes that each plant develops. If you thrust your hand into the soil around the plants, you can tell whether you have hilled them adequately.

As they grow, potatoes need an even, moderate supply of moisture—a little more than an inch of water a week. To control the various pests that may attack the plants—flea beetles, potato beetles, corn borers, aphids, leafhoppers, early blight, and late blight—treat the plants with a general-purpose garden dust or spray, or dust with rotenone, at the first sign of trouble. Repeat the application in a week. Then, when plants are 15 in. tall, apply a general-purpose garden dust (such as a mixture of methoxychlor, malathion, and captan) every week to ten days until harvest. The serious scab disease is most easily prevented by rotating crops, using potato varieties that are resistant to the disease, and keeping the soil acid. Late blight—another very serious disease—can be avoided by dusting as just described. However, it should be noted that late blight may attack plants very early in the season if the weather is damp; so if you at any time run into a prolonged bad spell, you should apply a general-purpose dust or spray with zineb.

"New" potatoes only an inch or two in diameter can be dug at any time they reach a desirable size. Potatoes for storing should not be dug until the plants have been dead for two weeks; if they are dug while the tops are green, they may rot in storage. In other words, potatoes are usually harvested a couple of weeks after a killing frost. You can, however, harvest them earlier if you cut off the tops and leave the tubers in the ground, well covered with soil, for two or three weeks. In no case should the tubers be allowed to freeze in the ground.

The day on which you dig potatoes for storage should be above 45°. Don't expose them to sun or wind any longer than necessary. Handle carefully to avoid bruising. Wash or brush off the dirt. Then place in a slatted crate or basket and store in a dark, humid place at 50°. If held at this temperature, potatoes will remain in good condition for three or four months. If you want to keep potatoes longer than this, hold them at 50° for two weeks after digging and then lower them to 40° or slightly less.

PUMPKINS

Large annuals with stems stretching to 7 or 8 ft. Grow in Zones 4–10. 1 packet produces 30 plants. Sow seeds ½ in. deep. Germination: 8 days.

Varieties

Connecticut Field. 115 days. Also called Big Tom. Huge pumpkins to 20 lb. or more; rounded but with flattened ends. Something to brag about.

Jack O'Lantern. 100 days. Medium-size, light orange, round to oblong fruits. More subject to rotting in field than others.

Small Sugar. 100 days. Excellent, deep orange pie pumpkin and good for freezing. Fruits weigh about 8 lb. and are round.

Culture

Grow like winter squash in the same space. Since pumpkins do well in partial shade, they are often grown in the corn patch; but because they compete for moisture and nutrients, they should there be spaced 6 ft. apart in rows 7 ft. wide.

To grow gigantic pumpkins—to almost 170 lb.—never let them run dry. Fertilize at least once a month (a Californian who grew a prize-winning pumpkin weighing 127 lb. fertilized once a week). Remove all fruits but one from a vine.

To keep ripening pumpkins from turning more or less white or rotting where they touch the ground, slip boards underneath.

Harvest fruits before a killing frost. They can, however, withstand light frost, because they are rather well protected by the leaves on the vines. Store in a dry, airy, dim place at 50° to 55°.

RADISHES

Small annuals about 6 in. high. Grow in Zones 1–10. 1 packet plants 20 ft. of row. Sow seeds ½ in. deep. Germination: 6 days.

Varieties

Note. The best known kinds of radish are the very fast-growing varieties which can be grown pretty much throughout the growing season. So-called winter radishes grow much more slowly and produce larger, more pungent roots.

Burpee White. 25 days. Roots round and white, to 1 in. across.

Champion. 28 days. Wine-red variety that stays firm even when large.

Cherry Belle. 23 days. Small, round, red roots; unusually short tops. Good outdoors and excellent under glass.

Chinese Rose. 52 days. Winter radish with deep red skin, white flesh. Roots to 7 in. long, 2 in. across.

Comet. 25 days. Small, red, round, or olive-shaped roots that remain crisp and firm longer than most early radishes.

Crimson Giant. 29 days. Old favorite with red roots that reach large size without becoming pithy. Stands heat better than most varieties and therefore does better in the summer.

Early Scarlet Globe. 22 days. There are two strains, one with a shorter top than the other. This is the type generally grown in home gardens. Roots are round and red. Also does well under glass.

French Breakfast. 23 days. Oblong roots are red on top, white below.

Long Black Spanish. 56 days. A winter radish. Roots up to 9 in. long and almost 3 in. across; have a black skin and white flesh.

Round Black Spanish. 56 days. A winter variety with round roots 4 in. in diameter. The skin is black; flesh, white.

Sparkler. 25 days. Round roots are red on top, white at the base.

White Icicle. 29 days. Roots are white and icicle-shaped; 5 in. long.

White Strasburg. 40 days. Grown for summer use. Tapering white roots are 5 in. long, 2 in. across.

Culture

Radishes can be grown throughout the growing season in cool climates; but in most areas they are grown in spring and fall, because they dislike intense summer heat. Sow seeds of quick-maturing varieties outdoors four weeks before mean date of the last spring freeze and make repeat sowings at one- or two-week intervals until late spring. Then make additional sowings in late summer and fall. In warm climates, radishes can be grown through the winter.

Sow seeds of winter varieties in time for them to reach mature size by about the mean date of the first fall freeze.

Sow a couple of seeds to the inch and thin small varieties to 1 to 1½ in. apart. Thin winter radishes to 3 in. Rows are 9 in. wide.

Radishes are easy to grow and undemanding; but they perform best and are tastiest when grown quickly. So mix a little humus into the soil and also 1 cup of balanced fertilizer per 25 ft. of row. Keep weeded and watered in dry weather. Since radishes lose their crispness and become pithy soon after reaching maturity, harvest them early and don't plant more at one time than you are likely to use. You'll get the best quality roots if you make frequent small sowings at fairly close intervals.

Winter radishes can be harvested when of desirable size. For winter use, store them in moist sand in a cool basement.

If root maggots are troublesome, mix a little chlordane dust into the soil at planting time, and dust additional chlordane around the plants once or twice until just before the roots start to form.

Special culture

Radishes are very easy to grow in cool greenhouses in all parts of the country and in coldframes in Zone 8. They can also be grown in cold-frames in Zone 7 if you take pains to cover the frames on coldest nights; but they will do better in hotbeds.

RHUBARB

A perennial to 30 in. Grows in Zones 1–10, but does best where the ground freezes in winter. Grows from divisions. Stalks of established plants mature in 30 days.

Varieties

MacDonald. An excellent red variety.

Valentine. Another fine red; big and sweet.

Victoria. Thick, broad stalks are green tinged with red.

Culture

Rhubarb can be raised from seed, but does not come true. You will do better to buy roots or to divide old crowns given you by a neighbor into several sections each with at least one eye.

Plant rhubarb at one side of the garden, where it is out of the way but easily cared for. If the soil is well drained and enriched with plenty of humus, preferably well-rotted manure, the plants will do well. Mix about ½ cup of 10-10-10 fertilizer into the soil for each plant a week or two before setting out the roots in early spring. Plant the roots about 2 in. deep and space them 3 to 4 ft. apart in rows 5 ft. wide. Well-developed plants take a lot of space. Do not pull any stalks the first year, and pull only a few the second in order to give the plants time to become strong and big.

Annual care includes shallow cultivation to keep down weeds, and ample moisture throughout the growing season. Sidedress each plant in early spring with about ½ cup of 10-10-10 and make a second application in late spring. During late spring and summer, treat regularly with a general-purpose garden spray to control insects and diseases. Cut out seed stalks as they appear; otherwise, they will reduce the plants' yield and vitality.

Harvest stalks when they reach the desired size by pulling, or breaking, them off at the base. Discard the leaves, which are toxic. You can continue harvesting stalks for eight to ten weeks, or even longer if you don't strip the plants at any time. Like all plants, rhubarb needs plenty of foliage to grow.

In most areas, rhubarb dies down naturally with the onset of cold weather. In warm climates, however, it never stops growing, so it is advisable to force the plants into dormancy by withholding water in the summer.

Plants that become very large should be divided. If plants are vigorous, you may have to do this every four years at least.

Special culture

Rhubarb is an easy vegetable to force in the basement in winter. Dig large, healthy clumps in the fall and leave them outdoors until they freeze. Then bring them into a dim but not black room where the temperature holds between 50° and 60°. Stand the clumps upright and close together in a box with a bottom layer of 2 in. of soil, and fill all around them with soil. Cover with a 2-in. layer. Water about once a week—just enough to keep the soil damp. The plants will produce a crop of usable stalks—without real leaf blades—in about a month; and when these are harvested, the plants will often produce a second crop. They should then be discarded because it is too much trouble to restore them to productive condition.

ROCAMBOLE

A perennial onion 3 ft. high which produces clusters of very small, purple-skinned, garlic-flavored onions in the tops of the plants. Grow from bulbs in Zones 6–10. Matures in 100 days.

Note: An onion relative similar to rocambole is the Egyptian multiplier onion. It is also a perennial, but produces much larger bulblets with a more distinct onion flavor.

Culture

Grow like onions. Plant the bulblets like onion sets in the early spring in rich, moist soil. Roots of parent plants may also be divided in the spring. Harvest the clusters of bulblets in midsummer when they begin to separate. Cut the stems below them and hang upside down in a dry, dark place. The bulblets keep better than garlic cloves.

After the bulblets are harvested, the plants die down. Then within about a month, they start putting up green sprouts which can be cut and used like chives.

RUTABAGAS

Also called Swede turnips. Rutabagas are very closely related to turnips, but grow to 20 in. The tops are inedible. Grow in Zones 1–8 but most popular in colder climates. 1 packet plants 50 ft. of row. Sow seeds ¼ to ½ in. deep. Germination: 9 days.

Varieties

American Purple Top. 90 days. Large roots have creamy yellow flesh. The skin is purple at the top, amber below. Old favorite.

Laurentian. 90 days. Like the above but the flesh has a somewhat finer grain.

Culture

Sow seeds outdoors three to three and a half months before mean date of the first fall freeze. In warm climates seeds may also be sown outdoors six to eight weeks before the last spring freeze. In Alaska seeds are sown in the spring when the soil can be worked.

Sow two or three seeds to the inch and thin to 6 to 8 in. in rows 15 in. wide. Grow like turnips. Harvest after frost, but don't allow the roots to freeze. Store in moist sand in a cold, but not freezing, basement or garage. Storage life can be extended if the roots are cleaned and then coated with paraffin before they are laid away in the basement.

SALSIFY

Also called oyster plant and vegetable oyster. Annuals to 3 ft. produce a slender, 8-in. carrot-like root with creamy-white flesh and an oyster-like flavor. Grow in Zones 4–10. 1 packet plants 20 ft. of row. Sow seeds ½ in. deep. Germination: 7 days.

Variety

Mammoth Sandwich Island. 120 days. The standard variety.

Culture

Sow seeds outdoors two weeks before mean date of the last spring freeze. Sow a couple of seeds to the inch and thin to 3 in. in rows 9 in. wide. Soil must be dug to a depth of 1 ft., picked free of stones, and mixed with a little humus and about 1 cup of balanced fertilizer per 25 ft. of row.

Keep weeded, and water in dry weather. Sidedress with a little more fertilizer when plants are half grown.

Dig the roots whenever they are of good size. For winter use, dig roots in the fall and store in moist sand in a cool basement or garage. Roots can also be left in the ground over winter for use in the early spring.

SHALLOTS

Onion relatives, 1½ ft. tall when in bloom, which produce clusters of small, brown-skinned onions of exceptionally fine flavor. The plants are perennials. Grow in Zones 5–10 from bulbs planted 1 in. deep. Mature in 100 days.

Culture

Grow like onion sets. The shallot bulbs should, however, be planted in early autumn. They will be ready to harvest the next summer, when most of the plant leaves have withered. Store in a cool, dry, dark place.

SORREL

Often called sour grass. Perennial to 18 in. with long leaves of slightly acid flavor that are used in salads, soup and as greens. Grow in Zones 3–7. 1 packet plants 30 ft. of row. Sow seeds ¼ in. deep. Germination: 10 days. Matures enough for use in 45 days.

Culture

Sow seeds outdoors as soon as the soil can be worked in the spring. Thin to 8 in. in rows 12 in. wide. If you don't want a crop the first year, seed can be sown outdoors any time until June 30.

Sorrel thrives in either sun or partial shade. The plant is a strong grower and is not particular about soil, but should be fertilized lightly every spring. Water in dry weather. Watch out for snails. Divide plants every other year.

Harvest leaves as you need them.

SOUTHERN PEAS

Also called cowpeas, table peas, and field peas. These are not really peas, but are related to them. They are annuals to 2 ft. and of varying growth habits which produce large pods of seeds. These are eaten fresh or are canned, frozen, or dried. Grow in Zones 6–10. ½ lb. plants 50 ft. of row. Sow seeds ½ in. deep. Germination: 10 days.

Varieties

Brown Crowder. 80 days. An old and still popular variety. Small, vining plants with light green seeds which turn light brown when dry. Good for freezing. Plants very susceptible to nematodes.

Dixielee. 80 days. Developed in Mississippi, one of the best varieties presently available. Compact plants. Pods to 8 in. with large seeds which are light green at their best eating stage. They turn brown when dry. Excellent for freezing. Very productive. Tolerant of nematodes.

Mississippi Silver. 65 days. New variety. Pods are a silvery color at green stage; straw colored when dry. Fairly compact plants with pods concentrated in the center. Has good resistance to diseases and nematodes.

Culture

The U.S. Department of Agriculture says of southern peas: "For the effort necessary to grow them, few if any other vegetables will pay higher dividends than southern table peas."

Unlike true peas, Southern peas do best in warm weather. Do not sow outdoors until all danger of frost has passed and soil has begun to warm up. Soil should be of average quality, with good drainage and ample humus. Mix in a low-nitrogen balanced fertilizer, such as 5-10-10 or 4-12-12, at a rate of 1½ to 2 cups per 50 ft. of row. Space seeds 1 to 3 in. apart and do not thin them. Rows are 2 ft. wide.

Water in dry spells and keep down weeds. Worst insect pest is the cowpea curculio, but it can be controlled by spraying with toxaphene as soon as blossoming starts and twice a week thereafter for a fortnight.

For fresh peas, pick the pods when the seeds mature to the desired size but are still green. For drying, let the pods hang on the plants until they turn to a full yellow or brown color.

SOYBEANS

Soybeans are erect, 3-ft., bushy plants loaded with pods containing several fat, oval, green beans which are cooked like green shell beans. Mature beans are cooked like lima beans. Grow in Zones 6–10. ½ lb. plants 75 ft. of row. Sow seeds 1 in. deep in heavy soil; 2 in. in light soil. Germination: 12 days.

Variety

Bansei. 96 days. Oval seeds. Old standby variety.
Kanrich. 103 days. Nearly round seeds. Freezes well.

Culture

In cooler areas, sow soybeans outdoors after last frost. In warm areas, sow any time in May. Soybeans are a short-day plant and their fruiting is controlled by length of darkness rather than by the number of days they grow in the garden.

Soybeans do better in heavy soil than light. Place fertilizer in bands 3 in. to either side of the seed drill and 3 in. below the drill. Use a balanced fertilizer with little or no nitrogen, such as 4-12-12. To help the beans produce their own nitrogen, treat the seed before planting with an inoculant. Sow ten seeds per foot. Rows are 3 ft. wide.

Keep weeds hoed out. It is advisable to cultivate soybeans from late morning on: in early morning the plants are brittle and easily injured. Water in long dry spells; but in the average growing season, the only time a little extra moisture is needed is when the pods start to fill out. If your garden is exposed to strong winds, it's a good idea to tie strings on both sides of the row to keep plants from being blown down.

Beans to be eaten fresh are harvested as soon as they plump up in the pods. Dried beans are left on the vine until pods and beans turn yellow.

SPINACH

An annual to 1 ft. Grow in Zones 3–10. It will grow in Alaska's still colder zones, but goes to seed too quickly in that state's long days. 1 packet plants 25 ft. of row. Sow seeds ½ in. deep. Germination: 8 days.

Varieties

America. 50 days. Extremely dark green, crumpled, and savoyed leaves. Sizable plants. Very slow to bolt.

Bloomsdale Long Standing. 48 days. Widely grown. Plants are compact; leaves dark green and crinkled. Stands heat better than most varieties.

Viking. 45 days. Large, spreading plants with smooth, dark green leaves. Slow bolting.

Virginia Savoy. 39 days. Medium-size plants with dark green, savoyed leaves. Blight resistant. Popular in the East and South. Plant for fall and winter crops.

Culture

Spinach is a very hardy plant that must have cool weather to grow. In hot weather it bolts to seed. Sow seeds outdoors in the spring as soon as soil can be worked, and make one or two succession plantings. For a fall crop, sow seeds six to eight weeks before mean date of the first fall freeze. In areas with cool summers, spinach can be grown continuously from spring to fall. And in areas with mild winters, it can be grown throughout the winter. In areas falling between mild and cold—Zone 7, for example—

spinach that is protected with a little hay or straw should also go through the winter.

Soil should be well drained, humusy, and moisture-retentive; and it must be nearly neutral in reaction, since spinach cannot tolerate a low pH. Mix in about 2 cups of 10-10-10 fertilizer per 50 ft. of row.

Sow a couple of seeds to an inch and thin to stand 4 to 5 in. apart in rows 1 ft. wide. Don't let the soil dry out. Harvest as soon as plants attain full size.

SQUASH—SUMMER

Annuals to 30 in. and very big around. Grow in Zones 1–10. 1 packet produces 50 plants. Plant seeds ½ in. deep. Germination: 7 days.

Varieties

Chefini. 55 days. A straight, cylindrical, zucchini-type squash with solid, dark green skin and crisp, white flesh.

Cocozelle. 60 days. Cucumber-like fruits have dark green skin striped with lighter green. Flesh is greenish-white and firm.

Early Prolific Straightneck. 50 days. Excellent, creamy-yellow squash with a tapering body that has no pronounced neck.

Early White Bush Scallop. 60 days. A patty pan squash. The fruits are creamy-white and shaped like a flat bowl with scalloped edges. The vines cover a little more ground than those of other summer squashes. Not recommended for Alaska except in mildest areas.

Golden Summer Crookneck. 53 days. Bright yellow squash of fine quality. Body is large; crookneck, small.

Greyzini. 52 days. A very productive, zucchini-type hybrid with straight, cylindrical fruits that have a grayish-green skin with dark green markings.

Long White Vegetable Marrow. 60 days. A popular variety in England. The fruits are oblong and faintly ribbed. Skin is smooth and creamy-white; the flesh, pale green and marrowy.

Culture

Summer squash is one of the most prolific vegetables you can grow if the soil is well supplied with humus and about 2 cups of balanced fertilizer per 25 ft. of row, if you keep it watered, and if you watch out for cucumber beetles, squash bugs, and mildew. So don't over-plant. Two or three plants each of a yellow squash, a patty pan and a zucchini should keep the average family *very* well supplied from mid-summer till frost.

Sow seeds outdoors after all danger of frost is past and the ground is warm. Some people plant in hills; I prefer rows. Sow two or three seeds to a foot and thin to 2 ft. apart. Rows are 4 ft. wide for all varieties except patty pans, which need 5 ft. and sometimes 6.

All summer-squash fruits will grow to enormous size if you let them or if you don't see them hidden under the big leaves and thick stems. What's more, at the height of their season, they grow with amazing speed: a slender 6-in. zucchini may become a fat 10- or 12-in. giant in 24 hours. As long as your thumbnail can easily penetrate the skin, the fruit is usable. Ideally, however, squashes should be harvested when they are only 6 to 8 in. long (3 in. across in the case of patty pans).

SQUASH—WINTER

Enormous, space-consuming annuals. Grow in Zones 3–10. 1 packet produces 50 plants. Sow seeds ½ in. deep. Germination: 9 days.

Varieties

Banana. 110 days. Popular in the West. Fruits are roughly banana-shaped —20 in. long; 5½ in. across. One strain has a blue-green skin; another, a pink skin. Flesh is orange-yellow and of fair quality.

Bush Table Queen. 80 days. Similar to Table Queen but the plants are bushier and take up less space.

Buttercup. 100 days. Excellent variety shaped like a turban with a some-what protruding button at the blossom end. The dark green skin has silvery-white stripes and gray spots. Fruits 6½ in. in diameter and 4½ in. thick. Deep orange flesh is dry, sweet, stringless, and excellent for freezing.

Butternut. 95 days. Shaped something like a large pear but with a very long, thick, cylindrical neck. Tan-skinned fruits up to 10 in. long and 5 in. across. Flesh is rather dry, fine-textured, and orange. Seed cavity very small. May not keep so well as other varieties but superior in all other ways. There are various strains differing mainly in size and maturity.

Gold Nugget. 85 days. Fruits are buttercup- or pumpkin-shaped, about 4 in. wide and 4 in. deep. Skin is orange; flesh, golden-orange, and of fine flavor and texture. Best of all—the plant is bush-shaped and occupies little space.

Hercules. 90 days. Like a Butternut, but a little fatter and more dumb-bell-shaped. Flesh very thick; seed cavity small.

Hubbard. 110 days. Fine for pies, baking, freezing, etc. Dark green, warty fruits measure about 12 in. long, 10 in. through. Flesh is deep orange-yellow. If you want even bigger fruits to brag about, try Blue Hubbard (115 days).

Culture

Winter squash requires a fertile, humusy soil. It should be enriched at time of seeding and again when plants are about two months old with balanced fertilizer, such as 5-10-10 or 10-10-10. Use about 2 cups per 25 sq. ft.

Except for the bushier varieties, which require a space measuring about 2 x 5 ft. per plant, winter squashes need plenty of space to roam. Plant in rows 7 ft. wide and thin plants to 30 in.

Seeds are usually planted outdoors after all danger of frost is past and soil has warmed; but for an earlier start, you can sow seeds under glass about a month earlier (see melons). Use of Hotkaps or Hotents over seedlings also permits a somewhat earlier start.

Water plants regularly. Cultivate shallowly to control weeds, or, better still, mulch the garden with hay or polyethylene film. Keep an eye open for cucumber beetles, squash bugs, and aphids. Squash vine borers, which may attack young plants, can be thwarted by dusting the plants and ground around them with rotenone or Sevin.

Allow winter squash to ripen before harvesting, but don't expose to frost. The skin should be hard enough to resist the pressure of your thumbnail. Handle carefully if you plan to store the fruits. Keep in a clean, dry place at a temperature of 50° to 55°. The air should be able to circulate freely around the fruits.

Fruits that have not been damaged in any way will keep for a number of months—perhaps until spring. Slightly damaged fruits should not be stored for much more than a month.

SWEET POTATOES

Sweet potatoes are vining plants, related to the morning glory, which form a low-growing groundcover. There are two types. One produces rather mealy, dry-fleshed tubers. The other has moist-fleshed tubers. In the South, the latter are known as yams. They are much more delicious than the dry type and have generally supplanted them. Sweet potatoes grow best in Zones 7–10, but in some parts of the country, such as the Middle West, they are also grown in 6. Grow from sprouts or tip cuttings. 50 sprouts plant 50 ft. of row. Plants mature in 140 days.

Varieties

Allgold. An orange-colored, dry-fleshed type. Does better than most varieties in soils of low fertility and under drought conditions. Fairly small vines. Wilt resistant.

Centennial. Widely grown yam-type with deep orange flesh. Very productive. Well adapted to varying climatic and soil conditions. Needs extra heat to speed development of sprouts.

Goldrush. Excellent-quality, yam-type sweet potato. Good for freezing. Early maturing. Resistant to wilt.

Onolena. Yam-type recommended for Hawaii, where it has better quality and higher yield than Porto Rico.

Porto Rico (Unit 1 strain). A first-rate, yam-type sweet potato. Widely grown but slowly giving way to newer varieties.

Culture

You'll save a lot of trouble if you buy vigorous, stocky plants produced from certified seed potatoes. You can, however, raise your own plants in an electrically heated hotbed. A half-dozen certified seed potatoes will provide in the neighborhood of 150 plants. To control possible diseases, dip the potatoes for ten minutes (no more) in a solution of ½ lb. borax and 3 gal. water. (Mix the borax in a little warm water before pouring it into cold water.) Then immediately lay the tubers horizontally in the hot-bed and cover with 3 to 4 in. of soil. This must be kept moist. When the sprouts produced by the tubers are 8 in. tall (this takes about six weeks), pull them from the tubers and plant in the garden. The tubers will produce several more crops of sprouts if you keep them watered and heated.

In Hawaii and other areas where sweet potatoes can be grown year round or for most of the year, stem cuttings taken from growing plants are used instead of sprouts. The cuttings are 8 to 12 in. long; and all but two or three of the bottom leaves are left on. The cuttings are planted at an angle with two-thirds of the stem covered. The advantage of starting plants in this way is that borers and diseases which may infest tubers are not passed on to the new plants.

Sweet potatoes are planted outdoors after all danger of frost is past. In warm climates with a long growing season, several plantings can be made. In warmest climates, such as Hawaii, sweet potatoes can be grown throughout the year.

Soil should be a rather acid and well-drained, light, sandy loam. Sweet potatoes do not do well in very rich, heavy soils; and they are not overly productive in very sandy soils. If nematodes are troublesome, fumigate the soil to get rid of them. Two weeks before setting out plants, dig the soil deeply and mix in about 2 cups of low-nitrogen balanced fertilizer, such as 5-10-10 or 4-12-8, per 50 sq. ft. Then shape the soil into ridges 24 to 30 in. wide and 8 in. high. Space the plants 1 ft. apart down the center of the ridges.

Cultivate shallowly to control weeds. See that plants receive about 1 in. of water every week. Spray or dust with Sevin if insects such as cucumber beetles, flea beetles, leafhoppers, leafrollers, and aphids become troublesome. Rogue out diseased plants and destroy them. (The best way to cope with sweet potato diseases is to start with plants from certified, treated seed potatoes and to rotate crops.)

Dig sweet potatoes when they are mature. Cut off the tops first to facilitate digging. Be very careful not to damage or bruise the tubers. Digging should be done when the soil is dry so that the tubers can be cleaned easily. If the soil is damp and clings to the tubers, don't try to wash or brush it off; put the tubers in a sheltered place until the soil dries instead. Do not under any circumstances leave tubers exposed to the sun for very long.

All tubers should be dug before the first fall freeze. If a freeze should strike before the harvest is completed, cut off the frosted tops immediately; otherwise the tubers will probably be ruined. (Without their tops, however, they can be left in the ground for a few days.)

Sweet potatoes can be cooked right after harvesting, but they are sweeter if they are first cured. Curing is essential if the tubers are to be stored. The process is complicated because it involves holding the tubers for seven to ten days in a room with very high temperature and very high humidity (the optimums are 85 degrees and 90 per cent relative humidity). The curing process is completed when all cuts on the tubers have developed a layer of corky cells. Following curing, tubers are stored at a temperature of 55° to 60°. Humidity should be high.

SWISS CHARD

Also called chard. This is a 15-in. beet relative which is used as a substitute for spinach. Grows in Zones 1–10. 1 packet plants 25 ft. of row. Sow seeds ½ to 1 in. deep. Germination: 8 days.

Varieties

Fordhook Giant. 60 days. Leaves large, very crumpled, and tender. White stalks are so thick that they are suggested as a substitute for asparagus.

Lucullus. 60 days. Old favorite still widely used.

Rhubarb. 60 days. Stalks are rhubarb red.

Culture

Grow like beets. Sow seeds outdoors in the spring a couple of weeks before mean date of last freeze. Sow one or two seeds to the inch and thin to 4 in.; then, when the plants begin to crowd a little, thin to 8 in. and eat those you remove. Rows are 1 ft. wide.

The usual method of harvesting is to cut off a few of the outer leaves of each plant. Handled in this way, the original spring planting will continue to produce until fall.

TAMPALA

A spinach substitute to 3 ft. Grow in Zones 3–10. 1 packet plants 30 ft. of row. Sow seeds ¼ in. deep. Germination: 7 days. Plants mature in 60 days.

Culture

Sow seeds outdoors after all danger of frost is past. Sow one or two seeds per inch and thin to 4 in. in rows 8 in. wide. Repeat sowings can be made at two-week intervals.

Tampala is undemanding if given some balanced fertilizer at the start and if watered in dry spells. Harvest the entire plants when they are 6 in. high. An alternative, which does not produce such tender greens, is to space plants 2 ft. apart in rows 18 in. wide and let them grow to maturity. Harvest 4- or 5-in. branch tips. If you don't take too many of these at one time, new growth will be produced and the plants will continue to supply greens until frost.

TOMATOES

Annuals to 6 ft. Grow in Zones 1–10, but not reliable in 1 and 2. 1 packet produces 150 plants. Sow seeds ¼ in. deep. Germination: 8 days.

Varieties

Note. Tomatoes grow in two ways. Most varieties are of the "indeterminate" type, with stems that continue to elongate. Some new varieties, on the other hand, are "determinate" in growth, which means that the stems terminate in a flower cluster that prevents further stem elongation. Because the latter varieties ripen a large percentage of their fruits at about the same time, they are widely grown on farms equipped with mechanical harvesters. Some are good for the home garden, however. In the descriptions following, the determinate varieties are identified.

Beefsteak. 80 days. There are better varieties, but this is one of the most popular because the red fruits are larger than any others.

Big Boy Giant Hybrid. 78 days. Red fruits weigh 1 to 2 lbs. Produces most heavily in mid-season, but continues into fall.

Big Early. 62 days. Hybrid. Exceptionally big, red fruits for a very early variety.

Burpee's Globe. 80 days. Medium-size, pink fruits.

Cardinal. 74 days. A hybrid. Big, red, crack-resistant fruits. Does well on rich, irrigated soils.

Delicious. 77 days. Very solid, red fruits averaging more than 1 lb.

Early Giant Hybrid. 60 days. Large, red fruits. Particularly recommended for Kentucky.

Fireball. 65 days. Medium-size, red fruits. Determinate. Recommended for cold areas such as Alaska and Maine.

Floralou. 70 days. Developed in Florida for Southern growers. Medium-size, red fruits. Those in the same cluster ripen close together. Resistant to fusarium wilt and several other diseases.

Glamour. 75 days. Medium-size, red fruits resist cracking. Highly recommended in numerous, scattered states.

Globemaster Hybrid. 65 days. Medium-large, red fruits resist cracking. Bears early and continues till frost.

Heinz 1350. 75 days. Red, crack-resistant fruits. Resistant to fusarium and verticillium wilts. Determinate. Excellent for canning.

Homestead 24. 82 days. Medium-large, red fruits. Has good resistance to fusarium. Determinate.

Jubilee. 72 days. Sizable, golden-orange fruits.

Large Red Cherry. 72 days. Red fruits 1 in. across.

Manalucie. 90 days. Medium-size, red fruits. Heavy foliage. A favorite in the South. Resistant to fusarium wilt and several other ailments.

Manapal. 80 days. Medium-size, red fruits. Also much grown in the South. Fairly resistant to fusarium and several other diseases.

Marglobe. 73 days. Large, red fruits. Somewhat resistant to fusarium.

Determinate tomatoes in front; indeterminate in back. Because the latter continue to grow taller throughout the growing season, they are usually staked. Determinate tomatoes, however, are shorter, and once they reach their full height they stop growing; so they are usually allowed to sprawl. Determinate tomatoes also set most of their fruits at one time.

Michigan-Ohio Hybrid. 75 days. Favorite large, red tomato for growing under glass. Resistant to fusarium.

Moreton Hybrid. 70 days. Big, red, solid fruits from early in the season till fall. Grown from North to South.

Nemared. 70 days. Medium-size, red fruits. Adapted to the South. Resistant to fusarium wilt and root-knot nematodes. Determinate.

New Yorker. 64 days. Medium-size, red fruits. Good for canning. Resistant to verticillium wilt.

Payette. 70 days. Dwarf plants with medium-size red fruits. Originated in Idaho and often planted in dry Western states. Resistant to curly-top disease.

Ponderosa. 85 days. Uneven-shaped, purplish-pink fruits averaging over half a pound but sometimes going to a pound and a half.

Porter. 80 days. Small red fruits. Recommended by the Oklahoma

Agricultural Experiment Station as a variety that sets fruit under adverse conditions of heat and drought.

Pritchard. 70 days. Medium-size, red fruits. Resistant to fusarium wilt. Determinate.

Red Pear. 75 days. Small, pear-shaped, red fruits.

Roma VF. 76 days. Red tomato for making paste or canning whole. Fruits up to 3 in. long; 1½ in. across. Very productive. Determinate.

Rutgers. 74 days. Old favorite in most areas. Fruits red, average about 7 oz. Heavy foliage. Fine for canning. Has fair resistance to fusarium.

Sheyenne. 66 days. Unusually large, red fruits for an early variety. Originated in North Dakota. Determinate.

Sioux. 70 days. Medium-size, red fruits. Developed in Nebraska for Mid-West conditions. Determinate.

Small Fry. 60 days. New, small, prize-winning hybrid with many tasty 1-in. red fruits. Resistant to fusarium and verticillium wilts.

Small Red Cherry. 72 days. Red fruits about ⅝ in. across. The best of the cocktail tomatoes.

Spring Giant Hybrid. 65 days. Medium-size, red fruits. Resistant to fusarium and verticillium wilts. Determinate.

Stokesdale. 72 days. Large, red fruits.

Stone. 81 days. Medium-large, red fruits.

Sunray. 83 days. Medium-size, yellow-orange fruits. Resistant to fusarium.

Supersonic. 79 days. A hybrid. Big, red, slightly flattened fruits. Resistant to fusarium and verticillium wilts.

Tiny Tim. 55 days. A novelty. Midget plants 15 in. tall with ¾ in. fruits. Can be grown in pots.

Tuckcross O. 70 days. A greenhouse variety recommended by the Mississippi Agricultural Experiment Station, among others. Small, red fruits.

Yellow Pear. 70 days. Pear-shaped, yellow fruits 1 in. across and up to 2 in. long.

Yellow Plum. 70 days. Oval, yellow fruits about 2 in. long. Good for preserving.

Culture

Sow seeds under glass and move plants into the garden as soon as all danger of frost is past. In warm climates it is especially important not to delay planting too much after this date because tomatoes often shed their blossoms in late spring and summer when the temperature goes over 90°. However, an advantage of living in a warm climate is that you can raise a late crop of tomatoes if you sow seeds in July or August.

Although tomatoes need full sun, they should be located where they get some protection from hot, dry winds which discourage fruit-setting. Space staked indeterminate varieties 2 ft. apart in rows 2 ft. wide. Space determinate varieties 30 in. apart in rows 3 ft. wide. Space unstaked indeterminate varieties 3 ft. apart in rows 4 to 5 ft. wide.

The soil should be well enriched with humus and have a pH of about 6.5. Work in 3 cups of 5-10-10 or 10-10-10 fertilizer per 50 sq. ft. Set plants an inch or two deeper than they previously grew: they will take root along the stem. Spindly plants should be set even deeper.

Indeterminate tomato varieties are usually staked because the plants take up less space and the fruits are likely to be larger, cleaner, and slightly freer of pests; however, they require more work and do not produce as much fruit as unstaked plants. Stakes used should be of 1 x 1-in. lumber and 6 to 8 ft. long. Plants are tied to these with soft twine which is first tied securely to the stakes and is then looped loosely around the stems, under each fruit cluster, and tied. Some people do very little pruning of staked tomatoes, but this is a poor practice because the heavy plants are easily knocked over by storms and it is hard to see all the fruits and to spray the vines thoroughly. Pruning each plant to one or two stems is a much better idea.

One-stem plants are produced by nipping out all suckers that appear in the leaf axils (corresponding to armpits). Two-stem plants, which are slightly larger and more productive than one-stem plants, are produced by nipping out all suckers except that just below the first fruit cluster.

Plants which are not staked can be allowed simply to sprawl, or if you want to keep the fruits off the ground, you can let them come up through a low flat "bench" of chicken wire or boards spaced a couple of inches apart.

Determinate tomato varieties are more compact than indeterminate varieties and are neither staked nor pruned.

Although the foliage of tomato vines sometimes seems excessive, it should not be thinned, since it shields the fruits to some extent from the sun and thus prevents them from being sunburned. It also puts additional strength into the plants.

Give tomato plants plenty of water until just before harvest starts; then reduce the supply somewhat. Excess moisture at this time may cause fruits to crack. Fertilize plants when they have been in the garden six to eight weeks and again about a month later. Use a balanced plant food and apply a scant handful each time.

In areas where night temperatures in the spring drop below 55°, blossoms formed at that time are likely to drop off, thus reducing the set of fruit. To prevent this, spray the first blossom cluster, when most of the flowers have opened fully, with a fruit-set hormone such as Sure Set, Blossom Set, or Tomato Tone. Earlier spraying is likely to result in misshapen fruit. Use a sprayer with a fine nozzle and direct the spray at the back of the flowers. Don't soak them so much that the liquid runs off. Keep the spray off leaves and stems as much as possible.

Keep weeds pulled, but avoid deep cultivation, because tomato roots are shallow.

Common pests to watch for are cutworms, hornworms, aphids, spider mites, nematodes, early blight, late blight, fusarium, verticillium and bacterial wilt, and blossom-end rot. Curly top disease is a problem in irrigated Western areas. Many people advocate dusting plants every week with a general-purpose tomato dust. I've never found this necessary, but maybe it is a good precaution.

When daily temperatures average 75° or below, allow the fruit to ripen to bright red on the vine before picking. The quality is superb. When temperatures are higher, however, the ripening process softens the fruit and the red color is slow to develop. It is, therefore, advisable to harvest the fruits when they are pink and ripen them in the house at a temperature of 60° to 70°.

In the autumn, when frost threatens, pick the fruits in the mature green

An unusual but excellent way to train tomatoes. The trellis need never be taken down. Because the soil in this garden is porous, the owner grows the plants in a long, narrow depression that catches whatever runoff water there is.

stage and ripen them indoors at about 60°. You can wrap them in paper or not, as you wish.

Special culture No. 1

Dwarf tomato plants can be grown in pots or other containers that are at least 12 in. across and 12 in. deep. Watch the water supply carefully, because soil in pots which are exposed to the sun dries out very rapidly.

Special culture No. 2

Tomatoes are also grown successfully in glass or plastic greenhouses in the dead of winter. For example, plants started June 1 and transplanted to the greenhouse about July 1 produce tomatoes from mid-September to mid-December. Similarly, plants started January 1 and transplanted to the greenhouse about March 1 produce tomatoes from mid-May to the end of July. You can, of course, operate on any schedule you like.

Use a variety recommended for greenhouse culture, such as Michigan-Ohio Hybrid or Tuckcross O. Plants are normally trained to a single stem and spaced 15 to 20 in. apart in rows 3 ft. apart. Temperature and ventilation must be carefully controlled at all times. During cloudy weather, a desirable night temperature is 57°–58°; day temperatures should range from 60° to 65°. During sunny weather, night temperatures should range from 58° to 60°; day temperatures, from 65° to 75°.

In order to produce a substantial crop, all greenhouse-grown tomatoes must be hand-pollinated. Ideally this should be done every day between the hours of 10 A.M. and 2 P.M. However, since pollen sheds only during sunny periods, there is no point in fussing with the plants on dark days. The pollinating is accomplished by tapping each flower cluster with your fingers when the blossoms are open. This tranfers the pollen from the anthers to the stigma.

TURNIPS

Annual root vegetables to 2 ft. Grow in Zones 1–10. 1 packet plants 50 ft. of row. Sow seeds ¼ to ½ in. deep. Germination: 7 days.

Varieties

Golden Ball. 60 days. Best yellow-fleshed turnip.

Just Right. 40 days. Roots are large, flattened, and white. Also produces good greens.

Purple-Top White Globe. 55 days. Favorite variety everywhere. Large, round, white roots are purple on top. Excellent for storage.

Seven Top. 45 days. Grown in the South as a winter crop and used strictly for the greens. Roots are inedible.

Shogoin. 45 days. Best variety for greens, which are produced in a few weeks and freeze well. Roots are small, flat, white, and tasty.

Tokyo Cross. 35 days. Excellent, new, pure white hybrid. Stays crisp even if left in the ground for several weeks after it matures.

Culture

Turnips are usually grown as a fall crop in the North; as a spring and fall crop in the middle South; and as a spring, fall, and winter crop in warmest climates.

In the spring, sow early-maturing varieties in the garden as soon as soil can be worked and make succession sowings at two-week intervals. For a fall crop, sow any variety outdoors in time for the roots to mature before a hard freeze.

Although some gardeners broadcast the seed, you will save work if you sow it in drills. Sow three or four seeds to the inch and thin to 3 to 4 in. in rows 8 in. wide. Use the tops of plants that are thinned as greens.

Turnips do well in almost any decent soil with a pH of 6.0 to 6.5. Mix in 1 cup of 5-10-10 fertilizer per 25 ft. of row before planting. Adding humus is also advisable.

Pests are much like those attacking cabbage.

Most of the varieties listed will produce roots 4 in. across; but they are best to eat when only 2 or 3 in. across. Leaves can be harvested at any time, but are most tender when young.

WATER CRESS

An aquatic perennial to 4 in. with small, oval, mildly pungent leaves used for garnishes and in salads. Grow in Zones 6–8. 1 packet produces about 200 plants. Sow seeds $\frac{1}{16}$ in. deep. Germination: 12 days. Plants mature in 60 days.

Culture

Water cress grows only in streams, shallow bogs, springs, or extremely wet soil. Scatter seeds into the stream or bog any time during the summer, and let them take care of themselves. Or sow the seeds—under glass or outdoors—in flats that are filled with a 50-50 mixture of soil and peat. The soil mixture must be kept wet at all times. When the plants are up, transplant them to a stream, etc. You might also try transplanting to a shady spot where the soil stays wet or grow them under fluorescent light.

Water cress should be harvested before the seed stalks form.

WATERMELONS

Sprawling annuals with branches 6 to 8 ft. long. Grow in Zones 3–10. 1 packet plants six hills. Sow seeds $\frac{1}{2}$ in. deep. Germination: 8 days.

Varieties

Blackstone. 87 days. One of the best in the South. Fruits are large, nearly round. Dark green skin. Flesh is bright red, sweet, and crisp. Tolerant of anthracnose and fusarium wilt.

Charleston Gray. 85 days. Large, 2 ft. long, and gray-green. The eating quality is excellent. Resistant to fusarium and anthracnose. Favorite variety in the Eastern half of the country.

Citron. 95 days. Not for eating but ideal for watermelon pickles and preserves. Round fruits 8 in. across. Flesh is white and inedible; seeds are red.

Crimson Sweet. 85 days. Not so large as some other late melons but fruits weigh 25 lbs. nonetheless. They are shaped somewhat like a barrel with rounded ends. Dark green stripes. Very sweet, red flesh. Resistant to fusarium and anthracnose.

Dixie Queen. 85 days. A big, heavy melon roughly 15 x 12 in. Striped skin. Very sweet, crisp flesh. Thin rind. Wilt resistant.

Klondike Striped. 83 days. 15 in. long. Striped skin. Thick rind. Very sweet, scarlet flesh. Tolerant of fusarium. Widely grown in California and other Western states.

New Hampshire Midget. 70 days. A tiny, round melon with a diameter of about 6 in. Thin rind. Sweet flesh. Skin light green with dark stripes. Made to order for cold climates.

Sugar Baby. 73 days. A favorite in Minnesota, North Dakota, and similar areas. Round fruits, 8 in. across, with dark green skin and hard, thin rind.

Culture

Watermelons are grown like melons, but require more territory. Space the hills 8 ft. apart and allow 7 to 8 ft. for the vines to grow to the sides. To produce large fruits in sizable numbers at this spacing, a large amount of humus—a bale would not be too much—should be incorporated in the soil along with 10-10-10 fertilizer at the rate of 2 cups per 50 sq. ft.

In areas with short growing seasons, plant the quick-maturing varieties. You may be able to bring through some of the 80-day varieties, however, by sowing seeds under glass and moving the plants outdoors under Hotkaps a week or two before the last spring frost.

Seeds can also be sown outdoors after all danger of frost is past and when the soil has warmed up.

When fruits are about 4 in. in diameter, if you decide that you would rather have a few huge melons rather than a lot of average ones, thin out the fruits to leave only three or four per hill.

It is hard to tell when watermelons are ready to harvest. One test is to thump the fruits with your fist. If they give off a metallic ring, they are probably not ready. But if they give off a dull, muffled sound, they are probably ripe. Another test is to examine the color of the skin touching the ground. If it is white, the melon is immature; but when it turns to light yellow, you're all set.

6

Growing Herbs

Without question, herbs are the most widely grown of all food plants. True, there are very few herb gardens that occupy as much as 50 sq. ft. But when you add all the pots of chives which grow on windowsills in city and country and all the patches of mint that flourish by the kitchen door to all the plants of sage and parsley and thyme that are carefully tucked in among the tomatoes or annuals, you total herb growers in the millions. Maybe tens of millions.

And little wonder: For centuries back herbs have been of tremendous importance to cooks (not to mention medicine men, expectant mothers, soothsayers, and perfumers). No matter that they have little food value and are rarely eaten for themselves. They bring to more conventional and nourishing foods a flavor, aroma, zest, subtlety—you name it—that makes nectar of the humdrum.

And for all that, they are easy to grow, take little time, occupy next to no space, and simultaneously add a touch of quiet beauty to any spot in the garden.

Small herb garden laid out as a knot garden. The larger plants are boxwood.

Herb gardens. Because they are attractive, usually small plants, herbs have long been grown for ornament as well as practical use. In the 1600s, for example, so-called knot gardens were the rage in Britain. These were rather small, often intricate, but always decorative geometric designs composed as a rule of tiny planting beds divided by narrow paths. Today these gardens are again in style, though their actual number in the U.S. is limited.

In the meantime, however, we have discovered or rediscovered other ways to use herbs decoratively. You can set them into soil-filled chinks in rock retaining walls; drop them into plant pockets made by lifting two or three bricks out of a terrace floor; grow them in containers of myriad designs; use them as edgings for walks and perennial borders; grow them with your annuals as foliage foils for the latter's bright flowers.

In addition, of course, you can line herbs out in the vegetable garden to add a little small-scale charm to that ultra-practical, ultra-efficient area.

How to raise herbs. No matter where you plant herbs, they are propagated and grown in the same way as vegetables. Since this is so, I shall save words and simply refer you to the first part of Chapter 5.

Harvesting. Herbs that are to be used fresh can be harvested whenever they have attained enough size to withstand the loss of some of their foliage. Leaves may be removed in their entirety, as in the case of parsley, or the tips may be nipped off, as in the case of chives. But in neither case should you remove too many.

If you are going to dry the leaves and stems of herbs, you should harvest them just before their flowers open. At this stage they are rich in the volatile oils that give them aroma and flavor. During and after flowering the oils are dissipated to some extent. Running the cut leaves under water to wash off dust does no harm; and it is a necessary precaution if you have used any insecticide or fungicide near the plants.

Herbs that are grown for their seeds must be allowed to flower. The seeds that then develop should be harvested as soon as they are ripe— before they scatter to the four winds.

ANGELICA

A biennial herb that grows to 6 ft. when in bloom but is only about 2½ ft. otherwise. The hollow stems are candied. Grows in Zones 3–7. 1 packet produces 100 plants. Sow seeds ¼ in. deep. Germination: 21 days. Plants mature in 70 days.

Culture

Sow seeds in the spring shortly before last frost or in late summer as soon as they ripen. Angelica requires a rich, humusy soil mixed with a handful of balanced fertilizer. It needs sun, but should be shaded at mid-day. Thin or transplant to stand 3 ft. apart in rows 2 ft. wide. Keep well watered. Fertilize again in the spring of the second year.

Cut young stems in the second year just before the flowers begin to open.

ANISE

Annual herb, 18. in. tall, with a mild licorice flavor. The green leaves are used in garnishes; seeds in cookies and candies. Grow in Zones 6–10.

1 packet produces 100 plants. Sow seeds ⅛ in. deep. Germination: 28 days. Plants mature in 75 days.

Culture

Sow seeds outdoors where plants are to grow on the mean date of the last spring freeze. Provide average soil, or better, and mix in some balanced fertilizer. Water as necessary. Thin plants to 6 to 8 in. apart in rows 9 in. wide, and hill them up slightly to hold them upright. Additional support may be needed later.

To harvest seed, gather on a dry day and put the seed heads on a stretched piece of cheesecloth in a dry, dim room where air can circulate around them. When thoroughly dry, remove seeds and seal in bottles.

BALM

Also called lemon balm. Two-ft., hardy perennial herb with lemon-scented leaves that are used in cold drinks. Dried leaves make tea. Grow in Zones 3–10. 1 packet produces 100 plants. Sow seeds ⅛ in. deep. Germination: 14 days. Plants mature enough for use in 60 days.

Culture

Sow seeds outdoors in the spring when the soil can be worked. Thin to 8 in. apart in rows 9 in. wide. Balm grows in sun or light shade, and is not overly particular about soil; but give it a little fertilizer and humus every year. Divide plants every two or three years. Runners produced after flowering can also be used to propagate new plants.

Pick fresh leaves as they are needed. For drying, gather leaves as the flowers open and place them on a stretched cheesecloth in a cool, dim place.

BASIL

An annual herb to 2 ft. Leaves with clove-like flavor are used in soups, stews, salads, meats, egg, and tomato dishes. Grow in Zones 3–10. 1 packet plants 30 ft. of row. Sow seeds ¼ in. deep. Germination: 5 days. Plants mature in 85 days.

Varieties

Dark Opal. 15 in. An ornamental basil usually grown for its attractive purplish foliage. But it can also be used for flavoring food.

Sweet Basil. 2 ft. This is the species usually grown as an herb.

Culture

Grow like summer savory. Space plants 8 to 12 in. apart, depending on the variety. Rows are 1 ft. wide. Water well. Pinch stem ends to promote branching. Cut sprigs when plants start to bloom and make one or two additional cuttings later. The sprigs can be frozen and held in a food freezer without blanching. To dry basil, cut plants before frost and hang them upside down in a dry, dark room; then crush and pack in tight containers.

Dark Opal makes a pleasant house plant in winter. Sow seeds outdoors in late spring and pot up and bring indoors before fall frost. Keep in a very sunny window.

BORAGE

A 2-ft. annual herb. Young leaves have a slight cucumber flavor and are used in salads and cool drinks. Grow in Zones 3–10. 1 packet plants 30 ft. of row. Sow seeds ⅛ in. deep. Germination: 14 days. Plants mature in 80 days.

Culture

Sow seeds outdoors on mean date of the last spring freeze and thin plants to 8 in. in rows 1 ft. wide. Mix humus and balanced fertilizer into the soil. Plants need little attention except for watering and weeding. Pick young leaves as you want them.

BURNET

A perennial herb to 18 in. Fresh young leaves have a cool, cucumber-like flavor; are used in salads and cool drinks. Grow in Zones 6–10. 1 packet produces 50 plants. Sow seeds ⅛ in. deep. Germination: 10 days. Established plants mature in 45 days.

Culture

Sow seeds outdoors in a seedbed or where they are to grow on about the mean date of the last spring freeze. Grow in full sun in almost any soil. Do not fertilize. Water in long dry spells, but generally burnet does not require a great amount of moisture (established plants may, in fact, rot in very wet weather). Space plants 9 in. apart in rows 1 ft. wide. Harvest young leaves before flowers open; and after flowering, cut back plants to encourage new growth, which can also be harvested.

Plants are difficult to divide, so don't bother. As older plants show signs of wearing out, start new ones to replace them.

Protect plants in cold climates with a winter mulch.

CARAWAY

A 2-ft. biennial herb with seeds that are used in breads, cookies, cakes, potato salad, and baked fruit. Young leaves may also be used in salads. Grow in Zones 3–10. 1 packet plants 30 ft. of row. Sow seeds ⅛ in. deep. Germination: 14 days. Plants mature in 70 days in their second year.

Culture

Caraway grows in light shade as well as sun. Sow seeds outdoors in the spring as soon as the soil can be worked. Soil should be deeply dug and mixed with humus and balanced fertilizer. Keep watered.

Early the next spring, sidedress with a little additional fertilizer. Plants should set seeds in about two months. Harvest the seed heads on a dry day and place in a dry, dim room on a stretched cheesecloth so that air can circulate around them. Remove the seeds when dry, and put in bottles.

CATNIP

Also called catmint. Hardy 2½-ft. perennial herb with mint-like leaves used green or dried as seasoning and in making tea. Grow in Zones 3–10. 1 packet plants 30 ft. of row. Sow seeds ⅛ in. deep. Germination: 8 days. Plants mature in 50 days.

Culture

Sow seeds where the plants are to grow any time to about the end of June. Plants may also be propagated from divisions of the roots. Grow in sun or, better, partial shade in average soil that has been treated with a little balanced fertilizer. Space plants 15 in. apart in rows 15 in. wide. Divide plants every three or four years. To harvest, cut leafy stems just before the flowers open, and hang them upside down in a dry, dark room.

CORIANDER

A hardy annual herb to 2 ft. The seeds, which taste and smell like orange, are used in bakery goods and salad dressings. Grow in Zones 3–10. 1 packet plants 30 ft. of row. Sow seeds ⅛ in. deep. Germination: 14 days. Plants mature in 90 days.

Culture

Sow seeds in the garden as soon as the ground can be worked in the spring. Thin plants to 8 in. in rows 12 in. wide. Soil should be of average quality, enriched with a little balanced fertilizer, and deeply dug. Harvest seed heads as soon as seeds are ripe and place on a stretched cheesecloth in a dark, dry room. When dry, remove seeds and put in jars.

CUMIN

Annual herb to 6 in. The seeds are used in pickles and for flavoring. Grow in Zones 3–10. 1 packet plants 20 ft. of row. Sow seeds ⅛ in. deep. Germination: 10 days. Plants mature in 90 days.

Culture

Start seeds under glass or sow outdoors after last spring frost. Space plants 10 in. apart in rows 8 in. wide. Water regularly and fertilize once.

When seeds ripen, cut down entire plant and hang it upside down in a dark, dry room.

CURLED CHERVIL

Annual herb to 2 ft. that looks like fine-leaved parsley and tastes like a cross between parsley and fennel. Leaves can be used, fresh or dried, in salads, soups, stews, meats, omelets. Grow in Zones 3–10. 1 packet plants 30 ft. of row. Sow seeds ⅛ in. deep. Germination: 14 days. Plants mature in 75 days.

Culture

Chervil does not tolerate heat. For a spring crop, sow seeds outdoors as soon as the soil can be worked. For a fall crop, sow in late summer or early fall in time for plants to mature before frost. Sow one or two seeds to an inch and thin to 6 in. in a row 1 ft. wide.

Plants do best in partial shade. Soil should have ample humus and ½ cup of balanced fertilizer per 25 ft. of row.

Frequent cutting of leaves discourages plants from flowering. Leaves can be used fresh and can also be frozen without blanching. To dry, cut leafy stems and place them on a stretched cheesecloth in a dry, dark room.

DILL

Annual herb to 2½ ft. The feathery foliage is used when green to flavor soups, sauces, and pickles. The seeds are used when dry. Grow in Zones 3–10. 1 packet plants 15 ft. of row. Sow seeds ¼ in. deep. Germination: 21 days. Foliage is ready for use in 70 days; seeds are ripe in 100 days.

Culture

Sow seeds outdoors where plants are to grow after danger of frost is past and soil is warm. Make one or more repeat sowings at two- or three-week intervals. Plants should be in a sunny spot that is somewhat protected from winds. Mix a little balanced fertilizer into the soil, which need be no better than average. When plants are up, thin them to 6 in. in rows 1 ft. wide.

Nip off leaves as they are needed. When seed is ripe, cut down the entire plant and hang it upside down in a dark, dry room.

HOREHOUND

Two-foot perenial herb with wooly, white leaves which are used for making candy. Grow in Zones 3–10. 1 packet produces 100 plants. Sow seeds ⅛ in. deep. Germination: 28 days. Plants mature in 45 days.

Culture

Sow seeds in the garden where plants are to grow in early spring or fall. Thin plants to 1 ft. in rows 1 ft. wide. Grow in sun in soil that contains a little humus. Sidedress with balanced fertilizer every spring. Gather leaves as flowers open and spread them on a stretched cheesecloth in a dry, dark place. When dry, seal in bottles.

LOVAGE

A 6-ft. perennial herb with celery-flavored leaves that are used dry or fresh for seasoning. Grow in Zones 5–8. 1 packet produces 100 plants Sow seeds ⅛ in. deep. Germination: 21 days. After the first year, plants mature in 40 days.

Culture

Sow freshly harvested seeds in late summer or early fall. Transplant seedlings the following spring into well drained, humusy soil. Space plants 2 ft. apart in rows 2 ft. wide. Sidedress every spring with balanced fertilizer. Water in dry spells. Plants grow best in full sun, but do well in partial shade. In warm climates, they must be shaded in the middle of the day. Divide clumps as necessary.

Harvest young leaves when you need them. To encourage production of leaves and to keep the plant down to a height of about 2 ft., cut off the flower stalk when it appears in late spring. To dry leaves, snip off some of the leafy stems and hang them upside down in a dry, dark place. Fresh leaves can also be frozen without blanching.

MINT

Hardy perennial herbs to 2 ft. Grow in Zones 1–10. Can be grown from seeds, but you save time if you start with divisions. Established plants mature in 30 days.

Varieties

Applemint. A tall species that requires less moisture than the others. Leaves are rounded, hairy, and have a faint fruity flavor.

Curly mint. A hybrid spearmint with wrinkled leaves.

Orange mint. Leaves 2 in. long, heart-shaped, and tinged with purple. They have an orange flavor.

Peppermint. Leaves 3 in. long and toothed. Usually taller than other mints, but some strains are not.

Spearmint. Most common type. 2-in. leaves are margined with widely spaced teeth.

Culture

Buy, beg, or steal plants and set them in the garden any time in the spring. Ideally the soil should be fertile and full of humus. Clay soil is also good. But the truth is that mint does not need anything very special so long as it manages to stay reasonably moist.

The plant also does well in either sun or partial shade. It forms a luxuriant summer border along the north foundation wall of a house.

Water in dry weather and pull out any weeds that are strong enough to
get a foothold in the mint thicket. Nip off 6- to 10-in. stem tips regularly
to keep the plants from getting too leggy and going to seed. Thin out the
bed every two to three years.

Mint can be dried by hanging leafy stems upside down in a dark, dry
room.

OREGANO

Also known as pot marjoram. A 2½-ft., hardy perennial herb with leaves
that are used, fresh or dried, for seasoning, particularly in Italian dishes.
Grow in Zones 4–10. 1 packet produces 100 plants. Just press seed into
the soil surface. Germination: 14 days. Plants mature in 45 days.

Culture

Sow seeds outdoors on about the mean date of the last spring freeze or
somewhat later. Transplant seedlings to stand 18 in. apart in rows 18 in.
wide. Grow in sun in average soil containing humus. Fertilize every year
with balanced plant food. Oregano is a vigorous grower and needs little
attention. Do not permit seeds to form. Clip leafy stems as flowers begin
to develop and hang them upside down in a dry, dark place. Divide plants
every couple of years to keep them from spreading too far.

PARSLEY

Biennial herb to 1 ft., commonly grown as an annual. Grow in Zones
1–10. 1 packet plants 30 ft. of row. Sow seeds ¼ in. deep. Germination:
14 days.

Varieties

Evergreen. 70 days. Large, curled leaves on long stems. Resists freezing
temperatures better than most varieties.

Hamburg. 90 days. Grown for the 6-in. long, 2 -in.-thick parsnip-like
roots, which are used to flavor soups, stews, etc., or are boiled like parsnips.

Moss Curled. 75 days. Upright, long-stemmed, and very curly. Widely
grown.

Paramount. 85 days. Dark green, very curly leaves. Plants are compact
and low.

Plain. 72 days. Also called Single. Leaves are deeply cut but flat, without
curls. Fine flavor.

Culture

Parsley is a cold-hardy plant which can be seeded directly in the garden;
but because the plants are fairly slow to develop, it is better to start them

in flats where you can keep an eye on them and don't have to worry too much about weeds. Sow seeds under glass eight weeks before mean date of the last spring freeze; harden off well, and move into the garden on the mean date or a little earlier. In warm climates, seeds can also be started in late summer or early fall.

Set plants 6 in. apart in rows 1 ft. wide. Parsley grows well in sun, but also does well in partial shade—as on the north side of buildings.

Soil of average quality is satisfactory. Mix in some balanced fertilizer before planting. Plants are not demanding, but need to be watered in dry weather and kept weeded. If you pick the outer leaves as you need them, the plants will continue to make new growth and keep you well supplied through the summer and into the fall, even after the first freeze. Mulching with straw helps to keep plants going for a long time; and in Zone 7 and even in 6b, if plants are well mulched and in a protected location, they are likely to go through the winter (although they die down) and then make new growth in the spring.

To keep supplied with parsley in winter, dig up plants with a good ball of earth, set in pots, and grow indoors in a very cool, sunny window. In moderate climates, plants moved into the coldframe will also keep you rather well supplied. You can also grow parsley very easily under fluorescent light.

Roots of Hamburg parsley are stored in sand and kept in a cool basement over winter.

Parsley is easily frozen without blanching. To dry it, place leaves on a mesh screen in a 400° oven for five minutes. Turn once. This should make leaves very crisp; if not, continue heating for a minute or so. Then rub leaves through a coarse sieve and bottle them tightly.

ROSE GERANIUM

A tender, 3-ft. perennial with broad, perfumed leaves that are used for garnishing and for flavoring apple jelly. Grow outdoors in Zones 9 and 10; grow indoors everywhere. Plants mature enough for use in 60 days.

Culture

Grow plants from stem cuttings taken in August and rooted in a moist mixture of sand and peat. Transplant into 2-in. pots filled with a mixture of three parts loam, one part peat and one part sand plus a pinch of bonemeal. As plants grow, repot them into successively larger pots.

Geraniums do best outdoors in the full sun until the weather turns cold; they should then be brought inside and kept in a south window well back from the glass (they dislike cold drafts). Water thoroughly but only when the soil surface turns dry. Fertilize lightly with liquid plant food once a month. Pinch stem ends occasionally to promote bushier, leafier plants (if you pinch too many branches, however, you will delay or prevent blooming). Move the plants outdoors in the spring when the weather is warm.

Don't try to carry geraniums over from year to year. Start new plants from cuttings every August.

A few leaves can be picked as they are needed.

ROSEMARY

A 3-ft. perennial herb with narrow leaves used, green or dried, to flavor soups, stews, meats, sauces. Grow in Zones 7–10. 1 packet plants 30 ft. of row. Sow seeds ¼ in. deep. Germination: 12 days. Established plants mature in 50 days.

Culture

Start seeds under glass or sow outdoors from last frost to the end of June. Grow in full sun. Soil should have a pH of about 7 or a little higher. Mix in a little balanced fertilizer and sidedress with fertilizer every spring thereafter. Space plants 3 ft. apart in rows 3 ft. wide. Water as needed. To harvest, cut stems and hang them upside down in a dark, dry place.

In Zone 6 and northward, rosemary will not survive the winter and should be grown in large pots or tubs that can be brought indoors into a cool, light place.

Cuttings taken from garden plants in September can be rooted in a sand-peat mixture and then potted up and grown in a cool, south window during the winter.

SAFFLOWER

Also called saffron. A hardy, 2-ft. annual herb with prickly leaves and dense flower clusters that turn from yellow to orange. The petals of the dried flowers are used as a yellow coloring substitute for the true saffron. (Farmers grow safflower for the seed.) Grow in Zones 5–10. 1 packet produces 50 plants. Sow seeds ¼ in. deep. Germination: 7 days. Plants mature (to opening of flowers) in 100 days.

Culture

Sow seeds outdoors in the spring as soon as the soil can be worked. Thin seedlings to 8 in. in rows 18 in. wide. The plants grow best in deep, fertile soil and require sun. Water regularly. Sidedress once with a little balanced fertilizer. To harvest, cut flower heads on a dry day when the flowers are fully open and place them on stretched cheesecloth in a dry, dark place. Then bottle the flower petals.

SAGE

A somewhat shrub-like, 2-ft. perennial herb with aromatic, gray leaves used to season meats, fish, poultry, stews, dressings, etc. Grow in Zones 6–10. 1 packet plants 30 ft. of row. Sow seeds ¼ in. deep. Germination: 12 days. Plants mature in 75 days.

Culture

Start seeds under glass or sow outdoors any time from last spring frost to June 1. For faster results, make divisions of established plants in early spring or fall. Space mature plants 2 ft. apart in rows 2 ft. wide. Mix balanced fertilizer into the soil when setting out plants; and sidedress the plants every spring thereafter. Water only sparingly in dry weather.

Cut some of the leafy branches when plants are starting to bloom, and hang them upside down to dry in a dark, dry room. Never remove all the leaves from a plant since this jeopardizes its chances of surviving the winter. In the spring, established plants can be cut to within a few inches of the ground.

Sage plants tend to become woody and less productive of succulent leaves as they age. It is, therefore, desirable to divide the plants every one or two years. Keep the young roots and stems and discard the rest.

SUMMER SAVORY

Easy-going annual herb, 1 ft. tall and somewhat sprawling. Use leaves, green or dried, to flavor salads, gravies, dressings, soups. Grow in Zones 3–10. 1 packet plants 30 ft. of row. Sow seeds ⅛ in. deep. Germination: 10 days. Plants mature in 60 days.

Culture

Start seeds under glass six to eight weeks before the mean date of the last spring freeze. Move into the garden after danger of frost has passed. Space plants 6 in. apart in rows 1 ft. wide. For a later crop, sow seeds in the garden when transplants are set out.

Soil should be reasonably good. Add about 1 cup of balanced fertilizer per 25 ft. of row. Water in dry weather.

Harvest leafy stems when plants are beginning to flower, and hang upside down in a dark, dry place.

SWEET CICELY

A 3-ft. perennial herb with fern-like, licorice-flavored leaves that are used fresh as a seasoning. Grow in Zones 3–10. 1 packet produces 50 plants. Sow seeds ¼ in. deep. Germination: 8 months. Plants mature in 60 days.

Culture

Sow seeds outdoors in late summer or fall. Transplant seedlings the following spring to stand 2 ft. apart in rows 18 in. wide. Sweet Cicely grows well in partial shade and is, like mint, a good plant to grow on the north side of buildings. Soil should be deep and mixed with a plentiful supply of humus. Sidedress plants with balanced fertilizer in the spring. Pick leaves as needed.

The deep roots can be divided occasionally to provide new plants. They can also be boiled and served as a vegetable.

SWEET FENNEL

A 2½-ft. perennial herb that is grown as an annual. The fragrant, licorice-flavored, fern-like foliage is used in soups, salads, and sauces. Grow in Zones 4–10. 1 packet plants 30 ft. of row. Sow seeds ¼ in. deep. Germination: 10 days. Plants mature in 45 days.

Culture

Sow seeds in the garden where they are to grow on about the mean date of the last spring freeze. Thin to 6 in. in rows 1 ft. wide. The soil should be reinforced with humus and a little balanced plant food. Water in dry weather. Cut leaves as they are needed.

SWEET MARJORAM

An 18-in., tender perennial herb usually grown as an annual. Leaves are used, fresh or dried, in poultry dressings, meats, soups, sausages, salads, beans. Grow in Zones 3–10. 1 packet plants 30 ft. of row. Sow seeds ⅛ in. deep. Germination: 10 days. Plant matures in 70 days.

Culture

Grow and harvest like summer savory, but do not expose little plants to bright sun until they are ready to be thinned. (Growing under fluorescent light is all right.) Space plants in the garden 8 to 10 in. apart in rows 1 ft. wide.

In frost-free climates, sweet marjoram will survive the winter. Divide the clumps every three or four years.

If you pot up a few plants before frost hits in the fall, they will grow indoors in a cool, sunny window.

TARRAGON

A 2½-ft. perennial herb which is used in making vinegar and for seasoning many dishes. Grow in Zones 4–10. Grow from divisions. Plants mature enough for use in 60 days.

Culture

The true tarragon is French tarragon. It does not set seed. The tarragon offered by seed growers is Russian tarragon, a larger plant with little flavor. It is not worth growing.

Divide established tarragon plants in early spring. Plant in full sun in well drained soil to which you have added plenty of humus and a little balanced fertilizer. Space plants 2 ft. apart in rows 18 in. wide. Water in dry weather, but don't overdo it and thus encourage plants to rot. Watch out for mildew. Divide plants every three years without fail.

Make a first cutting of leaves in early summer when the new stems are about a foot long. These are tender and succulent and can be used fresh or dried. Make a second cutting in late summer after the plants have branched and the stems and leaves are less succulent. Cut the plants to within a few inches of the ground before the first fall frost. Save the leaves for drying or for vinegar.

THYME

A perennial herb to 1 ft. The aromatic leaves are used in meats, poultry, dressings, gravies, soups, egg dishes. Grow in Zones 5–10. 1 packet plants 30 ft. of row. Sow seeds ⅛ in. deep. Germination: 10 days. Established plants mature in 50 days.

Varieties

There are innumerable species of thyme, but the common French thyme *(Thymus vulgaris)* is most often grown as an herb. Caraway thyme and Lemon thyme are also popular.

Culture

Start seeds under glass eight to ten weeks before the last spring freeze or sow them in the garden after the last freeze. Soil should be well drained and limed. Mix in a little balanced fertilizer and add more every spring thereafter. Until the small plants are established, keep them moist. After that, water only in dry spells. Space plants 8 in. apart in rows 1 ft. wide.

Cut leafy tops just before plants bloom and hang them upside down in a dark, dry room to dry.

In colder climates plants should be mulched in winter with salt hay or evergreen boughs. Divide plants every three or four years.

WINTER SAVORY

A 1-ft. perennial herb, nearly evergreen, used like summer savory. Grow from layers in Zones 4–10. Established plants mature in 45 days.

Culture

Established plants are readily layered by stretching some of the stems to the side and covering partially with soil. When rooted, cut the stems from the parent and plant them in a sunny location in good, well drained soil. Space plants 8 in. apart in rows 1 ft. wide. Planting can be done in early spring or fall. Sidedress all plants each spring with a little balanced plant food. Clip leafy shoots as needed. Tops are likely to stay green, even in fairly cold climates, if you tuck straw around the plants in the fall. Dry the leaves by hanging leafy stems upside down in a dark, dry place.

7

Growing Tree Fruits in Colder Climates

As a group, these "northern" tree fruits are the most important fruits grown in the United States. They are also the most popular. Yet many people who might well grow them studiously avoid doing so.

If you were to ask why they do this, you would probably be given three reasons: (1) The trees take a lot of space. (2) They demand attention if they are to produce quantities of good fruit. (3) Home-grown fruits are not enough better than those sold in stores to warrant the effort.

Only one of these arguments has any validity. That is the second. Without question, it takes a fair amount of work to raise delicious apples, peaches, pears, plums, cherries, etc. That is because the trees are afflicted by a good many pests and ailments.

But it is not true that tree fruits require a great deal of space. With the many excellent dwarfs that are now available, you can have a pretty sizable orchard in a small backyard. In fact, you can grow about a dozen dwarf fruit trees in the space occupied by a single, old-standard apple tree.

It is also not true that commercially grown fruits are as good as home-grown fruits. In selecting varieties to grow for the market, farmers must consider not only the quality of the fruit but also its ability to withstand mechanical harvesting, packing, and shipping. The home gardener, on the other hand, need be concerned only with the quality of the fruit he grows. This means that he can grow superior varieties which the farmer must bypass because they do not handle well.

Moreover the home gardener can allow his fruits to ripen on the trees while the commercial grower usually must pick his when slightly green. You have surely heard the statement that tree-ripened fruits are best. But just in case you have any doubts about it, consider the peach. Tests have shown that it gains as much as 300 per cent in quality when allowed to ripen on the tree.

Dwarf fruit trees. Interest in dwarf fruit trees has increased greatly in recent years; and you can now buy dwarf specimens of apples, pears, peaches, nectarines, apricots, plums, and cherries. Semi-dwarf specimens are also available.

The small trees are produced in two ways: In one instance, the variety desired is budded or grafted to the root—or rootstock, as it is generally called—of another variety or species that is of unusually small stature. In the second instance, a piece of the stem of a small-growing fruit tree is grafted to the trunk of the desired variety just above its roots

In addition, natural dwarfs sometimes occur among trees that bear fruits on stubby, stout twigs called spurs. These dwarfs and semi-dwarfs are known as spur-type trees because they have far more spurs than are usually found on standard trees.

But the principal point of interest to the home gardener is not how dwarf fruit trees are produced, but why they are desirable.

One reason, noted earlier, is that they take up much less garden space than standard trees. Dwarfs need a space only 10 to 12 ft. in diameter, and in hedges can be planted only 4 to 6 ft. apart. Semi-dwarfs need a 15- to 18-ft. space.

Other reasons for the growing popularity of the dwarf and semi-dwarf trees are the following:

You can prune and spray them and pick the fruits more easily; and you require less expensive, smaller equipment. (For example, I could spray the dwarf trees I planted in Greenwich with a 2½-gal. sprayer costing about $12. But to care for my standard trees in Lyme, I had to buy an 18-gal. wheelbarrow sprayer that shoots a stream for 30 ft. and cost $75.)

You can throw a netting over dwarf trees to protect the fruit from birds. And in cold climates you can readily protect them with heavy blankets against sudden freezes.

You can espalier them with very little work. You can also grow them in large containers.

You can harvest a first crop of fruit from them a year or two earlier than

Although this small backyard in New Jersey measures only about 60 by 60 ft. and is extensively landscaped, there is ample space for a number of heavy-bearing dwarf fruit trees. Owner keeps them heavily mulched.

from standard trees, and the fruits you get will usually be a little larger and more highly colored.

All of which are very good reasons to plant dwarf or semi-dwarf fruits rather than standards—especially if you have limited garden space. On the other hand, you must be prepared for several minor disappointments:

Dwarf trees cost a little more than standards. They do not produce so much fruit (a dwarf apple, for example, yields two to six bushels of fruit in contrast with a standard tree's ten to fifteen bushels). They do not live quite so long. And varieties that are grafted on to other rootstocks should be staked to keep them anchored in the ground (because of their small root systems, they blow over in strong winds).

Pollination of fruit trees. If in a burst of enthusiasm for raising fruit you were to go out tomorrow and buy one apple, one pear, one peach, and one sour cherry, you would be unhappily surprised in a couple of years to find that only the peach and cherry had any fruit; and no matter how long you waited or what you did, you would not get fruit from the apple and pear.

The explanation is quite simple: Some fruit trees (including tropical and bush fruits) are self-fruitful. They pollinate themselves. This means that you can plant just one tree and you will have fruit.

On the other hand, many fruit trees are self-unfruitful. For them to produce fruit, you must plant two or three different varieties fairly close to one another. What's more, you must make sure that the varieties you plant bloom at the same time, that they are compatible, and that at least one of them is a good pollinator or pollinizer (meaning that it produces large quantities of fertile pollen).

This is not so confusing a business as it sounds. In the encyclopedic section of this chapter you will see that it is really quite a simple matter to select varieties which will cooperate to give you a fine lot of fruit year after year.

Selecting fruit trees. In addition to considering the pollinating require-ments of the varieties you plant, there are a number of other things you must think about when choosing varieties:

Is the tree suited to your climate? In the North your main concern must be its ability to withstand winter cold. In warm climates you should ask whether the area in which you live has enough cold weather to satisfy the tree's need for winter chilling. (Most of the fruits covered in this chapter need a period of cold weather if they are to thrive and set fruit.)

Does the tree come into bloom before or after your last spring freeze? If it's before, you should bypass it, because it won't set fruit. In Virginia, for example, apricots are risky to plant because the buds respond to the first warm days of early spring and are usually killed by a freeze at a later date. For this reason the state Agricultural Extension Service says: "Unless protection can be provided, a crop can be expected no oftener than once every four or five years."

Has the tree natural resistance to serious diseases that may be prevalent in your area?

Does it bear biennially? This is a problem with some fruits, particularly apple varieties. They bear heavily one year and very little the next; and during their off year, they are poor pollinators. This is obviously not a good situation. But some biennial (also called alternate) bearers produce marvelous fruit, so you hate to overlook them. It is also possible sometimes to make such trees bear more regularly by thinning the fruits and pruning.

If you want to plant two or more varieties of the same tree, do they ripen their fruit at different times? They should, of course, because there is no sense in being inundated with fruit at one time and having none at other times. What most people want is a succession of crops. To have this, you should select early, midseason, and late varieties.

If you want to freeze or can fruit or make it into jams and jellies, are the varieties you select especially good for these purposes? For example, if you want to can peaches but have space for only a single tree, you should not put in an early variety because it is not so good for canning as mid-season and late varieties.

Is the tree a novelty that produces several varieties of fruit? Well, forget it. Such trees are usually disappointing and unusually demanding of attention.

When you actually get around to buying fruit trees, deal only with a nurseryman who has an established reputation for growing top-notch stock and who is willing to guarantee it. There are a number of national mail-order nurserymen who are particularly noted for their fruit trees.

Most fruit trees are sold as bare-root specimens. One-year-old plants are preferred; but two-year-olds are about as good. Trees advertised as "ready to bear" cost more, but do not perform so well. One-year-old trees actually start bearing about as soon as older trees; they establish themselves quickly and are easier to keep alive; and you can shape them with a minimum of pruning.

The trees must be planted when they are fully dormant. In colder areas, order them for delivery in early spring. In warmer areas, you can take delivery either in early spring or late fall.

Can you propagate your own trees? The answer is very simple: Yes, but don't. You can grow fruit trees from seeds, like Johnny Appleseed, but they will not come true. Propagation is done by budding or grafting, and I don't recommend either operation except to professionals. It's much easier to buy trees that have been budded or grafted by experts.

Where to locate your orchard. This is an academic matter if you have an average-size lot: you'll plant your trees where space exists. But if you have a large enough property to have a choice, you should give consideration to certain points:

To protect fruit trees from late spring freezes which damage or kill buds and blossoms, plant them in a spot where they get all-day sun and the air drainage is good. Ideally, they should be part way up a slope (preferably a gentle slope, which is easier to work on). They may also be at the top of the slope if they are not there exposed to hard winds.

Most people instinctively choose to plant on a southern slope because they figure that the sun warms the soil and gets the trees off to an early start in the spring. But experienced orchardists often prefer a northern slope—especially when planting trees that normally bloom very early in the spring—because the trees are exposed to less sun and, therefore, bloom later and are less likely to be hit by a late spring freeze. On the other hand, because a northern slope dries slowly after a rain, trees on it are somewhat more subject to insect attack and disease.

A good compromise is an eastern slope.

The soil in the orchard site should be fertile; but surprisingly, fertility is a less important requirement than some other requirements. (That's because you can easily add missing nutrients to soil, but cannot so easily change the structure of the soil.)

First of all, the soil must be well drained so that the tree roots can go to work early and keep on working—even in years of heavy rainfall—until late fall. In addition, there must be good surface drainage so that trees are not forced to stand in water for more than one day after a downpour.

Next, the soil must be deep enough to allow roots to develop to their fullest extent. It must also retain moisture well enough to tide trees over in case of scant rainfall. Sandy or gravelly soils should be 5 to 6 ft. deep; heavier soils, 3 to 5 ft. deep.

Planting fruit trees. As soon as the trees are delivered, open the bundle and examine the roots to see that they have not dried out. If they are dry and if you intend to plant them within a few hours, sprinkle with water and bundle them up again. If the trees are adequately damp when delivered, just keep them in their wrappings.

If for some reason you cannot plant your trees within a day after delivery, they should be "heeled in." Simply dig a trench anywhere in the garden, set in the trees so that the tops slope at a 45° angle to the southwest (this protects them against sunscald), and cover the roots completely with soil. Water well. Trees that are heeled in properly do not need to be planted for a week or two.

The planting holes for fruit trees should be at least 18 to 24 in. across and 18 in. deep. Separate the topsoil and subsoil that comes out of each hole into piles. Then return the topsoil, with whatever sods it contains, to the bottom of the hole, add a couple of spadefuls of humus, and mix thoroughly. Add sand or small crushed rock if the soil is heavy. Add limestone only if the soil has a pH of less than 5.5, since most of the cold-climate fruits prefer a slightly acid soil.

Snip off the ends of any broken roots, and then spread the roots out as naturally as possible in the hole. Standard fruit trees are set at the depth at which they previously grew or about an inch deeper. Dwarfs and semi-dwarfs which have been grafted on to other rootstocks must be planted so that the graft is above the soil level; otherwise, roots may form above the graft and counteract the dwarfing action of the rootstock. (Dwarfs that are produced by inserting a piece of stem into the trunk can be planted with the stem piece slightly below ground.)

Fill in around the roots with whatever topsoil remains; then throw in the subsoil (which should also be mixed with humus). Firm the soil well as you add more and more. Then, when the hole is three-quarters full, pour in water till it runs over the rim. When this has settled out of sight, fill in the rest of the way with soil and leave it loose on top.

Build a small dike of earth around the top edge of the hole to form a watering saucer. Fill this with water about every four days for the next two weeks.

Drive a 2-in. stake or iron pipe deep into the ground next to a dwarf tree on an alien rootstock and secure the tree to it with a wire inserted through a length of old garden hose. This should never be removed. A stake extending 4 ft. above ground in usually long enough to support even a full-grown tree.

In warm climates, to protect trees from sunburn, wrap the leafless part of the trunk with kraft paper or burlap, or paint it with whitewash. This protection should be maintained until the following fall.

General care. Throughout their lifetime, fruit trees should be watered deeply whenever long dry spells occur. In terms of quality fruit, an adequate moisture supply probably means more than anything else.

Surrounding the trees with an organic mulch conserves water and keeps down weeds. But its most important role is in adding humus to the soil. (It takes the place of the cover crops which commercial growers often plant in orchards.) The mulch should extend out to the ends of the branches, but should be pulled about 6 in. away from the trunk to discourage burrowing mice from eating the bark. The alternative, which is more troublesome but better, is to wrap ½-in. wire mesh around the trunk. This should extend from about 3 in. below ground to 18 to 24 in. above. It helps to protect against rabbits as well as mice.

Newly planted trees should not be fertilized until they start making good growth. You can then scatter a handful of nitrate of soda or balanced fertilizer in the watering saucer, scratch it into the soil (if it isn't covered with a mulch), and water well.

Thereafter trees are usually fertilized annually in early spring. If you maintain an organic mulch, you generally need to apply nitrogen alone because the mulch supplies phosphorus and potassium as it decomposes. Use nitrate of soda, ammonium nitrate, urea, or any other source of nitrogen. If you do not mulch the trees, you should use a balanced fertilizer such as 10-10-10. A balanced fertilizer is also used if grass, a ground cover, or cover crop is grown under the trees.

Government bulletins on raising fruit often specify the amount of *actual nitrogen* which should be applied. Table VIII shows how many pounds of several nitrogen fertilizers are needed to supply 1 lb. of actual nitrogen.

Semi-dwarf trees need about the same amount of fertilizer as standards; but dwarfs do well on about 40 per cent less.

Minor elements may also be required if the trees indicate they are not getting enough (see Table I). Magnesium is usually applied in dry form to the soil. Zinc and boron are applied in dry form or in foliar sprays. Copper, manganese, and molybdenum are usually applied in foliar sprays.

General fertilizing recommendations are made for the different fruits in the second section of this chapter. It should be noted, however, that the only way to determine accurately what your fruit trees need is to make a soil test. It should also be noted that it is usually better to under-feed most fruit trees than to over-feed them. This is especially true of trees that are mulched. Too much fertilizer is likely to result in too much vegetative growth.

As a rule, mature apple, pear, plum, sour cherry, and quince trees should make 8 to 10 in. of terminal growth per year. Mature peach, nectarine, and sweet cherry trees should make 10 to 20 in. of terminal growth. In all cases, young, non-bearing trees can be expected to make up to twice as much growth.

Pruning. The following material is taken from two excellent agricultural extension service publications. The statement on the principles of pruning was written in Kentucky; that on methods of training was written in Michigan.

A young apple tree before and after pruning. Note at left that at the end of its first year in the garden the tree had put up two leaders, of which only one was kept. In the future one of the two scaffold branches on the right side of the tree will be removed because they are growing in the same direction and are too close together. (New York State Agricultural Experiment Station)

TABLE VIII
Comparison of Some Common Forms of Nitrogen-Containing Fertilizers

FERTILIZER	% NITROGEN IN FERTILIZER	APPROX. LBS. REQUIRED TO SUPPLY 1 LB. NITROGEN	LBS. CONVERTED TO 8 OZ. CUPS
Ammonium sulfate	20.5	5.0	10
Calcium nitrate	16.0	6.3	12½
Sodium nitrate *(nitrate of soda)*	16.0	6.3	12½
Ammonium nitrate	33.0	3.0	6
Ammonium phosphate	16.0	6.3	12½
Anhydrous ammonia	81.0	1.2	2½
10-10-10	10.0	10.0	20

"Of the thousands of fruit trees planted in home gardens every year, very few have been pruned correctly. The pruning a tree receives the first five years of its life largely determines whether it will produce large crops of fruit during a long lifetime, or whether it will break down under large crops and be productive for only a relatively short time. To be able to prune intelligently, you must understand the basic principles:

"1. Pruning has a dwarfing effect, but a certain amount must be done to establish a strong framework and keep the tree symmetrical. During the first few years of the tree's life it must be properly pruned so that it has the right number and spacing of main branches. This practice dwarfs the tree and delays fruitfulness to a certain extent. However, since a tree is expected to produce heavy crops for many years, it must be prepared for this task by proper shaping while young. Snipping off small branches at this time will not have nearly the adverse effect that corrective pruning later would have. *However, any cuts in addition to the basic ones tend only to dwarf the tree and delay its fruitfulness.*

"2. Wide-angled branches form strong crotches. In selecting the main branches, care should be exercised to select those with wide angles, 45° – 90°. Narrow-angled branches are not joined at the crotch with strong woody tissue, but are weakened by the inclusion of bark in the angle. When the tree bears heavily, these branches may split off under the load.

"3. Pruning increases vigor but not total growth. The laterals from a branch that has been headed back are longer and more vigorous, and thus more good fruiting wood is formed. However, the total growth is not as much as on the unpruned limb. *Do not over-prune.* After the tree has been shaped by early pruning, the job consists mainly of pruning to keep it within bounds, removing broken and diseased limbs, some thinning out of limbs that become too thick, removing water sprouts, and removing branches that rub together.

"4. Upper branches compete with lower branches and shade them out. When selecting framework branches, never select one directly over another because the top one receives more light and manufactures more food and therefore will grow faster. The lower one will be shaded and starved so that it will not make a satisfactory growth.

"5. Pruning improves fruit size and quality, as more light is admitted to the tree and better fruit color results. More complete spray coverage is possible on pruned trees and better insect and disease control is accomplished. There is less competition among fruits for water and nutrients, and large fruits are borne on pruned trees.

"6. Pruning is best done in late winter or early spring. Winter injury may result when the pruning is done in the fall. This is especially true near large wounds. Also, by waiting, the grower can ascertain the amount of fruit-bud killing, and prune accordingly. If a large percentage of the fruit buds were killed, the tree may be pruned very lightly; but if most of them survived, the pruning should be heavier."

METHODS OF TRAINING

"Young fruit trees are trained either by (1) the modified leader or (2) the open-center method (also called vase method).

"Fruits pruned to the modified leader are apples, pears, cherries and European varieties of plums. Peaches and Japanese varieties of plums are pruned to the open-center method.

"Modified Leader Method. A well-developed modified leader tree is one with a central trunk or axis several feet long from which a number of main laterals or scaffold branches arise. These should form wide angles where they join the trunk, they should be spaced at least 6 in. apart, and none should be directly opposite or directly below another. Large one-year-old nursery trees are best for developing this type of tree. Two-year-old nursery trees of apple, pear, plum and sour cherry are often used.

"The method used to develop a modified leader tree varies with different kinds of fruits. Starting with a one-year-old nursery tree, the general procedure is as follows:

"First pruning—at the time of planting. Head or cut back large one-year-old unbranched trees to 3½ to 4 ft. above the ground. Trees 3½ ft. or less in height need no heading back. Prune well-branched two-year-old nursery trees in the same manner as that described below for the second pruning.

"Second pruning—in the spring, a year after planting. This is the first pruning of the two-year-old nursery tree when planted in the orchard.

"1. Save one of the most vigorous upright-growing shoots for a leader.

"2. Select for permanent scaffold branches one or more, preferably two, well-placed lateral branches that form wide angles with the trunk. The lowest scaffold branch on apples should be about 30 in. from the ground. On other fruit trees, the lowest should be 20 to 24 in. above the

These pears need thinning, but the job should have been done long ago. Then the tree would have concentrated its energy on producing a few, extra large and delicious fruits. Thinning at this stage might improve the size and quality of the remaining fruits, but not very much.

ground. Remove all sharp-angled branches. Keep the scaffold branches 6 in. or more apart.

"3. If the leader needs pruning, head it back to about 20 in. above the top scaffold. Shorten the laterals so that when you hold them upright their tips will be 6 in. lower than the tip of the leader.

"Third pruning—two years after planting.

"1. Select the highest shoot developed from the leader the previous season to continue as the leader.

"2. Save two or three lateral shoots from the leader for more scaffold branches. Head them back if need be to keep the leader dominant.

"3. During the previous season the branches saved for scaffolds will have rebranched, forming secondary shoots or laterals. On each scaffold, save two or three of these laterals that are 6 in. or more away from the leader. Remove or head back any that are longer than the leader or midrib of the main scaffold branch. Treat each scaffold as though it were a young tree.

"4. Leave the several parts of the tree in balance. Do not let the lower branches outgrow the upper portions of the tree, nor the upper branches grow longer and shade out the lower ones.

"5. Save short twigs and spurs that develop in the inside part of the tree. If these grow into vigorous shoots that tend to make the center of the tree thick and bushy, you can thin them out a year later.

"Fourth pruning—three years after planting. This pruning should encourage formation of more framework and keep a proper relationship among the present scaffolds. Choose two or three more scaffold branches as described for the third pruning. Keep the leader dominant. Correct any tendencies to develop weak crotches. Save short twigs and spurs. If opposite branching occurs on the trunk or along the main branches, remove the poorer one.

"Fifth year—four years after pruning. By this time the main framework of four to six scaffolds will be set up and you will not need to encourage the further development of the leader. Do not, however, head back the leader at this time. If necessary, you can cut it back to a well-placed, outward-growing lateral one or two years later. Most varieties need no heading back and very little thinning out until after the trees are in full bearing.

"Open-Center Method. This method is used mostly for training young peach trees. It differs from the modified leader method in that you remove the central leader at planting time and choose the branches for scaffolds along a fairly short space on the trunk.

"Steps in training a tree to the open-center method are as follows:

"1. Head back the one-year-old tree to 18 to 24 in. at planting time.

"2. Choose two or three scaffold branches that are well arranged around the trunk and that are as near as possible to the place where the tree was headed back. If the branches are large and uniform in size, you can leave them 10 to 12 in. long. If slender and uneven in size, cut them back to short stubs with one or two basal buds. Choose shoots which develop from these buds for the main scaffold branches.

"3. Inspect the trees two or three weeks after planting and remove all shoots with a sharp knife except those to be saved for scaffold branches. Make another inspection and a light shoot removal two weeks later. Rub off all new growth from the trunk of the tree.

"4. In the spring of the second year, remove any shoots other than those you have chosen to make the framework; head the three scaffolds to equal lengths so they will grow to be as nearly the same size as possible. Usually the trees need very little other pruning."

Thinning of fruits. This is often required on apples, apricots, peaches, pears, and Japanese plums. The operation helps to improve the size, quality, and color of the fruits left on the trees. It minimizes limb breakage, especially on dwarf trees. It somewhat simplifies spraying and dusting. It helps to assure production of a good crop of fruit the following year. And it induces regular annual bearing in certain varieties that tend to bear only every other year.

General agreement about when the thinning should be done is lacking. Some people advocate waiting until after "June drop"—the last of about three periods in which trees drop their fruit naturally. Other people say you should thin fruit within 20 days after trees are in full bloom. Take your pick.

The usual method of thinning is simply to pick off the excess fruits by hand. If you have a large orchard, however, you may want to consider the use of growth-regulator sprays. Table IX gives suggestions for spraying apples and peaches. In using any of these sprays, you must follow the spray manufacturer's directions carefully.

Controlling insects and diseases. Good sanitation practices will not solve your orchard problems, but will help. Here are some of the things you should make a habit of doing:

Burn the leaves of apples and cherries in the fall to destroy germs that cause scab and leaf spot.

Collect and destroy fruits that drop; and destroy damaged fruits that remain in the trees.

Burn diseased wood removed by pruning, fallen twigs and branches, and bark that scales off.

Cut out and burn black knots that develop on plums and sour cherries.

Tack screen wire over cavities in apple and pear trees. Small cavities may also be filled with asphalt roofing cement or concrete if you first scrape out the rotten and diseased wood inside. The cavities are good hiding places for codling moths and other insects.

Scrape loose bark from apple trees in winter. This destroys codling moth larvae.

A regular spray program is also essential to control tree-fruit pests. Except for the earliest spray applications, use one of the prepared general-purpose fruit sprays. They save a lot of time and work. If you prefer to save a little money, however, you can make your own general-purpose spray by mixing 2 tbs. captan 50 per cent wettable powder, 2 tbs. malathion 25 per cent wettable powder, and 3 tbs. methoxychlor 50 per cent wettable powder into 1 gal. water. Another excellent general-purpose spray is made with 3 tbs. captan 50 per cent wettable powder, 3 tbs. Sevin 50 per cent wettable powder, and 2 tbs. malathion 25 per cent wettable powder to 1 gal. water. The latter, however, should be used only after the middle of June because Sevin causes some trees to drop their fruit if applied early in the season.

TABLE IX
Suggestions for Chemical Thinning of Apples and Peaches
Source: Missouri Agricultural Extension Service.

CHEMICAL	COMMERCIAL FORMULATION	CONCENTRATION	VARIETIES	TIMING (DAYS AFTER FULL BLOOM)
		Apples		
Naphthalene-acetic acid (NAA)	Fruitone N, App-L-Set, Niagra Stick, Stafast, Kling-Tite, Nu-Tone, etc.	20–30 ppm.	York, Golden Delicious	10–14
		10 ppm.	Jonathan	10–14
		10–15 ppm.	Delicious, Winesap, others	10–14
Naphthyl-acetamide (NA)	Amid-Thin W, etc.	50–75 ppm.	Summer varieties	Petal fall to 7 days
		25–50 ppm.	Fall and winter varieties except Golden Delicious	Petal fall to 10 days
1-Naphthyl N-methyl carbamate	Sevin 50 W	1 lb./100 gal.	Winesap, Gano	12–22
		1–2 lb./100 gal.	Delicious, Jonathan, Rome Beauty	12–22
		2–3 lb./100 gal.	Golden Delicious, York, summer varieties	12–22
		Peaches		
N-1 Naphthyl-phthalamic acid (sodium salt)	Peach-Thin 322 Nip-A-Thin	100–150 ppm.	Light-setting varieties	Full bloom to 4 days after
		150–200 ppm.	Red Haven and other heavy-setting varieties	Full bloom to 4 days after

If using a prepared spray, follow either the application schedule recommended by the manufacturer or the schedule in Table X. This will take care of almost all pests except borers in peaches, nectarines, plums, and cherries.

If you have unusual pest problems in summer, you may make two more cover spray applications than called for in the table; and you may step up the frequency by allowing only two weeks between each application from the fourth to the eighth cover. No matter what schedule you follow, however, do not spray trees within seven days of harvest. (Some insecticides and fungicides are so lethal that an even longer period between last application and harvest must be allowed. Always read the label on the container through and through.)

Dormant oil spray must not be applied when the temperature is below 40° or when there is danger of a freeze before the spray dries. In summer, spraying should not be done if the temperature is over 90°.

One final precaution: Don't spray trees with an insecticide when they are in bloom, because you will kill the bees and other insects serving as pollinators. Wait until most of the petals have fallen. Fungicides can be applied safely during bloom, however.

Protecting trees against frost. Just before the flowers open, fruit tree buds can generally withstand temperatures down to about 24°; but open blossoms are killed at 27° or a bit higher.

If a hard freeze is predicted after flowers are open, there isn't much you can do to protect standard and semi-dwarf trees, although you can try to raise the air temperature around them with Tree-Heet bricks. The best way to protect dwarf trees is to throw tarpaulins or old blankets over them.

Espaliering fruit trees. Dwarf trees are perfect for this; and espaliering is perfect for them because it eliminates the necessity for supporting them with large stakes. But whether you have the time and patience to dwarf a fruit tree into one of the traditional espalier shapes, I cannot say. And I am not about to give you the how-to details because I think that espaliering is one of those fruit-gardening practices which is just outside the scope of this book.

I'll say this much, however: If you want one or more espaliered fruit trees to adorn a blank wall or to form a fence, the easiest and quickest way to get them is to buy them. There is a handful of nurserymen who specialize in developing espaliers. One of the most famous is Henry Leuthardt on Long Island. The espaliers he sells are six-year-old apple or pear trees of unspecified variety which have attained their permanent pattern but which will continue to grow somewhat larger. The cost of the trees varies with their size and the complexity of the espalier. For example, a tree trained in a single horizontal cordon and measuring 1½

Espaliered apples and pears form a charming and productive fence around a driveway.

ft. high and 6 to 8 ft. long costs about $8. By contrast, a six-armed palmette verrier measuring 65 in. wide and 5 to 6 ft. high costs about $35.

Whether you buy a ready-made espalier or train your own, you must establish a permanent framework to support it. This is most easily constructed with No. 10 galvanized wire stretched horizontally between strong posts. The wires are spaced about 1 ft. apart and must be taut. If the espalier is to be grown against a wall, the wires must be 6 in. out from the wall in order to allow for free circulation of air and easy care.

To bear a full crop of fruit, espaliers must be grown in full sun. If trained in front of a wall, it should in most regions be a south wall. In hot climates, however, a west wall is preferred because there is less danger of sunburning the tree.

Espaliers are cared for like natural trees. Most pruning, however, is done in summer. It is limited primarily to nipping off young, succulent growths.

Growing dwarf trees in containers. To do this, start a tree in a 12-in. pot and move it into increasingly larger containers every year or two until you reach a container about 18 in. across and 18 in. deep. This is about as large a container as a man can handle.

The containers must have drainage holes in the bottom; and if you want

TABLE X
Spray Schedule for Northern Tree Fruits
Source: Arkansas Agricultural Extension Service.

TIME TO SPRAY	PESTS	MATERIAL	TREES TO RECEIVE THE APPLICATION
Dormant—when leaves are off and before bud swell in spring	Scale insects Peach leaf curl	Dormant oil (¾ pint) plus Bordeaux mixture (2 oz. bluestone & 3 oz. hydrated lime) in 3 gals. water	All tree fruits*
Pink—just before blossoms open	Apple scab Cedar-apple rust	2 tbs. 75% Zineb or 2 tbs. 75% Ferbam in 3 gals. water	Apples only
Petal fall—when three-fourths of petals are off	Scab Codling moth Curculio Plant bugs	General purpose mix	All tree fruits*
First cover spray 14–21 days after petal fall	Scab Blotch Curculio Codling moth	General purpose mix	All tree fruits*
Second cover spray 10–14 days after first cover spray	Same	General purpose mix	All tree fruits*
Third cover spray 10 days after second cover spray	Apple scab Bitter rot Codling moth	General purpose mix	Apples, pears
Fourth cover spray 21 days after third cover spray	Bitter rot Black rot Codling moth Brown rot Curculio	General purpose mix	All tree fruits*
Fifth cover spray three weeks after fourth cover spray	Same as fourth cover spray	General purpose mix	Apples
Sixth cover spray three weeks after fifth cover spray	Same as fourth cover spray	General purpose mix	Apples

*All tree fruits includes apples, pears, plums, cherries, nectarines, peaches.

to be able to move them around on a terrace, they should be mounted on dollies.

Plant the trees in a mixture of two parts loam, one part peat and one-half part sand. Wait a month before fertilizing; then apply a little liquid plant food every 30 days throughout the growing season.

Water regularly and thoroughly—until it runs out the bottom of the container. Soil in containers dries out very rapidly, especially in hot, dry weather.

Keep the tree pruned so it does not exceed a height of much more than 4 ft.

When repotting from a smaller to a larger container, scrape or pick the soil off the outer edges of the rootball, until you reduce the size of the ball about 25 to 30 per cent. Trim back any large exposed roots to the margins of the ball. Then set the plant in its container and pack fresh soil in around it.

Once a tree is in its permanent container, repot it every year or two in the same way. All repotting should be done in the early spring, before the tree breaks dormancy.

In mild climates, potted trees can be left outdoors through the winter. In areas where the mercury dips below freezing, they should be moved into a garage, basement, or cool sunporch. The plants do not require light while dormant.

Resurrecting an old tree. Persuading an old tree to produce sizable crops of good fruit can be a hard job and is by no means certain of success. But if you form an attachment for such a tree, there is no harm in trying as long as the tree is not riddled with rot or hollow from top to bottom.

The first step is to cut out all dead and broken wood. Clean out holes to remove decayed wood, and then coat with tree paint.

The second step is to thin out live wood so that the sun can penetrate the crown and in order to encourage vigorous new growth. If the tree is not large, cut out all suckers as well as branches which cross, parallel one another closely, or grow up rather than out. If, however, the tree has grown so tall that you cannot spray it efficiently, cut out two or three of the large limbs close to the trunk; and then thin out some of the smaller branches. In either case, this kind of drastic pruning should be done over a period of two or three years; otherwise you'll put the tree into a state of shock.

Remove weeds from under the tree and apply a high-nitrogen fertilizer early every spring. Cover the soil with an organic mulch. Start spraying the tree religiously to control insects and diseases.

Your hard pruning will promote growth of new suckers. Remove the largest of these the second year after you start work on the tree, but save a few of the short ones to develop into fruiting wood. To encourage some of the older, smaller branches to bear better fruit, you should at the same time cut back their ends 6 to 12 in. This forces them to make new end growth which will result in good fruit set.

APPLES

Apples grow to about 50 ft. (if permitted), and when old and large they make very ornamental shade trees. But when you are growing them for fruit, you should keep them smaller. Dwarf and semi-dwarf varieties are numerous. Fruits are produced from mid-summer to late fall.

Apples grow in Zones 3–8. A few varieties will produce some fruit in milder parts of Alaska; and you might get some fruit from certain varieties in Zone 9; but such climate extremes are not to the apple's liking.

The trees are self-unfruitful. You must plant two and sometimes three varieties together. Be sure that they bloom at the same time. Note that red sports of older varieties are incompatible with these older varieties.

Varieties

Baldwin. Famous old variety but has many weaknesses. Dull red, medium-large fruits of fair eating quality but better for processing. Blooms medium late; ripens late. Starts bearing at eight years. Biennial producer. A poor pollinator. Zones 5–8.

Cortland. Old favorite. Big, red fruits with dark stripes. White flesh discolors slowly after cutting. Blooms medium late; ripens after mid-season. A good, annual bearer. Not compatible as a pollinator with Early McIntosh. Zones 4–7.

Dudley. Large, greenish-yellow fruits with crimson overtones. Firm, yellow flesh is a bit coarse but very good. Blooms medium late; ripens midseason. Productive. Hardy enough to grow in northern Maine. Zones 3–8.

Golden Delicious. Medium-size, cone-shaped, yellow fruits of top quality but poor keepers. Blooms medium late; ripens late. Biennial bearer. Good pollinator for Delicious and Gravenstein. Zones 5–8.

Gravenstein. Big, red fruits tops for cooking and eating. Blooms early; ripens in midseason. Poor pollinator; must be planted with two other varieties if you want all to bear. Red Gravenstein is a sport with a brighter red skin. Zones 6–8.

Grimes Golden. Much less popular than it used to be but still a very good variety. Medium-size, yellowish-green fruits—a delight to eat and splendid in pies. Blooms early; ripens in midseason. Old trees tend to produce small fruit. Zones 5–8.

Haralson. Medium-size, red fruits. Tart and juicy. Blooms early; ripens after midseason. Very popular in the Midwest for all purposes. Zones 3–8.

Jonathan. Small to medium-size, red fruits. Tart. Good for cooking and eating. Blooms early; ripens in midseason. Susceptible to fire blight, cedar-apple rust, and powdery mildew. Jonared and Blackjon are red sports of Jonathan which color earlier and more intensely. Zones 5–8.

Lodi. Large, yellow fruits good for cooking and eating. Store well. Blooms early; ripens early. Good pollinator for Gravenstein. In Oregon it is the only variety recommended for home gardens everywhere. Zones 4–8.

Macoun. Medium-size, dark red apples of fine flavor. Blooms late; ripens after midseason. Requires heavy thinning. Susceptible to scab. A good pollinator for Northern Spy. Zones 4–8.

Mantet. Medium-size, yellow fruits striped and blushed with red. Excellent fresh and cooked. Blooms early; ripens early. Hardy enough for all zones of North Dakota. Zones 3–7.

McIntosh. Superb variety. Handsome, large, red fruits with delicious flesh. Blooms medium late; ripens after midseason. A heavy, annual bearer. Leading variety in the Northeast. Zones 4–8.

Melba. Small, red-striped fruits with tender flesh—one of the finest early-season dessert apples. Blooms medium late; ripens early. Tends to bear heavily in alternate years and fruits tend to drop. Red Melba is a solid red sport. Zones 4–8; also 3 in favorable sites.

Milton. Large, pinkish-red fruits not always well shaped but good tasting. Blooms medium late; ripens in midseason. Zones 4–8.

Northern Spy. Large, delicious, red-striped fruits. Blooms late; ripens late. Often bears biennially and is unusually fussy about having a well-drained soil. Does not start bearing until about ten years old. A poor pollinator; must be planted with two other varieties if you want all to bear. Zones 4–8.

Patricia. Small to medium-size, pinkish-red fruits of very good quality. Blooms medium late; ripens after midseason. Heavy producer. Zones 3–8.

Red Delicious. Also called just plain Delicious. Old favorite and the most widely grown of all varieties. Fruits are red, somewhat cone-shaped, and excellent for eating fresh but not too good for cooking. Blooms medium late; ripens late. Zones 5–8. There are innumerable red sports of this variety. For the home gardener they offer few if any real advantages, except that they are of a richer red coloration. Some of the sports are also spur-type trees—semi-dwarfs that produce fruit spurs and fruit in practically all parts of the tree. Starkrimson, Redspur, and Oregon Red are just a few of these spur-type varieties. One drawback with the Delicious sports, however, is that they tend to revert; that is, the fruits they produce suddenly revert to the duller red color of the original Delicious. This reversion may involve an entire tree or only a single branch or spur; but once the change takes place, it is permanent.

Red Duchess. Medium-size, red fruits especially suited to cooking and jelly-making. Recommended in many of the Plains States. Blooms early; ripens early. Zones 3–8.

Rhode Island Greening. Very large, green apple, and very tart. What a pie it makes! Blooms medium-late; ripens late. Spreading tree, heavy producer, but sometimes a biennial bearer. Poor pollinator. Zones 5–8.

Rome Beauty. Big, red fruits fine for baking and pies. Blooms late; ripens unusually late. Tree is of drooping habit; produces heavily and annually. Susceptible to fire blight. Zones 5–8.

Stayman Winesap. Descendent of Winesap. Large, red-striped, juicy, all-purpose fruits, but outstanding as a dessert apple. Store well. Blooms medium late; ripens late. A poor pollinator; must be planted with two other varieties if you want all to bear. Zones 6–8.

Summer Pippin. Medium-large, green apples for pies and sauce. Blooms early; ripens very early. Productive, but tends to bear biennially. Zones 6–8.

Summer Rambo. Large apples which may have a little red striping or be almost entirely green. They're not pretty, but they're fine for cooking in late summer; and the last apples from the tree are also good to eat fresh (they are also more nearly red). Blooms medium late; ripens early. A poor pollinator. Zones 6–8.

Tydeman's Red. Also called Tydeman's Early. A McIntosh descendent with solid red, medium-size fruits of above average quality for an early apple. Blooms early: ripens early. Very popular in the Northwest. Zones 4–8.

Wealthy. Medium-size, red-striped variety for eating and cooking. Blooms early; ripens early. Long a favorite in the North Central states. Zones 3–7.

Winesap. An all-purpose apple. Small and red but crisp and toothsome. Keeps well. Blooms medium late; ripens late. A poor pollinator; must be planted with two other varieties. Zones 6–8. Reaches perfection in Virginia's Piedmont areas.

Yellow Transparent. The earliest *good* apple. In northern New Jersey, for example, harvest often starts in late June. Pale greenish-yellow fruits used for cooking. Blooms early. Zones 3–8. The only apple that is a reasonably consistent producer as far north as the Matanuska Valley in Alaska.

York Imperial. Fruits are red and lopsided but pleasant to eat and fine for processing. Blooms late; ripens late. Biennial bearer and susceptible to fire blight. Widely grown in Pennsylvania and Virginia. Zones 6-8.

Culture

I suppose the unavailability of land in suburban areas today discourages most people even from considering the possibility of planting a lot of fruit trees; so the point I am about to make borders on the academic. Nevertheless, it's a fact that the thing which seems to bother people most about raising apples is that they wind up with more fruit than they know what to do with.

Offhand, I can think of three people who put in or acquired small apple orchards who have completely quit working them. For instance, one of my neighbors here in Lyme bought a place with about 12 old trees which he promptly restored to good bearing condition. And now, five years later, he virtually ignores them simply because they produced bushels and bushels and bushels of fruit—more than he could use, more than his friends and neighbors could use. The waste appalled him. "Besides," he says, "just buying baskets to put the fruit in cost a lot of money—and no one bothers to return them."

The moral is obvious: Don't plant too many apple trees—especially standard-size trees that produce up to 15 bushels a year when they hit peak production along about their twelfth birthday.

Although apples, next to crabapples, are the hardiest of the deciduous tree fruits and rather late-blooming, you must plant them in a spot where they will not be damaged by late spring freezes. They should also be well removed from black walnuts, which have a toxic substance in the roots.

The soil should be well drained and well aerated, but it should also retain moisture. Add a good supply of humus; and if the pH is less than 6.0, add a little lime, too. Give each standard tree a space 35 ft. in diameter; each semi-dwarf, 18 ft; and each dwarf, 10 ft. Semi-dwarfs and dwarfs tend to have more roots on one side of the trunk than the other. Plant them with the bulk of the roots toward the prevailing wind, thus helping to improve their anchorage.

Apply a thick organic mulch around each newly planted tree in a 4- to 6-ft. circle; and increase the size of the circle every year so that it extends out as far as the branch tips.

After the young tree has developed full-size leaves, fertilize it with 1 cup of 10-10-10. In soils that are deficient in potassium and phosphorus, continue using 10-10-10 at a rate of 1 cup per year of tree age. Generally, however, the mulch will supply enough of these elements; so after the first year you can use nitrogen alone. If you use ammonium nitrate, apply ⅓ cup per year of tree age until you reach 10 cups. Level off there.

Apples are trained to a modified leader, as described in the first part of this chapter. Once you have selected a tree's scaffold branches, pruning should be kept at a minimum until the tree starts to bear enough fruit to weight down and spread the limbs. Your aim should be to keep the leader dominant and to maintain reasonable symmetry among the scaffolds. This means you should cut back scaffolds that get out of hand. And you should, of course, remove suckers and other undesirable growth. But leave small twigs that are not doing any harm, because they bear leaves which help to nourish the tree and hasten its development. If you want to speed up fruit-bud formation, tie the limbs down to a horizontal position. This will also develop stronger crotches.

When the leader attains a height of 16 to 18 ft., head it back to an outward-growing lateral. Don't let the tree grow higher than this.

Once a tree starts to bear heavily, annual pruning becomes a thinning operation designed to keep the crown open and not too high. Concentrate on the dead and diseased wood, suckers, small down-growing branches, small branches that are in the way of better branches and old unproductive spurs. There is little to be gained by removing branches over 3 in. in diameter unless they are sick or broken or unless a tree has been neglected.

Except for emergency work, pruning is best done in late winter before growth begins and when the temperature is above freezing. It can be done at any time during the dormant period, however.

Apples are borne on long-lived spurs; and some varieties also bear fruit on one-year shoots. Thinning of the fruits improves fruit size and

On apples and several other kinds of fruit trees, fruit is borne on spurs—short, stout stubs growing out from the branches.

color, reduces limb breakage, and promotes annual bearing. The job should be done after June drop. Apples left on the tree should be spaced an average of 6 in. apart. Largest fruits should be spaced 8 in. apart.

As pointed out in the first part of this chapter, thinning also helps to encourage a tree that bears biennially to bear every year. When this is your purpose, you should thin trees within 20 days after bloom and you should leave only one fruit per foot.

Another way to induce bearing, not only in trees that produce every other year but also in those which do not bear until they are fairly old (Northern Spy, for example), is by scoring. This is done by cutting through the bark with a knife in a full circle around the trunk just below the lowest branch. If you score a tree 12 to 16 days after full bloom, it will set more fruit the same year as well as the following year. Annual scoring is unnecessary.

Apples have more insect enemies and are afflicted by more diseases than almost any other fruit. But fortunately, these are not difficult to cope with. Follow the spray schedule in Table X. If borers start tunneling into a tree, dig them out as soon as possible with a wire or spray repeatedly with malathion. Borers attract woodpeckers which open up holes that let in disease germs.

Fire blight attacks some varieties of apples more than others. If you run into it, reduce the amount of fertilizer given infected trees; and cut out and burn the blighted growths immediately. For more about dealing with fire blight, see pears.

The great majority of apple varieties start to bear at four to seven years of age, and bear efficiently for 20 to 25 years. Allow fruits to ripen on the tree and then pick them soon, because if they are left hanging too long, they become mealy. Ripe apples are fully colored and have a waxy coating. If you can't determine ripeness by the appearance of the fruits, take a bite.

Apples to be stored are picked just before they are ripe. Keep them in a cool, somewhat humid spot. If you place them in a plastic bag in the coldest part of your refrigerator's fresh-food compartment, you can keep them for a good many months.

APRICOTS

Apricots are much like peaches, but the fruits are generally less than 2 in. across. The fruits ripen in mid-summer and are eaten fresh, cooked, frozen, canned, and dried. The trees are deciduous and reach about 25 ft. Dwarf varieties are available.

Apricots are most widely grown in California and Washington, but can be grown almost anywhere in Zones 5–8. Several varieties also grow in 4 and perhaps even 3. Self-fruitful with some exceptions.

Varieties

Alfred. Hardy and productive. Said to be one of the most regular in bearing of any apricots tested at Geneva, New York. Medium-size, bright orange fruits of very good quality. Midseason.

Blenheim. Old variety similar to Royal and widely grown in the West. Midseason.

Erli-Orange. Large, orange-skinned fruits ripen early. An example of a very good variety that grew from a seed.

Farmingdale. Hardy and productive. Medium-size, soft, orange fruits in midseason.

Moongold. Developed in Minnesota; does well in Zone 4 and is worth trying in favorable locations in Zone 3. Spreading tree with slightly flattened, golden, freestone fruits. Midseason. Self-unfruitful; is best planted with Sungold.

Moorpark. Old variety, widely planted. Large, sweet, freestone fruits are deep yellow with a red cheek. Late. Tree is rather tender, but blooms late and thus escapes many spring freezes.

Riland. Another Western variety. Early, medium-size fruits with red-blushed skin and fine flavor. Tree rather easily damaged by wind.

Royal. A very old variety that is widely grown in California. Medium-large fruits with orange skin and fine texture. Good for processing. Mid-season.

Sungold. A companion to Moongold but matures a little later. Freestone fruits are golden-orange. Buds are exceptionally hardy; tree does well in Zone 4 and is worth a trial in 3. Self-unfruitful.

Wenatchee Moorpark. Widely grown in Washington. Large, orange fruits.

Culture

It's easy to grow apricots from seeds, but they will not come true. Nevertheless, many of the best varieties have originated in this way (and there have also been a great many poor varieties).

Because apricots bloom very early, they should be planted in a relatively frost-free spot. Ideally, they should also be on a north slope or on the north side of the house where they will more or less escape the warming rays of the late winter-early spring sun.

The soil can be of average quality, but must be very well drained and should have a good supply of humus. Since the trees are susceptible to verticillium wilt, do not plant them on land that has been planted to tomatoes, potatoes, peppers, melons, strawberries, or raspberries within five years. Give each tree a space 20 ft. across.

Grow like peaches. Fertilize with 10-10-10 for the first three or four years. Start with 1 cup and add 1 cup with each succeeding year. From five years of age on, use ammonium nitrate at the rate of $\frac{1}{2}$ cup per year of tree age. The maximum application should be 6 to 8 cups.

Prune trees to an open center by cutting out excess interior branches. Also remove branches that grow downward. Bearing trees make 12 to 18 in. of terminal shoot growth each year. Head back shoots that make the longest growth. Most fruit is borne on spurs up to about three years of age; so keep the youngest spurs and remove those that are no longer productive.

If a tree's fruit production declines despite annual pruning, it can be rejuvenated by complete removal of a good number of the older branches. Such drastic pruning should, however, be done over a period of about three years.

When fruits are about the size of small cherries, thin them to 3 to 4 in.

Spray trees with a dormant oil in very early spring. Then spray them with a general-purpose fruit spray (1) when petals fall, (2) ten days later, (3) ten days later, (4) ten days later, (5) ten days later. Trees are very susceptible to brown rot if warm, humid weather occurs at bloom and in the three-week period before harvest. To prevent this, spray with captan every three days while trees are in bloom; and spray with captan weekly (or twice a week in very wet weather) for three weeks before harvest. If borers are a nuisance, spray as for peaches.

Apricots start to bear in four or five years. Allow fruits to ripen on the tree before picking those that you intend to eat fresh. For cooking and processing, pick before the fruits are fully ripe. In either case, handle with care.

CHERRIES—SOUR

These are spreading, deciduous trees to 35 ft. which produce tart red fruits in late spring and early summer. Dwarf varieties are available, but are so small and produce so few fruits that some nurseries have given them up and now carry semi-dwarfs only. Grow in Zones 4–7, and in the case of one variety, in 8 at high elevations. Self-fruitful.

Varieties

Early Richmond. Soft, medium-quality fruits. Earliest of all.

English Morello. Medium-size, dark red, crack-resistant fruits are extremely tart. Two weeks later than Montmorency. Small, hardy trees, not too vigorous or productive.

Meteor. Twelve-ft. trees with large, light red, tart fruits for cooking and processing. Along with North Star, it is one of the hardiest varieties.

Montearly. A sport of Montmorency and a little earlier.

Montmorency. By far the most widely grown sour cherry. Fruits unusually large and attractive, with skin that rarely cracks. Tart but pleasant to eat fresh when fully ripe. There are various strains of slightly different shades of red.

North Star. A naturally dwarf (to 8 ft.) tree originated in Minnesota. Grows from Zone 4 to parts of Zone 8. Big, red, juicy, tart fruits. Midseason.

Culture

Sour cherries need good air drainage and soil drainage. The ideal soil is also reasonably light, deep, and reinforced with organic matter. Give each standard tree a space 20 to 25 ft. in diameter. English Morellos, however, need only about 18 ft.

When planting, take special pains to keep the roots from drying. If they are dry on delivery, soak in water for several hours. If the entire tree is dry, cover it with damp soil for several days.

Apply ⅓ cup of ammonium nitrate per year of tree age until the trees are 15 years old; then level off. Since the trees fruit very early in the growing season, fertilizer to be of any value must be applied several weeks before the buds break.

Prune young trees to develop a system of three scaffold branches. Then, after two or three years, cut back the leader to a strong, outward lateral; and develop two or three more of the upper branches as scaffolds (thus creating a vase-shaped tree with six or seven strong scaffold branches). Thereafter, prune lightly until trees start to bear: too much cutting will delay fruiting.

Mature trees should be kept thinned out in the center. Side branches should also be thinned and cut back to strong laterals so that the lower and side limbs will remain productive. The effect of this pruning is to produce larger fruits in all parts of the trees.

To control pests, apply a dormant oil spray in early spring. Then apply a general-purpose fruit spray when most of the petals fall; ten days later; and ten days after that. Spray with ferbam after all fruits have been harvested. If warm, humid weather occurs during bloom period, spray with captan every week to prevent brown rot; and spray with captan every week for three weeks before harvest if weather at that time is also warm and humid. Watch out also for borers, and spray as for peaches if necessary.

Throwing netting over the trees just before fruit is harvested keeps off birds.

Sour cherries start to bear in four or five years, reach maximum production at eight years, and are efficient producers for fifteen to eighteen years.

Allow cherries to ripen on the tree before picking. Unless you are going to make a pie immediately, pick the fruits with the stems on: they will not lose juice and will keep better.

CHERRIES—SWEET

Sweet cherries are upright, deciduous trees to 50 ft., but dwarf and semi-dwarf varieties are available. They produce sweet, red, black, or yellow fruits toward the end of spring. Grow in Zones 6 and 7; also in 5 in protected places. Self-unfruitful; you must plant two or more varieties. Note, however, that Bing, Lambert, Napoleon and Emperor Francis will not pollinate one another. (Sour cherry varieties will also pollinate sweet cherries, but they rarely are in bloom at the right time.)

Varieties

Note. Duke cherries are crosses between sweet and sour cherries and have some characteristics of each type, but are more nearly like sweet cherries. There are several varieties with good fruit—May Duke, Royal Duke, Olivet, and Reine Hortense—but they are hard to find; and they really don't offer anything which you cannot find today in standard sweet and sour cherries. Dukes are self-unfruitful.

Bing. Big fruits are such a dark red that they are almost black. Flesh is sweet and firm. Midseason. Subject to cracking. Tree will not cross with Lambert or Napoleon.

Black Tartarian. Medium-size, purple-black fruits of excellent quality. Fairly early. An old favorite.

Early Rivers. Big, firm, crimson-black fruits of excellent quality. One of the earliest.

Emperor Francis. Large, red, and yellow fruits of top-notch flavor and juicy. Midseason. Fruits have better than average resistance to cracking. Vigorous and productive tree.

Giant. Resembles Bing, but often rated higher.

Lambert. Large, purple-red fruits are sweet and luscious. Late. The tree is hardy enough to be raised on a commercial scale on the east shore of Flathead Lake in Montana. Will not cross with Bing or Napoleon. A self-fruitful sport of Lambert has been introduced.

Napoleon. Also called Royal Ann. This yellow and red cherry is much better for the fruit-packing industry than the home gardener, although it

The best way to keep birds out of a cherry tree—and also away from blueberries and other small fruits: surround the tree with netting. (Unfortunately, while the owner of this tree succeeded in foiling our feathered friends, he failed to protect the tree against a disease which has almost defoliated it.)

is often grown by the latter. Midseason. Fruits crack in wet weather. Tree is less hardy than most, finicky about soil and susceptible to brown rot. Will not cross with Bing or Lambert.

Seneca. About the earliest good variety. Fruits are purple-black, soft, juicy, and tasty.

Windsor. One of the latest varieties. Big, purplish-red fruits with crisp, sweet flesh. Vigorous and productive tree.

Yellow Spanish. Light yellow fruits with a red cheek. Midseason. Hardy, vigorous trees. Good pollinator for Napoleon.

Culture

Sweet cherries are a little more demanding about climate and soil than sour cherries, but they are grown in the same way. Give each tree a space 25 to 30 ft. in diameter.

The trees are of upright habit, but are pruned in about the same way as sour cherries. The scaffold branches should be spaced further—about 12 in.—apart up and down the trunk. On mature trees, cut back branches that grow vertically to a lateral or bud that is growing outward.

Sweet cherries start bearing at five to seven years of age and produce best when eight to twelve.

CRABAPPLES

Deciduous trees to 30 ft. Grow in Zones 2–8. Self-fruitful.

Varieties

Note. All listed here are grown primarily for their fruit, which is used in making jelly, pies, and for pickling.

Adam. Fruits less than 1 in. across, yellow striped with red. Rather puckery but make excellent jelly. Early. Tree has been called the hardiest of the hardy.

Dolgo. Small, oval, bright red fruits make a ruby-red jelly. Ripen in late summer.

Hyslop. Large, red fruits with a purplish bloom. They are a little astringent and very good for jelly. A bit later than Dolgo.

Jacques. Another very hardy variety with medium fruits considered excellent for pies and sauce. Fruits are yellowish-green washed with red, and are borne in tight clusters.

Rescue. Small, greenish-yellow fruits blushed with red. Sweet and of good quality; may be eaten fresh. Early. Very hardy.

Young America. Large, red fruits produce an attractive clear red jelly. Midseason.

Culture

Grow like apples.

NECTARINES

Nectarines are almost exact duplicates of peaches except that the fruits are smaller, fuzzless, and taste a little different. They ripen in midsummer (all varieties listed below are ahead of the Elberta peach). Dwarf varieties are available. Grow in Zones 5–8. Self-fruitful.

Varieties

Cavalier. Smallish, yellow and red fruits with firm yellow flesh of aromatic flavor. Freestone. Vigorous tree.

Cherokee. Large, yellow-fleshed, semi-clingstone fruits of very good quality. Very early to ripen. Blossoms are unusually tolerant of frost.

Lexington. A very hardy, very vigorous tree with yellow-fleshed, freestone fruits. Medium-early buds moderately tolerant of frost.

Pocahontas. Very early, yellow-fleshed fruits; mild and good. Semi-clingstone. Fruits are easier to protect against brown rot than those of other varieties.

Redbud. Firm, white-fleshed, freestone fruits. Early.

Redchief. Medium-size, bright red fruits with firm, white flesh and a strong but fine flavor. Freestone. Midseason. Trees more resistant to brown rot than most varieties, but blossoms tender to frost.

Rivers Orange. An old variety but still among the best. Small fruits are almost completely covered with a red blush. Yellow flesh. Freestone.

Culture

Grow like peaches. But trees are more susceptible to brown rot and need to be sprayed more often with captan during humid weather.

PAWPAW

Also called papaw. Not to be confused with the papaya, which is also occasionally called pawpaw.

The pawpaw is an interesting deciduous tree to 40 ft. but usually much less. In the autumn it produces somewhat misshapen, dark brown fruits 3 to 6 in. long and 1 to 1½ in. across. The fruits have either a white, inedible flesh or, on desirable trees, a soft, yellow, aromatic flesh with a banana-like flavor. These are eaten raw or are sometimes cooked.

Pawpaws grow in Zones 5–8 in the Eastern half of the country. Self-fruitful.

Varieties

Named varieties are available, but except for the fact that they all have edible fruits, they have little to offer.

Culture

Grafted trees may be purchased or you can grow your own from seed with about the same results. The seed should be extracted from the ripe fruit and planted immediately in good, moist soil where the tree is to grow (transplanting is rather difficult). An alternative recommended by some people is to plant an entire fruit. Cover seed or fruit with ¾ in. of soil. Germination will not take place till the following July at the earliest and may not take place until the spring after that.

Pawpaws grow naturally in or on the edges of forests and are rare among fruit trees in that they grow well in light shade. They need a fertile, well-drained, but moisture-retentive soil which is rich in humus.

Given sufficient water in dry weather, an organic mulch, and spring applications of several cups of balanced fertilizer, pawpaws should grow well and demand little additional attention. Pruning is unnecessary except to keep out dead, broken, and excess wood. Don't worry if the trees make slow growth for the first few years: that is their nature.

The trees start to bear at six to eight years of age. Pick fruits when they are soft.

PEACHES

Peach trees reach 25 ft., but there are dwarf and semi-dwarf varieties, and a few dwarfs which are veritable midgets. The luscious fruits mature in late spring and summer.

Peaches grow best in Zones 6–8. When the temperature drops rather suddenly to 10° below, a majority of the fruit buds are likely to be killed; and at 18° to 20° below, the wood tissues are killed. Nevertheless, peaches can be grown in Zone 5 if you give them protection and select hardier varieties. There are also a few varieties that will do well in Zone 9.

Varieties

Elberta. This is the standard commercial variety by which all others are judged. The fruits are large, attractive, yellow with a bright blush. The yellow flesh is sweet but a little coarse. Freestone. Very good for processing. Fruits ripen in late midseason—about two-thirds of the way through the entire peach season. They are susceptible to dropping before they are ready for harvest. Tree is large, productive, but rather tender.

Blake. Large, yellow, freestone fruits of excellent texture and flavor. They freeze unusually well. Ripens just before Elberta. Tree tends to set light crops.

Bonanza. A genetic dwarf that starts bearing at 3 ft. (usually the second year after planting) and never grows to more than 7 ft. It can be kept at about 4 ft. with relatively little pruning. Large, yellow fruits with yellow flesh are freestone and of fair quality. They ripen with Elberta. Tree is ornamental, with dense foliage and pretty blossoms. Easily grown in containers as well as in the garden.

Dixired. The best of the very early varieties (it ripens more than six weeks ahead of Elberta). Fruits of good size, soft and with pleasing flavor. Yellow flesh. Semi-freestone. Not good for processing.

George IV. White-fleshed freestone of outstanding flavor and with very high Vitamin C content. Ripens with Elberta. Not a commercial variety and hard to come by.

Georgia Belle. White-fleshed, freestone fruits of extremely fine quality. Ripens shortly before Elberta. Tree very susceptible to brown rot.

Golden Jubilee. Big, attractive, yellow-fleshed, freestone fruits. Good for home canning and eating fresh, but bruises easily. Better than four weeks ahead of Elberta. Productive.

Halehaven. Excellent freestone with yellow flesh. Fruits are big and numerous. Ripens three weeks ahead of Elberta. Excellent processor. Hardy.

J. H. Hale. A very famous variety but mostly grown for the market. Large, firm fruits with yellow flesh and a free stone. Makes an excellent frozen product. Tree lacks hardiness and vigor and is also self-unfruitful. Ripens just before Elberta.

Keystone. Recommended especially for Zone 9. Yellow-fleshed, freestone fruits ripen about three weeks ahead of Elberta. Above average for processing.

Lizzie. Large, yellow-fleshed, freestone fruits two weeks after Elberta. Good quality. Productive.

Redhaven. Fruits so highly blushed that it is difficult to judge when they are really ripe. Yellow flesh. Semi-freestone. Do not turn brown when exposed to air. Best eaten fresh, but produces a good canned or frozen product. Five weeks ahead of Elberta. Heavy producer.

Redrose. Freestone fruits of good flavor and with firm, white flesh. Ripens three weeks before Elberta.

Redskin. Another excellent variety for Zone 9. Medium-large, freestone fruits with yellow flesh of melting texture. Ripens five weeks before Elberta; but in more Northern areas, where it is also well thought of, it ripens along with Elberta. Good for processing. Very productive.

Rio Oso Gem. Big, firm fruits with yellow flesh. Freestone. Excellent for freezing. Ripens a week after Elberta.

Southland. Medium-size, yellow-fleshed, freestone fruits which don't turn brown when exposed to air. Rated exceptional for canning and freezing; also excellent for eating fresh. Ripens about three weeks before Elberta.

Springtime. An extremely early variety for the South. In south Mississippi it ripens on May 15—two months ahead of Elberta. White-fleshed clingstone.

Triogem. Yellow-fleshed freestone of very good quality. Ripens four weeks before Elberta. Vigorous, productive tree.

Vedette. Only variety which has survived the winters at the Maine Experiment Station farm (Zone 5); but it has been damaged by low temperatures. A Canadian introduction. Yellow-fleshed, freestone fruits are attractive and good. Ripens almost three weeks before Elberta.

Culture

Since peaches are among the early bloomers, you should plant them where they will not be awakened too early in the spring by the warming sun. A north slope or north side of a building is good. The location must, of course, have very good air drainage so that late spring frosts will pass by.

The soil must be well drained and deep. If it does not meet these requirements, you can expect poor performance by your trees and they will die long before their time. On this score, Table XI is extremely revealing.

TABLE XI
Soil Effects on Peach Productivity and Longevity in
Niagara County, New York, 1926 to 1935
Source: Cornell University Experiment Station.

Soil description	Yield per tree (bushels)		Trees remaining after— (per cent)	
	5- TO 6-YR. TREES	13- TO 14-YR. TREES	6 YRS.	14 YRS.
Shallow and imperfectly drained soils	0.73	0.54	80	19
Soils intermediate in depth and drainage	0.89	1.13	73	62
Deep, well-drained soils	1.07	1.76	91	81

The ideal soil is a sandy loam into which you mix a good supply of humus. The pH should be 6.0 to 6.5—definitely not below 5.5. Fumigate to get rid of nematodes if these are troublesome. However, you should note that even though you exterminate these pests, you cannot be sure that peach trees will survive if planted in an old peach orchard that has been cut down. There is no explanation for this. Just accept the fact that if you plant a young peach tree in the hole formerly occupied by another peach tree, it will probably die in short order. And it may die if planted anywhere near the hole.

Give each tree a space 20 ft. in diameter. Surround it with an organic mulch to add nutrients to the soil, to control weeds, and to eliminate the need for watering except in dry spells. Adequate soil moisture throughout fruit development *right up through "final swell"* (the final month before harvest) is one of the most important factors in peach production

Mature peach trees should make about 15 in. of terminal growth each year (young trees should make even more). Apply just enough fertilizer to maintain this growth. Trees that make too much growth produce poorer fruits and are more likely to be damaged by winter weather.

A good average feeding schedule calls for application of 1 cup of 10-10-10 or 8-8-8 per year of tree age for the first three years. Thereafter apply pure nitrogen unless a soil test indicates your soil is deficient in potassium, phosphorus, or a minor element. If you use ammonium sulfate, apply ¼ cup the first year and add ½ cup each succeeding year until you reach 10 cups. As a rule, this is as much nitrogen as a tree needs unless it is not making adequate annual growth.

Fertilizer should be applied just before trees bloom.

Peach trees are trained in a vase shape with an open center. Commercial growers keep even the oldest trees very low—to only about 7 or 8 ft.—so they will be easier to manage. You don't have to take such drastic action, but this is an indication of how much pruning peaches can stand.

If the tree you buy has branches, cut them back at planting to very short stubs with one bud at the base and head the leader back to about 24 in. above the ground. By June or July strong new shoots will develop. You should then select three or four to become your scaffold branches and remove the others.

From this point on, all pruning is done in late winter.

At the start of the second year, remove any excess branches that have developed and cut back the scaffolds slightly to the same length. Remove some of the weak laterals on the scaffolds.

In the next two years, prune only enough to eliminate crossing and crowding branches.

Peaches are borne on wood of the previous year's growth. Once trees start to bear, they should be pruned annually to keep them low and open. Cut back the new growth of the previous year about 50 per cent or a little more. Remove long branches that are high out of reach. Branches that are too vertical should be cut back to laterals that are growing outward. Remove excess growth in the center of the trees.

In addition to pruning, you should thin the fruits each year when they are about the size of a dime. Those remaining are spaced 6 to 8 in. apart. Use the smaller spacing for fruits in the top and outer parts of the tree, because the branches there are more vigorous than those in the center of the tree and can support more fruits. Use the 8-in. spacing for fruits on the weak wood inside the tree.

Follow the spray schedule given in Table X to control peach pests. If the weather at the time of bloom and in the three-week period before harvest is wet and humid, you may have a lot of trouble with brown rot. This can be controlled, however, by applying captan. Spray about every three days during bloom; every week or more often during the pre-harvest period.

Peach tree borers, if present, are combatted in summer with malathion sprays. They are also controlled by fumigating the soil in the fall with para-dichlorobenzene.

Peach trees start bearing when three or four years of age and reach maximum production a year or two later. They are efficient producers for about ten years, but will, of course, continue to bear much longer.

Pick fruits just before they are fully ripe. They feel firm; the skin of yellow-fleshed varieties is fully yellow while that of white-fleshed varieties is fully white; the reddish blush has reached maximum intensity and size. When pulling a peach from the tree, hold it in the palm of your hand with your fingers around it; don't pull it with the fingertips only, because you will bruise the flesh.

Firm ripe peaches (not soft ones) can be stored in the coldest part of your refrigerator's fresh-food compartment for two to four weeks.

PEARS

Pears are deciduous trees to 40 ft., but are usually kept much lower. Dwarf and semi-dwarf varieties are available. The fruits ripen in late summer and early fall. Grow best in Zones 5–8, but some varieties can be grown in 3 and 4 and others in 9. Usually self-unfruitful; two or more varieties must be planted together. Most varieties are compatible and most bloom at about the same time.

Varieties

Anjou. An old favorite. The medium-large, oval fruits are yellowish-green and slightly russeted. They are of excellent dessert quality even after several months' storage. Late. Zones 5–7, but does best in the West.

Baldwin. A good variety for Zone 9; also grows farther North. Tender; good flavored; excellent for processing. Early. Has good resistance to fire blight.

Bartlett. Top favorite. Medium-large, yellow fruits are juicy and sweet; perfect for eating and processing. Ripens about the end of August. Fruits can be stored for about two months. Tree is vigorous and productive but unfortunately susceptible to fire blight. Cannot be pollinated by Seckel. Zones 5–7.

Beurre Bosc. Medium-large fruits with long necks are yellow overlaid with bronze. Smooth, juicy, and rich in flavor. Late. Fruits store well in the refrigerator. Productive tree very susceptible to fire blight. Excellent pollinator for Bartlett. Zones 5–7.

Clapp's Favorite. Medium-large, symmetrical fruits of fine quality and flavor, but soften very quickly and should, therefore, be picked while quite firm. Two or three weeks earlier than Bartlett. Very susceptible to fire blight.

Comice. Generally rated the outstanding dessert pear. Medium-large, yellow fruits are juicy and melting. Late. Zones 5–8 but rather finicky about the climate; at its best in the West, particularly at higher elevations.

Duchess. Excellent fruit for eating fresh and processing. Very big, greenish yellow. Self-fruitful. Zones 5–7.

Flemish Beauty. Medium-large, rounded fruits with a spicy flavor. Mid-season. Tree is susceptible to fire blight and scab, but very hardy—will grow in Zone 4.

Gorham. Large, yellow fruits delicious fresh and processed. Late. Vigorous tree susceptible to fire blight.

Kieffer. Large, yellow fruits of fair quality fresh but excellent when processed. Late. Tolerant of fire blight. Zones 4–9.

Lincoln. Recommended for Oklahoma and similar areas. Large, good quality fruits in late summer. Tree is dependable, moderately blight-resistant, but susceptible to scab.

Magness. A new cross between Seckel and Comice. Medium-size fruits are greenish with russeting, sweet, and aromatic. They will store for a couple of months. Midseason. Vigorous, thorny tree resistant to fire blight. Not a good pollinator; must be planted with at least two other varieties if all are to bear fruit. Zones 5–7.

Maxine. Large, late, yellow fruits of fair quality. Best eaten fresh but good for processing. Because of the tree's high resistance to fire blight, it is recommended especially for areas where this is a severe problem. Zones 5–7.

Moonglow. Another new, vigorous, blight-resistant variety. Big fruits, not so juicy as some, but good fresh and for processing. Early. Zones 5–8.

Orient. Very large, rounded fruits good to eat and to process. Keep well. Midseason. Vigorous, spreading tree resistant to fire blight. Grows from Zone 9 northward.

Seckel. Small, brownish-yellow fruits with a red blush. Delicious when fully ripe. Rather late. Very popular. Productive tree but slow to get started. Has good resistance to fire blight. Is not pollinated by Bartlett. Zones 5–7.

Tait Dropmore. Medium-size pear of fair quality but useful because of its hardiness. Recommended for planting throughout North Dakota, including that part in Zone 3.

Culture

Pears bloom fairly late and the flowers are somewhat more resistant to cold than those of peaches and sweet cherries; nevertheless it is risky to grow them in areas where the mean date of the last spring freeze is May 10 or later. Plant trees in a reasonably frost-free spot. The soil should be well drained and deep to accommodate the deep roots. A good loam is preferred. Give each tree a space 20 ft. in diameter.

Keeping the trees mulched with organic matter generally takes care of their moisture requirements (although you must water them in dry spells) and also enriches the soil. The last point is important because pears are susceptible—in some cases, very susceptible—to fire blight, a disease which particularly attacks trees that are making very vigorous growth. You must be careful, therefore, not to give them too much dry fertilizer; yet if you want good fruit, you obviously cannot ignore their nutritional requirements entirely.

The best program for feeding pears is this—assuming that you mulch them: (1) Do not fertilize young trees for a year. Or if you cannot bear doling out such cruel treatment, give them only a couple of handfuls of

10-10-10. (2) From the second year until the trees start to bear, give them 1 cup of ammonium nitrate per year. Then increase to 2 cups until the tree is ten years old; to 3 cups until the tree is fifteen years old; and to 4 cups thereafter. Mature trees that are performing badly might be given 6 cups of ammonium nitrate per year, but this is the absolute maximum

Although more upright in growth, pears are pruned more or less like apples. Train each tree when young to a single leader with four or five scaffold branches. After that, until the tree starts to bear, prune just enough to keep the leader dominant (longer than the scaffolds), but head it back a little if you need to develop better scaffolds than you started with. Remove suckers. Bearing trees that are properly developed need only light annual thinning out to keep the tops open. Unproductive, slow-growing spurs should be reinvigorated by reducing them to half their length. On Comice and Anjou pears, you should cut back most of the spurs to promote larger fruits.

Pruning must be done in winter to reduce the danger of spreading fire blight. However, you should cut out blighted twigs and branches *whenever* you discover them. Make cuts at least 6 in. below the blighted area. Dip your tools in denatured alcohol after each cut.

Suckers that arise from the trunk, roots, and lower parts of the scaffold branches in early summer should also be cut out at once to eliminate tender wood that is particularly susceptible to blight.

Other diseases and insects are controlled by a spray schedule similar to that in Table X.

Thin the fruits after June drop to 6 to 8 in.

Pears start to bear in four or five years, reach maximum production about the tenth year, and are efficient producers for twenty to twenty-five years. Fruits must be picked before they ripen on the tree. They are ready for picking when the green skin begins to yellow and when the stems separate from the spurs with a very light tug (Bartlett and Kieffer fruits require a stronger tug). The fruits should then be ripened in a cool (60°–70°), shady place—ideally a basement. The process usually takes only a few days, but winter pears take longer.

To hasten ripening, dip the fruits in tepid water for an hour or two. To delay ripening, move the fruits directly from the tree to the coldest section of the fresh-food compartment in your refrigerator. Bartletts can be held for two months; Bosc for three, and Anjou for four.

Ripe fruits should be stored in the refrigerator.

PERSIMMONS

These are handsome deciduous trees bearing sizable orange or red fruits which are usually eaten fresh. They mature in the fall. Two species of persimmons grow in the United States. The native species grows to 50 ft. or more; bears oval or oblong fruits up to 2 in. in diameter. These grow in Zones 5–9, but are reliable in 5 and 6 only if the fruit ripens in early

October before a hard freeze. The oriental, or Japanese, persimmon is a much smaller tree with larger, more highly esteemed fruits. It grows in Zones 7b–10.

To produce fruit, you must plant male and female specimens of native persimmons. Some Oriental persimmons are self-fruitful, and in other cases you should plant male and female trees.

Varieties

Fuyu. Oriental. Medium-size, tomato-shaped, deep red fruits with light orange flesh. Seedless or nearly so. Not astringent; you can pick and eat them while still firm. Usually self-fruitful.

Gailey. Oriental. Fruit is small, dull red, and not at all choice. But this variety is useful because it regularly produces a large quantity of pollen and is, therefore, excellent to plant with oriental varieties that are self-unfruitful or doubtfully self-fruitful.

Garretson. Native. Orange-yellow fruits about 1¼ in. in diameter have soft, non-astringent flesh superior to other native varieties. Early. Has been grown at the experiment station in Geneva, New York, and is there rated the best.

Great Wall. Oriental. Smallish, more or less square fruits are astringent until fully ripe. They ripen in midautumn. Tree is hardy in colder areas, such as the warmer sections of Maryland.

Hachiya. Oriental. By far the favorite variety in California. Large, oblong fruits taper to a point; have orange-red skin and yellow flesh. Astringent until soft. Seedless and self-fruitful in California, but you probably need male and female trees elsewhere.

John Rich. Native. Originated in Illinois. Fruits larger than Garretson, have a heavy red blush, and are of fine quality. Early.

New Hampshire No. 1. Native. Hardier than most. Fruits are larger than other native varieties but not attractive. Reasonably good quality. Slightly astringent.

Peiping. Oriental. Medium-size, peach-like fruits astringent until soft. Tree is hardier than most; will grow in Washington, D.C., area. Usually self-fruitful.

Tamopan. Oriental. Large, oddly shaped, reddish-orange fruits with light orange flesh. Astringent till soft. Seedless. Ripens in late fall. Usually self-fruitful.

Tanenashi. Oriental. Medium-large, somewhat conical fruits with light orange skin turning to light red when ripe. Seedless, yellow flesh is astringent till ripe. Early. Self-fruitful. Favorite variety in the Southeast.

Culture

The California Agricultural Extension Service says: "Persimmons require very little attention. They are one of the best trees for the home gardener who has little time or inclination to control the usual fruit garden pests and diseases."

Persimmons have very deep roots, so you should be sure to start with one-year-old plants which can be moved without too much damage to the root system. The planting holes must be unusually deep, and the soil must be well drained and enriched with a large quantity of humus. Give each Oriental variety a space 20 ft. in diameter. Give a native 25 ft.

Because the trees grow fast—especially if the soil is good—and have large crowns, they should be supported with sturdy stakes for the first three or four years.

Water deeply when the soil dries out. Mulch the soil. Fertilize rather lightly with a nitrogenous fertilizer. Start with ⅓ cup of nitrate of soda and increase the application gradually to about 4 cups in the sixth year. Continue at that rate thereafter.

Develop a system of four or five scaffold branches when the trees are young. After that, prune in late winter to keep the tops open. Since fruits are borne on the current season's growth, cut back a few of the longest branches to force development of new side branches. But pruning should not be extensive.

Trees start to bear in four or five years. Allow fruits to ripen on the tree, then cut them off with clippers. Take a bit of stem with them. Keep ripe fruits in the refrigerator.

PLUMS

Plums are deciduous fruits to 25 ft. Dwarf and semi-dwarf varieties are available. Three types are grown: European plums with mainly blue fruits; Japanese plums with mainly red fruits; and native plums with red or yellow fruits. The best varieties of the natives are usually hybrids resulting from crossing with Japanese varieties. All plums ripen from midsummer on.

European plums grow in Zones 5–7 and are worth a trial in protected locations in 4. Japanese plums grow in Zones 5–9 and some are also worth a trial in 4. Native plums grow in Zones 3–7. Most plum varieties are self-unfruitful, and even the few that are self-fruitful do better if planted with another variety. European plums cannot pollinate Japanese plums or vice versa. Native varieties are pollinated either by other native varieties, by sandcherry-plum hybrids, or, in the case of native-Japanese hybrids, by Japanese varieties.

Varieties

Abundance. Japanese. Excellent plum for eating fresh. Large, red, juicy, and sweet. Very susceptible to brown rot.

Elephant Ear. Japanese. Big, red fruits with red flesh and a superior flavor. Midseason. Prefers dry Western areas and sandy soils, and does not do well in many areas.

French Damson. European. Large, dark blue fruits of top quality when mature and also good for preserves. Midseason to late. Fruits hang on trees for a long time without deteriorating badly. Better than Shropshire, but trees are not so long lived. Self-fruitful.

Green Gage. European. Fruits are medium-small, yellowish-green with red mottlings. Freestone. Midseason. Self-fruitful.

Imperial Epineuse. European. Largest prune-type plum. Skin is an un-attractive reddish-purple, but the greenish-yellow flesh is delicious fresh and also good for canning and drying. Semi-clingstone. Midseason. Susceptible to brown rot. Self-fruitful.

Methley. Japanese. Early, purple-red plums with red flesh that is delicious fresh. Clingstone. Very productive but tends to biennial bearing. Does better than most varieties in warm climates such as Hawaii.

Oneida. European. A late, reddish-black, prune-type variety. Fruits fairly large, freestone, and of good quality. Self-fruitful.

Queen Ann. Japanese. Big, heart-shaped fruits with a dark mahogany skin and amber flesh. Tree is weak, but the fruits are delicious.

Red Coat. Native. Medium-size, dark red fruits especially good for cooking but only fair for fresh use. Freestone. Midseason.

Santa Rosa. Japanese. An outstanding variety developed by Luther Burbank. Big, red fruits change to purple just before they ripen. Clingstone. Prolific. Widely grown, especially in California.

Shropshire. European. A variety of Damson plum, satisfactory for eating and splendid for jam. Small, blue, very tart fruits. Midseason. Hardy. Self-fruitful.

South Dakota. Native. Very sweet, medium-size, red-skinned fruits. Midseason. A good pollinator for other natives.

Stanley. European. Large, freestone, dark blue fruits excellent fresh and for cooking. Midseason. Reliably self-fruitful. Trunks susceptible to damage from winter weather unless whitewashed.

Superior. Native. A little less hardy than other natives. Big, heart-shaped, red fruits of excellent quality. Midseason. So productive that fruits often need thinning.

Tecumseh. Native. Medium-size, red-skinned fruits good for cooking and eating. Juicy. Clingstone. Early.

Underwood. Native. Large, dark red fruits of excellent quality. Clingstone. Early.

Culture

Plant plums in well-drained, average soil containing plenty of organic matter. The location should be reasonably frost-free; and since Japanese varieties bloom early, they should be on a north slope or north side of the house. Give each tree a space 20 ft. in diameter.

Fertilize with nitrogen in early spring. If using nitrate of soda, apply ⅔ cup per year of tree age up to a maximum of 10 cups. Native varieties can do with a little less.

Prune trees as you do apples. European plums actually need very little pruning to develop into good bearing specimens. Japanese and native plums grow more vigorously and need more pruning, including some heading back almost every year. In any case, once a system of three to four scaffold branches is formed, the main aim in pruning is to keep the top open so that sun can reach the long-lived fruit-bearing spurs inside the tree. Since plums generally have ample bloom every year, they do not need a great deal of pruning to keep them vigorous and productive.

Fruits of European plums generally need little thinning; but those of Japanese varieties almost always should be thinned to 3 to 4 in. apart. Some of the natives need to be thinned in the same way.

Spray trees with dormant oil in very early spring or late winter. Then spray with a general-purpose fruit spray (1) when petals fall, (2) ten days later, (3) ten days later, (4) at two-week intervals until a month (or less if pests are very troublesome) before fruit ripens. To prevent brown rot, spray with captan if weather is warm and humid at time of bloom and in the three-week period prior to harvest. Spray three or four days apart during bloom; at least every week before harvest.

If borers are troublesome, spray as for peaches.

Plums start to bear at four to six years of age. European and native plums are most delicious when allowed to ripen on the tree. Since Japanese plums deteriorate rather quickly once they are fully ripe, it's a better idea to pick them a few days early and allow them to ripen in a cool place.

QUINCE

The quince grown for its large, yellow, or orange fruits should not be confused with the flowering quince, which is a completely different plant. The fruiting quince is a deciduous, 15-ft., shrub-like tree with crooked branches. A few dwarf varieties are available. The fruit, which ripens in the fall, has a delicious aroma, but is used only for making jelly (one of the finest you ever tasted) and preserves. Trees grow in Zones 5–8. Self-fruitful.

Varieties

Champion. Fruits are yellow and somewhat pear-shaped. Late.
Orange. Most widely planted. Fruits resemble orange apples. Early.
Pineapple. Grown in California. Fruits have a vague pineapple flavor.
Van Deman. Offspring of Orange. Large and early.

Culture

Quinces grow in almost any soil, but live longer in heavier soils. Good drainage is essential; good humus content, desirable. Give each tree a space 15 ft. in diameter.

Because quinces grow slowly, you may be tempted to feed them heavily. Don't. This increases danger of fire blight. The best practice is to keep the trees mulched with an organic material. Fertilize in early spring with nitrate of soda. Give newly planted trees ⅓ cup and increase the application by ⅓ cup each year until you reach 4 cups. Level off there.

If you want a quince to develop as a tree, prune it at planting as you would an apple. But if you want to train it as a shrub, cut it back to within a foot of the ground. Thereafter you need to do relatively little pruning to shape the plant; and you must be careful not to cut it back indiscriminately for any other reason, because the fruits are borne at the terminal ends of twigs of the current season's growth. (In other words, anyone foolish enough to shear the entire tree would wind up that year with very little fruit.)

However, dead and damaged branches must be removed; and if a tree becomes too thick with branches, a few should be cut out entirely in order to open up the top. To stimulate development of new fruit-bearing twigs, you should also cut out some of the older branches and shoots inside the tree.

Quinces are subject to fire blight and most of the other diseases and insects that attack apples and pears; so spray them regularly in the same way.

Trees start to bear when about four years old and reach maximum production when ten. Pick fruits as they reach their full color. Wormy fruits, though much more troublesome to prepare for jelly than sound ones, are perfectly good to use.

SANDCHERRY-PLUM HYBRIDS

Also called cherry-plums. Deciduous fruits which range from 4-ft. shrubs like the native sandcherry to 25-ft. trees like the plum. Fruits also vary from ½ in. to 1¼ in. in size. These have green, red, or purple skins and yellow to purple flesh. Maturing in late summer, they may be eaten fresh or made into jams, jellies, or sauce.

Sandcherry-plum hybrids grow in Zones 2–6. They are especially popular in the northern Plains States, where many other fruits do not survive. Self-unfruitful; plants are pollinated either by other varieties of sandcherry-plums or by plums.

Varieties

Compass. Small, dark red fruits with yellow flesh. Tart and juicy. Late. Good for canning. Plant is a good pollinator.

Deep Purple. Unusually large, almost black fruits with purple flesh and a small stone that is almost free. Can be left on tree for a couple of weeks after ripening. Best used in jams and jellies. Midseason. Hardy.

Dura. Medium-size, juicy, purple-skinned fruits with red flesh. Midseason. Fruits keep well on the tree.

Opata. Medium-small, red-purple fruits with green flesh. Sweet. Midseason.

Culture

Grow like plums. In semi-arid regions such as North Dakota, each tree is given a space 20 ft. across; but in wetter regions, the space for small varieties can be reduced. Plants require rather hard pruning to produce plenty of young growth on which the best fruit is borne. Probably the best procedure is to cut out entire branches after they have fruited for three or four years.

8

Growing Small Fruits

If you never raised fruit of any description, the chances are that the small fruits—more commonly referred to as berries and including straw-berries, raspberries, blueberries, grapes, etc.—will be the ones you try first. This, at least, is the way most people act.

Because the small fruits grow on fairly small plants, they look easier to grow than tree fruits—and they are. They obviously take up less space. And since some of the plants are ornamental, they can even be tucked into flower beds and shrubbery borders where there isn't room for a tree. (Come to think of it, is there any more delightful way to shade a sunny terrace than to cover it with a grape vine dripping clusters of sweet, purple fruits?)

One other point in favor of starting out with small fruits is that they seem to have shot up in price at the grocery store far more steeply than their larger cousins.

How many plants should you start with? Don't let the size of the plants deceive you: if they are grown even moderately well, they will produce an awful lot of delicious food. Table XII shows what you can expect from the most popular of the fruits.

TABLE XII
Yield, Life, and Spacing of Small Fruits

| | | | Minimum space requirements in feet | |
	AVERAGE ANNUAL YIELD PER PLANT	PRODUCTIVE YEARS OF PLANTS	WIDTH OF ROW	SPACE BETWEEN PLANTS
Blueberries	3–4 qts.	20–30	6	6
Blackberries, erect	1 qt.	8–12	6	4
Blackberries, trailing	1½–3 qts.	8–10	6	6
Currants	3–4 qts.	12–15	6	4
Gooseberries	3–4 qts.	12–15	6	4
Grapes, bunch	15 lbs.	20–30	5	10
Grapes, muscadine	25 lbs.	20–30	6	10
Raspberries, red	1½ qts.	8–10	5	3
Raspberries, black	1–1½ qts.	8–10	6	3
Raspberries, purple	1–1½ qts.	8–10	6	3
Strawberries, June	½ qt.	3	2	1
Strawberries, everbearing	½ qt.	2	2	1

Size and layout of the berry patch. Table XII will help you figure out how large a berry patch you need once you have decided how many plants of this and that you want. But be sure to bear this point in mind: The table gives the *actual width of each plant row.* It does not make any allowance for you to walk and work between the rows. The space required for this is about 21 in. minimum. That's wide enough for you to pass between the plants without getting hung up in the branches and scratched by the thorns. It also allows for operation of a small rotary tiller to keep down weeds. (In strawberry beds, however, 12 in. between rows is enough if you use a hoe rather than a tiller.)

The rules for laying out a berry patch are about the same as those for laying out a vegetable garden:

Don't arbitrarily make the garden a rectangle if some other shape makes more efficient use of the available space.

If you plant on a slope, run the rows across the slope to slow water run-off.

If you use power equipment, make the rows as long as practicable.

Don't hesitate to make curving or sinuous rows if this improves land utilization.

Don't waste space on inside garden paths that parallel plant rows. In a large garden, however, you are likely to find that an inside path at right angles to the rows simplifies gardening operations.

If possible, place tall-growing fruits, such as elderberries and grapes, to the north of lower-growing fruits so that the latter will not be shaded.

Although all small fruits are perennials, strawberries are comparatively short-lived and are best grown along one side of the garden. Then you will be able to replace them every few years without disturbing the other plants so much.

If you are establishing your berry patch in what was your vegetable garden (a very good idea, because the soil should then be in prime shape for the fruits), remember that strawberries and bramble fruits should not be planted in the same place where tomatoes, potatoes, peppers, eggplants, melons, and okra grew within the preceding three years. This is because these fruits and vegetables are susceptible to the same diseases, and the fruits might be wiped out by the bacteria lingering after the vegetables.

Locating the garden. Small fruits do best if exposed to the sun all day, but they will not suffer greatly if they are in the shade for an hour or two. Ideally, you should try to locate the garden on an open southern slope or in an open space on the south side of a building or hedge. The area should have good air drainage so that the plants will not be injured or killed by a late spring freeze. It should also be protected from strong prevailing winds.

Preparing the soil. The nutritional needs of small fruits are somewhat different from those of tree fruits, and they require more careful soil preparation because, once they are planted, it is rather difficult to work humus into the soil around their shallow roots.

The best procedure is to start preparing the soil one year prior to planting the fruits. The following steps should be taken:

1. In the spring plow under whatever non-woody plants are growing in the garden space.

2. During the summer you have three alternatives all designed, in part, to get rid of as many weeds as possible: (a) Plant the space to corn or beans, keep them cultivated, and then, after harvest, chop them up and plow them under. (b) Cover the soil with an inch or more of peat, plow it in, and keep the soil tilled. This does not make such good use of the garden area as A, but adds more humus to the soil. (c) Spread on the soil all the grass clippings, hay, leaves, etc., that you accumulate and till them under regularly. This has the same disadvantage as B.

3. In the fall, plant a cover crop of rye and fertilize it with 10-10-10 at the rate of 4 cups per 100 sq. ft. Unless you are planting blueberries, you should also add limestone if the soil pH is below 5.5. Small fruits generally do best when the pH is between 5.5 and 6.5. Blueberries, however, require a pH below 5.2.

If you cannot follow this procedure, you should at least plow the garden space in the fall before setting out the fruit plants. And by all means mix in as much humus as you can lay hands on.

Selecting plants. Buy small fruits from a reputable source that will guarantee them to be true to name and healthy. If virus-free varieties—particularly strawberry varieties—are available, they are well worth the slight premium they command.

As a rule, the best plants to put in are one year old. Blueberries, however, should be two years old.

You can also propagate a number of the small fruits yourself. This is done in several ways but frequently by layering. To layer plants that root at the tips of the stems—blackberries, for example—bend a young cane to the ground and bury the tip to a depth of several inches. When roots form, cut off the cane about 6 in. above ground level, dig up the new plant, and set it out wherever you want it.

To stem-layer plants such as grapes, lay a one-year-old cane on the ground or in a shallow trench and cover a foot of it with soil. Then cut back the tip of the cane to about two buds. When roots form, cut off the cane on the parent-plant side.

To mound-layer plants such as currants and gooseberries, simply mound soil high over the entire crown of a plant. Each cane will then form roots.

All layering operations are started in the spring. The new plants should be well rooted and ready to be moved in the following spring.

Planting is best done in the spring, but may also be done in the fall in warm climates. Open and inspect the plants as soon as they are delivered. If they are dry, soak the roots in water for an hour or two and plant immediately. If planting must be delayed, rewrap the plants in polyethylene film and store them in the vegetable drawer of your refrigerator. They can be stored safely for as long as a week. The alternative is to dig a trench in a shady place and heel in the plants. Place the plants side by side and only one layer deep; cover the roots with soil, and water thoroughly.

Except for strawberries and grapes, small fruits are planted about 1 in. deeper than they previously grew, and the roots are spread out slightly in the hole. Firm the soil around them and water well. Applying a cupful of starter solution is advisable.

Balled-and-burlapped and canned plants need not be pruned; but the tops of bare-root plants are generally cut back a bit.

Routine care. Until your new plants are making good growth, cultivate the soil around them regularly. With the exceptions of elderberries and strawberries, they should then be mulched with an organic material. The decomposed part of this is scratched lightly into the soil every spring, and new material should then be added. Pull the mulch away from the plants a little in winter so mice cannot hide in it and feed on the stems.

During the growing season, water the plants whenever the soil under the mulch dries out. Like other edible plants, small fruits need ample moisture to grow and set sizable crops.

Fertilize the plants according to the general directions in the encyclopedic section following. They need nitrogen most of all; but unlike the tree fruits, they may also need phosphorus and potassium. If a soil test or inadequate plant growth indicates this, use a 10-10-10 balanced fertilizer or something similar. This should be applied at three to five times the rate specified for straight nitrogen fertilizers such as ammonium nitrate and ammonium sulfate (see Table VIII).

Minor elements may be required, too. Magnesium deficiencies are especially common.

Other care depends on what you grow.

Building trellises. Several of the small fruits are best grown on trellises. These are all constructed in the same way, although the designs may vary to some extent.

For posts, use 4 x 4-in. timbers or 4-in.-diameter poles. If you cannot get hold of black locust or cedar poles or don't want to spend the money for redwood, buy pine or fir posts that have been pressure-treated at the mill with wood preservative. Set the end posts in a trellis 3 ft. into the ground; others, 2 ft. You may have to guy the end posts in a grape trellis.

No. 12 galvanized wire is generally strong enough, but No. 9 is usually required for the top support wires in grape trellises.

BEACH PLUMS

Beach plums are 6 ft. deciduous shrubs which produce in late summer numerous clusters of small purplish plums with a heavy bloom. These are used to make superb jelly and jam. Grow in Zones 6–8 near the ocean. They are particularly common on Cape Cod. Self-fruitful.

Culture

Dig up plants from the wild or buy them from a nursery (which probably dug them up from the wild). Plant in sandy soil of average quality. The shrubs need full sun but little attention otherwise. It won't hurt, however, to water them in long dry spells, fertilize them lightly with balanced plant food in the early spring, and keep dead, broken, and unnecessarily thick growth cut out.

Beach plums start to bear in two or three years. Harvest fruits any time after they reach the almost-ripe stage.

BLACKBERRIES

Blackberries are vigorous, thorny, deciduous plants producing large, black, rather seedy but delicious fruits in midsummer. They form two types of plants which differ considerably in hardiness. Erect or semi-erect types grow in Zones 5–8. Trailing types—commonly called dewberries—grow in Zones 7–8. Self-fruitful.

Varieties

Bailey. Erect. A good midseason variety but not the equal of Darrow. Susceptible to orange rust.

Boysen. Also called Boysenberry. Trailing. Very large berries with a reddish-purple cast and excellent flavor. Big seeds. Susceptible to some diseases and inclined to be a shy bearer but does well if you fuss over it. A thornless strain is available.

Brazos. Erect type originated in Texas and recommended only for warmer climates. Exceptionally large berries good for processing as well as eating fresh. Very early.

Darrow. About the best erect type. Large, top-quality berries ripen early and over a long period—even into the fall. Very productive.

Early Harvest. Erect. Good, medium-size berries. Early. Hardy from Zone 6 southward. Recommended in a number of Midwestern states. Susceptible to orange rust.

Early Wonder. Erect. Medium-size fruits produced in great numbers early in the season. Less thorny than some varieties. For warmer climates.

Flint. Semi-erect. Large, jet-black fruits ripening in midseason and over a six-week period. For warmer climates.

Humble. Erect but inclined to trail. Large, sweet fruits recommended only for home gardens because they are too soft to ship. Early. Rapid grower. For warmer climates.

Jerseyblack. Semi-trailing. Medium-large, firm berries on very productive and thorny plants. Zone 7 and southward.

Lucretia. Trailing. Large berries of good quality. Early. Susceptible to anthracnose and leaf spot. A little hardier than Boysen and Young.

Smoothstem. Erect. Medium-large berries ripen late and continue for a long time. Thornless plant is very productive. Zones 6–8.

Thornfree. Erect. Medium-large, semi-firm, semi-acid berries ripen late. Plant is thornless.

Young. Also called Youngberry. Trailing. Delicious, large berries with only a few big seeds. Early. Vigorous plant is very prickly.

Culture

Buy plants that are certified to be free of disease. Or you can propagate your own plants in many cases by layering the tips of canes of established plants or by taking ¼-in. root cuttings. If a variety is difficult to propagate one way, try it the other way.

Grow blackberries in full sun in a spot that has good air drainage. The area should not have been planted in earlier years to raspberries, blackberries, tomatoes, potatoes, eggplants, or peppers. Kill all wild brambles within several hundred feet.

Blackberries are planted with the same precautions as red raspberries and are spaced and grown in the same way. Erect varieties do not require supporting, but are better with it; trailing varieties are definitely better with it. If grown in hedgerows, space the plants 4 ft. apart in rows 6 ft. wide.

Blackberries are produced on two-year-old growth. They generally require no pruning during the first year after planting, but if they do not appear to be sending out very many lateral branches, summer pruning as below is essential.

From the second year on, pruning of erect varieties is started in early spring. At that time, you should cut out the weak canes leaving the strong canes 4 to 6 in. apart. You should also remove weak or dead laterals and cut back the remaining laterals to 12 to 18 in. In summer, when the new shoots put up from the base of an unsupported plant reach 30 in., pinch out the growing tips to force them to branch out. Supported plants are pinched when they reach 36 to 40 in. Immediately after harvest, cut out the canes which bore fruit to make room for new ones. (The summer and post-harvest pruning operations often coincide.)

Trailing and semi-erect blackberries require less pruning. Just remove the fruit-bearing canes after harvest and thin out some of the others if crowded. Then, in early spring, remove all but eight to twelve of the best canes, tie them to their trellis, and head them back to about 5 ft.

Always burn the wood you cut out. This is the best and easiest way to keep pests under control, but does not obviate the need for spraying as for red raspberries.

In recent years some blackberry varieties have shown disturbing signs of sterility. The plants that are affected make good growth and bloom profusely, but set only a few malformed berries. Such plants should be rogued out as soon as you discover them. They will not infect other plants, but are a waste of good garden space.

BLUEBERRIES

Blueberries are handsome deciduous shrubs producing their increasingly popular fruits in the summer. There are three types. The highbush varieties, growing to 12 ft. and the most widely planted, grow in Zones 5–7. Rabbiteye varieties, reaching 15 ft., grow in Zones 7–9. Lowbush blueberries, which are only 2 ft. tall and are rarely cultivated except in eastern Canada, grow in Zones 3–5.

Blueberries are generally self-unfruitful. For best fruit production, plant two different varieties of the same type.

Varieties

Bluecrop. Large clusters of large, very light blue berries. Midseason. You can count on it to be productive. One of the hardiest varieties, it is worth a trial in Zone 4.

Collins. Much like Earliblue but ripens about a week later.

Concord. Big, rather dark blue berries of very good quality. Very hardy.

Coville. Very late variety with unusually large berries that are tart and light blue. Productive.

Darrow. Like Coville but more consistently productive.

Earliblue. The best extra-early variety. Large, light blue berries in medium clusters. Upright plant.

Herbert. Excellent for the home garden. Exceptionally large, delicious, medium blue berries in big clusters. Rather late.

Jersey. Old favorite planted more widely than other varieties. Very hardy and reliable. Big, light blue berries. Midseason.

Pemberton. Extremely vigorous and always productive. Good, big, dark blue berries. Midseason.

Rubel. If, like many people, you have a feeling that the great big blueberries we so often see today are not the best, this variety discovered in the Michigan wilds will be to your liking. The berries are small but ever so numerous.

Tifblue. A rabbiteye variety. Large, bright blue berries of very good quality. Considered a midseason variety in the deep South, where it ripens from late May through June.

Woodard. Another first-rate, midseason rabbiteye variety. Very big, medium blue, tasty berries.

Culture

Among fruits, blueberries are unusual in demanding a soil with a pH of 4.0 to 5.2. They can be grown in sweeter soil only if given continuous extraordinary care. Lowering soil pH can be done by mixing in sulfur every spring to a depth of about 6 in. Use no more than ¼ cup per plant in sandy soil; ½ cup in heavier soil; and to avoid injury to the roots, it is a good idea to apply it in several small doses a week or so apart. But even this treatment is uncertain if you start out with a heavy clay soil with a normal pH of 6.0 or higher.

In the long run, the best way to give blueberries a satisfactorily acid soil is to mix the soil in the planting hole with an equal volume of well-rotted oak leaves, well-rotted pine needles, peat, or sawdust. Keep the plants mulched heavily with one of these materials. This treatment makes almost any soil, except one with a neutral or alkaline reaction, right for blueberries. But there is one further requirement: The soil must be well drained.

Plant blueberries in full sun in a spot with good air circulation. Avoid frost pockets. If plants are set in the lawn or on the edges of a shrubbery border, give each one a space 6 ft. across. In the berry patch, space plants 6 ft. apart in rows 6 ft. wide.

Start with two-year-old plants and plant them at the depth at which they grew in the nursery. Spread the roots out well in large holes. Keep watered.

Fertilize new plants after they start making strong growth. At that time apply ¼ cup of ammonium sulfate. Thereafter make two applications annually—one in early spring and the other about six weeks later. In the second year apply a total of ½ cup in two equal doses; in the third year, ¾ cup; in the fourth year, 1 cup; in the fifth year, 1½ cups; and in the sixth and all subsequent years, 2 cups.

Cut the tops of plants back one third at planting. During the next two years remove weak, low-hanging branches. Continue this practice in subsequent years. In addition, you should cut out at the base all but six to eight sturdy, upright canes. These should be divided between two one-year-old canes, two two-year-olds, two three-year-olds, and two four-year-olds.

Keep suckers and weak, twiggy growth pruned out. And to prevent plants from setting huge crops of tiny berries, cut back some of the new shoot growth bearing large numbers of the big, plump, round fruit buds. Another way to reduce the number of fruit buds is simply to rub off the buds, leaving one for each 3 in. of shoot growth.

All pruning is done in late winter or early spring.

Birds are the worst pests of blueberries, but will give no trouble if you cover the plants with netting. Spray or dust for other problems if and when they arise—which is not often.

Blueberries start bearing at two to three years of age and reach maximum production at about six years. Pick berries two or three days after they become fully colored if you want maximum sweetness. Berries can, however, be left on the plant for a few days after they are fully ripe: They do not deteriorate so rapidly as blackberries or raspberries. After harvesting, store them in the refrigerator.

CURRANTS

Currants are deciduous shrubs to 6 ft. They produce small, red, black, or white berries in midsummer. These are used mainly for jelly. Grow in Zones 3–8, but do best in the colder climates. Self-fruitful.

Currants—especially black currants—are alternate hosts for the white pine blister rust which kills white pines. Many of the states in which white pines flourish forbid planting of currants, and you should, therefore, check with your state agricultural extension service or forestry department before considering this fruit. This does not mean, however, that if you buy a property on which currants and pines are already growing, you must instantly rip out the currants. If there has been no trouble with the pines so far, the spores of the disease are not present in the area. But if one of your neighbors should innocently plant an infected currant or gooseberry, then your currants and white pines would probably become infected, too.

Varieties

Boskoop Giant. Black currant especially recommended for the home because of the fine quality and large size of its fruit. But not so productive as other varieties.

Cascade. Red currant. Popular, old variety with big berries in compact clusters.

Perfection. Big, bright red berries on a somewhat spreading bush. Fairly productive.

Red Lake. First-rate, large, red berries in big clusters hang on long after ripening. Vigorous, upright plant.

Viking. Red currant. Productive and late. May be immune to the white pine blister rust.

White Grape. Medium-size, white berries in clusters which don't always fill out. The standard white variety but less good than the next.

White Imperial. The best of the white-fruited varieties.

Wilder. One of the choice varieties. Dark, red berries on a big, upright, productive plant. Early.

Culture

You can easily propagate currants by mounding the soil up about 6 to 8 in. over the base of the canes in the spring. In summer, roots will form on the canes. These can then be cut from the plant very early the following spring and planted where they are to grow.

Whether you propagate your own plants or buy them, cut the tops back at planting to about 8 in. Set the plants 1 or 2 in. deeper than they previously grew, spread the roots well, and firm the soil around them. This forces plants to develop a bush form rather than have only one stem.

Although they are hardy, currants must be planted where they will not be nipped by late spring freezes. Planting on the north side of a building or hedge or on a north slope keeps them from bursting into bloom too early and also gives them some protection from summer heat, which they hate. In warmer climates plants should grow in partial shade. Space plants 4 ft. apart in rows 6 ft. wide, or 5 ft. apart in rows 5 ft. wide.

The ideal soil is rich, rather heavy, moisture-retentive, and well drained. However, currants grow well in average soil and even in rather light soil if you mix in plenty of humus.

Fertilize new plants after they have made good growth with a handful of balanced fertilizer, such as 10-10-10. Increase to two handfuls early the following spring. Thereafter apply ½ cup of nitrate of soda or 1½ cups of balanced fertilizer every year.

Prune in late winter. In the second year after planting, cut out all but six or eight of the strongest canes. In the third year, cut out all but four or five one-year-old canes and three or four two-year-old canes. From the fourth year on, you should prune so that each plant starts the growing season with three each of one-, two-, and three-year-old canes. Keep the upright canes, not those growing more or less horizontally.

Red and white currants produce some fruit on one-year-old canes, but produce their best fruit on two- and three-year-old canes. Four-year-old and older canes are more or less fruitless. Black currants produce their best fruit on one-year-old canes. You should, therefore, prune out all but six to eight canes of this age every spring.

The most troublesome pests—and they are rarely much of a nuisance —are cane borers, aphids, black-spotted currant worms, anthracnose, and cane blight. When pruning, look for hollow stems which indicate the presence of borers, and then cut out those with enlarged nodes (a sign that the canes are infested). Spray with a general-purpose fruit spray containing ferbam rather than captan when plants are fully leafed out and two weeks later.

Currants start to bear when three years of age. Those used for jelly are picked just before they are fully ripe. But if you don't pick them then, don't worry: The berries will hang on the plant for several weeks without deteriorating. Don't leave picked fruit in the sun.

ELDERBERRIES

There are numerous species of elders. Those raised for food are deciduous shrubs to 15 ft. with large clusters of small, sweet, blue, purple, or red fruits with exceptionally high Vitamin C content. These ripen from late summer to midautumn and even later in warm climates. They are used in jam, jelly, pies, and wine.

Elders grow in Zones 3–9. Partially self-unfruitful; plant two or more varieties to assure fruit production.

Varieties

Adams No. 1. Very juicy, purple berries excellent for pies. Late. Heavy producer. Zones 5–8.

Johns. Produces more fruit than other varieties. Very large clusters of medium-size, purple-black, juicy berries. Early. Big plant. Zones 5–8.

Nova. Big producer, having a large number of medium-size clusters bearing small, purple-black fruits. Especially good for jelly. Zones 5–8.

Redman. Bright red fruits on compact plants. Developed in Manitoba, it grows northward into Zone 3.

Superb. Originated by Luther Burbank at Santa Rosa, California. Blue fruits are produced right through the fall. They are blander than other varieties but good for cooking. When dried, they resemble raisins. Zones 6–9.

York. Unusually big, productive plant with very big berries. Late.

Culture

Elderberries are most easily propagated by dormant hardwood cuttings 10 to 18 in. long and with three sets of opposite buds. Early in the spring the entire cutting is buried in the ground with only the top buds showing.

Plant rooted plants in well-drained soil with a good humus content. Space plants 8 to 10 ft. apart in rows 8 to 10 ft. wide. Do not mulch: studies made in Pennsylvania indicate that elders grown in cultivated, weedfree soil produce more heavily. This means, however, that the soil dries out more quickly, so you must water the plants more often in dry weather.

Fertilize in the spring with ammonium nitrate at the rate of ⅛ cup per year of plant age up to a maximum of 2 cups. The alternative is to use 2 cups of 5-20-10 fertilizer per year of plant age up to a maximum of 8 cups.

Prune in early spring. Cut out all but five or six vigorous, erect, one-year-old canes and one or two two-year-old canes. All these canes should be grouped within a 2-ft. circle. At the same time trim 6 to 8 in. off the tips of the laterals on the older canes. Burn all trimmings to destroy borers which may be in them.

Pests include birds, cane borers, mildew, and mites, but are usually not troublesome enough to worry about.

Elderberries start to bear when two or three years of age. Allow fruits to ripen on the plant before picking. Cook or process soon afterwards.

GOOSEBERRIES

Gooseberries are very spiny, deciduous shrubs to 4 ft. with tart, green, or red berries in midsummer. These are used in pies and jam and are sometimes eaten fresh. Grow in Zones 3–8 but do best in the colder areas. Self-fruitful.

Gooseberries are alternate hosts for the white pine blister rust and planting is prohibited in some states. See the introductory note under currants.

Varieties

Note. American varieties are healthier and more productive and generally better adapted to conditions in the United States than European varieties. The latter have larger, more flavorful fruit, however.

Chautauqua. Large, greenish-yellow berries on a small, somewhat spreading bush. Fairly early.

Downing. Medium-size, green fruits of excellent quality. Very productive plant. Probably the most widely planted American variety.

Fredonia. A European variety with very large, dark red berries. Late.

Glendale. Medium-size, dull red berries on a big, vigorous plant. Bush withstands heat better than other varieties and is accordingly recommended especially for warmer zones.

Pixwell. Widely planted in the North Central states. Medium-large, green berries turn red when ripe. Heavy yielder. The plant is not too thorny.

Culture

Propagate, grow, and prune like currants. However, the plants need even better air circulation than currants to help protect them against powdery mildew. Also to control mildew, spray the plants frequently with sulfur during humid weather.

Gooseberries start bearing at three years of age. Wear gloves when you harvest the fruit. Berries to be used in pies and jams should be picked at full size but before they turn reddish-brown and become fully ripe. Berries can be left on the plants for several weeks without deteriorating.

GRAPES—BUNCH

Bunch grapes—also called American grapes—are mainly descended from the fox grape native to the East and from the frost grape. They form large (to 50 ft. if not controlled), vigorous, woody vines with handsome deciduous foliage and tendrils that twine around anything within reach. The large bunches of luscious, usually slip-skin fruits mature in midsummer in warm climates; late summer and early fall farther north.

Bunch grapes grow in Zones 3–10, but are at their best in Zones 5–7. They do not do well in arid areas, areas with very short growing seasons, areas with extremely low temperatures or areas with high temperatures combined with very high humidity. They are generally self-fruitful.

Varieties

Note. Varieties listed here are keyed to a special regional map prepared by the U.S. Department of Agriculture and reproduced on page 211.

Beta. Small, black berries good for juice and jelly but not of table quality. Early. Regions 1 and 5.

Blue Jay. Small, blue berries for juice and jelly; also good to eat fresh if fully ripe. Very hardy. Region 1. Self-unfruitful.

Blue Lake. Blue grape with unusual flavor recommended for home use in making jelly and juice. A Florida development. Region 4.

A gooseberry before and after pruning. Plant at left had not been touched in years and bore only a few fruits. At right, old canes have been cut out at ground level to give new canes a chance. Several of the small fruits, along with gooseberries, are pruned to leave only a few young canes.

Brighton. Delicious, midseason, red variety. Fruit and clusters of medium size. Self-unfruitful. Regions 2 and 3.

Catawba. Medium-size, purplish-red berries delicious fresh but more often made into wine. Late. Regions 2, 3, and 4.

Champanel. Black berries of medium size good for juice. Late. Vigorous vines should be spaced and pruned like muscadine grapes. Region 4.

Concord. The standard bunch grape to which all others are compared. Most widely planted; thrives in every region except 1 and 5. Large, black fruits of delicious flavor ripen in midseason. Adapts to many soils but subject to chlorosis in those which are alkaline.

Delaware. An outstanding grape by any standard. Small, light red, and early. Great for eating and wine making. Stores well. Fairly weak vine but quite productive. Regions 2, 3, 4, and 6.

Ellen Scott. Excellent variety for the drier parts of Regions 3 and 6. Tender, juicy, blue fruits. Late. Susceptible to anthracnose.

Extra. Big, blue fruits with a flavor like that of the wild post oak grape, from which it is descended. Region 4; especially popular in the Southeast.

Fredonia. Big, black berries much like Concord but two weeks earlier. Regions 2, 3, and 4.

Golden Muscat. Popular home-grown, yellow variety of a mild but very pleasant flavor. Unusually large berries. Regions 3, 6, and 7.

Himrod. Fine, greenish-white, seedless variety very similar to Interlaken Seedless but a few days later. Not a slipskin. Regions 2, 3, and 6.

Interlaken Seedless. Earliest seedless variety. Small, greenish-white berries almost as good to eat as Thompson seedless, from which it is descended. Birds love them. Not a slipskin. Vigorous, productive, hardy vine. Regions 2, 3, and 6. Especially recommended for Washington and milder parts of New York.

Isabella. A large, purplish-black, Concord-like grape. The only variety recommended for Hawaii. Also grows in Region 8 and the warmest parts of 4. A bud sport—the Pierce—is recommended by the Arizona Agricultural Extension Service.

Lake Emerald. Developed in Florida. Green to golden fruits for the table and wine-making. Region 4.

Moore Early. A Concord-like, purplish-black variety that ripens early. Good quality but not outstanding. Region 2.

Niabell. Large, blue grape developed in California. Eat it fresh or turn it into wine. Regions 7 and 8.

Niagara. Top white variety (actually yellowish-green). Big fruits that you are bound to enjoy. Midseason. Not so hardy as Concord but grows in Regions 2, 3, 4, 6, and 7.

Norton. Small, blue fruits that produce a marvelous juice or wine. Slow-growing vine but hardy and vigorous. Region 3.

Ontario. Another good white variety for the table and jelly-making. Very early. Region 2.

Portland. The U.S. Department of Agriculture rates this as "probably the best very early variety for home planting." Large, white fruits with tender skins. Zones 2 and 3.

Seneca. Small, white fruits in big clusters. Luscious. Early. Requires more care than some other varieties. Region 2.

Van Buren. Rated as the earliest good Concord-like variety. Medium-size, blue fruits. Region 2; worth a trial in 1.

Worden. A Concord seedling that ripens a bit earlier. Big, purplish-black berries of high quality but with a tendency to crack. Regions 2, 3, 6, and 7.

Culture

You can propagate your own grape vines by layering vigorous one-year-old canes in the spring. These should be well rooted and ready for planting the following spring. The easier alternative is to buy one-year-old plants with good root systems.

Plant grapes in a sunny location with good air drainage. In colder climates you should also take pains to select a location that is protected from winter winds. The soil should be well drained (but not too sandy), reasonably fertile, full of humus, and have pH of 5.5 to 6.5. Dig large, deep holes for your plants because they put down very deep roots. Spread out the roots, firm the soil around them, and water well. Remove all but one vigorous cane and cut it back to eight buds. The vines should be spaced 8 to 10 ft. apart in rows 5 ft. wide.

Mulch with organic matter. Water in dry weather, but reduce the supply somewhat in late summer in order to reduce shoot growth and to aid in the maturing of fruit and canes. In the fall, after harvest, give the vines another heavy irrigation to help protect them against winter injury.

Vines that are growing well do not require feeding; and even those that are not doing so well as they should require only light feeding. Use ammonium nitrate and apply it in early spring at the rate of ½ cup per plant or less.

Because grapes form large, heavy plants that are easily banged around by the wind, they must be grown on very sturdy trellises. Space the posts 20 ft. apart. Brace the end posts well. Use No. 9 galvanized wire for the top wire or wires; No. 10 or 12 wire for lower wires. Run the wires through holes drilled through the posts so they will be well supported and can be tightened from time to time. The slightly easier but less desirable alternative is to attach the wires to the posts with heavy staples which are left loose enough so the wires can be tightened.

The actual design of the trellis depends on the training and pruning system you use.

All pruning is done in late winter, and it must be quite severe if you want strong vines producing large clusters of first-class fruit. Grapes are produced on pencil-size shoots which grow during the current year from canes that developed the previous year. As the Wisconsin Agricultural Extension Service points out: "High production of good quality fruit depends on (1)

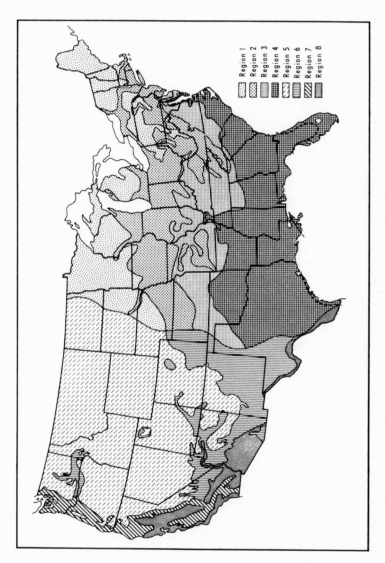

This map prepared by the U.S. Department of Agriculture shows where the varieties of bunch grape listed in this chapter grow.

balancing the fruit load with the productive potential of the vine and (2) on providing for new fruiting canes for the following year."

The most commonly used training system is the Four-Arm Kniffin System. This requires a trellis in which one wire is secured to the posts at a height of 30 in. and a second wire is secured 30 in. higher. If you want a slightly larger crop of fruit or if you live in a climate with a short growing season, increase the above-ground height of the posts to 6 ft. and set the top wire about 42 in. above the bottom. This exposes the vines to more sunlight.

Erect the trellis before or soon after the vines are planted, and plant the vines between the posts. Plants set against the posts might be injured by the preservative used on the posts and they would almost certainly be injured when the posts were replaced.

During the first year, when the two uppermost shoots put out on the cane you keep are an inch long, rub off all the others below. In the second spring, cut out the less vigorous of these shoots, tie the other to the top wire, and cut it off just above the wire. If the cane does not reach the top wire, tie it to the bottom wire and then tie it to the top wire the following season. This cane becomes the trunk of the vine.

During the third or fourth spring select four strong canes for the arms. Two should be at the top wire on the left and right of the trunk; two at the bottom wire on either side of the trunk. Cut them back to ten buds and tie them to the wires. Then select four other canes that originate close to the four arms and cut these back to two or three buds. These are your renewal spurs. The canes that grow from them will provide the arms for the following year. Remove all other growth from the vine.

Pruning in subsequent years is done in the same way. You select four vigorous young canes for the arms, and four other canes for renewal spurs; and you cut out the arms that produced fruit the preceding season and all other growth. The best canes to use for arms are more than $\frac{1}{4}$ in. in diameter and have buds spaced no more than 7 in. apart.

How much you should cut back the fruiting arms at time of pruning depends on how vigorously the vine is growing. The most accurate way of determining this is to rough-prune the vines, weigh the prunings, and then leave a certain number of buds for the first pound of prunings and an additional number for each additional pound. But this is troublesome for home gardeners who are not trying, in effect, to milk their grapevines of every last berry. A simpler approach is to make an educated guess about the vine's vigor. If it is weak, leave only ten buds on each fruiting arm. If it is strong, leave 15 buds or even two or three more.

In the Umbrella Kniffin System the same type of trellis is used and each vine is grown to a single trunk extending to the upper wire. In the third or fourth spring, choose two to four of the canes near the top of the trunk for arms. If you have two arms, cut them back to 20 buds each; if you have four arms, cut them back to ten buds each. Then loop the arms over the top wire, bend them sharply down to the bottom wire, and tie the ends securely. Save two to four more canes for renewal spurs and cut them back to two buds. Remove all other growth.

The Munson Training System is especially suited to humid climates since the fruit is high above ground where it is exposed to more air movement and is less subject to disease. The trellis is made by nailing 2-ft. cross-arms to the posts 5 ft. above ground. Two wires are attached to the ends of the cross-arms and a third wire is attached to the posts about 8 in. below.

The vine is trained to a single trunk up to the low wire. Two canes are then converted into arms which are tied to the low wire; two more are cut back to form renewal spurs; and all others are removed. The shoots developing from the arms are draped over the outer wires. As in other systems, the renewal spurs provide the arms for the following season.

The Modified Chautauqua System is for cold climates where it is necessary to protect semi-hardy grape vines. The trellis has three wires attached to posts at 12, 28, and 44 in. above the ground.

In the fall following planting—after the vine has gone dormant—remove all but one vigorous cane, cut that back to 30 in., lay it on the ground, and cover with 6 in. of soil to protect it against winter damage. The following spring, uncover the cane, angle it up to the bottom wire, and tie it. Shoots put out during the summer are tied to the two upper wires.

In the second fall, cut the shoots back to two-bud spurs, but don't touch the one at the end of the trunk. Untie the vine, lay it on the ground, and again cover with soil.

Over the following years, the same procedure is followed except that you cut back all shoots arising from the trunk. The end-of-trunk cane that you saved in the second fall is allowed to grow and become an exten-

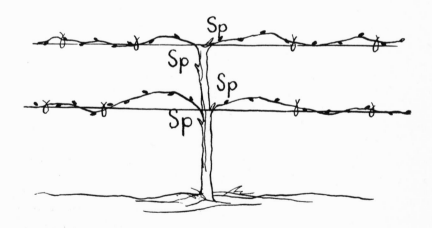

Four-Arm Kniffin System of training grape vines. "Sp" indicates the renewal spurs that will replace this year's branches next year.

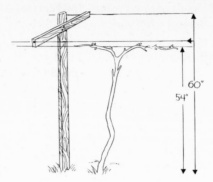

Munson Training System.

sion of the trunk. The maximum length of the trunk should be approximately 7 ft. In time, if the trunk gets too stiff to be covered in the winter, it should be replaced with a new trunk.

The Geneva Double Curtain System is a new system developed in New York to increase a vine's exposure to the sun and thus improve fruit yield and quality. It is recommended especially for such vigorous varieties as Catawba, Concord, Delaware, and Niagara.

In the trellis, posts are spaced 24 ft. apart (and vines 8 ft. apart). Four-foot cross-arms are secured to each post at about 6 ft. above the ground. Two wires are attached to the ends of the cross-arms and a third wire to the posts 52 in. above ground.

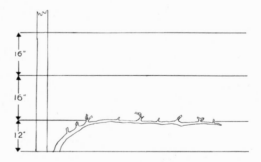

Modified Chautauqua Training System.

The vine is trained to two trunks which are tied first to the bottom wire and then to one of the top wires. (The neighboring vines are tied to the other top wire; thus each plant has about 16 ft. of wire to grow on.) One cane at the tip of each trunk is chosen to become a cordon, or permanent extension of the trunk. These are trained in opposite directions and tied to the top wire.

In spring, strong canes put out from the cordons are cut back to five buds, and additional canes are cut back to one bud to form renewal spurs.

Shoots arising from the canes during the growing season are draped over the top wires and downward to form a solid curtain of foliage on both sides of the trellis.

Vines grown on arbors are generally less productive than those trained to any of the preceding systems; but their appeal in the home landscape is undeniable. For best results, stretch two or three horizontal wires along the sides of the arbor and cover the top with a network of wires or with very open mesh. Train the vines to single trunks which extend up and slightly over the top of the arbor. Allow arms to develop along the side wires as in the Four-Arm Kniffin System; and allow an additional pair of arms to develop at the top of the arbor. Replace these arms each year.

Geneva Double Curtain System. A shows the cordons; B, the canes; C, the renewal spurs.

Another way to train a vine on an arbor is to allow the trunk to grow to the height of the arbor and then to develop three or four large horizontal branches, or cordons, radiating in all directions from the trunk. Canes growing from these put out shoots which produce fruit. Annual pruning is similar to that in the Geneva Double Curtain System.

If it becomes necessary at some time to renew a vine because it is injured or becomes unproductive, the job is easily done by selecting as a new trunk one of the canes that arise at the base of the vine. Train this up to the top wire as you did the original trunk. Then over a two-year period allow the growth developing from the new trunk to replace that from the old. Finally, cut out the old trunk entirely.

If a vine that has just started to make growth in the spring is nipped by a late frost, cut off *all* the new growth, whether injured or not. The vine will then make second growth and you should have a partial crop. However, if the vine is hit by frost after its first growth is several inches long, leave it alone. You may or may not get a partial crop.

Don't be alarmed if your grape vines bleed when you prune them. This does not harm the the plants or their fruiting ability.

Grape vines which are exposed to moving air and properly cared for are not bothered greatly by pests. But to guard against unexpected trouble, it is well to apply a dormant oil spray in late winter; then apply a general-purpose fruit spray when new shoots are 8 in. long, just before the vines bloom, right after bloom and two weeks after that. If Japanese beetles start to ravage your vines (which they seem to crave), spray repeatedly with Sevin. Birds can be held at bay by throwing netting over the vines or by tying paper bags around the fruit bunches.

Grape vines may start to bear the second season after planting, but you would be smart to follow the commercial grower's practice of letting the plants grow one more year before setting fruit. This produces stronger vines.

Pick berries when a taste test tells you they are fully ripe. Skin color is not always an indicator of ripeness. Grapes picked before they are ripe do not, like other fruits, continue to get sweeter. Those picked long after they have ripened may crack and start to rot.

When picking, hold the clusters gently in your hand and cut the stems with shears. Store the fruit in the refrigerator.

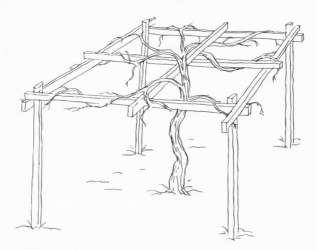

This is a common way of training grapes on arbors in Hawaii: three or four large branches radiate in all directions from the trunk. It is a simple system which can be used anywhere.

GRAPES—MUSCADINE

Muscadine grapes form very large, vigorous vines (to 90 ft.) on which the grapes grow singly or in loose clusters. They ripen in late summer and well into the fall. Grow in Zones 7–9.

Most varieties have imperfect flowers and in the past they had to be pollinated by male plants if they were to bear fruit. In 1946, however, a perfect-flowered (self-fruitful) variety was introduced; and since then several others have come along. So you can now plant these alone; or you can use them instead of non-producing male vines to pollinate the self-unfruitful varieties (which have better fruit than the self-fruitful varieties).

Though very attractive, grapes on arbors are less productive than those on trellises because, like the vines here, they are not pruned so severely as they should be.

Varieties

Burgaw. Fair to good, reddish-black, musty-flavored fruits. Self-fruitful and a good pollinator.

Creek. Slightly tart, reddish-purple berries good for juice and wine-making. Late. Self-unfruitful.

Dearing. Very sweet, medium-size, white fruits. Flavor superior to that of other perfect-flowered varieties. Self-fruitful; a good pollinator.

Dulcet. Red-purple berries of small size, but sweet and delicious. Early. Self-unfruitful.

Higgins. Very productive new variety with large, bronze fruits. Late. Self-unfruitful.

Hunt. Excellent, all-purpose, large, black grapes. Early. Favorite for jelly and jam. Self-unfruitful.

Magoon. Small, black fruits of excellent quality. Early. Self-fruitful.

Scuppernong. Oldest and best known variety. Bronze-skinned fruits in small clusters. Distinctive flavor. Early. Self-unfruitful.

Thomas. Another old variety. Small to medium-size, reddish-black fruits of excellent quality and very sweet. Very good for juice. Midseason. Self-unfruitful.

Topsail. Medium-large, greenish-bronze fruits are the sweetest of all muscadines. Midseason. Vigorous grower. Self-unfruitful.

Culture

Muscadines are one of the easiest fruits you can grow, but they require plenty of space.

Although they thrive in many kinds of soil, make sure it is well drained and mix in a good quantity of humus. Dig large holes 18 in. deep. Space plants 20 ft. apart in rows 6 ft. wide.

Grow like bunch grapes.

Train the vines to a vertical two-wire trellis similar to that used in the Four-Arm Kniffin System for bunch grapes. During the first two years, prune each plant in the summer and winter to form a main trunk with four strong arms. The latter should not be cut back until they meet the arms of the neighboring vines. From then on, annual pruning consists of removing dead wood, side growth on the trunk, and tendrils that encircle the arms and trunk. Thin out weak canes, and cut all others back to two or three buds.

In warmest climates, annual pruning is best done within six weeks after the first killing frost. Vines do not bleed at this time. In colder areas, it is better to delay pruning until early spring. The vines will bleed badly at this time, but research has established that this does not damage the plants.

If one of the vine's four arms dies and needs to be replaced at any time, cut if off and train the largest cane growing from the trunk near the dead arm's base as a replacement. You can also replace the trunk by training a strong shoot arising from its base to the trellis, and then establishing new arms.

Muscadines grown on an arbor are trained in the same way except that the trunk must extend 6 to 7 ft. up before it is allowed to branch out. The wires to which the arms are trained run the length of the trellis and are laid side by side rather than one above the other.

Muscadine grapes have few pests and there are some years when spraying is unnecessary. In other years, you should spray with an insecticide such as malathion or a fungicide such as captan when trouble appears.

The vines start to bear at three years of age. Pick berries when ripe and use them soon because they deteriorate rather quickly.

GRAPES — VINIFERA

Also called European grapes, because they originated in the Old World and were grown there for centuries before their introduction to California by the Spanish priests. These are generally considered to have the finest fruits for table eating and for wine-making. Some varieties are also used for raisins. The berries are produced in very large clusters. Skins and pulp are inseparable.

The vinifera grapes do best where the summers are long, warm, and dry and the winters cool; but thanks to the development of new hardier varieties, some can now be grown in Zones 6–10. In California, where they are at their best, they ripen from late spring to midautumn, depending on the variety and location. Self-fruitful.

Varieties

Alicante Bouschet. Medium-size, brilliantly black berries with red juice. Midseason. Used for wine.

Black Monukka. Berries seedless, reddish-black to black, small to medium size, and with pleasing flavor. The clusters are large and very long. Midseason.

Cardinal. Big berries are a rich, dark red and have a slight Muscat flavor which improves as they become fully ripe. Early.

Csaba. Medium-small, yellowish-white fruits with a slight Muscat flavor. Very early. One of the hardiest varieties.

Delight. A good table grape. Berries seedless, oval, dark greenish-yellow, and with a slight Muscat flavor.

Exotic. Medium-large, crisp, blue berries on a very vigorous vine.

Flame Tokay. Beautiful, very large, red fruits after midseason. A superb table grape. Plant is productive but rather tender.

Muscat Hamburg. Recommended only for the home garden. Rather small, green berries of fine flavor and aroma.

Johannesberg Riesling. Medium-size, greenish-yellow fruits with russet spots. Fairly early.

Muscat of Alexandria. Large, oval, dull green grapes with Muscat flavor. Rather late. Used as a table grape, for wine and raisins. Tender.

Perlette. Extremely vigorous, productive seedless grape ripening very early. The yellow to pale green berries are a third larger than Thompson Seedless. Big, compact clusters. Vine slow to develop but increases in growth rate as it ages.

Seibel 5279. Early, pink-white grape for dessert use and wine-making. Hardy; grows in Zone 6 and southward.

Thompson Seedless. Famous green to yellow, sweet, seedless grape used for all purposes. The vine has excellent vigor and produces a lot of fruit early in the season.

Zinfandel. Famous wine grape. Berries are medium-size and reddish to black. Fairly early.

Culture

Vinifera grapes are susceptible to a deadly pest named *phylloxera viti-folia,* so be sure to buy vines which are grafted on to resistant rootstocks. Grow like bunch grapes.

In warm climates, most vinifera grapes are trained to the Four-Arm Kniffin System (although it is usually called the Long-Cane System). However, some varieties such as Csaba, Cardinal, Perlette, and Exotic are trained to the Spur System. This varies but is essentially a Four-Arm Kniffin System in which the arms are permanent rather than renewable. Each arm has six to eight vertical fruiting spurs containing two or three buds apiece. The buds produce the shoots on which fruit clusters are borne.

In colder climates, where the more tender varieties need to be taken down from the trellis and covered with soil in the winter, vines should be trained either to the Modified Chautauqua System or to the Fan System. In the latter, the vines have very short trunks and two short arms from which two to four canes fan upward on a conventional two-wire trellis.

Fruit thinning is recommended for vinifera grapes, which are unusually heavy producers, to improve the size of the fruit. On varieties that have loose or straggly fruit clusters, the usual practice is to remove some of the immature flower clusters which appear with the new growth in early spring. On varieties with very large or compact fruit clusters (Thompson Seedless and Perlette, for example), thinning is done by removing individual berries right after the fruit is set.

All vines can also be improved by removing entire fruit clusters soon after the fruits are set. Depending on the size and vigor of the vine, you can reduce the number of clusters to 20 or 30 per vine.

To control powdery mildew, one of the most common diseases of vinifera grapes, dust vines with sulfur when the shoots are 6 to 8 in. long and again when they are 18 to 24 in. long. Several additional applications at two-week intervals may be made.

HAWTHORN

Several hawthorns produce red fruits which are made into an excellent jelly. The best known of these is the Mayhaw *(Crataegus aestivalis),* a 30-ft. tree growing in Zones 7–9. Its fruit ripens in mid- and late spring.

C. arnoldiana, also 30 ft., grows in Zones 5–6 and ripens its fruit in late summer. *C. mollis,* 30 ft., grows in Zones 5–7 and ripens its unusually large fruit in late summer and early fall. All three trees are deciduous and self-fruitful.

Culture

Although hawthorns can be grown from seed, the process takes a long time. Buy plants instead in early spring. Plant in full sun in average, well-drained soil. For best development, give each tree a space about 18 ft. across.

Water deeply in dry weather. Fertilize newly set-out trees with a cup of balanced fertilizer, and increase the amount each year until you reach 4 cups. The trees need little pruning except to remove dead and broken wood. Pruning can be done before or after the trees bloom in the spring. You lose fruit either way, but you can at least enjoy the flowers if you prune after they bloom.

Hawthorns are susceptible to a number of insects and diseases, but don't worry too much about them unless they become troublesome. However, if the trees are attacked by fire blight (see pears), cut back the dead wood at once. If cankers appear on branches, cut out the entire branches and burn.

Harvest berries as soon as they are ripe, because they do not hang on the trees very long.

HIGHBUSH CRANBERRY

Also called cranberrybush, *Viburnum trilobum* is a handsome, 10-ft. deciduous shrub with small, acid, red cranberry-like fruits in midsummer. These are made into an excellent jelly. The shrub grows in Zones 3–6, but is particularly useful in the colder areas where fewer fruits can be grown. Self-fruitful.

Varieties

Take what you can get. However, Manito, developed at the agricultural research station at Morden, Manitoba, is especially desirable because of its large fruits.

Culture

The highbush cranberry can be propagated by layering, but you'll do better to buy plants. Plant in the sun or partial shade in average soil. Provide a growing space about 6 ft. across.

Water in dry spells and fertilize in early spring with 2 cups of balanced plant food. Prune in late winter to remove unnecessary and broken branches.

The plants start to bear when about three years old. Berries should be collected just before they start to soften.

HUCKLEBERRIES

These are rather handsome deciduous shrubs producing clusters of blue or black berries resembling blueberries in mid- and late summer. They grow in Zones 3–8, especially in the East and Northwest. There are several species, the best being a 6-ft. shrub with blue fruit. Self-fruitful.

Huckleberries are seedier than blueberries and generally considered inferior. But they are not by any means to be scorned, because they make fine pies and jam.

Culture

Plants are easily moved from the wild, where they flourish in open and burned-over fields. Plant and raise them like blueberries. They do well in light shade as well as sun.

LOGANBERRIES

The loganberry is a deciduous bramble fruit with large, blackberry-like, acid, red fruits. These are produced in the summer on long (8 ft.), trailing stems. Grow in Zones 8–10, but most common in the Pacific states. Self-fruitful.

Culture

Grow like the trailing type of blackberry, to which it is closely related.

RASPBERRIES—RED AND YELLOW

Thorny, deciduous plants to 6 ft. producing red and occasionally yellow fruits. Standard varieties, sometimes called July-bearing, ripen in early summer. Everbearing varieties ripen in the fall and the following early summer. Grow in Zones 3–7. Self-fruitful.

Varieties

Amber. New yellow variety (actually the berries are amber) of much better quality than other yellows and on a par with or better than most reds. Late. Hardy only to Zone 4.

Boyne. Red raspberry from Manitoba that is recommended in North Dakota. Good quality. Very hardy and vigorous.

Canby. Large, firm red berries good for freezing. Canes are thornless or nearly so. Plants do not sucker so freely as some varieties.

Chief. Small, red berries of fair quality but profuse. Maine rates it the hardiest raspberry.

Early Red. Very early, red variety of superior flavor. Good for canning and freezing. Hardy.

Indian Summer. Everbearing red variety with soft, crumbly but tasty fruits. Vigorous plant.

Latham. Widely planted. Productive, tolerant of virus diseases, and adapted to many locations. One of the hardiest. Big, red berries tend to crumble and are of only fair quality.

Meeker. Developed in Washington in 1967, this has not been so thoroughly tested as some varieties, but early results are promising. Red berries are very large and delicious. Fine to eat, freeze, and make into jam.

Milton. Sizable, red berries of good quality. Good for freezing. Plants have considerable resistance to mosaic.

MR 158. A red variety showing great promise for the warmest parts of Zone 7. In Mississippi it has far outproduced the named varieties listed here.

September. Everbearing red raspberry a little earlier than Indian Summer and, therefore, more likely to escape early fall frosts.

Sumner. Red berries are big and ripen over a long period. Good for freezing; excellent for jam. Better adapted to heavy soils than other varieties. Dependable.

Taylor. Large, red berries of top quality. Plant is vigorous, productive, erect, and hardy. Susceptible to mosaic but resistant to some other virus diseases.

Culture

If possible, buy plants that are certified to be virus-free. Or you can propagate your own plants—if disease-free—by digging up and planting rooted suckers in early spring.

Plant raspberries in a spot which is protected from wind and has good air drainage. Avoid locations where raspberries, tomatoes, potatoes, peppers, or eggplants grew in the preceding three years. Kill all wild brambles, which might harbor diseases, within several hundred feet. Do not plant red or yellow raspberries within 300 ft. of black or purple raspberries.

The ideal soil is a deep, sandy loam containing a lot of organic matter; but any decent, well-drained soil will do. Dig large holes to accommodate the roots and set the plants 1 or 2 in. deeper than they previously grew. Plants usually come from the nursery with about 6 in. of the old cane attached. This serves as a "handle" in setting the plants. As soon as new growth starts, cut the handle off at the ground.

Spacing of plants depends on the way you plan to train them. In the hill system, which is particularly well suited to small gardens, set the plants at least 4 ft. apart each way. In the hedgerow system, set plants 3 ft. apart in rows 5 ft. wide.

Cultivate new plants shallowly until about midsummer, then apply a mulch of organic matter. This should be maintained from then on. Water in dry weather, especially just before and during harvest, when the plants draw heavily on the moisture in the soil.

Fertilize new plants after they start to make good growth with a handful of balanced fertilizer such as 10-10-10. After that, fertilize every spring.

If you maintain an organic mulch, apply about 2½ cups of ammonium nitrate per 50 ft. of row or ⅛ cup per hill. If you use a 10-10-10, apply 5 cups per 50 ft. of row or ¼ cup per hill.

Raspberry plants do not require support, but supported canes are easier to care for, fruit is cleaner, and there is less breakage as a result of storms. If you use the hill system, a 2-in. stake is driven into the ground next to each plant, and the plant is trained to five to eight canes. These are tied loosely to the stake about 3 ft. above ground and also at 4 to 4½ ft. If you use the hedgerow system, the plants are allowed to grow toward each other to form a hedge 1 ft. wide at the base. To support the plants, drive posts into the ground about 25 ft. apart; nail 18-in. cross-arms to each at a height of 3 ft. or a little more; and stretch two wires between the ends of the arms. The canes are guided up through the wires. No tying is necessary.

Do not prune red and yellow raspberries during their first growing season. In early spring of the second year, trim off dead wood and cut canes which are not supported back to 3 ft. From then on you should prune twice a year. As soon as you harvest the berries from summer-bearing varieties, cut out and burn the canes on which these were produced. You may at the same time thin out a few of the suckers put up by the plants. Early the following spring, cut out all but three or four strong canes per foot of row, or eight canes per hill. Then head these back slightly, but not more than one-quarter the total length of the canes (unless they have been damaged or winter-killed), and remove all side branches.

Everbearing varieties are pruned in the same way. However, the canes that bear fruit in the fall at their tips will bear additional fruit lower down during the next summer, so they should not be cut out until after the summer crop.

Another way to handle everbearing raspberries is to grow them only for their autumn berries, which are produced abundantly on canes of the current season's growth. In this case, all canes are cut to within 2 in. of the ground after you harvest the fall crop. This procedure saves pruning, prevents winter injury, and helps to control fungus diseases.

Prompt burning of all prunings and elimination of excess canes do much to keep pests under control. Nevertheless, a regular spray program pays dividends. The following is recommended: Apply lime sulfur when new growth starts in the spring. Then apply a general-purpose fruit spray just before bloom, ten days after bloom, and as soon as you have harvested the fruit and completed your summer pruning.

In very severe climates and on exposed sites, plants should be given winter protection by bending the canes gently to the ground and tossing enough soil on the tips to hold them down. The bent canes trap the snow, which protects them against biting cold.

Everbearing raspberries may produce some fruit the first year, but do much better the second. Summer-bearing varieties start bearing in the second year. Allow berries to ripen on the plants before picking.

RASPBERRIES—BLACK AND PURPLE

These are generally similar to red raspberries; however, both form larger plants and are more productive, both are more tender and withstand more heat, both are more susceptible to diseases, and both are used mainly for jam and jelly. The black raspberries, or blackcaps, ripen first. The purples ripen last, have the largest fruit and a distinctive flavor. Grow in Zones 4–8a. Self-fruitful.

Varieties

Allen. Very productive black raspberry. Fruits of good dessert quality ripen more or less at the same time. Early.

Black Hawk. Black. The latest good variety but not so productive as some others. Hardy.

Bristol. A very popular black variety with firm, luscious berries. Fruit is hard to pick until fully mature. Midseason. Plants do much better in some areas than in others.

Cumberland. An old favorite among the blacks, but very susceptible to anthracnose and other virus diseases. Late.

Dundee. Rather dull black fruits of good quality. Plant more tolerant of poorly drained soil than other varieties.

Manteo. Black variety originated in North Carolina. It has done better in central Mississippi (Zone 8b) than any other variety.

Marion. Purple berries ripening after Sodus. Productive.

Morrison. A late black variety of better-than-average eating quality.

Munger. Recommended for Oregon and Washington as the best black variety.

New Logan. Medium-large, black berries on good-yielding plants. Early.

Sodus. Leading purple raspberry. Very large berries are tart but good, ripen later than most red and black varieties. Upright, vigorous plant. One of the few purple varieties that is recommended in all five climate zones.

Culture

This is similar to red raspberry culture, but note these differences:

Both black and purple raspberries are propagated by tip-layering— bending the long, arching branches to the ground and covering the tips with soil.

In the hedgerow system, black raspberries should be spaced 3½ to 4 ft. apart in the row.

Set the plants only 1 in. deeper than they previously grew.

Prune plants in summer, early spring, and after harvest. In the summer, the canes that come up should be pinched back about 3 in. when they reach the desired height. This is called tipping. The desired height for black raspberries grown without supports is 24 in.; for those with supports, 30 in. The desired height for purple raspberries is 6 to 12 in. more.

In the early spring, before the plants break dormancy, cut out all weak canes at the ground, leaving four to six strong canes per plant. Cut out weak or dead laterals. Then cut back the remaining laterals on black raspberries to 8 to 10 in.; on purple raspberries, to 12 to 18 in.

After harvest, all canes that bore fruit should be cut off at the ground. In all cases, prunings should be burned promptly.

SASKATOONS

The saskatoon belongs to the genus *Amelanchier* and is a close relative of the shadbush and serviceberry. It is an 18-ft. deciduous shrub producing clusters of ½ to ⅝-in., usually bluish-purple berries in late spring and early summer. These are eaten fresh, made into pie, jelly and wine, and frozen. Extremely hardy, the fruit is one of the few that thrives in our coldest climates. Grows in Zones 2–4, especially on the northern prairies. Varieties listed here are self-fruitful.

Varieties

Forestburg. Has larger fruits than the following varieties, but their quality is less good. Ripens slightly later.

Pembina. Large, fleshy, sweet fruits in long clusters. Upright, slightly spreading plant.

Smoky. Large fruits in medium-size clusters are sweet but a little milder than Pembina. Spreading shrub only 8 ft. tall.

Culture

Saskatoons grow readily from seed, but do not come true. You should propagate them by the rooted suckers that spring up around the plants. Cut the tops back to within 2 in. of the roots and plant in a nursery bed until the plants grow to about 1 ft. or a little less. Then transplant to a sunny spot that is not subject to late spring freezes. The soil can be of average quality, but should be well drained. Give each shrub a space 8 ft. in diameter, or plant 6 ft. apart in a hedgerow. When transplanting, take pains not to injure too many of the roots, keep them damp, and don't expose them to sunlight for even a few minutes.

Mulching eliminates the need for cultivation, which must otherwise be done shallowly and carefully to avoid damaging the roots and causing them to sucker excessively. Little water or fertilizer are required, but don't neglect the plants completely.

Prune before growth starts in the spring but after danger of severe cold weather is past. Keep the shrubs headed back to about 6 ft. to make them easier to manage. The best fruit is produced on wood of the previous season's growth, and some fruit is also produced on older wood; so when you thin the shrubs to let in the sun, remove the older branches. Remove low branches also.

Saskatoons are attacked by various insects and diseases, but these can generally be kept under control by spraying when the petals fall with malathion and captan.

The plants start to bear when two to four years of age. Fruit to be made into jelly or to be frozen is picked when it is barely ripe, at which point it has a higher Vitamin C and pectin content. Fruit to be eaten fresh or made into desserts or wine is picked when fully ripe and sweetest.

STRAWBERRIES

Strawberries are perennials which are in their fruit-bearing prime for only one or two years, but which send out runners to perpetuate themselves indefinitely. Standard varieties produce a single crop in the spring. Usually called June-bearing, they grow in Zones 3–10. Everbearing strawberries are popular with home gardeners because they produce one crop in the fall and two more the following spring and fall, but the fruit is of poorer quality than that of the June-bearing varieties. They grow in Zones 3–6b. High temperatures in summer and fall lower the quality of the fall crop in warm climates. Self-fruitful.

Varieties

Note. There are innumerable good varieties of strawberries in addition to those listed below. In reading catalogs, you will find that the berries are usually classified as firm or soft. Although you may take use of these words to mean that firm berries are better than soft, the truth is that they are equal in quality. The difference is that firm berries ship better than soft. Or putting it another way—one of the best uses for soft-berried varieties is in the home garden.

Catskill. June-bearing. Very large, soft, bright crimson berries with an extra-sweet flavor. Midseason. Good for freezing. Productive plants are very resistant to verticillium wilt.

Charles V. Everbearing. A so-called wild French strawberry or French woodland strawberry (fraises des bois). Prolific plants producing very small, toothsome berries of unusual flavor. Runnerless.

Dixieland. June-bearing. Big, firm berries. Early. Adapted to many areas but particularly good in the South. Be sure to buy plants that are resistant to yellows.

Dunlap. Sometimes called Senator Dunlap. Old, old favorite. June-bearing. Medium-size, rich red fruits in midseason. Good for freezing. Hardy plants.

Earlibelle. June-bearing. Medium-large, bright red berries turn dark red. Very early. Does best in the deep South.

Earlidawn. June-bearing. Very early, large, tart fruits freeze well. A high yielder. Rated outstanding in Ohio. Very susceptible to verticillium wilt.

Fairfax. June-bearing. Large berries of top quality and superb flavor. Fruit becomes very dark when fully ripe. Midseason. Not very productive.

Fairpeake. June-bearing. Very good berries for late in the season.

Fletcher. June-bearing. Outstanding for freezing. Medium-size berries. Late. Does best in cool but not cold zones.

Florida 90. June-bearing. Standard variety for Florida gardens. Should not be grown north of Georgia. Big, long berries.

Fraises Espalier. A so-called climbing strawberry which puts out very long runners that are tied to a trellis. Everbearer from France. Sizable berries of good flavor.

Geneva. Large, excellent, fairly late berries which have an unfortunate tendency to rot in wet weather. Rated the best everbearing variety in New York.

Luscious Red. Everbearing variety from Minnesota. Medium-size, long, pointed berries. Moderately vigorous plants.

Midway. June-bearing. Exceptionally heavy producer. Berries large, tart, and of good quality. Midseason. Resistant to red stele but very susceptible to verticillium wilt.

Northwest. June-bearing. Leading variety in the state of Washington. Medium-large, firm fruits excellent for freezing. Midseason. Very productive.

Number 25. A cross between a wild strawberry and a fruiting variety, this forms a good ornamental groundcover up to 15 in. high. It also produces fruit in the spring. The plants must be mowed early every spring to force growth and fruit production.

Ogallala. Everbearing. Large, dark red, soft berries with a faint wild-strawberry flavor. Productive. Recommended in North Dakota but not in Missouri, indicating it is best grown in colder climates. Drought-resistant.

Ozark Beauty. Originated in Arkansas but hardy in much colder climates. Berries are attractive, wedge-shaped, and sweet. One of the most productive everbearing varieties.

Pocahontas. June-bearing. Vigorous plants with bright red berries, good fresh and for freezing. Especially recommended in temperate, mid-country zones.

Premier. June-bearing. Medium-size berries early in the season. A standard commercial variety also good for home use.

Puget Beauty. June-bearing. Long, medium-large berries are aromatic and sweet when eaten fresh; make excellent preserves. Early. Grown in the Northwest.

Redglow. June-bearing. Not a big producer, but the medium-large berries are particularly good. Early. A fine freezer. Resistant to red stele.

Rockhill. Everbearing variety popular west of the Rockies, from Arizona to Washington. Rated the highest quality everbearer in Idaho.

Sonjana. Another climbing strawberry. Everbearing. The fruits are pleasant but not notable.

Sparkle. June-bearing. A late-season, medium-size, dark red variety of top quality. Excellent for freezing. Very productive. Red stele resistant.

Superfection. One of the most popular everbearing varieties. Rounded, tart, light red berries. Hardy. Brilliant and Gem are almost identical varieties.

Surecrop. June-bearing. Large fruits are everything you can desire. Good for freezing. Resistant to red stele and moderately resistant to verticillium wilt.

Suwanee. June-bearing. Old favorite in the South. It was once practically wiped out by a virus, but virus-free stock is now available. Big, light red berries.

Tennessee Beauty. June-bearing. Medium-size berries in midseason. Widely grown in the middle South.

Vermillion. June-bearing. Medium-size berries, a bit soft and good. Midseason. Resistant to red stele and verticillium wilt.

Culture

Strawberries propagate themselves by the runner plants they put out; and you can speed the process a bit by covering the runners at the base of the little plants with soil. However, it is not advisable to continue propagating your own plants for more than three or four years, because strawberries are very susceptible to viruses and you may wind up with diseased stock. In short, you should start out with virus-free plants from a reputable nursery; and you should replant the garden every few years with additional purchased virus-free plants.

Whether you should also start out with varieties that are resistant to red stele and verticillium wilt, two serious soil-borne diseases, is a hard-to-answer question. If neighboring strawberry growers have not been troubled by these diseases, you probably won't be troubled either. On the other hand, if your neighbors have had trouble, you *may*, too. In the latter instance, you may take several precautions:

If red stele is present in neighboring gardens, you can either buy varieties resistant to this disease or you can fumigate your soil before planting with Vapam or Mylone. Since the fumigants also kill nematodes and several other soil pests and since they also help to control weeds during the following year, they are probably a better answer to a *possible* red stele infestation than resistant varieties. If red stele is *known* to infest your soil, however, you should definitely buy resistant varieties.

One way to forestall a possible attack by verticillium wilt is not to plant strawberries in soil in which tomatoes, peppers, potatoes, and eggplants have been grown within the preceding three years. The alternative is to plant wilt-resistant varieties such as Surecrop or Vermillion. There is no other known way to control this disease.

Strawberries should be planted in a sunny spot on the upper side of your garden where they will escape late spring freezes. The soil should be well drained, not too heavy and rich in humus. If you always grow strawberries, rotate them with some other crop about every two or three years. Ideally, the other crop should be a cover crop such as clover, rye, vetch, or soybeans followed by a crop, such as corn, that requires intensive cultivation.

Rotation improves the fertility and humus content of the soil, discourages weeds, and reduces insect and disease problems.

The best time to plant strawberries in most parts of the country is in early spring. In warmest areas, however, fall planting is recommended because it gives the plants an opportunity to make good root growth during the winter months when rainfall is usually plentiful.

If plants are dry on delivery, sprinkle them with water and wrap them in plastic film or some other reasonably water-tight covering until planting. Do not expose them to the sun or air any longer than necessary. If planting must be delayed, you can store the plants in the fresh-food compartment of your refrigerator for several days, or you can heel them into the ground in a shady spot.

To set plants in the garden, simply drive a spade or trowel straight down into the soil about 6 in. and move the handle back and forth to open the hole. Trim roots to a length of 5 or 6 in. if they are longer than this. Spread them slightly and drop them straight down into the hole. The crown of the plant *must be level* with the soil surface. Remove big, old leaves. Firm the soil around the roots and apply a half cup of starter solution.

Strawberries are trained in two ways. In the matted-row system, which is commonly used for June-bearing varieties, the rows are spaced 3 to 4 ft. apart and the plants are spaced 2 ft. apart in the row. (Actually, varieties that are not vigorous runner producers, such as Earlidawn, may be spaced 18 in. apart, while those that are very vigorous runner producers, such as Dunlap, may be spaced 30 in. apart. But 2 ft. is a good compromise.) Runners produced by the plants are allowed to form a mat 15 to 18 in. wide, with at least 6 in. between plants. Once enough plants have been established to fill the row, new runners should be removed.

In the hill system, which may be used for June-bearing varieties to produce unusually large berries and which is recommended for all everbearing varieties, the plants are set 1 ft. apart and all runners are kept cut off. The plants may be in a single row about 1 ft. wide; in double rows totaling about 2 ft. in width; in triple rows about 3 ft. in width; or in quadruple rows about 4 ft. in width. As a rule, the triple-row system is favored by agricultural experts. Leave a 1- to 2-ft. space between one triple row and another.

During the first year, water as necessary so the plants will receive at least 1 in. a week. Sidedress the plants with a balanced fertilizer such as 10-10-10 as soon as growth starts (about two weeks after planting), when runners start to form, and in mid-August. Apply about 2 cups per 50 ft. of row at each feeding.

Weed control is essential. The hard way to achieve it is to hoe the bed regularly throughout the growing season. An easier way is to apply a mulch of hay, straw, or other organic material as soon as all plants comprising a matted row have been established or as soon as plants in a hill system are thriving. An alternative—applicable only to strawberries grown in the hill system—is to cover the bed before it is planted with black polyethlene film; and then to plant the strawberries through 4-in. slits in the film.

During the summer the plastic should be covered with a thin layer of hay, leaves, etc., to keep it from becoming very hot and injuring the plants. This is especially important in the deep South and Southwest.

Remove all flowers as they appear until July 1 to July 15: if fruit is allowed to develop during this period, it will limit vegetative growth and reduce the crop the next year. After early July, everbearing varieties will continue to flower and, within about a month, will start to bear fruit. The harvest should continue until frost.

In the Southwest, where the hot sun, high temperatures, and drying winds play havoc with plants, you can reduce maintenance of your planting and improve production by erecting a lath screen over the plants during the summer.

In the fall, from Zone 7 northward, you must mulch all plants with straw or hay to protect them against heaving and other winter injury. The mulch is applied as soon as the temperature has dropped to just above 20°, but not later than the end of November. Cover the soil between rows to a depth of 3 in. (a little deeper in very cold areas). Cover the plants also. In coldest regions the plants are covered as deeply as the soil; but in warmer areas, such as Zone 7, part of the strawberry leaves should be visible.

The next spring most of the mulch on top of the plants must be removed. Don't be in a hurry about doing this, because the mulch helps to protect

A strawberry plant in a matted row. The daughter plants are spaced around the parent plant, and when they fill out, they will form a mat 15 to 18 in. wide.

the blossoms against late frosts. Wait until growth is well started. However, if the leaves turn yellow, remove the covering at once.

On the other hand, if you are anxious for an early crop of berries, you can remove all the mulch as soon as growth starts. But keep an eye on the thermometer and be prepared to re-cover the plants at night when frost threatens.

Do not fertilize strawberries in the spring in which they fruit: it tends to reduce rather than to improve the yield. But give them plenty of water if the weather is dry.

Pick berries as soon as they are fully colored. They will keep better if picked early in the morning. Do not expose them to any more sun than necessary. The berries should be pinched off with a bit of the stem attached; those that are pulled off are likely to be bruised. Store the fruit in the refrigerator and don't wash it until you are ready to use it. If the plants are well mulched, there is probably no need for washing anyway.

After the spring harvest, everbearing strawberries should be fertilized with about 2 cups of balanced fertilizer per 50 ft. of row. Keep the plants

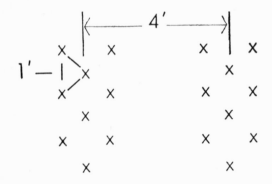

This is how strawberries should be planted in a three-row hill system.

weeded and watered during the summer, and they will produce a new, smaller crop in the fall. Then tear out the plants and start fresh. The plants would continue to bear for another year or two, but the size, quality, and quantity of berries would decline.

June-bearing varieties also go down hill if they are fruited for more than two years. And sometimes they are in such poor condition following production of their first crop that they should be destroyed right then and there. Usually, however, you can renovate the bed and enjoy a second harvest in the third spring after the plants are set out. Here is what you should do:

As soon as the last berry has been picked, remove the mulch and reduce the width of each matted row to 15 to 18 in. by hoeing or tilling out the plants along one or both sides. Cut the plant tops to within 1 in. of the crowns with a rotary mower. Broadcast 2 cups of balanced fertilizer over 50 ft. of row for its entire width, and water in thoroughly. Then when the plants start to develop new leaves, thin them out to stand about 8 in. apart.

Keep the plants watered and weeded during the summer. Apply a mulch between the rows and between the plants once they are well established. Remove runner plants unless you need them to fill in large gaps. Make a second 2-cup application of fertilizer in the middle of August. Apply a winter mulch in late fall.

Another way of renovating a June-bearing strawberry bed planted to the matted-row system is to reduce the row width to about 7 in. Then you allow the plants to put out new runner plants to restore the row to its normal 15- to 18-in. width. All other treatment is the same.

Although strawberries are attacked by a good many insects and diseases, these are usually not too much of a problem in the home garden as long as you (1) start out with virus-free, disease-resistant plants; (2) fumigate the soil, if necessary, before planting; (3) keep out weeds and destroy diseased or injured plant parts; and (4) rotate plantings. Should any trouble arise, you can generally cope with it by immediately applying a general-purpose fruit spray. To control birds, which sometimes go on rampages in strawberry beds, cover the plants with netting.

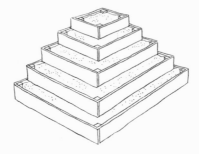

How to construct a pyramid bed for strawberries. Each bench (bed) is 12 to 24 in. deep. Round and triangular pyramids are also built.

Special culture No. 1.

If you have poorly drained soil or lack space in your garden, a good way to raise strawberries is to build a square pyramid of redwood boards and soil. The boards should be 6 to 8 in. wide. Each level of the pyramid should be 12 to 24 in. less in width than the one below it. Plant each level with one row of plants spaced 1 ft. apart. keep runners cut off.

A good soil mixture to use in the pyramid consists of three parts loam, one part peat, one part sand, and 1 tbs. of balanced fertilizer per sack of sand. The soil must be tamped well at each level to support the framework for the level next above.

Plant and care for the strawberries as if they were in the garden.

Special culture No. 2

Growing strawberries in strawberry barrels and jars has been a popular home pastime for generations. Red-clay jars holding about a dozen plants must be purchased. You can make your own strawberry barrel out of almost any kind or size of barrel, but a whiskey barrel is best because it is extremely sturdy.

First drill about four 2-in. holes in the bottom of the barrel to allow excess water to drain out. Then, starting 6 in. from the bottom, drill rings of 2-in. holes through the sides. Space the holes in each ring 10 to 12 in. apart and space the rings 6 to 8 in. apart vertically. Center the holes in every even-numbered ring between those in the odd-numbered rings, otherwise the plants will not get as much sun as they need.

Pour a 2-in layer of gravel in the bottom of the barrel. And then con-

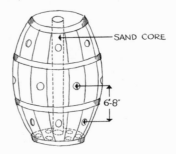

A strawberry barrel.

struct a central core of sand from the bottom of the barrel to the top so that water will readily reach the lowest plants. To make the core, cut the ends from a 1-lb. coffee can. Place the can in the center of the barrel and fill it with sand. Then fill around it with the same soil mixture recommended for a pyramid planting. Then raise the can, leaving the sand behind, and repeat the process.

The strawberries are planted as you fill the barrel with soil. Spread the roots inside the barrel so that they are slanted slightly upwards. As the soil packs down upon them, they will settle in a horizontal or downward-slanting position. The crowns of the plants should be nearly level with the vertical soil surface.

Set a few plants in the open top of the barrel, too.

When the planting is completed, water thoroughly down through the sand core and keep the soil slightly moist thereafter. Fertilize every two to four weeks with a liquid plant food. Keep the barrel in the sunniest spot you can find and turn it half way around every other day so that all plants will receive the maximum amount of sunlight. If the barrel is large, mounting it on a dolly makes the turning much easier.

Move the barrel into a frost-free basement in the winter. Plants will not survive the low temperatures otherwise. However, since they probably will produce poorly in the second year, it makes more sense to start new plants every year.

Everbearing varieties are best for barrels and jars.

Special culture No. 3

Climbing strawberries are interesting as novelties; and if you're lucky, they will give you a fair quantity of fruit. Set the plants about 15 in. apart in front of a 4-ft. trellis of wood or wire. Tie the long runners to this. In late summer, however, some of the runners should be taken down from the trellis and allowed to root so you will have a continuing supply of plants. In cold climates, cut off all runners, except those you have rooted, in the fall.

9

Growing Tropical and Sub-Tropical Fruits

Tropical fruits will grow in only a few parts of the U.S. mainland and in Hawaii. They belong in Zone 10 or still warmer climates. Sub-tropical fruits grow in Zone 9 (but not in all areas) and also in Zone 10. But from this point on, for the sake of simplicity, I refer to them all as "tropicals."

Except for bananas, citrus, pineapples, and avocados, most of these warm-climate plants seem strange and even a bit unreal to the great majority of Americans; and surprisingly, they are also rather strange and unreal to many of the people who are able to grow them. This is a shame, because the fruits range from good to superb; they are no more difficult to grow than more familiar fruits; and in many cases they make exceedingly handsome ornamentals.

Acquiring plants. The easiest way to acquire tropical fruit plants is to buy them in containers from a nursery specializing in tropicals. You may also be able to buy bare-root plants, which are cheaper but which are also more troublesome to plant. In the case of the more popular fruits, you have a choice of varieties; and you would be well advised to ask the grower which he recommends for your particular situation. In the case of the more unusual fruits, however, you may have to take whatever variety the grower happens to have. The reason for this is that American interest in many of the tropical fruits is quite new, and there are few if any commercial growers who have started to concern themselves about varietal differences and merits.

If buying plants does not seem like much fun to you, the obvious alternative is to propagate them yourself. But I recommend that you try this only if the plants can be reproduced from seeds or by making divisions, cuttings, layers, or air-layers. Grafting and budding (a form of grafting) are not difficult, but they are demanding.

How to divide plants is covered in Chapter 5 on page 62. Layering is described in Chapter 8 on page 199.

Air-layering is done by cutting a slight notch in a one-year-old branch or stem on a growing plant and dusting it with a rooting hormone. Soak sphagnum moss in water and squeeze a large handful of it as dry as possible. Then wrap the moss tightly around the notch and overwrap it with plastic film. Seal the ends with cellulose tape. When roots develop in two to three months to a length of ½ in. or more, cut off the branch just below the notch and plant it.

Cuttings are taken from several parts of plants but most commonly from roots and stems. Root cuttings are very easily made by cutting live roots into 4- to 6-in. lengths and burying them shallowly in soil.

Stem cuttings are trickier. The best time for making them is when the parent plant is making strong growth. In the case of tropical fruits, the stems used are young, green, vigorous shoots.

Cut through a stem diagonally about ½ in. below the fifth, sixth, or seventh leaf. Trim off all but the four top leaves, and dip the bottom of the stem in a rooting hormone.

Mix two parts shredded peat with one part sand. Wet it slightly but evenly; squeeze as dry as possible; and put a 4- or 5-in. layer in the bottom of a large plastic bag of the type used in the kitchen. Firm the mixture well; poke a small hole about 3 in. deep in it; insert the bare stem of the cutting; and press the mixture around it. Dampen the leaves just a little. Then close the top of the bag tightly with a rubber band, and set the bag in a warm, lightly shaded place. The leaves should not touch the plastic.

Examine the cutting occasionally to make sure it is not drying out. If it is, open the bag, sprinkle the rooting mixture with water, and close the bag again. This is usually unnecessary, however. Watch out also for fungus on the cutting. Should it appear, spray with captan.

When the cutting develops ½-in. roots, pot it up in a mixture of two parts loam, one part peat, and one part sand. Keep it in the shade for a few days; then gradually expose it to full sun. As the plant grows, it can be moved into larger and larger containers or transplanted to the garden.

Plants propagated by cuttings, layers, and divisions are faithful repro-

ductions of their parents. On the other hand, tropical fruits that are propagated by seeds may or may not come true, depending on the species or
variety. Those that almost always come true include the papaya, Barbados
cherry, bignay, Surinam cherry, and passion fruit. Citrus often comes true,
and mangoes may.

As a rule, the seeds used to grow topical fruits should be planted right
out of the fruits. Rinse them in water and dry; then dust with a fungicide
such as Spergon or captan to protect them against rot and disease. Plant
in a seedbed or container in a well-drained loam containing plenty of
humus. Except for avocados, which do not come true, the seeds should
be covered with about ¼ in. of soil. Keep the seedbed moist and protect
it from sun until the plants are up. The warmer the weather, the faster the
seeds will germinate.

Required growing conditions. With a few exceptions noted in the second
part of this chapter, tropical fruits must be grown in full sun. But all small
plants that you propagate yourself should be grown in mixed sun and shade
until they become stocky.

Always plant tropicals on a high point of land or a slope—never in a
depression where they may be hit by frost. Provide a windbreak if they are
exposed to strong winds.

The soil should contain plenty of humus and have pH of about 6.0 to
6.5   It must be well drained, especially in the top foot where 75 to 90 per
cent of the fruits' roots are to be found. And it must be very well aerated—
much better aerated than the soil for other kinds of fruits.

Planting tropical fruits. The directions given in Chapter 7 for planting
deciduous fruits are equally applicable to tropical fruits except for one
point: Because a tropical must have lots of oxygen at the roots, the root
crown must be level with the soil surface—no lower. In fact, M. J. Soule,
Jr., associate professor of fruit crops at the University of Florida and co-
author of *Tropical and Sub-Tropical Agriculture,* tells me that a good
way to plant tropical fruits—if you take pains to stabilize them against wind
—is to put the roots right on top of the ground and then cover them with
soil!

Planting is best done in the spring, when tropicals make their strongest
flush of growth; but it can be done at any other time the plants are making
vigorous growth. (Unlike northern plants, which may make only one or
two spurts of growth a year, tropicals have three, four, even as many as
twelve flushes a year.)

Routine care. Although some people question the advisability of mulching tropical fruits because, they say, it may encourage disease, Dr. Soule
and his co-authors—all foremost authorities on tropical agriculture—
advocate it strongly. Their principal reason: Mulches of organic material,
gravel, or light-colored sand protect the soil against the burning tropical
sun and thus reduce and stabilize soil temperatures. In addition, mulches

hold in moisture and keep down weeds; and organic mulches add to the humus content of the soil.

Water plants in dry periods which occur when the plants normally are making growth, blossoming, and developing fruit. However, if plants are not making growth, no watering is necessary. (Most tropical plants, like temperate plants, have dormant periods. But whereas dormancy in temperate plants is controlled by low temperatures, tropical plants go more or less dormant during normal, seasonal periods of low rainfall and you should not upset their schedule at this time by watering them.)

Fertilize according to the schedules given for the different fruits in the following pages. Use the balanced fertilizer that is recommended for your garden as a result of a soil test, and add magnesium in the event this is not specified. Tropical fruits require an unusual amount of this element. If other minor elements are needed—as they often are—apply zinc, manganese, boron, molybdenum, and copper in foliar sprays. Iron is usually applied to the soil in a solution of iron chelates.

Pruning of tropical fruits is rather limited. As with deciduous fruits, the main aim is to develop in young trees a good scaffold system of three to six large branches spaced around and up and down the trunk close to the ground. Then, starting in the trees' third year, the secondary branches are allowed to fill in.

After that, you should usually prune just enough to keep the crowns of the trees reasonably open. Cut back branches that grow too long. Eliminate weak, broken, and diseased branches; those with weak crotches, and those that cross. Also eliminate unnecessary suckers.

In the West, pruning is best done just before the end of the dry season. In other areas, where rainfall is more evenly distributed, prune trees any time during a reasonably long dry spell when they are making little growth.

Freeze damage. If plants are injured by a freeze (young plants are much more susceptible to cold than old), don't do anything to them for several weeks. The chances are they will start making growth again, and when they do, you can determine how much if any pruning is called for. Should drastic treatment be required, allow about six months to lapse before undertaking it; otherwise you may compound the damage already done.

Fruitfulness of tropical fruits. If anything, the tropicals are even more mixed up than other fruits. Many are self-fruitful, which means that you need to put in only one plant to have fruit. But a number are self-unfruitful and must be planted close to a different variety of the same fruit. In still other cases, you need both male and female plants. Avocados are a law unto themselves.

AMBARELLA

Also called Otaheite-apple. A straight, high-branched, deciduous tree to 60 ft. It bears yellow or orange, plum-like fruits about 3 in. long in fall and winter. The flesh is firm, very juicy, and has been said to taste like an apple, pineapple, or very bad mango. You may not like it, especially if you eat it fresh; but it makes interesting preserves, relishes, and pickles. Grows in Zone 10. Self-fruitful.

Culture

Ambarellas are easily propagated by stem cuttings. In fact, you can cut off a branch 2 or 3 in. in diameter, stick it in moist soil in the garden where you want a new tree to grow, and it will probably root for you quickly.

Plant in any decent soil. Each tree needs a space about 40 ft. in diameter. Young trees should be lightly shaded at midday for a couple of years.

Water in dry weather. Fertilize annually when trees start making active growth. Begin with a cup of balanced fertilizer for young trees and double the amount annually through the fifth year. From the sixth year on, feed 20 cups a year.

Ambarellas start to bear at six years of age. Allow fruits to ripen on the trees before picking.

AVOCADOS

The avocado is presumably an evergreen, but some varieties lose their leaves briefly before flowering. The trees grow to 25 ft. and are of varying habit. The fruit is also variable, ranging from pear-shaped to round and with a skin color of green, black, purple, or reddish. Fruits of different varieties mature in all seasons.

Avocados grow in Zones 9b and 10. Some varieties can withstand temperatures as low as about 24°; others are damaged at the freezing mark.

Avocado varieties are classified into A and B types according to the schedule they follow in opening and closing their flowers. To ensure fruit set, you should plant both A and B types.

Varieties

Note. Avocado varieties are separated into three races: West Indian, Guatemalan, and Mexican. The West Indians are most sensitive to cold and do best at low elevations. They are most widely grown in Florida. Guatemalan and Mexican varieties are highland natives and more resistant to cold and drought. They are grown in California and Hawaii. Guatemalan varieties are also grown in Florida. West Indian varieties generally mature their fruits in summer and autumn; Guatemalan, in winter and spring; and Mexican, in summer.

Anaheim. Guatemalan. Type A. Large fruits mature in summer. Grown in California and Hawaii.

Beardslee. Guatemalan. Type A. Very large fruits of rich, nutty flavor mature in the fall. Grown in Hawaii.

Booth 8. A hybrid. Type B. Trees bear large quantities of medium-size fruits in the fall. Moderately resistant to scab. Grown in Florida. Booth 7 is much the same.

Choquette. Guatemalan. Type A. Very large fruits mature in late fall to midwinter. Resistant to scab. Grown in Florida.

Fuerte. A hybrid. Type B. Fruit matures from midfall to midspring in California; from midsummer to early winter in Hawaii. Extensively planted in California. Fruits are small but very good. Trees bear every other year. Moderately resistant to cold.

Hass. Guatemalan. Type A. Small fruits mature in summer in California; in winter in Hawaii.

MacArthur. A hybrid. Type B. Fruits mature from midfall to midspring. Similar to Fuerte but bears more reliably.

Nabal. Guatemalan. Type A. Fruits mature in summer in California; for the first six months of the year in Hawaii; for the first two months in Florida. Trees are very heavy bearers of large fruits.

Pollock. West Indian. Type B. Very large, rich fruits of good quality mature in midsummer. But yield is low and uneven. Tree is susceptible to cold but resistant to scab. Grown in Florida.

Taylor. Guatemalan. Type A. One of the best varieties in Florida. Fruits are small but tasty, mature in late fall to midwinter. Plants have good cold tolerance and are moderately resistant to scab.

Culture

Avocados are very easily grown from fresh seeds, but they do not come true to variety and they take a long time to start bearing. So buy grafted trees.

Give each tree a space 25 ft. in diameter and protect it from strong winds. Any decent soil will do provided it is very well drained. Avocados do not tolerate wet feet. In California you should not plant the trees in an area where previous avocados failed, because there is a good chance the soil is infested with root-rot fungus.

Since there is a difference in the way avocados are fertilized in the three principal U.S. growing regions, I quote here the recommendations of the different state agricultural extension services:

California. "The chief nutrient needed is nitrogen. Broadcast the fertilizer uniformly over the whole area under the tree to slightly beyond the the drip-line.

"Mature trees need about 1 lb. of actual nitrogen each year. (The Hass variety requires about 2 lb.) For a more even supply to the tree, especially on sandy soils, apply one-half the fertilizer before the end of the rainy season, usually in February, and the other half in June or July.

"To supply approximately ½ lb. of nitrogen, apply 3.2 lb. (a little over 6 cups) of calcium nitrate, or 2.4 lb. (4¼ cups) of ammonium sulfate, or 1.5 lbs. (2¼ cups) of ammonium nitrate.

"Young, non-bearing trees require much less nitrogen. They can be damaged by too much fertilizer. The following amounts of ammonium nitrate per tree are suggested:

"First year—1 tsp. every second or third irrigation.

"Second year—¼ cup in February and again in June.

"Third year—½ lb. (1 cup) broadcast in February and again in June.

"Fourth year—1½ lb. (3 cups) broadcast in January or February."

Florida. "Young trees should receive fertilizer applications every two months during the first year, beginning with ¼ lb. (½ cup) and increasing to 1 lb. (2 cups). Thereafter, three or four applications per year in amounts proportionate to the increasing size of the tree are sufficient. Fertilizer mixtures containing 6 to 10 per cent nitrogen, 6 to 10 percent available phosphoric acid, 6 to 10 per cent potash and 4 to 6 per cent magnesium give satisfactory results with young trees. For bearing trees, available phosphoric acid should be reduced to 2 to 4 per cent. Plants growing in calcareous soils should receive annual nutritional sprays of copper, zinc and manganese for the first four to five years. Thereafter only zinc and manganese are necessary. Avocado trees are susceptible to iron deficiency under alkaline conditions. Soil applications of iron chelates designed for alkaline conditions will correct this deficiency."

Hawaii. "A tree with a heavy crop of fruits will require more fertilizer than a tree with a light crop. A complete fertilizer is usually used. An example is the general garden fertilizer 8-10-8. During the first year a small grafted tree will be given approximately 1 lb. (2 cups) divided into three applications: At planting time—¼ lb. (½ cup): four months later—¼ lb.; eight months later—½ lb. (1 cup). Usually an extra handful of superphosphate is put at the bottom of the hole and covered with an inch-thick layer of soil at the time of planting.

"In the second year the amount of fertilizer may be 1½–3 times more than the first year. The amount is divided into two or three applications spaced equally apart.

"After the second year, a rule-of-thumb method is used as a guide: A tree should be fertilized with a minimum of 1 lb. (2 cups) of fertilizer for every inch diameter of tree trunk. In many instances, however, as in the case of hot and dry areas, or areas where the soil is poor, the amount is doubled so that a tree with a 10-in.–diameter trunk will receive 20 lb. for the year. Usually a high nitrogen and potash fertilizer such as 10-5-20 is desirable for bearing trees."

Irrigate avocados deeply about once a week during dry seasons. If your water is highly saline, be sure to apply water very heavily once in a while to leach the salts out of the root zone. This problem and its solution are discussed at length in Chapter 3.

If trees are properly trained when young, they should require little pruning later on. However, some gardeners like to keep the tops cut back to simplify spraying and harvesting. Such pruning should be done soon after the fruits are picked.

Thinning of fruits is rarely necessary except when a young tree produces an unusually heavy crop.

Insect pests are not overly troublesome as a rule. Monthly spraying with a copper fungicide for three months before fruits mature helps to control most diseases. But where scab is a problem, you should use resistant varieties.

Grafted varieties begin to bear about three years after setting in the garden. Fruits do not ripen until they fall or are picked. If they are mature, they will then ripen in three to eight days. If they are immature at picking, the flesh will become soft and rubbery. Green-skinned varieties are usually ready to pick as the green is replaced by a yellowish tinge and the fruit becomes smoother. Dark varieties are usually mature when they start to turn from green to dark color. When picking, do not pull off the fruits, but cut the stems close.

BANANAS

The banana is a tree-like herbaceous perennial. Large varieties grow to almost 25 ft.; the dwarfs, to only 6. The plants have magnificent leaves and put up a series of stems, or suckers, each of which produces one bunch of fruit. Bunches sometimes have several hundred fruits. They are produced in all seasons.

Bananas grow in Zones 9b and 10. They tolerate a few degrees of frost. Self-fruitful.

Species and varieties

Cavendish. Also called Chinese or dwarf banana. This is a species. A small plant, it does better in windy locations than other bananas. It also withstands more cold, and because of its size, can be easily protected. Fruit is small but sweeter than that of Gros Michel. Common in Hawaii and Florida.

Gros Michel. A variety of the common, tall-growing banana species. Very widely planted, it keeps U.S. supermarkets filled with yellow fruits. Its main claim to fame is that the fruit ships and keeps well; but the quality is rated low in comparison with that of other bananas. Trees are susceptible to two dread diseases.

Lady Finger. Another variety of the common, tall-growing banana. Outstandingly delicious fruit. Does well in U.S. banana-growing areas.

Plantain. A species used only for cooking. Fruits are large, firm, starchy, and less sweet than those eaten fresh.

Culture

Bananas require full sun; good protection from wind (grow them on the lee side of a building or dense hedge); and a rich, well-drained, neutral to slightly acid soil containing large amounts of humus. The soil should be fumigated if nematodes are present. Give each tall-growing plant a space 15 ft. in diameter, each dwarf, a space 8 ft. in diameter.

Bananas are commonly propagated by the suckers they produce. Large suckers 4 to 8 ft. high are best; but smaller may be used. Cut the suckers very carefully from the parent stalk and remove all the fibrous roots and expanded leaves. Soak the bottoms for 48 hours in water to help prevent infestations of root borers. Then dry the suckers in a shady place for several days until the cut surfaces heal.

Dig large, 18-in.-deep planting holes. Throw the subsoil away. Surround the roots with topsoil only. This should be mixed with humus, limestone, and about a cup of balanced fertilizer, such as 10-10-10. Set the suckers in the holes a couple of inches deeper than they previously grew; pack the soil in around them; and water well.

Since bananas are extremely thirsty plants, keep the soil evenly moist at all times. Do not, however, permit water to stand around the plants. Mulching with a deep organic material reduces evaporation, smothers weeds, and thus eliminates the need for cultivation (which would have to be done very carefully, since the roots are shallow), and keeps the soil from being over-heated by the sun.

Feed young plants every month for about six months. Start with ¼ cup of fertilizer after the first month and work up to a full cup. Thereafter the plants, together with the suckers they produce, should be given about 10 cups of balanced fertilizer a year. This should be applied in three to five equal doses.

As banana plants develop, they throw up suckers around themselves. The cluster thus created is called a mat. In fertile soil a mat should include no more than four stems at any time. One of these is the stem that is next going to produce fruit. The other stems should be nine, six, and three months old. This arrangement makes it possible for you to have bananas more or less the year round.

Pruning of bananas consists of regularly removing the weak suckers that pop up so that the three strong suckers you save and the fruiting stem will develop well. Pruning cuts must be made carefully to avoid injuring the parent plant and the fruiting stems that follow. You can use the suckers you cut off to propagate new plants.

The two serious diseases that attack the Gros Michel banana have not presented a problem in the U.S. But other pests may be troublesome. Mealybugs can be controlled by washing them out of the plants with strong streams of water. The freckle disease which makes spots on leaves and fruits of dwarf bananas can be controlled by spraying with Bordeaux mixture. The Hawaiian Agricultural Extension Service also advises that "some protection is obtained by wrapping the fruit on the plant with paper before it matures to prevent the disease spores from spreading to the bunch from the leaves above. This wrapping is also beneficial as it keeps fruit flies away in case fruits become ripe before they are harvested." Rats and mongooses, which often eat fruit ripening on the stalks, should be shot or trapped.

A banana stem will bear its one and only bunch of fruits within 12 to 18 months after planting or after it spears up out of the ground around a parent plant. Fruit ripens best when picked green. It is also damaged less by fruit flies.

Fruit is ready to harvest when it reaches full size and the angles start to soften. Cut each bunch with 1½ to 2 ft. of stem, and leave the stem on the bunch to help keep the fruits fresh as they mature. If the bunch is out of reach, chop through the trunk about half way up on the side the bunch will fall. Then place a heavy stick against the trunk and let the weight of the fruit slowly bring it down to the ground. Be careful not to damage the fruit or the other plants in the mat.

After the fruit is harvested, cut down the entire plant close to the ground so the surrounding plants can develop.

BARBADOS CHERRIES

The Barbados cherry is a spreading, 9-ft., evergreen shrub with pink flowers followed in spring and summer by bright red, cherry-like fruits with a soft flesh that is often too sour to enjoy fresh. The fruits make good jelly and jam, however. They have exceptionally high Vitamin C content.

The shrub grows in Zones 9b and 10. Self-fruitful.

Culture

Propagate by seeds or air-layering. Plant in well-drained soil containing lots of humus. Fumigating the soil to get rid of nematodes is advisable. Individual plants need a space about 10 ft. in diameter; but you can set a group of plants closer together to form a handsome hedge.

Water in dry weather. Fertilize the first year with a cup of balanced plant food. Thereafter apply 2 cups—one just before the plants bloom; the other in June.

If plants are attacked by scale, spray with malathion. If scale persists, spray the following winter with dormant oil.

Pick fruits when they mature. If you want to try eating them fresh, allow them to soften somewhat.

BIGNAY

A handsome evergreen tree to 60 ft. in the Far East, but in Florida only a third of that height and generally shrub-like. In summer and fall it bears clusters of small, blue-black, currant-like fruits with a high pectin content. These make an excellent jelly.

Bignays grow in Zones 9b and 10. They withstand temperatures into the 20s. You must plant a male and female specimen to have fruit. If grown on a large scale, you need one male for every ten females.

Culture

Propagate by seeds, air-layers, or stem cuttings.

The plants must be grown in a place protected from the winds, since the wood is weak. Allow a 10-ft.-diameter space for each plant, and give it a humusy soil of good quality.

Water as necessary when fruit is developing. Fertilize annually before active growth begins in the spring. One cup is enough for plants before they reach bearing age; use 2 cups after that.

Shrubs grown from seed start bearing when they are about six years of age. The fruits in each cluster ripen one by one for several weeks. You can pick them individually as they are ready; or Dr. Soule suggests that you wait until a third to a half are ripe, then pick the entire cluster. The green fruits can be used with the black in making jelly, because they are unusually rich in pectin.

CALAMONDINS

Upright, evergreen, citrus trees to 20 ft. (dwarf specimens to 8 ft.). They have beautiful foliage and are planted more for ornament than for eating. The fruits are shaped like small, yellow to orange tangerines and have very acid pulp. They are used only as substitutes for lemons and limes. Ripen in spring, summer, and fall.

Calamondins are among the hardiest of the citrus trees and grow in Zones 9b and 10. Self-fruitful.

Culture

Grow like oranges. Each tree requires a space about 15 ft. in diameter. Trees are best grown on trifoliate orange rootstocks.

CARAMBOLA

The carambola is a 20-ft., evergreen tree of somewhat irregular shape. In spring and summer and occasionally in other seasons it bears waxy, yellow, 5-in. fruits that are star-shaped in cross-section. In the best forms of the tree, the fruits are big, juicy, tartly sweet, fragrant, and delicious to eat fresh. But some trees have small, sour fruits that are good only for cooking.

Grows in Zone 10. Mature trees can withstand a little frost, but young ones cannot. Self-fruitful.

Culture

Buy grafted trees; seedlings are likely to have poor fruits.

Plant in well-drained, humusy soil. Give each tree a space 18 to 20 ft. in diameter. Water regularly, especially when trees are young, because at that stage they are on the delicate side.

Fertilize newly planted trees every three months, but sparingly. Once established, they can be fed two or three times a year while in active growth. Gradually work up to giving them a total of 12 to 15 cups of balanced fertilizer, such as 8-4-4, when they are five years of age. After trunks attain a diameter of 6 in., fertilize at the rate of 20 cups a year.

Trees start to bear four years after planting. Pick fruits as they mature.

CHERIMOYA

The cherimoya is a deciduous tree about 20 ft. tall. In early spring it bears a few large fruits with a soft, creamy-white, oddly acid flesh that many people think is beyond compare. The shape and appearance of the fruits vary widely, depending on the tree. Some are heart-shaped, others oval or conical; some have a fairly smooth skin, others a warty skin.

Cherimoyas grow in Zone 10, but need fairly high elevations and a rather dry climate to fruit. They do poorly in Florida, for example, but well in southern California on the coastal hills. Mature trees withstand temperatures to 26°. Self-fruitful.

Culture

Cherimoyas can be grown from seed, but you will be better off to start with grafted plants derived from trees known to produce top-quality fruits.

Plant in well-drained loam that is substantially reinforced with humus (well rotted manure is ideal) and sand. Provide a space 20 ft. in diameter for each tree (trees grown from seed require more space).

Water sparingly in dry weather. Watch out for mealybugs. Give about 16 cups of balanced fertilizer annually to bearing trees. Start newly planted trees with 1 or 2 cups.

Prune trees while without their leaves. On the Island of Madeira, where cherimoyas do spectacularly well—fruits up to 16 lb. have been reported— the trees are often grown on trellises like grapes, or are espaliered. Training starts with two-year-old plants.

Cherimoyas begin to bear when four years old—perhaps a year earlier; but even full-grown trees never produce many fruits. Pick fruits when they are mature and allow them to ripen for several days before eating.

CHINESE GOOSEBERRY

Also called kiwi and yangtao, the Chinese gooseberry is a handsome, twining, deciduous vine to 30 ft. In late fall and early winter it produces ugly, egg-sized, fuzzy brown fruit with delicious, unusually flavored, translucent green flesh shading to cream at the center. This has a high vitamin C content, may be eaten fresh or made into pie, preserves, ice cream, or sherbet.

The vines are most often grown in California, but do well in almost any part of Zones 8b–10. They can also be grown as far north as 7b, but must be well protected in winter and rarely produce usable fruit. Male and female plants are required for pollination. Although there are several varieties, there is little difference between them.

Culture

Buy grafted plants and set them 30 ft. apart. The vines do best in the sun although they also grow in light shade. Avoid locations where they will be nipped by late spring and early fall frosts.

Chinese gooseberries are grown much like grapes on the same kind of trellis as is used in the Kniffin system of training (see grapes, bunch). They may also be grown on pergolas. The soil should be of good quality and free of nematodes, to which the plants are susceptible. Mulch plants with organic matter and give them ample water during the growing season. Fertilize in the spring with about ½ cup of ammonium nitrate and give them a second feeding in midsummer if they are not making adequate growth (but this is rarely necessary).

Prune in the winter after leaf fall. As with grapes, young plants should be trained to a sturdy trunk with several branches stretching to the sides. Once established, the vines are cut back moderately every year to control their size and promote fruit production.

Diseases and insects cause little trouble.

The fruits attain almost full size in the summer, but do not ripen until November or December. They can then be harvested and used or stored in the refrigerator for some time. They can also be left on the vine for a month or two.

Plants may start to bear at three years of age. They reach good production at five years, and very heavy production at seven.

CITRON

The citron is a shrubby, evergreen, citrus tree to 12 ft. The yellow, lemon-shaped fruits, which mature in winter, are as much as 10 in. long and 6 in. across. They have very little pulp and a very thick, fragrant peel, which is candied. (This fruit should not be confused with the watermelon variety, called citron, which is used in preserves.) Citrons are very susceptible to cold and grow only in Zone 10. Self-fruitful.

Culture

Grow like oranges. Give each tree a space 15 ft. in diameter. New plants are usually propagated by stem cuttings.

DATES

The date palm is a handsome, straight, evergreen to 60 ft. It has a large crown of arching leaves sprouting from the top of the trunk. The huge clusters of richly sweet fruits are harvested from September through November.

Dates are successful only in the southern desert of Arizona and California. The trees require long, hot summers; mild winters; low humidity, and little rainfall in late summer and fall. Trees will, however, grow elsewhere in Zone 10; and every once in a while they may produce a few fruits. Male and female plants are required to set fruit.

Varieties

There are a good many of these; but since the date palm has the peculiar habit of producing offshoots only when five or six years old, and because there have not been many trees planted in recent years, you don't have much choice about what you can plant today. Fortunately, one variety that is in reasonably good supply is Medjool. The Arizona Agricultural Extension Service rates it highly for both homes and commercial plantings. In midautumn it produces large, firm, rich fruits which ripen to amber and cure to reddish brown.

Culture

Buy offshoots or get an expert to remove a couple from parent plants for you: the offshoots are large and must be cut off with a special chisel and sledge hammer. Dates can be grown from seeds, but they do not come true and rarely produce good fruit.

Trees do best in a soil that is a fertile, well-drained but moisture-retentive loam containing a large amount of humus—preferably well-rotted manure. Give each plant a space at least 30 ft. in diameter.

The best time to set out new plants is in May and June. Before planting an offshoot, cut off the leaves close to the stem; but leave about a dozen young ones at the top. Gather these together and tie them tightly about 30 in. above the stem; then cut off the portion above the string.

The planting hole should be at least twice as wide and deep as the base of the offshoot. Dig it in the center of a watering saucer that is 5 ft. across and about 10 in. below the level of the surrounding soil. Plant the offshoot so that its widest part is level with the bottom of the saucer, and pack soil around it firmly. Wrap the entire offshoot almost to the top of the stubbed leaves with burlap to protect it against wind and sun. (The wrapping should not be removed until the following spring.) Then water copiously, and when the water has sunk out of sight, apply a mulch of hay or straw.

Water the young plant again after about 48 hours. Thereafter, for the next six months, you should never allow the soil surface under the mulch to dry out. When applying water, however, do not pour so much into the saucer that it comes up close to the loose fiber at the crown of the plant.

Although the date palm is very resistant to drought, it requires much water to produce good fruit. This means that as the trees grow you should water frequently and deeply so that the soil is kept moist to a depth of 6 to 8 ft. You should also enlarge the watering saucer occasionally to make sure that the water is getting to the roots that spread away from the trunk.

Trees need little fertilizer if you start them off in rich soil and if you maintain a mulch of organic matter which is worked into the top few inches of soil about once a year.

Experience and experiments have shown that date palms are most productive when they have close to 100 leaves. The leaves stay on the tree for as long as seven years; but as they grow older, they manufacture less and less of the sugar needed by the tree. Pruning, therefore, consists of removing enough of the oldest leaves to reduce the total number on the tree to about 100. This operation is done in May. Cut the leaves off as close as possible to the fiber at their base.

Since the trees produce approximately 20 new leaves each year, it is obvious that pruning should not be started until a tree is about five or six years of age. From that point on, if you remove the 20 oldest leaves each year, your trees should be in good fruiting condition. When new leaves are a year old, cut off the spines that project from their ribs. This will make working in the trees a lot less painful. (To estimate how many leaves are on a tree, count the number in one of the spiral columns in which the leaves grow, and multiply by 13.)

Date palms start to bear four to six years after they are planted. In home gardens pollination of the flowers on the female tree is usually left to Nature; but if you want maximum fruit production, you should adopt the professional's practice of pollinating flowers by hand. The best way to do this is to stick three or four strands from a newly opened male flower upside down in a newly opened female flower cluster. The alternative is to place an entire male flower cluster in the top of a palm among the female flowers and let the bees do the rest.

A date offshoot planted in the center of a deep, 5-ft. watering saucer and mulched with hay or straw. The plant is wrapped almost to the top in burlap to protect it against drying and cold injury. (Arizona Agricultural Extension Service)

When fruits reach about ¼ in. diameter—usually in June—they must be thinned to improve their size and quality, to reduce the weight of the bunches, and to ensure adequate flowering the next year. The first step is to remove entire bunches that are undersized. Leave only one bunch for every eight or nine leaves. The next step is to cut out from the center of each bunch a third or a little more of the long stems on which the fruits are borne. Try to remove the same number of stems from each bunch. If you are growing the Medjool variety, which produces unusually large dates, a third step is to remove from each fruiting stem all but about 20 fruits.

During the summer, as the fruit bunches gain in weight, they droop down through the leaves and require support to keep the main stems from breaking and to keep the bunches from being banged about in the wind. To provide this support, simply tie each fruit stem just above the bunch to a nearby leaf or cluster of leaves.

Dates may be damaged by rain and high humidity, fungi, and beetles. Commercial growers commonly cover the bunches of fruit, when they are mature, with tight, waterproof, paper tents; but it is doubtful that you will want to go to this trouble because it is a more complicated undertaking than it sounds and if you're not careful, there may be more damage to the fruit then you would have had if you left them uncovered.

Fungi, which may appear in humid weather, can be controlled by dusting the fruit in late August with Thiomate 19. If beetles start causing trouble in September, spray or dust with malathion.

To keep away birds, cover the fruit bunches with cheesecloth. Dates of the soft type, such as Medjool, are more attractive to our feathered friends than dryer types.

When dates ripen, the flesh becomes soft, pliable, and light brown in color. It looks somewhat translucent. Do not pick the fruits until they reach this stage. If they are not to be eaten within a week or two, put them in the meat keeper in the refrigerator. For longer storage, they can be frozen and held at zero.

If low temperatures and wet weather arrive before all your dates ripen, pick the fruits when the tips begin to soften. Wipe them off with a moist Turkish towel (never wash them). Then spread them in a single layer in a shallow tray with a bottom of ¼ to ½ in. wire mesh. (You can also spread them on cookie sheets, but the results are not so good.) Then preheat your kitchen oven to 180° or 200°, turn it off, and put in the dates. Leave them until they have partially cooled. Then remove them and repeat the process. Continue in this way until the fruits are soft and pliable.

FIGS

Deciduous trees to 25 ft. which produce rather small, seedy, sweet fruits of several colors in summer and fall. The fruits are eaten fresh or are dried, canned, preserved, or made into jam. The trees grow in Zones

A large cluster of dates is thinned by pulling out a third or more of the fruiting stems. (Arizona Agricultural Extension Service)

8–10 and may also be grown in 7 if given winter protection. They are killed by temperatures below 10°. Common figs, the only type which can be grown in the South and Southeast, are self-fruitful. Smyrna figs, which are grown only in California, need to be planted with a caprifig containing fig wasps. They are not recommended for home gardens.

Varieties

Note. All varieties listed are common figs.

Brown Turkey. Also called Southeastern Brown Turkey, Everbearing, Harrison, Ramsey, Lee's Perpetual, and Texas Everbearing. Not to be confused with the Brown Turkey variety grown in California. Widely grown in the South. Medium-size, bronze fruits ripen in summer and fall. One of the best varieties for colder areas because, even after it is frozen, it will put out growth which will bear a good crop of fruit.

Celeste. Also called Celestial, Blue Celeste, Little Brown, Celeste Violette, and Malta. Very widely grown. Small fruits are violet to light brown and have a very good flavor. Ripen in midsummer. Will not bear fruit the same year it suffers severe freeze damage.

Green Ischia. Also called Ischia Green, White Ischia, and Ischia Verte. Medium-size, green fruits in midsummer are of excellent quality but very seedy. Fruits are less attractive to birds than other varieties. Will not bear fruit in the same year it has been frozen.

Hunt. Small to medium fruits with white-flecked, dull bronze skin. Midsummer. Mostly grown in Louisiana. Will not bear fruit the same year it has been frozen.

Kadota. Also called Florentine and Dottato. Large, smooth, yellow fruits in midsummer and early fall are excellent for eating and preserving. They spot and may turn sour in wet weather. Mostly grown in California's hot interior valleys, Texas, and Louisiana. Sets fruit fairly well the same year it is frozen.

Magnolia. Also called Brunswick in California. Medium-size, midsummer fruits are bronze with white flecks. Excellent for preserving. Fruits sour and split badly in wet weather. If frozen, tree will produce fruit on new growth the same year.

Mission. Recommended as the most satisfactory home garden fig in California. Purple-black fruits in summer are splendid for jam, for drying, and for eating fresh. Does not require annual pruning.

San Piero. Also called Thomson, Brown Turkey, and California Brown Turkey. Very large, purplish-green fruits ripen in summer and early fall, but sour and split badly in wet weather.

Culture

You can propagate your own figs speedily and easily by stem cuttings taken in the summer. Or buy plants.

The trees must be planted where they will receive sun all day long. An excellent location is on the south side of your house about 4 ft. from the foundations. Some commercial growers plant figs on a sunny, north slope in order to delay growth in the spring and thus protect the plants from late freezes.

The soil should be well drained and of good quality. Fumigate it if infested with nematodes. If figs are to be trained as trees, each plant needs a space 20 ft. across. It should be planted 2 in. deeper than it previously grew. (In California, give trees even more space.) However, if you train figs as shrubs, they need a space only 10 ft. across. Set the plants 4 in. deeper than they previously grew.

Tree-type plants are recommended only for the warmest climates, where trees are not likely to be damaged by freezing weather. Newly planted trees are headed back to 2 ft. to promote development of three or four scaffold branches. After that, pruning is limited to removal of dead and diseased wood, suckers, and branches that clutter the center of the tree.

Bush-type plants are cut back at planting to half of their original height. Allow the shoots that develop to go through the summer; then during the winter, cut out all but four to six strong stems spaced 4 to 5 in. apart and then trim these back to within a foot of the ground. Thereafter, in the spring after frost danger is past, trim off about half of the growth made by the stems in the previous year. Remove suckers, dead wood, and low-growing side branches.

Keep your trees mulched and watered in dry weather. They need a uniform moisture supply. Fertilize in early spring and about six weeks later with an 8-8-8 fertilizer. The total application should be at the rate of 2 cups per year of tree age up to ten years. Level off at 20 cups. Stems and shoots should grow 12 to 18 in. a year.

Take care not to fertilize in late summer or water heavily in the fall lest you force trees to put out succulent growth which will be killed by cold.

To control fig rust and leaf blight, spray with Bordeaux mixture in the spring when the leaves have reached full size, again four weeks later, and again after fruit is picked. Cover foliage thoroughly. Insect pests include mealybugs, scales, the three-lined fig borer, and several beetles that feed on or in the fruits. The best control for these is to keep your trees healthy and to clean up and burn dead wood, fallen leaves, and fruit, etc. If mites cause leaves to drop, spray with a miticide.

In Zone 8, one- and two-year-old fig trees should be protected in winter by mounding clean soil up around them to a height of 1 or 2 ft.

In colder climates, all figs, regardless of age, must be well protected against low temperatures. After the leaves fall, before the first hard freeze, prune the shrubby tree to desired height, gather the branches together loosely, and tie them. Fill the center of the plant with straw; then wrap more straw around the outside and overwrap with old blankets or burlap. Wrap polyethylene film over this, and seal the top seams so rain and snow cannot enter.

An easier way to raise figs in cool and even in cold climates is to grow them in tubs which are brought into a cool greenhouse, sunporch, or basement in the winter.

Fig trees start to bear two or three years after planting and reach maximum production in about five years. Many varieties produce two crops per season—a small breba (first) crop followed by a large second crop. The breba fruits, borne on the previous year's growth, are slightly inferior. The second crop is produced in the axils of the leaves of the current season's growth.

Fruits ripen from the bottom of the tree up. For eating fresh, pick the fruits as soon as they are ripe. For preserving, pick several days before fruits are ripe. Leave the stem attached to the fruit. Wear gloves to protect your hands against the irritating juice.

GRAPEFRUIT

The largest trees in the citrus family, grapefruits grow to 25 ft. in height and as much as 30 ft. across. They are evergreen and handsome, but less hardy than oranges. Dwarf trees grow to 8 ft.—less if kept in containers. They do not live very long.

Grapefruits grow in Zone 10; also in 9b, but the quality of the fruit is not very good. Self-fruitful.

Varieties

Marsh. Leading commercial variety and very widely planted; but excellent for the home garden, too. Trees are big, vigorous, dense, and consistent bearers. Fruits are seedless and quite juicy. Mature in late fall, winter, and spring, depending on the location.

Royal. Fruits are much smaller than most and more orange colored. They also have a good many seeds. But the juice is unusually sweet. Ripen in the winter; at peak maturity in early March.

Ruby. Also called Redblush. Like Marsh except that the flesh is rosy-red and the rind has a reddish tinge. This and other pink grapefruits are the type most widely planted in Texas. They do not color well in California.

Triumph. Much like Royal, though a little larger. Seedy fruits are very sweet and juicy. Ripen in the winter.

Culture

Grow like oranges. Give each tree a space 30 ft. in diameter.

Like other citrus trees, grapefruits normally shed their old leaves gradually, although the heaviest fall is in the spring. Occasionally, however, something unusual happens to cause a sudden large fall at other times of year. For instance, extremely hot weather with drying winds may cause a heavy leaf drop in the late summer. Young trees may lose a lot of leaves at any time if over-fertilized. Lack of water at any time may also cause trouble.

Such heavy leaf falls generally do no harm: trees recover in fairly short order. In the case of grapefruits, however, you may find that many of the twigs also die back. When that happens, remove as much of the dead wood as you can.

GRUMICHANA

Grumichanas are attractive evergreen trees to 20 ft. and of compact growth. The sweet, cherry-sized fruits produced in summer and fall are usually red but may be black. They are delicious fresh, as a jelly or in pie. The trees grow in Zones 9b and 10. They tolerate temperatures down to about 26°. Self-fruitful.

Culture

Grow from seeds or buy grafted plants.

Plant in a good loam containing humus and sand. Each tree needs a space about 15 ft. in diameter. Give plenty of water, especially when fruit is developing. Apply a balanced fertilizer containing the important minor elements when active growth starts. Young plants need 1 or 2 cups. Increase the amount each year until trees start to bear at the age of five or six. From then on give 12 to 15 cups a year.

Fruits ripen and are ready to pick about a month after flowering.

GUAVA

The guava is a spreading, shrubby, evergreen tree reaching 30 ft. It bears fruits which vary widely in appearance, but which generally have a yellow skin and white, yellow, pink, or red flesh with high Vitamin C content. These are used primarily in jelly, jam, and paste, because they taste sour when fresh; but superior varieties may be eaten fresh. The fruits are most heavily produced in the summer, but are to be had almost the year round.

Guavas grow in Zone 10. Mature trees are not seriously damaged if exposed briefly to 26° temperature; but young trees are killed at somewhat higher readings. Trees are occasionally self-fruitful, but for good fruiting you should plant at least two specimens.

Varieties

Improved varieties which are good to eat fresh but which may produce second-rate preserves include *Blitch, Fan Retief,* and *Malherbe* (pink fleshed), *Miami Red* and *Miami White, Patillo* and *Rolfs* (pink fleshed), *Ruby* (red fleshed) and *Supreme* (white fleshed). But these are hard to find.

Strawberry guava is a relative of the common guava. It has small, red fruits that taste better when fresh and that also make good jelly. Of shrubby growth, the tree reaches only 15 ft., makes a good hedge plant. It grows in Zones 9 and 10.

Culture

You can grow guavas easily from seed, but they do not come true and have inferior fruit; so it is better to air-layer trees that are known to bear superior fruit or to take rooted suckers from them. Or buy grafted plants growing in 5 gal. or larger cans (plants in small cans may have weak roots).

Plant in any decent soil that retains moisture and is well drained. Each tree should have a space about 15 ft. in diameter—more if you do not keep it pruned.

Water as necessary to supplement rainfall when plants are making strong growth and developing fruits. Fruits that ripen in a drought period are small. For maximum fruit production, fertilize rather heavily with an 8-3-8 mixture containing 4 per cent magnesium. Shortly after planting, apply ½ cup; and make repeat applications at the same rate every two months for the first year. During the second year, apply 2 cups every two months. After this, use a total of 10 cups per year per inch of trunk diameter. This should be applied in four to six equal doses. Minor nutrients such as zinc, manganese, copper, and iron may also be needed; and if you want a truly big crop of fruit, give each tree a couple of cups of ammonium nitrate about a month before the main flowering season.

Train young trees to a single trunk with a well-developed system of five to eight scaffold branches. Thereafter trees respond well to winter pruning that keeps them down to 12 to 15 ft. Remove all suckers and thin out older branches in the top. This promotes growth of vigorous young branches which bear larger fruits. It also makes the trees easier to manage in every way.

Spray plants with a copper fungicide if red algae appear on the leaves —usually in very humid weather. Use an oil spray to control whiteflies and scale. Malathion is the best control for fruit flies which burrow in the fruits, but not very successful even so.

Guavas start to bear at three years of age. Allow fruits to be eaten fresh to turn yellow and become soft before picking. Fruits to be preserved should be picked when they are yellow but still quite firm. Ripe fruits can be stored in a refrigerator for two weeks.

If trees are frozen and severely damaged by a sharp freeze, they will generally put up new growth and start producing again in a couple of years.

JABOTICABA

The jaboticaba is an attractive and interesting evergreen tree to 30 ft. in Brazil but only half that here. The branches, which start low on the trunk, are quite contorted; but the entire crown is dense and symmetrical.

The small, purple or black fruits, which mature in flushes almost from the beginning to the end of the year, are produced right on the trunk and main limbs. They taste like Concord grapes and are used fresh, in jelly and for juice.

Trees grow only in Zone 10 because they can withstand little frost. Self-fruitful.

Culture

Propagated by seeds or grafting.

Plant in rich, humusy, well-drained soil. Each tree needs a space 15 ft. in diameter. If you want the maximum amount of fruit, do not let the tree go thirsty for very long at any time. Fertilize two or three times a year at the end of the tree's relatively inactive periods. Give young trees 1 cup of balanced fertilizer and increase 1 cup a year until you reach 12. Level off here.

Seedling trees do not start to bear until they are about ten years of age. This is a good reason for planting grafted trees, because they get to work several years earlier. Pick fruits when ripe.

JAMBOLAN

Jambolans are massive evergreen trees to 40 ft. In spring and summer they bear 1-in. purple fruits which, at their best, are juicy and somewhat astringent but not unpleasant. You may not like them fresh, but they make good jelly. The trees are also useful as windbreaks. Grow in Zones 9b and 10. Self-fruitful.

Culture

Grow from seeds. Plant in average soil. Give each tree a space about 40 ft. in diameter. They do not require watering. Fertilize in late winter. Mature trees can use 20 cups of balanced plant food, but young trees should be fed at one-tenth this rate.

Trees bear when five years old. Pick fruits when ripe.

JUJUBE

Also called Chinese date. The jujube is a very ornamental, deciduous tree to 30 ft. with slender, prickly, drooping branches. The fruits, which look like dates, have reddish-brown, parchment-like skin and a sweet, pithy flesh. They ripen in September and October and may be eaten fresh or dried. They are also used in preserves.

Trees are quite hardy but need a long summer with high temperatures to do well. They grow in Zones 7b–10, but are most common in California's warm interior valleys. Self-fruitful.

Varieties

Lang. Fruits somewhat pear-shaped, up to 2 in. long and 1 in. across.
Li. Round fruits 2 in. in diameter. The seed is very small.

Culture

Although jujubes are easily grown from seeds, the trees thus produced do not always have the best fruit. You should either propagate good varieties by stem cuttings or buy grafted plants.

Plant in any good, well-drained soil except heavy clay. The tree is unusually tolerant of saline soils and water.

Water occasionally but deeply during dry weather. The California Agricultural Extension Service suggests that plants need 4 to 6 in. per month during the summer. Keep mulched to hold moisture in the soil and, particularly, to kill weeds, because unless trees are cultivated with care, you may damage the roots and cause them to sucker. Fertilize in late winter with 6 to 8 cups of ammonium nitrate. Pests rarely cause trouble.

The trees start to bear three years after planting. Fruit to be eaten fresh or put up in syrup should be picked when the skin is still smooth and has turned reddish brown. Fruits left on the tree become wrinkled and darker and are a little less acid. They make an excellent dried product which keeps for many months if they are spread out in the sun for a day or two after they are picked.

KUMQUATS

The kumquat is a very ornamental, evergreen, citrus tree. It grows to about 12 ft. high and across, and makes a good hedge plant. The fruits, which are produced in late fall and winter, are like 1-in. oranges. They are eaten fresh, peel and all, and are also used in preserves. Grow in Zones 9b and 10. Trees are about equal to calamondins in hardiness. Self-fruitful.

Varieties

Marumi. Fruits are round and fairly sweet.
Meiwa. Round, fairly sweet fruits. Trees are less vigorous than the variety below.
Nagami. Fruits are oblong and acid. This variety is also available as an 8-ft. dwarf.

Culture

Grow like oranges. Each tree needs a space about 15 ft. in diameter. Kumquats should be grown on trifoliate orange rootstocks.

LEMONS

Lemons are evergreen trees to 20 ft. (dwarfs to 8 ft. unless confined in containers). Because they are almost as susceptible to cold as limes, they should be grown only in Zone 10. They do best in southern California. Self-fruitful.

Varieties

Eureka. Especially good for home gardens. Bears the year round. Tree is open and spreading.

Lisbon. A top-notch variety though you may not appreciate its thorns. Tree is vigorous, dense, and upright; a little more cold-resistant than other varieties. Fruits are produced pretty much the year round, but most heavily in autumn.

Meyer. This is not a true lemon. The tree is somewhat smaller. Fruits are almost orange colored, contain a lot of mild juice, and have unusually tender flesh. The peel is smooth and very thin. Trees are more resistant to cold and disease than the true lemons. This is the only variety that is recommended without some reservation for Florida and Louisiana.

Ponderosa. Huge fruits weigh as much as 2½ lb., but do not compare in quality to those of other varieties.

Culture

Grow like oranges. Give each tree a space 15 ft. in diameter. As a rule, plants on sweet orange rootstocks perform best.

LIMES

Evergreen citrus trees to 25 ft. (dwarfs to 8 ft. unless confined in containers). The acid, green fruits are borne more or less the year round, although they have peak seasons which vary somewhat between Florida and the West. Since these are the least hardy citrus trees, they should be grown only in Zone 10. Self-fruitful.

Varieties

Bearss. Most popular variety in California and Arizona. Fruits are seedless, a little smaller than lemons, and less acid than Mexican limes. Round, medium-size trees are somewhat hardier than other varieties.

Mexican. Also called Key. The 1-in.-diameter fruits are round or oval and very acid. Tree is small and can be trained as a shrub. It is extremely thorny. This variety is very susceptible to frost injury and anthracnose.

Persian. Also called Tahiti. Recommended for the southernmost parts of Florida. Large, oval, dark-green fruits are very juicy.

Rangpur. Not a true lime, though called one. It is probably a mandarin. It reaches 15 ft. and because it is hardier than the true lime, it can be grown in Zone 9b. Fruits are the size of a small lemon, round or oval, orange outside and in. They are acid and flavorful.

Culture

Grow like oranges. Provide a space 15 ft. in diameter for each tree.

LOQUATS

A handsome evergreen, the loquat grows to 25 ft., has a rounded, compact crown and long, dark, glossy green leaves. Fine panicles of fragrant, white flowers in late fall and winter are followed in late winter and early spring by clusters of oval, large-olive-sized fruits. These have a yellow or orange skin; white to orange flesh that is juicy, delicious, sometimes sweet, and sometimes slightly acid. The fruits are eaten fresh or used for jellies, preserves, and pies.

Loquats grow in Zones 9b and 10. In Hawaii they do best at higher elevations. Mature trees are not seriously injured by brief exposure to 10° temperature; but flowers and fruits are killed at 27° or a bit higher. Self-fruitful.

Varieties

Advance, Premier and **Tanaka.** Three quite similar varieties producing lots of sweet, yellow-fleshed fruits.

Champagne. Sweet, white-fleshed fruits. Heavy bearing.

Culture

For fruit, buy grafted trees. Loquats are easy to raise from seed, but are useful only for ornament.

The trees grow in average soil, but prefer a rich, rather heavy one. It must be well drained and should contain a lot of humus in any case. Although loquats fruit best in dry climates, such as California, supply ample water while they are blooming and developing fruit. Give each tree a space 20 ft. in diameter.

Fertilize two or three times a year with a balanced plant food, such as 8-4-4, plus magnesium. Young plants need about 3 cups. Increase this gradually until, starting at the age of five, you are giving them about 8 cups annually. Over-feeding encourages fire blight.

Once the shape of young trees has been established, they require little pruning. They will, however, produce bigger, better fruits if you remove excess branches and keep the crown open enough for the sun to get in. Fruit size can also be increased by thinning the fruits when they are small.

The worst pests are fire blight, scab, and birds. Spraying with Bordeaux mixture after blossoms fall helps to control scab. Blighted trees should be rid of infested wood at once. Handle like pears.

Trees start to bear in about three years and should be producing heavily at five. Fruits to be eaten fresh are allowed to ripen on the tree; those to be cooked are picked when still a little tart.

LYCHEE

Also called litchi and leechee. Pronounced "lee-chee." An ornamental evergreen tree to 40 ft. with a dense, rounded crown that extends almost to the ground. The 1- to 1½-in. fruits borne in large clusters have a rough skin with a red color, but are sometimes yellow. The white, succulent flesh is delicious. Fruits mature in late spring and summer.

The tree grows in Zone 10, but is a reliable fruit-producer only in areas where the weather is cool and dry for a few months before flowers appear in midwinter. Old trees are badly damaged by several hours' exposure to 25°; young trees are damaged by temperatures just below freezing. Self-fruitful.

Varieties

Brewster. Widely planted but is rather off and on in producing fruit. In Florida it averages under 50 lb. of fruit a year; in Hawaii, 20 lb. It bears a really big crop only about once in four years.

Groff. Upright tree producing an average of 40 lb. of fruit in late summer. Bears more consistently than other varieties. Fruits are dull red, fairly sweet.

Hak Ip. Compact, slow-growing tree producing slightly less fruit and at a somewhat later date than Kwai Mi. Fruits dark red and fairly sweet.

Kwai Mi. Most popular and earliest ripening in Hawaii. Tree is vigorous and wide spreading. Light red fruits in large clusters; acid until fully ripe. Trees average 30 lb. of fruit per year.

Culture

Trees are best propagated by air-layering. This can be done at almost any time, but generally gives best results in the spring. Newly rooted plants should be potted in a humusy soil and kept in the shade for about two months, during which time you should mist them at least once a day with water. They can then be moved gradually into a brighter location and spraying can be reduced. Plant the trees in the garden about six months after the layering wrappings are removed.

If you buy trees, use potted or canned specimens only. Bare-root trees are difficult to get started.

Plant trees in well-drained, acid soil containing a large amount of humus. Protect from wind. This is especially important in the case of young trees; they are, therefore, sometimes surrounded with lath fencing or burlap. However, mature trees are brittle and lose their flowers easily, so they, too, need protection. Give each tree a space about 40 ft. in diameter.

Water regularly until young trees are established. Thereafter, see to it that trees get ample moisture when blossoming and developing fruit; but withhold water (and fertilizer) during their rest period.

Fertilize young trees every two months with a handful of 8-4-4 fertilizer plus a little magnesium. After a year, increase the amount to a total of 6 cups and apply this in three more or less equal doses when trees start making growth in the winter, four months later, and again four months later. In the third year, make three 4-cup applications; and in the fourth and succeeding years, make three 8-cup applications. Trees in limestone soils must also be treated about three times a year with iron, zinc, and manganese.

Since air-layered trees tend to develop narrow, V-shaped crotches and too many branches near the ground, you must take care to prune lychees when young so that they have a system of a few strong scaffold branches with wide crotches. Allow only one leader to develop. Once started in this way, trees need comparatively little pruning to keep them shapely, healthy, and productive.

Mites and scales are the most troublesome pests, but can be kept under control with malathion sprays.

Trees start to bear in about four years. Allow fruit to ripen on the trees before picking. Within a few days after picking, fruits lose their bright red color although their flavor is unchanged. They can, however, be kept pretty for about three weeks if placed in plastic bags and stored in the coldest part of the fresh-food compartment of your refrigerator. They can also be frozen whole and stored for a year.

Mature trees that produce poorly or very erratically can sometimes be made to mend their ways if you score the trunk in the manner described on page 175. The timing of the operation is tricky, however; and trees may not respond as you want them to. Furthermore, you can score a tree only once every few years. So you may be smart to let Nature take its course.

MANDARINS

Mandarins include tangerines and satsumas. They are evergreen citrus trees to 20 ft. which produce flat fruits with loose, easy-peeling skins. Dwarf specimens grow to 8 ft. Among the hardier citrus trees, mandarins grow in Zones 9b and 10. Most (but not all) varieties are self-fruitful.

Varieties

Clementine mandarin. Also called Algerian tangerine. Deep orange fruits are of fine flavor and with few seeds, but are produced erratically. Ripen November to January. Unpicked fruits stay in good condition longer than most mandarins. Self-unfruitful.

Dancy tangerine. Most widely planted tangerine. Especially suited to the desert. The trees have good cold resistance, but fruits do not. Fruits of medium size, reddish orange and with a flavorful, deep orange pulp. Produced in winter, they should be picked promptly when ripe.

Kinnow mandarin. Good-sized, yellowish-orange fruits of excellent flavor are produced in early winter in desert areas; in late winter and spring elsewhere. Trees are upright and vigorous, but tend to bear every other year. Fruits must be thinned in heavy-set years, otherwise they are small.

King orange. This is actually a mandarin. The big, oblate, deep orange fruits are unusually delicious. They are borne in March and April.

Ponkan mandarin. Tree is small, upright, and very ornamental. Large, deep orange fruits are exceptionally flavorful. Unfortunately, they are produced in large quantities only every other year. This tendency can be corrected by using Cleopatra mandarin or Troyer citrange for rootstock.

Satsuma. One of the most cold-tolerant mandarins—especially when grown on trifoliate orange rootstock—but not suited to desert areas. Trees rarely over 10 ft. and have a weeping-willow–like habit. Yellowish-orange fruits are small to medium size; have few seeds. They ripen in late fall and early winter. Fruits must be picked within a fortnight after they mature; if left on the tree, they deteriorate rapidly. They can be stored for a long time, however. Owari is an especially good strain. Armstrong is similarly good and a little earlier.

Culture

Grow like oranges. Most varieties need a space 20 ft. in diameter, but satsumas need only 15.

MANGOES

The mango is a gorgeous, dense, evergreen tree to 90 ft. It has large panicles of pinkish flowers in the winter which are followed in late spring and summer by delicious, greenish, yellow, or red fruits of variable size and shape but generally suggestive of a nectarine. These are usually eaten fresh, but are also made into jam, jelly, pie, etc. Few fruits are more highly rated.

Mangoes grow in Zone 10 and the warmest parts of 9b. Trees seem to do best in hot, dry areas. Mature trees are not injured by brief periods of 25° temperature. Self-fruitful.

Varieties

Earlygold. Medium-size fruits have pink and yellow skin; are usually seedless; mature in May and June. Production is only fair. Trees are resistant to anthracnose.

Haden. Most widely planted mango in the United States. Fruits weigh a pound or more but are not rated as highly for flavor and texture as some

Like many other tropical fruit trees, the mango is beautiful enough to be a focal point of any garden. The large, juicy fruits hang in clusters.

other varieties. Production is inconsistent. Fruits mature in June and July.

Joe Welch. Medium-size fruits are rated about with the above. Production is very good. Most fruits mature in July, but there are usually some in other seasons.

Kent. Originated in Florida and also highly considered in Hawaii. Fruits to 2½ lb. are dark red and yellow; very sweet. They mature in July to September.

Momi K. Medium-size, oblong fruits of excellent quality ripen in June and July. Trees bear moderately but regularly. A Hawaiian panel has ranked the variety just below Pope.

Pirie. Half-pound fruits are very rich, juicy, and sweet; mature in July. Fruit production is inconsistent, however.

Pope. Hawaiians are very enthusiastic about this variety. The 1-lb. fruits, maturing in late July and August, have orange-yellow flesh with excellent flavor and texture. Trees are consistent producers, usually flowering and setting fruit even after the first flowers are destroyed by anthracnose.

Zill. Fruits less than a half pound but have a fine flavor. Mature in June and July. Production good and fairly consistent.

Culture

Buy grafted plants in cans. Those grown from seed do not always come true.

Mangoes grow in any good soil provided it is well drained and neither very heavy nor very light. The trees will also grow in either sun or partial shade, but are heavier-yielding when they get full sun all day long. Protection from the wind is essential, especially during the flowering and fruiting season. Give each tree a space approximately 35 to 40 ft. in diameter, although in shallow, less fertile soils, they can do with less space.

When setting out trees, dig holes at least three times the width and twice the depth of the cans. Set the plants at the depth they previously grew or a little deeper. Water frequently, as the weather requires, for about a month.

Fertilize with 10-10-10, and in Florida add 4 to 6 per cent magnesium. Give each tree ½ cup at planting time, ½ cup three months later, ¾ cup six months later and again nine months later, and 1 cup at the end of a year. From then on, make three applications annually when the tree is growing vigorously. During the second year, apply 1 cup of fertilizer at each feeding; in the third year, 2 cups; in the fourth year, 4 cups; and from then on, 6 cups—or more for very large trees and those with a heavy set of fruit. Bearing trees should also be given a light dose of muriate of potash when flowering starts.

Mangoes usually start to blossom during the dry months of the year, and do not want any excess moisture to speak of during this period. After that, however, they should be watered well if the weather turns unexpectedly dry.

The trees do not need to be pruned unless you want to keep them small and easy to manage. In that case, do your cutting right after fruit is harvested.

Insect attacks are rarely serious although mites, thrips, and scales may need to be brought under control now and then. Diseases can be troublesome, however. This is particularly true of anthracnose, which often causes fruits and flowers to blacken and drop during damp or wet weather. The only way to control it is to spray the trees every week with captan or copper fungicide from the time flowers open until the fruits are well developed.

Grafted mangoes start to bear three to five years after planting. It's a good idea to remove the fruits from three-year-old trees to encourage further growth. As indicated in the descriptions of varieties, mangoes often fruit erratically, setting a good crop one year and almost none the next. The trees also have the disconcerting habit of setting many fewer fruits than their large flower clusters would seem to call for. In fact, even the most fruitful varieties may produce only a couple of fruits per flower panicle. Unfortunately, there is little that you can do about this.

Allow fruits to ripen on the tree before picking them.

NATAL PLUMS

The natal plum is a spiny, evergreen shrub growing to 15 ft. It has big, white, fragrant flowers followed in the summer by 1-in.-long, red fruits that taste like cranberries and make a very good jelly and sauce. To add to the tree's virtues, it makes a splendid hedge plant and keeps right on fruiting even when trimmed. It tolerates salt spray. Grows in Zone 10. Can be grown in 9b, but does not bear fruit. Self-fruitful.

Culture

Buy grafted plants or propagate by cuttings or layers. Plant in average, well-drained soil. If grown as a specimen plant, give each shrub a space about 8 ft. in diameter. In hedges, plant 4 ft. apart.

During dry weather, water deeply every couple of weeks. Fertilize in the spring, before bloom starts, with a balanced plant food. Apply 1 cup to small shrubs; 2 cups to those bearing fruit.

Prune moderately every year to encourage the new growths which bear the fruit.

Plants start to fruit when three years old. Pick fruits when ripe.

Special culture

Natal plum makes a good house plant. Pot up in a large container filled with two parts loam, one part humus, and one part sand. Keep well watered and fertilize sparingly every two months. Grow in a south window in a warm room. Move outdoors as soon as weather is reliably warm. Bring in before frost. Don't count on many fruits, but you should get some.

OLIVES

The olive is a handsome, long-lived, evergreen tree to 25 ft. Its blackish fruits, which are harvested in the fall, are pickled. The trees grow in Zones 8b–10, but they produce best in areas with fairly cold winters (but not below 15°) and warm, fog-free summers. Virtually all commercial orchards are in California—particularly in the southern part of the San Joaquin Valley and the northern part of the Sacramento Valley. Since olives are doubtfully self-fruitful, you should plant two varieties.

Varieties

Ascolano. Fruits almost as large as Sevillano, of excellent quality, but easily bruised. Early. Tree has good resistance to low temperatures.

Manzanillo. Most widely planted variety. Fruits larger and fleshier than Mission and mature early enough usually to avoid frost damage. Low, spreading tree bears regularly.

Mission. Widely planted, but the fruits are the smallest of the varieties listed and are hard to harvest because the tree is tall. Fruits mature rather late and may be damaged by early freezes. Tree tends to bear biennially.

Sevillano. Largest fruits with the largest pits. Fairly early. Harvesting is easy because tree is spreading.

Culture

Olives must be planted where they will escape early fall frosts which damage the fruit and late spring frosts which injure the fruiting wood and flowers. They tolerate a wide variety of soils provided these are well drained, not excessively alkaline, and not infested with the verticillium wilt microbes which attack tomatoes, strawberries and other plants, including olives. Trees on very deep, fertile soil grow larger, but are less productive than those on average soil.

Buy trees in gallon cans: they can be planted at any time and require less work. Bare-root trees must be planted from December through February.

Both canned and bare-root trees are planted at the depth at which they previously grew. Cut the tops of bare-root trees back to a single trunk without branches. Whitewash the trunks or wrap them in paper to protect against sunburn. Keep well watered at all times. Mulch the soil around them. Give each tree a space at least 30 ft. across.

Although olive trees are very tolerant of drought, successful California growers irrigate them regularly throughout the year. One particularly critical period is in the spring after an unusually dry winter. In such a year, you must soak the trees once or twice before they bloom if you are to have a good set of fruit. Another especially critical period is in the summer after the fruit is set, because if the trees do not get enough water at this time, the fruit will shrivel.

The best practice while trees are making growth is to water them deeply whenever the soil in the root zone becomes dry to a depth of 1 ft. (Note that olives are less affected by saline waters than many other plants.)

Keep the ground under trees mulched, or seed it to grass, which should be kept mowed. The olive is unusual in that commercial growers often grow it in sod.

Fertilize trees in late December or January with ammonium nitrate. Start with 1 cup for newly set out trees and increase the application by 1 cup each year until you reach a total of 12. Level off here. Other elements are rarely required.

Pruning is done in the summer. In the first year your aim is to develop three good scaffold branches 12 to 24 in. above ground. Rub out or nip off all other growths. During the next three years prune only to remove suckers and broken and crossing branches. After trees start to bear, you should develop a secondary system of three scaffold branches on each of the primary scaffolds. Work on only one branch a year, lest you force the trees into excessive vegetative growth.

Olives are borne laterally along the shoots of the previous season's growth from the periphery of the tree in toward the center 2 to 3 ft. In a mature tree, annual moderate pruning is required to stimulate growth of new fruiting wood. Cut out dead and unfruitful twigs. Remove branches that grow straight up in the center of the tree. Once a tree reaches 15 to 18 ft., cut top limbs back judiciously so that the tree will be low enough for easy harvesting. Cutting back the side branches may be necessary if trees spread so wide that they crowd against one another or against buildings. Branches growing in shade die.

If trees are damaged by a freeze, don't prune them until June or July, when you can more easily determine which branches really need to be cut.

Trees that bear heavily in alternate years can often be made to behave by pruning just after the fruits are set in a heavy-bearing year. You should then cut out some of the small branches and twigs which are laden with large numbers of fruits. Do not touch the branches with only a few fruits. Your aim is to remove as much fruit as possible while removing a minimum number of leaves.

Another and better way to prevent or at least minimize alternate bearing is to thin out fruits on overloaded trees. This also produces larger and better fruits at an earlier date. Thinning should be done between June 15 and July 10. Wear heavy rubber gloves and strip the fruits from heavily laden twigs. Leave only three to five fruits per foot of twig. The alternative is to spray with naphthaleneacetic acid when the fruits are $\frac{1}{8}$ to $\frac{3}{16}$ in. across.

The principal insect pest of the olive are scales. Verticillium wilt, peacock spot, and olive knot are the worst diseases. Peacock spot, which occurs in rainy seasons and causes black circular spots on the leaves, is controlled by spraying with zineb. Olive knot, which causes galls, is beyond control, but can be prevented by doing all pruning in the summer—never in the winter.

Olive trees start to bear when four or five years old, but their yield is low until they are seven or eight. Maximum production starts at 20 years and may continue for a century.

A mature olive yields a white juice when you squeeze it. Ascolano and Manzanillo olives are picked when they range from an even pale green to a straw color; Mission olives, when they range from an even pale green to dark red; Sevillano olives, when straw colored. Set the fruits aside in the deep shade immediately, and deliver them to a processor the same day. Or pickle them yourself.

ORANGES

Sweet oranges (as they should be called to distinguish them from sour oranges) form handsome, dense, evergreen trees which, depending on variety, mature their fruits from midautumn to the end of spring. As in the case of some other citrus trees, the fruits can be left on the tree for several months after they are ripe. Dwarf specimens of many varieties are available. They reach about 8 ft. in the garden, but are much smaller when grown in containers. They are rather short-lived.

Oranges grow in Zones 9b and 10. Self-fruitful.

Varieties

Hamlin. Often rated as the best of the early varieties. Fruits ripen in December and can be harvested over a three-month period. They are small, sweet, and relatively seedless. Particularly good for home plantings.

Murcott Honey Orange. Like the Temple orange, this is really a tangor— a cross between a tangerine and a sweet orange. It has very sweet, juicy, red flesh and an unfortunate number of seeds. At its peak in midwinter.

Parson Brown. Similar in many ways to Hamlin, but the fruits are larger, seedier, and more highly colored.

Pineapple. Very productive variety bearing heavily every year. Fruits are not quite as good as Hamlin, and a little later. Also quite seedy, but a new strain called Plaquemines Sweet is seedless.

Temple. This is a tangor. It produces big, red-orange, seedy fruits of excellent flavor. They peel fairly well. Fruits mature from midwinter to early spring.

Valencia. Although this is a leading commercial variety, it is also recommended for home gardens. Fine for juice as well as for eating. Fruits are big, deep orange and nearly seedless. They mature in the spring, but can be left on the tree until midautumn. Because they are late-maturing, they are risky to plant in Texas and other areas where freezing temperatures are encountered every few years.

Washington Navel. Seedless fruits of fine flavor ripen in late fall and early winter, but can be left on the tree for three to four months. Very popular in the West, but yields inferior fruits in most other areas.

Culture

Oranges can be grown from fresh seeds (which should not be allowed to dry), but the trees are unusually large and upright and may not be so well adapted to your area as they should be. You should, accordingly, start with trees which have been grafted on to rootstocks best suited to your climate and soil. The stocks most often used are trifoliate orange, sweet orange, Troyer citrange, Cleopatra mandarin, and rough lemon. All have advantages and disadvantages. For example, trifoliate orange is particularly desirable in cold areas and if you want semi-dwarf trees. Rough lemon generally produces heavy-bearing trees, but fruit is of poorer quality. And so on.

Because the question of which rootstock is best is complex, you will be smart not to worry about it unduly. When buying young trees, just tell a reliable nurseryman where you live and what your soil is like, and trust him to give you trees on the right rootstocks. Dealing with a local nursery-man is a sound idea.

The best trees to buy are one-year-old specimens with trunks of ½ to ¾ in. diameter or two-year-old specimens with trunks of ¾ to 1¼ in. diameter (measurements are made 1 in. above the graft). The trees should be balled-and-burlapped, or canned. Select trees with big, bright green leaves, straight trunks, clean bark, grafts at least 3 in. above the ground level. If available, by all means buy trees that are state-registered to be free of certain serious virus diseases.

Oranges will grow in almost any soil that has good drainage and a pH of 6.0 to 6.5. But for best results, look for a spot with a loam or sandy-

Bareroot and potted orange trees only a few feet tall but already bearing fruit. The potted trees are much better to plant because they suffer no shock when they are set out. On a bareroot plant, if the rootlets dry out—which they do very quickly when exposed to the air—they cease to function. (Florida Agricultural Extension Service)

loam soil and add a good quantity of humus. If drainage is poor because of a high water-table or an impervious layer close to the surface of the soil, build up an earth mound that is at least 18 in. high, 8 ft. in diameter at the top, and 12 ft. in diameter at the base.

Oranges should be grown in a location where they get full sun all day long. Never plant them in low spots, where they may be hit by frost. If you live in an area where frost is not too uncommon, placing the trees on the south side of a building or hedge or next to a pond will help to protect them. Avoid planting near septic tanks and drain fields. Give each tree a space 25 ft. in diameter.

Plant in late winter or early spring. The trees should be set just a little higher than they formerly grew. Ideally the top roots should branch out at about ground level. Trees planted too deep are subject to gummosis disease.

After planting, form a watering basin around the tree and fill with water. Then wrap the trunk, from the ground to the branches, in a loose covering of newspaper or wrapping paper to prevent sunburning. This should be kept on for a year. If danger of frost has not passed, bank the tree with soil rather than wrapping in paper. Banking is done after you have given the newly planted trees at least two and preferably three irrigations. Use clean, trash-free soil and mound it up to a height of 15 to 20 in.

Once established, orange trees need good care to assure top production of fruit.

In areas prone to frost, trees that have not developed a low-hanging canopy of branches should be banked with earth in late November. Remove this as soon as danger of frost is past in the spring. Larger trees are best protected from freezing temperature by burning Tree-Heet bricks or orchard heaters on cold nights. If trees are frost-damaged, wait until they put out new growth before pruning, because you may find they need very little. Should severe pruning be needed, wait at least half a year before undertaking it: this gives the trees time to recover from the shock of being frozen.

Annual pruning, which is done before the trees start making growth in the spring, should be avoided if possible on young trees and limited on bearing specimens. All you should do is cut out dead and broken wood and the suckers that grow up from the trunk and main limbs in the center of the tree.

Keep the ground around trees mulched in a circle that grows as the trees spread; but in order to keep the trunk dry and safe from fungi and other pests, allow a space of 6 in. between it and the mulch. This is the easiest way to conserve moisture and eliminate weeds and grass that would compete with the tree for the nutrients in the soil. The alternative—if you consider a mulch unsightly—is to keep the ground bare in a 4-ft. or larger circle around the trunk.

Orange trees need ample moisture, especially in their first three years. It has been figured that they require a minimum of 36 in. of water annually.

Fortunately for Florida and Louisiana gardeners, Nature usually provides enough water to keep trees happy except in unusual dry spells. Elsewhere in the country, you must apply water systematically during the dry season. The California Agricultural Extension Service recommends that, under most conditions, you should water trees every seven to ten days during their first year, and every two weeks during the next two years. Thereafter, trees should be watered every two to six weeks, depending on the soil and the climate. Make a very deep soaking now and then if your water and/or soil are saline.

The simplest way to apply water is to pour it into a shallow watering basin that extends at least a foot beyond the outermost branches. To keep the trunk as dry as possible and thus protect it against gummosis, build a dike of earth close around it.

Do not fertilize newly planted trees until they begin to put out new growth. Then scatter the fertilizer on the ground over the roots and water in well. This is the way citrus trees should always be fed. Applying fertilizer in holes may sound like a good idea if a tree is not doing well, but it's a bad practice because the roots may be burned.

Following are the Agricultural Extension Service recommendations for fertilizing oranges that are growing in bare ground or under a mulch. (If trees are growing in sod or a ground cover, the recommended fertilizer applications must be increased about 40 per cent.)

Arizona. In most cases, nitrogen is the only nutrient required. Although any nitrogen fertilizer may be used, ammonium sulfate seems to be best. During the first year, apply a total of 3 cups in four to six equal doses from midwinter to the end of summer. In the second year, apply a total of 5 cups in equal doses in February, March, May, and August. In the third year, apply 7½ cups on the same schedule. And in the fourth and fifth years, continue with 7½ cups, but make only two equal applications—in February and May.

Mature trees in good condition need 20 cups of ammonium sulfate annually. Half is applied in February and the other half in May. Slightly heavier feedings may be made on sandy Yuma Mesa soils.

California. Give mature trees ammonium sulfate at the same rate recommended for Arizona. Apply in four equal doses—the first in January or February and the others at about monthly intervals thereafter.

Ammonium sulfate is also used for young trees, but the suggested rate of application is much lighter than for Arizona.

Phosphorus may be needed in some areas, but apply it only if local commercial growers are using it.

The only other element which oranges are likely to lack is zinc. A deficiency in this causes a nutritional disease known as mottle-leaf. The leaves turn yellow between the veins and are smaller toward the ends of the twigs. To prevent or correct this problem, spray all the leaves in late winter or early spring with a mixture of 1 oz. zinc sulfate and 1 oz. washing soda in 1 gal. water.

Florida. Use a 6-6-6 citrus fertilizer containing 4 per cent magnesium, 0.75 per cent manganese, and 0.25 per cent copper. Give newly planted trees 1 cup to start. Gradually increase succeeding applications—which should be made at six-week intervals—until each tree is receiving approximately 2¼ cups at the last application. This final feeding should be made about August 15 in northern areas; two to four weeks later further south.

In the second year, starting February 1 or a couple of weeks later in cold areas, follow the same six-week schedule; but gradually increase applications from 2¼ to 4¼ cups. Repeat this schedule in the third year, but start with 4¼ cups and work up to 8 cups. In the fourth year, apply 8 cups in early February, again in May or June, and once again in October or November.

Follow this three-times-a-year schedule thereafter. Until a tree reaches ten years of age, each application should be at the rate of 1⅓ cups of fertilizer per year of tree age. Trees over 30 years old should be given no more than 60 cups (30 lb.) of fertilizer per feeding—or a total of 180 cups (90 lbs.) per year.

Trees growing in alkaline soil should also be sprayed in winter, just before growth begins, with a mixture of copper, zinc, manganese, and lime. Most garden stores carry prepared mixtures.

Louisiana. Use a 6-12-6 or 8-8-8 fertilizer. In late January or early February apply 3 cups per year of tree age up to 12 years; then level off. In addition, you should apply in late May or June ½ cup of ammonium sulfate per year of tree age up to 12 years. Then increase to 7 cups and level off at this amount.

Texas. Follow the California schedule. If trees growing in alkaline soil develop chlorosis, apply 20 cups of ferrous sulfate to the soil. Add manganese to your zinc spray if leaves become mottled but show no signs of dwarfing.

Oranges, like apples, are subject to many diseases and also have a goodly number of insect and animal enemies. Fortunately, several of the worst diseases—tristeza (quick decline), exocortis, psorosis (California scaly bark), xyloporosis, and stubborn disease—can be avoided if you buy healthy, virus-free trees on properly selected rootstocks. Another serious disease—gummosis—is best prevented by selecting trees on Cleopatra mandarin, Troyer citrange, or trifoliate orange rootstock, planting them at the proper height and not allowing wet soil to remain in contact with the bark for long periods. (But refer to Chapter 4.)

Melanose and scab are common fungus diseases for which control measures are given in Chapter 4.

Insects that may become a nuisance are scales, mites, aphids, mealybugs, thrips, leafrollers, cutworms, katydids, citrus nematodes, orange dogs, and orange tortrix. To control these, follow a simplified spray schedule like that in Table XIII.

Deer have a liking for young tree leaves. Gophers, land turtles, and armadillos sometimes build their burrows under banked trees in winter and mutilate the roots.

TABLE XIII
Spray Schedule for Citrus Fruits
Source: Florida Agricultural Extension Service.

1. *Post-Bloom Spray* (March–April).—Applied immediately after flower petals have fallen and before young fruits are ¾ inch in diameter. A suggested combination spray follows.

	AMOUNT OF PESTICIDE FOR	
	50 GALS. WATER	1 GAL. WATER
Malathion (57%) emulsifiable concentrate	1 pint	2 teaspoons
plus		
Kelthane (18½%) emulsifiable concentrate	1 pint	2 teaspoons

NOTE: A neutral copper may be added (a) for melanose control on older trees; (b) for scab control on Temple, Satsuma, grapefruit, tangelos, Murcott honey orange, and lemons; and (c) to aid in greasy spot control.

2. *Pre-Summer Spray* (May).—Same as Fall Spray below.
3. *Summer Spray* (June 15–July 15).—A suggested combination follows.

	AMOUNT OF PESTICIDE FOR	
	50 GALS. WATER	1 GAL. WATER
Oil Emulsion (80–90% oil)	3 pints	2 tablespoons
plus		
Ethion (25%) emulsifiable concentrate	1 pint	2 teaspoons

4. *Fall Spray* (Between October 15 and November 15).—A suggested combination follows.

	AMOUNT OF PESTICIDE FOR	
	50 GALS. WATER	1 GAL. WATER
Malathion (57%) emulsifiable concentrate	1 pint	2 teaspoons
plus		
Kelthane (18½%) emulsifiable concentrate	1 pint	2 teaspoons

5. *Dormant Spray* (Usually in January).—This may be omitted unless scab is a problem (on Temple, Satsuma, grapefruit, tangelos, Murcott honey orange, and lemons) or mites or scales show signs of building up to high populations. Neutral copper should be used for scab, malathion for scales, and Kelthane for mites.

Long exposure to the sun often causes the bark on trunks and branches to become hard and brittle and peel off in patches. But this can be prevented by applying whitewash to the exposed wood of young trees until the canopy grows large enough and low enough to shade them.

A final problem that bothers many home gardeners is fruit-splitting. The cause is unknown, but is generally thought to be either a lack of minor nutrients (especially copper) or an extremely uneven moisture supply in late summer or early fall. Valencias are among the varieties in which splitting most often occurs.

Orange trees start to bear about the third year after planting; but the fruits are of poor quality and should be picked and thrown away. Fourth-year fruits are better, though not perfect, and are usually kept. From the fifth year on, excellent fruits should be produced in good volume.

Allow the fruits to ripen on the tree before picking. They can be left there for a long time without deteriorating; but they may, of course, be damaged by wind and frost and they will in time become inedible.

Fruits picked soon after they mature can be stored in open boxes in a 60° room for a number of weeks. But the longer fruits remain on the tree, the shorter the storage period. In any case, fruits to be stored must not be bruised or cut, because they will spoil rapidly. Do not yank the fruits from the tree, but cut the stems close.

Special culture

Dwarf orange trees perform well in well-drained containers 14 to 18 in. across, or larger. Plant in a mixture of three parts loam and one part peat. The graft should be an inch or so above the soil surface. The latter should be 3 in. below the container rim so that when you water you can apply plenty.

Water tree at planting and repeat in two or three days, and then three or four days after that. Then water whenever the soil surface dries out.

Grow the tree in a sunny spot in a protected part of the garden or terrace. Fertilize monthly with a high-nitrogen plant food and apply a foliar spray of zinc and manganese in spring and fall. Bring the plant indoors for the night when frost threatens or drape an old blanket over it.

PAPAYAS

The papaya is a slender, tree-like, evergreen perennial about 25 ft. tall and with enormous, deeply lobed leaves. It bears large, long, juicy fruits that are more or less yellow and have orange flesh. These are eaten fresh as a rule, but may be made into jam, juice, etc. The fruits are borne on the main stem in winter, spring, and summer.

Papayas grow in Zones 9b and 10, but have been virtually driven out of Florida by mosaic disease. (They will grow there for perhaps a year—if you're lucky.) Trees are killed by subfreezing temperatures, but because they are fast-growing and cheap, there is no reason why you shouldn't take a chance on them in areas with occasional frosts. To ensure production of fruit, you should plant both male and female trees. There are also self-fruitful, bisexual trees, which can be grown alone, but they do not produce such good fruits in such numbers as female trees.

Varieties

There are a number of these, but they are not sufficiently choice to worry about. Take what you can get.

Culture

Grow papayas from seeds picked from ripe fruits, freed from the gelatinous envelopes that encase them, and dried. These may be planted immediately or stored in air-tight containers for several years. Seeds can be sown directly in the garden and covered with ¼ in. of soil. But you get better results in the long run by planting them in sterile peat pots. Plant two to four seeds to a pot and thin to one plant. Seeds germinate in two weeks.

Transplant to the garden when seedlings have four leaves. Shade the little plants with a lath screen, or the equivalent, for a fortnight. Water well every day.

Like many other tropicals, papayas grow in a wide range of soils. In fact, on the island of Hawaii some of the best trees grow in almost pure lava rock. If possible, however, you should give them a soil of good quality and with plenty of humus. It must be well drained. To get the seedlings off to a fast start, dig ample holes and mix 1 cup of superphosphate with the soil at the bottom, below the base of the peat pots. Plant the seedlings, in their pots, a little deeper than they previously grew. Firm the soil around them well. Sidedress them about a week after planting with a handful of balanced fertilizer.

Individual papayas need a space 7 to 8 ft. in diameter. However, since it is impossible to tell the sex of seedling trees, you should plant two or three seedlings about a foot apart in clumps, spaced 7 to 8 ft. apart. Then when the trees begin to flower at the age of about five months, remove from each clump all but one of the desired sex. Flowers on female trees have short stems, large petals and pistils only. Flowers on male trees are small, have ten stamens, and grow in hanging clusters on long stems. You need one male tree for every ten to fifteen female trees.

All papayas must be well screened from wind.

Until you thin the young trees, they should receive about 1 in. of water a week. After that you can, if you wish, reduce the supply about 50 per cent, provided the soil in the root zone retains some moisture. If trees go without moisture for a prolonged period, growth and fruiting will slow down.

Papayas also need to be fed regularly and heavily. Use 10-10-10 or 5-10-10. Apply ½ cup to each tree after it has been in the garden one month. Increase to ¾ cup the second month; 1 cup the third month; 1½ cups the fourth month; 2 cups the fifth month and every month thereafter.

Mulch plants to keep down weeds that fight for fertilizer and water. Keep a lookout for mites and fruit flies. Do not prune trees. You may, however, need to thin the fruits, especially if two or more develop close together; then the smaller and deformed fruits should be removed. This is done about three weeks after the fruits have been set.

Papayas start to bear when a year old. Pick fruits as soon as they turn completely yellow. Handle carefully because they bruise easily. Since the trees are not strong, you should not place a ladder against them to reach the fruits at the top. Use a stepladder; or you can borrow a trick from commercial growers who do their picking with the bell-shaped rubber tool known as a plumber's friend. This is mounted at the end of a long pole. Place the bell against the bottom of a fruit and push upward with the pole. This snaps off the fruit, which either falls into the bell or is caught by hand on its descent to the ground.

Trees continue in good production for about five years; but by the end of three years they are so tall that harvesting is difficult.

PASSION FRUIT

Also called granadilla and lilikoi. The passion fruit is a vigorous, evergreen vine growing to 25 ft. It climbs by tendrils. The oval or round, 2-in.–diameter fruits produced in midsummer and midwinter have a leathery rind and a yellowish, juicy, aromatic flesh of tart but delightful flavor. The fruits are eaten fresh or used for juices and sherberts. In the United States, passion fruit is most widely grown in Hawaii, but can be grown elsewhere in Zone 10 if plants are given good protection against cold for the first year. Two or more plants are required to ensure fruiting.

Varieties

Purple passion fruit. Fruits are purple and considered somewhat superior in flavor and aroma to yellow fruits. This variety grows best above 2,500 ft. elevation.

Yellow passion fruit. Fruits are yellow. Plants are larger, more vigorous and more productive than the purple variety. They grow best from sea level to 2,500 ft. This is the variety most widely grown for commercial purposes in Hawaii.

Note. Other members of the passiflora genus bear fruit; but while palatable, these are much inferior to the fruits of the above varieties.

Culture

Passion fruit is usually grown from seed, but can also be easily propagated by cuttings and layers. Do not bother to remove the pulp from around seeds before planting. If possible, seeds as well as cuttings and layers should be taken only from plants that produce oval fruits since they are juicier than round fruits. You should also avoid plants that produce fruits with orange-colored rinds.

When seedlings are 2 in. tall, move them into small pots. Plant them in the garden when they are 6 in. tall.

Passion fruit grows well in various soils, but does best in one containing much humus. The soil must be very well drained. Apply lime to soil that is extremely acid. Fumigate soil that is infested with nematodes.

Plants should be grown in a location where they are not battered by winds. Train them on a trellis made with three heavy-gauge (No. 9) wires stretched between posts 10 ft. apart. The top wire should not be less than 6 ft., and should preferably be 7 ft., above ground. The middle wire is 18 in. below the top; and the bottom, 18 in. below the middle. Because the vines are very heavy, run the wires through holes bored in the posts; don't just staple them to the posts.

Plant one vine at the base of each post; and to help it climb to the first wire as quickly as possible, drop a string down to it from the wire. If healthy, it will go up this like Jack on the beanstalk.

Vines should be pruned after the winter harvest but only very lightly. Remove the stems that trail or threaten to trail on the ground. Beyond that, you should remove no more growth than is necessary to keep the vines neat and reasonably lightweight, to facilitate spraying and to allow ripe fruits to fall through to the ground.

Water vines during dry spells that may occur when they are growing actively.

The Hawaiian Agricultural Extension Service recommends use of a 10-5-20 fertilizer in that state, where all soils lack nitrogen. In other areas you can use a fertilizer with lower nitrogen content. Give each young plant, soon after planting, 4 cups of fertilizer; and make a second application of the same size six to eight weeks later. Plants over a year old should be given a total of 24 to 30 cups a year in four equal doses. Make one application when plants start into active growth before the summer and winter crops, and make a second about midway through each growth period.

Fruit flies and mites are the worst pests. The former can be controlled by spraying with malathion as they appear. This may also take care of the mites; if not, use a sulfur spray. To avoid killing too many of the bees and other beneficial insects that serve as pollinators, all sprays should be applied when the flowers on the vines are closed. (Purple passion fruit flowers open early in the morning and close before noon; yellow passion fruit flowers open after noon and close at night.)

Passion fruit vines should start bearing within a year after they are started from seed. Harvest fruits as soon as possible after they fall to the ground. Spread them out on a counter, or store in a slatted, open crate in a cool, ventilated, sunless place until you use them.

PINEAPPLE

The pineapple is a 3-ft. perennial with sword-like leaves that usually have wicked spines. The leaves are arranged in a large rosette around a stem on which a single fruit is borne. Fruits generally mature in the summer.

Pineapples grow in Zone 10 and, with luck, in 9b. Self-fruitful.

Varieties

Eleuthera. Also called Pernambuco. A good home variety. Sweet, juicy flesh is a faintly yellow white. Fruits weigh up to 4 lb. Spiny leaves.

Natal Queen. Highly recommended for home growing. Yellow-fleshed fruits weigh about 3 lb., have an excellent flavor, and keep well. Leaves are spiny.

Smooth Cayenne. Outstanding and most widely planted variety. Cylindrical, yellow-fleshed fruits weigh up to 6 lb. Leaves are spineless.

Culture

You can easily propagate your own pineapples in several ways: (1) Cut off the crown of leaves from the top of a fruit, trim off the flesh at the base,

and then cut the bottom of the stem until you see root buds. Then strip
off three or four of the basal leaves and place the crown upside down in
a dry, shady place for about a week. When the cut end hardens a bit, plant
the crown right side up in soil. This should be brought up around the stem
just far enough to hold the crown upright. Do not get soil into the leaves.
(2) Remove the small slips, or suckers, that sprout from the stem below the
fruit and handle like a crown. If there is a knob at the base of a slip, cut it
off before drying. (3) Plant the large suckers which develop near the base
of the stem in the leaf axils. Handle like a crown. (4) Plant the underground
suckers, called ratoons, which sprout around the pineapple. Unlike the
other plant materials, these should be planted quickly so that the roots
cannot dry out.

To keep out mealybugs, which are a major pest once they infest a
pineapple planting, dip all plants before setting them in the garden in 2

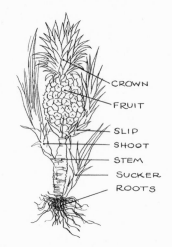

The parts of a pineapple.

tsp. malathion mixed in 1 gal. water. If nematodes are active in your area,
fumigate the soil before planting.

In Florida pineapples should be planted in partial shade, as in a lath
house or in the lee of a high-crowned tree. Elsewhere they are grown in
full sun.

Pineapples are most successful in a fertile, sandy, very humusy, somewhat acid soil that has good drainage and also retains moisture. Space
plants 18 in. apart in rows 2 ft. wide. Fertilize lightly with a balanced material with a low phosphorus content, such as 7-2-7 or 8-3-8. Make a first
application of a heaping tablespoonful four months after the plants are
set in the garden; and make repeat applications at the same rate every four
months thereafter. An alternative, after making the first feeding of balanced fertilizer, is to apply a foliar spray of urea (nitrogen) at four-month
intervals. Make the spray with ¾ lb. urea in 1 gal. water. A spray of iron
applied at the same time is generally advisable.

Give plants plenty of water, but do not let them stand in it. Weed faithfully, because pineapples cannot stand the competition. The alternative, of course, is to apply a mulch—usually black polyethlene film.

If mealybugs infest your plants, drench them with malathion sprays up to one week before harvesting fruit. Keeping ants out of the garden helps to keep out mealybugs. Should a plant develop heart-rot—a fungus disease that blackens and loosens the center leaves—you may be able to save it by pouring captan into it; but you'd be better advised to destroy it at once.

Depending on the way you start them, pineapples will mature fruits in 15 to 24 months. Crowns are slowest; suckers fastest. Cut off the fruits just below the base when they turn yellow all over.

As noted earlier, pineapples generally fruit in the summer. They can, however, be forced to fruit at almost any season if you spray the terminal buds with naphthaleneacetic acid or BOH. This must be done only to mature plants that are growing vigorously. They will ripen fruit within five to seven months after the treatment.

Each plant produces one fruit. After this is picked, one of the ratoons will throw up a new fruit. However, plants that are left to carry on in this way produce increasingly smaller fruits. So the best practice is to discard plants that have fruited and start new ones in their place.

Special culture No. 1

Pineapples grow beautifully in 3- to 5-gal. cans if the roots are kept at a temperature above 70°. Fertilize with a foliar spray of 20-20-20 plus magnesium and iron once a month. Take care not to expose plants to gas fumes.

Special culture No. 2

Pineapples have long been favorite house plants. They are usually started in 8-in. pots and then transplanted into 12-in. pots. Grow like plants in cans or in the garden.

In winter, keep the plants indoors in a warm, sunny window which is covered with a storm sash (cold seeping through a single-paned window at night can injure pineapples). Or you can grow them under fluorescent lights in any room. In summer, move the plants outdoors into a sunny, protected spot.

PINEAPPLE GUAVA

A close relative of the guava, the pineapple guava is a 15-ft., wide-spreading, evergreen shrub. It is ornamental, especially when in bloom in the spring; and in the fall it produces oblong, 2-in., gray-green fruits with a pineapple-like flavor. These are eaten fresh, cooked, or preserved.

Pineapple guava grows in Zones 9 and 10, especially in areas which have a definite cool season. They withstand short periods of temperatures to 15° with little damage. May be self-fruitful; but to be sure of fruit, you should put in two plants.

Culture

The pineapple guava can be layered if you want to perpetuate an unusually productive specimen; but it is usually raised from seeds started in partial shade. Germination: 3 weeks. Transplant seedlings into individual pots, and after they make further growth, move them into a sunny place in the garden. The soil can be of average quality, but should contain a lot of humus. Good drainage is important. Give each plant a space about 15 ft. in diameter.

Water in dry weather when shrubs are making growth and developing fruit. (Note, however, that if your water is extremely saline, it will kill the plants.) Fertilize in early spring with a couple of cups of balanced fertilizer with a low nitrogen content. Prune only enough to keep the plants shapely. There are few pests to worry about.

A splendid way to grow pineapples: in large cans. Several varieties are shown here in an experimental greenhouse at the University of Florida.

Shrubs grown from seed begin to bear in about the fourth year. Layered shrubs start a year earlier. Mature fruits fall to the ground. They should be allowed to soften slightly in a cool place before they are eaten.

POMEGRANATES

The pomegranate is a 15-ft. tree producing large, usually red fruits which are filled with seeds covered with a juicy, slightly acid, pleasant-tasting pulp. The fruits, which mature in the fall, are eaten fresh or made into juice and grenadine syrup. Trees are deciduous, but in warmer areas are without leaves for only a short period. They are very pretty when their scarlet flowers are open.

Pomegranates grow in Zones 8b–10. They withstand brief periods of 15° temperature without severe damage. Self-fruitful.

Varieties

Paper Shell. Not the equal of the last, but good.

Spanish Ruby. Large, bright red fruits with sweet crimson flesh.

Wonderful. An old variety but still about the best. Vigorous and very productive. The purple-red fruits have deep crimson flesh of excellent quality.

Culture

Pomegranates are readily grown from rooted suckers taken from around the base of trees. They may also be layered and grown from seeds.

The plants are not very exacting about soil, but perform best in rather heavy, humusy loams. Give each tree a space 15 ft. in diameter. Trees can, however, be grown in hedges, in which case they are spaced about 7 ft. apart.

Although pomegranates can withstand long dry spells, they fruit best if watered regularly through spring and summer. Fertilize established plants annually in early spring with 4 to 6 cups of balanced fertilizer.

Because pomegranates left to themselves make thick, shrubby growth, you should train them from time of planting as single-trunked trees with a good system of scaffold branches. After three years, when the desired shape has been established, prune regularly in late winter to remove all suckers in and around the trees.

Trees start bearing at three to four years of age. Pick fruits before they are fully mature, because they tend to split if ripened on the tree. They should also be dry when picked. Ripen in a cool, dry, shady place.

PRICKLY PEAR

Also called Indian fig or tuna, the prickly pear is a cactus belonging to the *Opuntia* genus. The species most commonly grown for food are *ficus-indica* and *tuna.* The former is more tree-like and has larger fruit; the latter is wide-spreading. Both reach 10 ft. or more and have wicked spines and bristles. The more or less pear-shaped fruits are usually yellow, covered with bristles and sweet. They are produced from about July into late fall and are eaten fresh. The plants grow best in Zones 8-10 in the Southwest, but can be grown in 6 and 7 though they are not likely to ripen their fruit. Self-fruitful.

Culture

Prickly pears require as much sun as you can give them. The soil must be exceedingly well drained but of only average quality.

Plant in the spring. To propagate, break or cut off one of the fleshy, leaf-like joints from an old plant and allow it to dry for about a week in light shade. Then plant the joint cut-side down in just enough soil to hold it upright. Do not water for about four days; then dampen the soil slightly. For the next two months, dampen the soil slightly about every fourth day. Once the plant is rooted and established, it generally makes good growth, flowers, and fruits without attention. You may, however, water it occasionally in spring and summer, and you may also give it a cup of balanced fertilizer or bonemeal in early spring.

Individual plants require a space about 8 ft. in diameter, but may be planted a couple of feet closer together if you want an impenetrable hedge.

Plants start to bear in three years. To harvest fruits, first rub off the bristles with straw or leaves. Wear heavy gloves. Then break the fruits from the joints.

SAPODILLA

A very handsome, slow-growing, evergreen tree to 60 ft. with a dense, spreading crown. It bears brown-skinned, scurfy fruits ranging from 2 to 4 in. in diameter and from round to oval. The flesh is light brown, sweet, and savory. Some fruits have no seeds; others have as many as 12. Fruits are most plentiful in the summer, but mature throughout the year.

Sapodillas grow in Zone 10—best in coastal lowlands. Young trees are likely to be injured or killed at the freezing point. Large trees generally show little damage if exposed to a 26° temperature for a brief period. Self-fruitful.

Varieties

Prolific. Tree is irregular when mature but pyramid-shaped when young. Produces four to six bushels of smooth, richly sweet fruits. Recommended in Florida.

Russell. Fruits are larger than Prolific's but more granular in texture. Young trees are vase-shaped; old trees, irregular.

Culture

Sapodillas can be grown from seeds, but the trees are often poor producers of inferior fruit. So it is better to buy grafted plants.

Unlike many tropical fruits, sapodillas have high resistance to uprooting and breakage and can accordingly be planted in very exposed locations. They are also rather indifferent to the kind of soil they grow in as long as it is well drained. And they do not require a great deal of water.

Each tree needs a space about 20 ft. in diameter.

The Florida Agricultural Extension Service recommends feeding with a mixture containing 6 to 8 per cent nitrogen, 2 to 4 per cent phosphoric acid and 6 to 8 per cent potash. Apply ½ cup to newly planted trees after they have been in the ground several weeks. Make two additional ½-cup applications at three-month intervals. Then step up to 1-cup applications—twice at three-month intervals—then to 1½-cup applications—twice at three-month intervals. Then increase applications to 2 cups. Continue feeding at this rate for five years; then increase to a total of about 12 cups a year.

Trees may be infested with scale insects which cause a sooty mold on leaves. These can be controlled with miscible oil sprays. Use copper fungicides if trees are attacked by rust (usually in winter or spring). A more difficult pest is the Caribbean fruit fly, the larvae of which feed on the fruit. There is no control.

Harvest fruits when fully mature and allow them to soften a few days. Trees start to bear at about five years of age.

SHADDOCKS

Also called pummelos. Evergreen trees very similar to the grapefruit and about the same size. They bear very large, yellow, pear-shaped or more or less round fruits with yellow or pink flesh, depending on the variety. (All varieties are hard to find in the United States.) The fruits, which Americans generally consider inferior to grapefruits, ripen in late fall and winter. Trees grow in Zone 10. Self-fruitful.

Culture

Grow like oranges. Give each tree a space 25 ft. in diameter. Trees are commonly propagated by seeds.

SOUR ORANGE

Also called Seville orange. In the United States the sour orange is used primarily as a rootstock for other citrus trees; but in Spain it is grown to provide the somewhat flattened, acid fruits which the English make into the world's best marmalade. The trees are evergreen, spiny, and reach about 20 ft. in height. Grow in Zones 9b and 10. Self-fruitful.

Culture

Grow like oranges. Give each tree a space 15 ft. in diameter. The sour orange does better on wet soils than other citrus, but don't abuse them. Take care not to bruise the fruit skin when harvesting.

SUGAR APPLES

A 20-ft. deciduous tree closely related to the cherimoya, the sugar apple bears apple-sized, yellow-green fruits which look like a fat artichoke or strawberry. The white flesh surrounding a plethora of seeds is custardy, sweet, and delicious. You eat it by breaking it into pieces. The fruits mature in midsummer and fall. Trees grow in Zones 9b and 10 at low altitudes. As opposed to the cherimoya, they do well in Florida and poorly in California. Self-fruitful.

Culture

Buy grafted plants and grow like cherimoya. Pick fruits before they are fully ripe, because if left on the tree too long, they are likely to burst. Ripen in the house several days before eating.

Heavier yields result if plants are hand-pollinated.

SURINAM CHERRY

Also called pitanga. An evergreen shrub to 15 ft. In spring and again in fall the Surinam cherry bears small, round fruits with eight prominent ribs. These are usually red, but in one form of the shrub, they are almost black. They are juicy, aromatic, but too acid to enjoy when fresh; so use them for making an excellent jelly. Grows in Zones 9b and 10. Withstands temperatures in the low 20s. Self-fruitful.

Culture

This is an easy plant to grow from seed. Just make sure that the seeds come from a shrub that produces lots of sizable, tasty fruits. Grafted plants are also available and are generally more reliable.

Plant in good soil. Allow a space 10 to 12 ft. in diameter for each shrub. If planted in a hedge, they produce few fruits.

Surinam cherry is not a very demanding plant, but like most fruits does its best when cared for. See that it receives ample moisture when blossoming and fruiting. And fertilize it twice a year as it starts to set fruit. Apply 1 cup of balanced plant food each time.

Prune as little as possible if you don't want to reduce the fruit crop temporarily.

Shrubs start to bear when two or three years old. Let the fruits ripen on the plants before picking.

TANGELOS

Tangelos are crosses between mandarins and grapefruit. They are evergreen trees to 20 ft. (dwarfs to 8 ft.) and have very juicy, orange-size fruits. Grow in Zones 9b and 10. Some varieties are self-unfruitful.

Varieties

Minneola. Fruits have excellent flavor, few seeds, and a reddish-orange skin that peels easily. They are about the size of a Temple orange; ripen from December to April, depending on the area. Self-unfruitful.

Nova. One of the earliest tangelos, ripening in October and November. Medium-size fruits are more highly colored and sweeter than Orlando.

Orlando. Fruits are orange-colored, mandarin-shaped, and have a mild, pleasing flavor. They ripen in late fall and winter. Trees are less vigorous than other varieties, but grow rapidly. Self-unfruitful.

Culture

Grow like oranges. Give each tree a space 20 ft. across.

WHITE SAPOTE

An ornamental tree to 25 ft. with glossy, evergreen foliage. The orange-size fruits have a thin, yellowish, soft skin and yellow flesh of pleasant but variable flavor. Fruits mature from midspring to early fall. They are eaten fresh or made into preserves. Trees grow in Zones 9b and 10.

The white sapote is not widely grown and has been given little study. Take any variety you can find. Trees are self-fruitful.

Culture

Buy grafted plants. Seedlings take too long to start bearing and yield inferior fruit.

Give each tree a space 20 ft. in diameter. Plant in any decent soil with good drainage. Newly set out plants need to be watered well, but established plants get along with less moisture. Watering should not be ignored in dry spells, however.

Fertilize young plants about three times a year with 1 cup of balanced 8-4-4 fertilizer. Increase applications gradually as trees grow. After five years, you can give them a total of 8 to 12 cups annually.

Spray with malathion if scale insects become troublesome.

White sapotes start bearing at about five or six years of age. Pick fruits when they are mature but hard, and allow them to ripen in a warm place for several days before eating.

10

Growing Nuts

If you want to grow food plants with a very minimum of effort, raise nuts. They return bigger dividends for a small investment of time and energy than anything else. Consider exactly what they yield:

A delicious, uniquely flavored food—one so good that you cannot stop eating it once you start.

A food with high nutritional values.

A food that attracts amusing (and sometimes pestiferous) small animals and birds to your garden.

Beauty—many of the nut trees are magnificent ornamentals.

Shade.

Valuable lumber—although this is of possible interest only if you have a plantation of nut trees.

And as I said at the outset, they require little work.

Except for peanuts, which are legumes, the nuts we raise in the United States grow on trees and, in one case, shrubs. At least one will grow in every zone south of Alaska, so there is no reason why the vast majority of American gardeners should not grow them.

The process is essentially the same as that used in growing northern tree fruits, so I refer you to Chapter 7 and will simply summarize matters here:

Selecting nut trees. There are no dwarf or semi-dwarf nut trees. In the parlance of fruit growers, all are "standards" and most of them attain gigantic proportions. This is of no real concern if you have about a third of an acre or more. But on a small lot you might feel swamped by anything other than almonds, coconuts, filberts, and pistachios (all of which happen to grow in mild or warm climates).

Varieties of nut trees are numerous, but except for species which are cropped on a broad scale (almonds, filberts, pecans, and Persian walnuts), the choice is not terribly clear-cut. This is partly because varieties that do well in one state do not always do well in an adjoining state with the same general type of soil and climate. For this reason, if you have any doubts about varieties, you should be guided by what a local nurseryman is offering.

Finally, you must concern yourself with the pollination habits of the species you plant. Relatively few nut trees are reliably self-fruitful. A peculiar failing of a number of the trees is that, although male and female flowers are borne on the same tree, they do not open at the same time. As a result, you must plant two or more varieties to get a good crop of nuts.

Obtaining plants. The easiest thing to do is to buy trees from a nursery you trust. As a rule, one- or two-year-old plants are the best buy; but of greater importance—especially in the case of the largest trees—is the condition of the roots. These must be large and well branched if the tree is to survive.

The other way of obtaining nut trees is to grow your own from seeds (filberts, however, are usually tip-layered). This produces fine trees, but they very rarely are exactly the same as their parents. Occasionally they are better; but often they are not.

Be this as it may, the way to grow temperate-climate nut trees from seed is to stratify newly harvested nuts of the largest size you can find. (There is a correlation between the size of the planted nuts and the size of the nuts on the trees they produce.) You can stratify by putting a few nuts (in their shells) in a plastic bag filled with moist peat and storing them in the fresh-food compartment of your refrigerator. Or you can place nuts between layers of sand in a box with an open but screened top and bottom. This is set outside on a small mound of earth (so water will drain away) and covered with leaves, straw, or fiberglass insulation to protect the nuts from extreme temperature changes.

In the spring, before the nuts develop sizable sprouts, they should be planted on their side in a nursery bed or wherever the trees are to grow. A somewhat sandy soil is desirable, because it promotes growth of more fibrous roots. Bury small nuts 1 in. deep; large nuts, 2 in. deep. Keep the soil moist and weeded. The seeds should germinate and make good growth before the summer is over; but sometimes hickories and walnuts do not appear for a year. In any case, when the seedling trees are well developed, give them a light dose of balanced fertilizer. Protect them from the broiling summer sun with a lath screen.

An alternative procedure is to sow nuts in the fall directly in the garden. Handle them as described above. They must be covered with wire mesh to protect them from rodents. When the soil freezes, cover it with an organic mulch to prevent heaving.

Planting nut trees is like planting fruit trees. The two differences: Nut trees are not only big but also long-lived and they should have exceptionally good, well-prepared soil. And because of their large root systems and in some cases very deep tap roots, the holes must be dug unusually deep and wide. (The first time I planted pecan trees, I didn't think I would ever get the holes dug.)

General care can be summed up quickly: Give the trees plenty of water throughout the growing season. Fertilize every year even though the trees look so big and healthy that you doubt whether they need any more nourishment. Train to a sturdy, desirable shape and prune annually in the winter thereafter.

Unless the trees are planted in an area where a mulch would be unsightly, most expert nut growers recommend maintenance of a mulch, especially around young trees. I favor an organic mulch since it adds valuable nutrients to the soil and also holds in moisture, controls weeds, and maintains a desirable soil temperature. Of course, such a mulch causes a problem when nuts mature and fall from the tree, because it swallows them up. But during this period it can be pulled to one side to expose the ground; or under a small tree, it might be covered with plastic film or tarpaulins.

Controlling pests. This is a more difficult job on nut trees than on fruits, not because the nuts have more pests (quite the opposite) but because the trees are usually so much larger. In fact, mature nut trees are likely to be of such dimensions that only a professional tree man with large spraying equipment can do the job. This is not frightfully expensive if only a single application of insecticide and/or fungicide is called for: but if the trees require several treatments, the cost of spraying may outweigh the value of the crop you harvest.

What is the alternative? Good garden sanitation measures: Select varieties that are resistant to diseases which are known to be bothersome in your area. Sterilize your pruning tools when pruning diseased trees. Clean out rotten wood and apply tree paint to the sound wood that is left exposed. Cover cavities with screen wire to keep codling moths, etc., from hiding in them. Keep litter that falls from the trees cleaned up and burned. In the fall and again in the early spring do a really thorough job of raking up and burning nuts, twigs, and diseased leaves.

Admittedly, these measures are not going to give you complete protection in every year against pests. There will be times when spraying is indicated; but those times should be so few that, hopefully, the work and expense of spraying will seem quite reasonable.

ALMONDS

Almonds are deciduous trees to 30 ft. They are related to peaches, plums, and other stone fruits. The sweet, creamy white nuts mature in early fall.

Almonds grow in Zones 7–9, but they are reliable producers only in 9. They do best in the Sacramento and San Joaquin Valleys of California, where the summers are long, hot, and dry; winters are moderately cold; and spring comes early. Usually self-unfruitful; two different varieties are needed.

Varieties

Hall's Hardy. A late-blooming variety that just might produce a few nuts for you in Zones 7 and 8. Shells are hard; kernels not up to other varieties in quality. Tree is self-fruitful.

Ne Plus Ultra. Well-known variety but of poorer quality. Midseason. Susceptible to fungus disease. Flowers are often hit by frost.

Nonpareil. Best and most commonly planted variety. Uniform, smooth nuts in paper-thin shells. Early.

Texas Prolific. Also called Texas. Good nuts but not quite the equal of the above. Hard shells. Late. Vigorous tree but may be damaged by saline soils.

Culture

Buy grafted plants.

Because almonds bloom earlier than other nut and fruit trees and because the flowers are very tender, trees should be planted on a north slope or north side of the house. Be very careful to avoid locations where frosts settle. Give each tree a space 25 to 30 ft. in diameter. The trees are very tolerant of poor to average soil, but perform best in good, well-drained, humusy soil.

Water occasionally but deeply. Too much water encourages crown rot. For this reason it is best not to plant trees in lawn areas or other spots that require frequent watering. The obvious alternative is to maintain a deep mulch around each tree over the better part of its root system.

Fertilize in the spring. Apply about a cup of balanced fertilizer the first year, then use ammonium nitrate alone. Apply 1 cup the second year, and thereafter add 1 cup a year until you reach 6. This is usually enough. Applications of zinc, copper, or boron may also be needed.

Cut back trees at planting to 30 in. and trim branches to two buds. Train to a modified leader with three scaffold branches. Once the shape is established, trees do not require a great deal of pruning, but should be kept thinned out so that light will get into the center. Old trees especially need attention to encourage them to make new growth.

To control insects and diseases, apply a general-purpose fruit spray according to the schedule for peaches in Table X. Keep an eye out for red spiders in midsummer, and spray with a mite-killer if they appear.

Almonds start to bear in the fourth year after planting and should be producing well by the seventh year.

When almonds mature, the hull splits open, allowing the shell and kernel to dry out. Splitting occurs first on the outside nuts, then on the inside. Harvesting is best done after most of the inside nuts have opened. All may then be picked or knocked on to sheets on the ground. Allow them to dry for several days longer under the tree; then remove the hulls and spread the nuts in a shady spot to dry or put them into an oven at a very low temperature (about 110°).

Dried almonds can be stored in a cool, dry place in sacks for several months. Shelled kernels are best kept in the fresh-food compartment of the refrigerator.

BUTTERNUTS

The butternut is a fast-growing walnut with white wood (which is why it is sometimes called white walnut). It grows to 90 ft. and produces in the fall rough, thick-shelled, hard-to-crack nuts similar to but smaller than black walnuts. The kernels are sweet and oily.

Butternuts grow in Zones 3–8, but best in the eastern half of the country. Probably self-fruitful, but not reliably so.

Varieties

Craxeasy, Kenworthy, and Kinneyglen are superior varieties with fine nuts that crack out better than most; but there is little to choose between them, and they are not widely available. You had better just take what you can get.

Culture

Grow like black walnuts. Butternuts are often killed by a fungus disease called dieback and the bunch disease which also attacks black walnuts. There is no cure for these.

CHESTNUTS

The only reliable chestnut with good nuts to grow in the United States is the Chinese species. It is resistant to the blight which has almost wiped out the American chestnut and which also attacks other species. The tree is deciduous, grows to 50 ft., and spreads even wider. The nuts, which mature in the fall, are cooked before they are eaten.

The Chinese chestnut grows in Zones 5–8 and will usually survive in sheltered spots in 4b. Self-unfruitful; two or more varieties or seedlings must be planted to assure production of nuts.

Varieties

Abundance. Has the smallest nuts of any variety listed here, but they have excellent flavor.

Crane. Big, dark red nuts keep better than those of any other variety. A very precocious tree, it occasionally bears in the first year.

Kuling. Large, dark brown nuts. Upright tree.

Meiling. Light brown nuts on an upright tree. Along with Kuling, this variety is especially good for small yards because of its growth habit.

Nanking. Big, dark brown nuts of fine quality. Starts bearing early. Widely planted.

Orrin. Big nuts, nearly black, are flavorful and keep well.

Culture

Chestnuts are easily grown from seeds and many of the trees available for sale have been propagated in this way. Grafted trees are also available. The latter are true to type, produce somewhat larger nuts, and start bearing at an earlier age. However, they often die young because of failure of the graft. The exact cause of this is unknown, but seems to be related to winter injury. If you live in the North, therefore, you probably should plant seedling rather than grafted trees.

Chestnuts bloom in late spring, but the swollen buds are likely to be killed by frost; so be sure to plant the trees in a frost-free location. The soil should be well drained, slightly acid, and humusy. Although trees planted in poor soil will produce nuts, they are much inferior to the nuts of trees planted in good soil. Give each tree a space 50 ft. in diameter.

Fertilize newly planted trees very lightly after they put out growth. In subsequent years, give the trees a 10-10-10 fertilizer in early spring at the rate of 2 cups per inch of trunk diameter. However, if you have planted grafted trees in a cold climate, it might be advisable to reduce this amount somewhat until you are reasonably certain the graft is not going to fail: too much fertilizer may cause excessively vigorous growth leading to winter injury which precipitates graft failure.

Chestnut weevils are the worst insect pests and can be controlled by spraying trees three or four times in August with Sevin. An easier control, however, is to rake up and burn all nuts you don't want and store the rest in polyethylene bags from which the larvae cannot escape. Chestnut diseases are more difficult to control, but you will probably escape trouble if you keep the garden clean.

Cut back the tops of newly planted trees about one-third. Then train the trees to a modified leader with four or five scaffold branches. Be sure that all branches have wide crotches, because chestnut wood is brittle and narrow crotches frequently split. Cut back high, outspreading branches that shade lower branches; or remove the lower branches entirely (they have a tendency to arch downward and hide from the sun).

Grafted chestnuts generally start to bear at four or five years of age, although some varieties start much earlier. Seedling trees start bearing a couple of years later. Nuts are borne on the current season's growth, and are usually larger in young trees than in old. But old trees bear more heavily.

Chestnuts are harvested when the burs in which they are enclosed open and the nuts fall to the ground. Occasionally, however, the burs fall without releasing the nuts; in which case, you must open them by hand. Pick up the nuts every day, because they deteriorate if left in the sun. They must then be cured for three to seven days—until they feel a little soft—in order to reduce their moisture content and increase their sugar content. This is done by placing them in a shady, airy place either in trays or in open containers.

Store nuts in ventilated plastic bags in the fresh-food compartment of your refrigerator. Large quantities of nuts can be mixed with barely damp peat, placed in light plastic bags and stored in a garage or basement at a temperature just above freezing (this storage method is preferred if chestnut weevils are known or thought to be present). They will keep for months.

COCONUTS

Beautiful evergreen palm trees to 100 ft. with clean, slender, leaning trunks, large crowns of fronds, and clusters of enormous nuts which are enjoyed for their white flesh and "milk." Nuts mature one by one more or less the year round.

Coconuts grow in Zone 10. In the United States they do best in Hawaii; less well in southern Florida. It is one of the best trees for planting along the seashore, since it is quite tolerant of salt spray and can put its roots down to tap the moisture in the soil. Self-fruitful.

Varieties

There are numerous varieties of coconuts, but it is difficult to buy any that are true to their name because all coconuts are grown from seed and varieties cross-pollinate freely. Your best bet is to grow your own from seed taken from any tree that is a reliable producer of large quantities of superior nuts.

Culture

To grow a coconut palm, allow a nut to mature on a tree. When the husk turns brown and starts to dry, cut down the nut and plant it in a partially shaded seedbed without removing the husk. The nut is laid horizontally with the eye end slightly higher and with the longest side of the husk on top. Cover all but the upper third of the husk with soil which has been forti-

Coconut palms thrive near the sea despite salt spray and driving winds. This is a fairly young tree on the island of Hawaii.

fied with humus. Keep moist. The nut will germinate in three months or more. Although it has three eyes, it will send up only a single sprout.

When the sprout is 6 to 12 in. high, transplant it with the nut still attached to its permanent place in the garden or to a 5-gal. can for further growing. In the garden, coconuts are often planted in groups of three spaced about 8 ft. apart, or single specimens may be planted in a space about 20 ft. across. Do not place them where the nuts falling from the trees will endanger people, automobiles, your terrace roof, etc.

Although coconuts grow wild in areas that have rather thin, sandy soil, your tree will do best if you dig a very large planting hole and fill it with sandy loam and a large amount of humus. Set the seedling tree in the center and cover the husk with a very thin layer of soil.

Keep the young plant well watered until it has made substantial growth. Thereafter, water regularly in dry spells. Coconuts can endure considerable drought, but to do well they need about 1 in. of water a week throughout the year.

Nitrogen and potash are the elements most important to coconut growth, but the usual practice is to apply a balanced fertilizer such as 10-10-10. Make the first application of about ½ cup several months after the tree is set in its permanent place, and make two or three more applications at the same rate at three-month intervals. In the next year, make four applications of 1 cup every three months. Increase to 2 cups per application the third year; 4 cups the fourth year; 8 cups the fifth year. Level off here —at a total of 30 to 32 cups per year. You may, however, reduce the number of applications to two or three.

Coconuts do not require pruning or thinning. Keep the soil in a circle around young trees free of vegetation to reduce competition for moisture and nutrients. An easy way to do this is to mulch the soil with several inches of pebbles. Old trees can also be mulched or you can allow lawn grass to grow up to their bases as long as you keep it mowed.

Pests are rarely a serious problem, although young trees may be attacked by scale insects. These are controlled with oil or malathion sprays.

Coconut palms start bearing at five to ten years of age. Nuts to be used for their "milk" are harvested when the husks are full size but still green. Those to be used for their flesh are allowed to mature until the husks turn brown and start to dry.

FILBERTS

Also called hazelnuts or hazels, filberts are deciduous shrubs to 30 ft. which produce small nuts in the fall. They grow best in Zones 8 and 9 in the Northwest, but do reasonably well in 6 and 7 pretty much throughout the country. Self-unfruitful; plant at least two varieties.

Varieties

Note. European varieties of filberts produce the largest crops and nuts. They are the type grown in the Northwest. American varieties are hardier, but produce such small crops and nuts that they are rarely worth growing. Crosses between the European and American filberts have most of the best features of the parents and appear to be the best varieties for colder climates.

Barcelona. European. Standard variety in the Northwest and by far the most widely planted in Oregon. Medium-large nuts. Vigorous, productive, spreading tree. Good pollinator for other varieties. Tends to bear well every other year.

Brixnut. European. Large nuts. Heavy producer, especially when young.

DuChilly. European. Large, long nuts. Medium production. Popular in Washington.

Daviana. European. Good, thin-shelled, medium-size nuts, but lightly produced. Excellent pollinator for Barcelona because it sheds pollen at a time when a large number of the latter's flowers are receptive.

Medium Long. One of the hardiest European varieties, it grows in Zone 6. Medium-size nuts of good flavor.

Nooksack. European. Widely grown in Washington. Except for Medium Long, hardier than other European varieties listed here.

Potomac. Hybrid. Large nuts of excellent flavor produced in abundance. Grows in Zone 6.

Reed. Hybrid. Medium-size, very tasty nuts. Zone 6.

Winkler. American. Low shrub but a prolific producer of good, small nuts. Very hardy.

Culture

Filberts are easily and most commonly propagated by tip-layering—bending a shoot downward and burying the tip in an upright position 6 to 8 in. deep.

Plant filberts in a spot protected from bitter winter winds. The plants do not have tap roots, but put down very deep roots, so they should have a deep, well-drained, fertile, humusy soil. In colder climates, where plants are small, they need a space only 10 to 12 ft. across. In the Northwest, however, they need 20 ft. and on exceptionally good soils, 25 ft.

Planting is done in the early winter in the Northwest; in early spring elsewhere. To protect the trunks against sun-scald and winter injury, paint with whitewash or wrap in kraft paper. This protection should be maintained for two or three years.

Because filberts are small, it is more practical to mulch them than larger nut trees. Use hay, leaves, or other organic material. The nutrients they contribute to the soil are important to maintenance of vigorous growth and good nut production. Further to promote growth, you should fertilize the plants with a balanced fertilizer such as 20-10-10. Apply ½ cup after the young plants are making growth; 1 cup the next year; and from then on increase the dosage by 1 cup a year until you reach 6. This is about the maximum for cold climates; but in milder areas, you can increase the supply 30 to 50 per cent.

In the Northwest, filberts are trained as vase-shaped trees with a single trunk. Cut them back at planting to a height of 24 to 30 in. and allow three to five scaffold branches to develop. Do not remove the short laterals that branch from the scaffolds even though there are a great many of them: some of them will bear an early crop of nuts and will then be shaded out or can be cut out. Immediate removal of such branches encourages development of water sprouts, which interfere with tree growth.

Suckers that proliferate around the base of filberts should be removed promptly while they are still soft. To do the job properly—so that suckering will be greatly discouraged in the later years—scrape the soil away from the tree roots and nip the suckers off at their point of origin.

Pruning of young bearing trees consists of cleaning out undesirable and unnecessary branches. But to maintain vigor of trees over ten years of age, you should head the trees back severely. If this is done every three years, the cuts are made in wood that was produced three years earlier. If the cut branches are more than 1½ in. across, the Oregon Agricultural Extension Service recommends that the wounds be allowed to dry for two weeks or more. They are then painted with a paste made by mixing powdered Bordeaux mixture into raw linseed oil. When pruning trees up to five years of age, sterilize your tools after working on each tree.

In colder climates, where filberts are often damaged by low temperatures, the plants are grown as shrubs with five or six large stems. Keep suckers cut out. Head back stems and laterals as necessary (but it is probable that the weather will do much of this work for you).

Good sanitary practices help to control weevils that sometimes lay eggs in nuts. They can also be killed with Sevin. Keep an eye out also for aphids. Spray in late summer with 6-3-100 Bordeaux mixture to control filbert blight.

Filberts start to bear two or three years after they are planted; reach good production three or four years later, but are likely to become erratic after ten years unless they are pruned severely.

Nuts are harvested from the ground after they drop. If the husks remain, these must be removed. The nuts should then be spread out in a warm, dry, shady place to dry.

HEARTNUTS

The heartnut is a variety of the Siebold walnut (Japanese walnut). It is a wide-spreading, ornamental tree to 50 ft. with luxuriant foliage and hanging strings of small, smooth, heart-shaped nuts in the fall. The kernels taste something like butternuts. Grow in Zones 5–8. Self-fruitful.

Varieties

Canoka. Large nuts of good flavor, easily cracked. Bears heavily.

Fodermaier. Large nuts which are well filled and easy to crack. Very productive.

Wright. Medium-size nuts of fine flavor. Prolific.

Culture

Grow like black walnuts.

HICKORY

The outstanding hickory nuts are pecans (which see). But good nuts rather similar to pecans are also borne by the shagbark and shellbark hickories. Both of these are huge (over 120 ft.), deciduous trees with very shaggy trunks. Nuts of the shagbark are smaller than those of the shellbark, but are much easier to crack.

Shagbark hickories grow in the eastern half of the country in Zones 4–8; shellbarks, in 5–8. Since the fruitfulness of the different varieties is not fully established, you should plant two varieties to assure production of nuts.

Varieties

There are a good many named varieties of shagbark and shellbark hickories, but their performance is so erratic that there is little consensus about which are the best. The safest way to select varieties, therefore, is to use those which originated in or near your area or which are especially recommended by local nurserymen who know nut trees. Some of the better shagbark varieties and their place of origin are: *Abscoda* (Michigan), *Davis* and *Fox* (New York), *Glover* (Connecticut), *Grainger* (Tennessee), *Harold* (Wisconsin), *Shinerling* and *Weschcke* (Iowa), and *Wilcox* (Ohio). Good shellbark varieties are: *Keystone* (Pennsylvania), *Ross* (Illinois), *Scholl* (Ohio), and *Stephens* (Kansas).

A number of hybrid hickory nuts are also available, but they are generally very shy bearers. The best are crosses between the pecan and shagbark or pecan and shellbark. They are called hicans. *Burton* is the best variety.

Culture

Grow like pecans.

Hickories are very difficult to transplant successfully because the long taproot is often cut too short and there are not enough side roots to make up for the loss. But if you deal with a nurseryman who specializes in nut trees, you should have no problem.

Hickories do not start bearing until they are about ten years old. They tend to bear every other year.

MACADAMIA

Evergreen trees to 60 ft. with holly-like leaves and small, round nuts with sweet, white kernels. Peak harvest is in summer and fall. Grows in Zone 10 at elevations up to 2,500 ft. and in areas with more than 45 in. of annual rainfall. Doubtfully self-fruitful; to assure good nut production, plant two varieties.

Varieties

Beaumont. Best variety in California. An attractive tree for landscaping. Large producer of fine nuts more or less the year round.

Ikaika. Hardy, productive, vigorous and more wind-resistant than other varieties. Also does better on relatively poor soils. But nuts are inferior to the following.

Keauhou. Excellent nuts a bit bigger than other varieties. Has best resistance to anthracnose; but tree is not quite so rugged or productive as the above.

Culture

Buy grafted trees only and be sure they have been root-pruned several months before transplanting. The trunks should be no more than ¾ in. in diameter. Macadamias can be grown from freshly fallen seeds, but are much less productive.

The trees must be planted in full sun in an area that has very good protection from strong winds. The soil should be reasonably fertile, deep, enriched with organic matter, and well drained. "Red soils" which are high in manganese should generally be avoided. In areas where macadamias grow well—in the Kona section of the island of Hawaii, for example—give each tree a space 35 ft. in diameter. Elsewhere 30 ft. is sufficient.

Plant the trees during the rainy season. Dig holes 2 ft. deep and about 1½ ft. across and mix a handful of 10-10-10 with the topsoil placed in the bottom. Set trees at the same depth they previously grew. Cut them back to a single stem 2 to 2½ ft. high, and remove all but eight of the leaves.

When the new trees begin to make growth in about two months, give them another handful of fertilizer and continue to feed them at this rate every two months until a year after planting. The Hawaii Agricultural Experiment Station suggests that trees should then be given 1½ cups of balanced fertilizer per year of tree age. This can be applied in two equal doses in early summer and early fall or in four or five equal doses about two months apart if you live in an area with heavy rainfall. Use a 10-10-10 mixture. In addition to this, the trees should be given ½ cup of ammonium sulfate per year of tree age just before their peak blossoming period. The

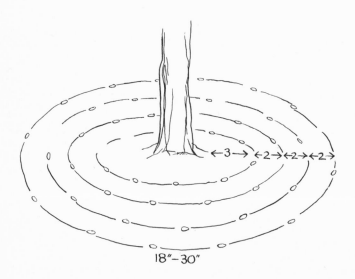

To feed a macadamia tree (and also a pecan growing in a lawn), make holes in the ground at 18- to 30-in. intervals in circles 2 ft. apart and distribute fertilizer evenly among them. The outer ring of holes should be about 2 ft. beyond the branch tips.

fertilizer is best placed in 18-in.-deep holes made with a crowbar at 2-ft. intervals under the canopy of the tree.

During the first two years, prune the trees to develop a single trunk with several sets of scaffold branches (left to its own devices, the macadamia tends to develop several leaders). To keep trees from becoming top-heavy, the lowest scaffolds should be 2 to 3 ft. above ground level. Successive groups of scaffolds should be spaced about 2 ft. higher.

Mature trees that have been well developed need only minimum pruning to remove broken, dead, and diseased wood. Also cut out branches that are getting in the way of stronger branches.

The three principal pests of the macadamia are anthracnose, nut borers, and rats. The first is controlled by planting resistant varieties. The second generally do not do enough damage to worry about. Rats are destroyed with Warfarin baits.

Macadamia trees start bearing four or five years after planting, but are relatively sparse producers until about the seventh year. Nuts fall from the tree when mature and are then picked up off the ground. Harvest them fairly often: if left on the ground too long they will start to rot, mold, or germinate. They may also be taken home by rodents.

The fleshy, green husks enclosing the nuts must be removed within three days to prevent fermentation. The nuts are then spread on wire racks in a shady place to dry for two to three weeks. After this they can be stored in sacks in a cool, dry, airy place for four months or longer.

PEANUTS

Peanuts are not nuts but annual vegetables related to peas. They are 18-in. plants which produce a dozen or more seed pods underground at the ends of stalks growing from the branches above ground. Nuts mature in the fall.

Peanuts grow in Zones 6–10, but do best in 7 and 8 in the Southeast, Texas, and Oklahoma. Self-fruitful. ¼ lb. plants 125 to 300 ft. of row, depending on variety. Plant seeds 1 in. deep. Germination: 18 days.

Varieties

Note. Peanuts grow in two ways. One is a runner type of plant which forms a somewhat sprawling vine. The other is a bunch type of plant, which is more compact, upright, and bushy.

Commercial growers also classify peanuts as runner types, Spanish types, Virginia types, and Valencia types; but if you start worrying about the differences between these, you will be hopelessly confused.

Argentine. Matures in 120 days. Bunch type. Very small nuts in almost straight shells. Productive.

Early Runner. 135 days. Runner type. Medium-large seeds in long, constricted shells. Commonest variety in the Southeast.

Florigiant. 140 days. Runner type. Very large seeds, averaging under

500 per pound (vs. 1,200 for Argentine). Pods are straight and cylindrical. High yielding.

NC-2. 140 days. Bunch type. Seeds almost as large as Florigiant. Thin shells tend to split.

Starr. 120 days. Bunch type. High-yielding plants with slightly larger nuts and thicker shells than Argentine.

Culture

If you are not particular about varieties, you can grow peanuts from the seed pods you buy at your favorite nut shop provided they have not been roasted. But whether you buy from this source or from a seed house, shell the seeds carefully and do not remove the thin skin covering them. Plant three or four seeds to the foot and later thin bunch varieties to 9 in., runner varieties to 12 in. Sow seeds after all danger of frost is past. Rows are 2 ft. wide.

The soil should be a well-drained, sandy loam containing some organic matter. Mix in 6 cups of 5-10-10 fertilizer per 100 sq. ft. No further feeding should be necessary.

Keep the new planting weeded as you do any other vegetable crop; then after the flower stalks bearing the nuts are "rooted" in the soil, apply an organic mulch. Water in dry weather.

The plants are not greatly bothered by pests although you may run into some problems with leafhoppers and corn borers.

To harvest the nuts, lift the entire plant with a fork when the foliage yellows and the soil is fairly dry. Shake reasonably free of dirt and spread the plants out in a warm, shady, airy place for two to three weeks. Then pick off nuts and roast them.

PECANS

Pecans—pronounced "pee-cons," with the accent on the second syllable—are a species of hickory growing to 120 ft. in the wild. The sweet, brown, oblong nuts are produced in the fall. Although the trees are hardy fairly far North, they require five to seven months of warm weather to mature their nuts. They grow best in Zone 8 from Georgia to New Mexico; but they also grow in Zones 5b, 6, 7, and 9.

Although pecans are self-fruitful, they are not reliably so because they often shed pollen at a time when the pistils are only partly receptive. Furthermore the nuts are of inferior quality. You should, therefore, plant two varieties—one that sheds its pollen early and the other that sheds its pollen late.

Varieties

Note. Pecans are divided into three groups: Eastern varieties are particularly adapted to the humid Southeast, although they do well farther west. They have above-average resistance to scab and other diseases. Western varieties grow from central Texas westward. They are well adapted to a fairly dry climate and alkaline soil, but they are very susceptible to scab and other diseases. Northern varieties mature their nuts in an unusually short time. They are tolerant of disease.

Apache. Western. Large, chunky nuts in big quantities. Midseason. Late pollen shedder.

Barton. Eastern. Long, thin-shelled nuts. Early. Tolerant of scab. Early pollen shedder.

Desirable. Eastern. Big, blocky, flavorful nuts. Midseason. Tree starts bearing fairly early and is prolific at maturity. Resistant to scab. Early pollen shedder.

Elliot. Eastern. Rather small, round nuts, easily shelled. Midseason. Moderately productive. Resistant to scab. Late pollen shedder.

Giles. Northern. Medium-large nuts with thin shells and tasty kernels. Midseason. Early pollen shedder.

Greenriver. Northern. Sizable nuts with plump, tasty kernels. Later than most northern varieties so cannot be grown too far north. Tolerant of scab. Late pollen shedder.

Mahan. Eastern. Extra-large nuts in midseason. Tree starts bearing at an early age. But a poor variety otherwise. Late pollen shedder.

Major. Standard northern variety. Medium-size nuts of excellent quality. Early. Good resistance to disease. Early pollen shedder.

Peruque. Northern. Medium-size, thin-shelled nuts. Early. Scab resistant. Early pollen shedder.

San Saba Improved. Western. Medium-size, high-quality, easy-to-shell nuts. Midseason. Late to· start bearing and tends to overbear with age. Early pollen shedder.

Schley. Eastern. Widely planted. Medium-size nuts of very good quality. Thin shells. Midseason. Shy bearer and late to start. Very susceptible to scab. Late pollen shedder.

Sioux. Western. Small nuts of excellent quality. Easily shelled. Late. Bears young and quite heavily. Late pollen shedder.

Stuart. Eastern. Most popular variety in the Southeast. Medium-large, fat nuts. Midseason. Tends to biennial bearing and late to start bearing. Tolerant of scab but susceptible to some other diseases. Late pollen shedder.

Success. Eastern. Big, delicious nuts but not always well filled. Midseason. Tree bears heavily and regularly. Susceptible to scab and other diseases. Early pollen shedder.

Culture

Buy 4- to 6-ft., one-year-old trees. Keep them moist until they are planted—which should not be delayed too long.

Pecans are very deep rooted, so they require a very deep soil. This should be a good loam, well drained and containing humus. Sandy and clay soils are much less desirable, although they can be improved to make the trees reasonably at home. Fumigate soils infested with nematodes. The planting holes must be at least 6 in. deeper than the tap roots and about 30 in. wide. Don't trim the roots unless damaged. Set the trees at the depth they previously grew or an inch deeper.

Give each tree a space 60 to 70 ft. in diameter.

At planting, cut the top of each tree back one-quarter to one-third, leaving a trunk 30 to 36 in. high. Wrap the trunk to within 6 to 8 in. of the top with burlap or kraft paper to protect it against sunscald. Don't remove this wrapping for two years. When the little tree starts making growth, select one of the upper branches as the extension of the trunk and train it upward by tying it to a stake. The first scaffold branch will be put out from this trunk extension at a height of 5 to 6 ft. Three or four additional scaffolds will also be put out from the trunk extension. Each should be 18 in. higher than the one before it and growing out from the trunk in a different direction. Branches developing below the first scaffold should not be removed for three or four years: they shade the trunk and provide the leaf area needed for vigorous growth.

If properly trained at the start, mature pecans need little pruning except to remove dead or damaged branches. Trees with very heavy canopies should also be thinned out in the top to let in the sun.

During their first summer pecans must be treated with solicitude to help them survive. Undoubtedly the most important thing you can do is to water them frequently so that moisture reaches down to the bottom of the tap root. Mulching with a thick layer of hay or other organic material is recommended.

In subsequent years, water as necessary to maintain an even supply of moisture around the roots from the time the trees start making growth in the spring until the nuts are harvested in the fall. A lack of moisture at any time during this period will adversely affect the growth and output of the trees not only in the current year but also in the year following.

Fertilize newly planted trees when they put out growth with ½ cup of 10-10-10. Apply an additional ½ cup six to eight weeks later, but not after July 30 in more northern areas. Thereafter the trees can usually be fertilized with ammonium sulfate (or other nitrogen fertilizer). Apply this in early spring at the rate of about 1½ cups per year of tree age. If trees are growing in an orchard where the ground is cultivated or mulched, the fertilizer should be broadcast over the entire root area. If trees are growing in a lawn or ornamental garden area, however, the heavy applications of fertilizer required for the mature trees would probably kill the grass and other small plants if it were broadcast. So you should place it in holes made with a crowbar at 2-ft. intervals throughout the root zone.

Pecans are attacked by numerous insects and diseases; but if you take time to rake up and burn fallen nuts, leaves, and twigs in the fall and again in very early spring, you should avoid most of these. To be completely safe, you may also want to spray small trees on a regular schedule. If your trees are susceptible to scab, use dodine (Cyprex) and malathion; other-

A Northern pecan tree four months after planting. The shoot growing straight up from the trunk will form the trunk extension; and eventually, when the scaffold branches develop from it, the lower branches seen here will be removed. But for the moment they are needed to nourish the tree.

Pecan tree at left has been pruned so that limbs are spaced about 15 in. apart and come off the trunk at wide angles. Tree at right has too many limbs growing from one point and the crotches are rather narrow, thus making a weaker tree. (Arizona Agricultural Extension Service)

wise, use zineb and malathion. Applications of dodine or zineb alone are made when buds are bursting and first leaves are showing, and when leaves are half grown. After that, add malathion and make applications when tips of young nuts start to turn brown, and at three- to four-week intervals thereafter.

One other common disease of pecans is a physiological disorder called rosette. This is characterized by yellowing of the leaves, thickening of the leaf veins, and a bunching up of small leaves at the ends of short, thin twigs. The cause is a zinc deficiency which can be corrected by applying 2 cups of zinc sulfate for each inch of trunk diameter. Broadcast this over the root area and work it in well. An annual application of about 6 cups will prevent further trouble.

The tendency of some pecan trees to bear nuts every other year can be prevented by giving them mother-hen care—plenty of moisture, a proper amount of fertilizer, and good insect and disease control. The same kind of care also helps to assure that the kernels will fill the shells (however, trees that tend to overbear are pretty much beyond help on this score).

Pecans start to bear about five years after planting, but you will not harvest very many nuts until they are ten. If trees are healthy and vigorous, production increases steadily after this. Texas, for example, has a 100-year-old native tree which produced half a ton of nuts in 1956.

Nuts are ready for harvesting when the husks lose their bright green color and open at the tips. The easiest system of harvesting is to leave the nuts on the tree until they cure and fall naturally. The alternative is to knock them from the tree with light bamboo poles. They should be allowed to dry thoroughly before they are placed in sacks.

If stored at a temperature of just under 40°, pecans can be held for two or three months. For longer storage, they should be held at 32°–34°.

If you buy a property with an old pecan tree that does not produce well, you can probably persuade it to mend its ways by pruning out the dead, damaged, and unnecessary limbs; clearing the ground underneath and applying a heavy dose of fertilizer; and watering well. If Spanish moss infests the tree, it should be removed by spraying with copper sulfate. Don't expect an immediate huge crop of nuts, however: you will probably have to continue this treatment for a couple of years.

PISTACHIO

Ornamental evergreen tree to 20 ft. with clusters of small, oblong, red nuts containing sweet, green kernels of unusual flavor. Nuts mature in late summer and early autumn. Grows in Zones 7b–9, but you can count on nuts only in certain parts of 9—notably the Sacramento and San Joaquin Valleys of California. The trees require long, hot, dry summers and somewhat cold winters. Self-unfruitful; you must plant both male and female specimens.

Varieties

Bronte. A good producer but not up to the following. Early. Very green kernels.

Kerman. Favorite commercial variety and good for the home garden. Delicious, large nuts in ample quantity. Kernels are yellowish. Late. Nuts often have cankers, which spoil them.

Peters. Best used as a pollinator, since its bloom period overlaps that of several good nut-bearing varieties. Trees produce a lot of pollen, but are not very vigorous growers.

Culture

Buy grafted trees. Plant in very deep, well-drained, sandy soil to which you have added lime to provide a pH of about 7.0. When planting, be very careful not to let the roots get dry. Give each tree a space 30 ft. in diameter.

Like some other trees, pistachios are very drought-resistant once they are established; but they should be watered well when young. Mature trees should also be watered deeply several times during the growing season.

Fertilize in early spring with nitrate of soda, ammonium nitrate, or other nitrogen fertilizer. Since pistachios are not widely grown in the United States, the amount required is not known. But it would not be unreasonable to follow the schedule for olives, which are somewhat similar in habit and fruiting and grow in the same region.

Prune trees to a modified leader. Since the main branches of young trees are usually very long, slender, and inclined to droop, they should be cut back slightly at the first sign of bending. Established trees need only light pruning. Nuts are borne on growth of the previous season.

The trees have very few pests.

Pistachios start to bear the fourth or fifth year after they are planted and reach top production in about the tenth year. Nuts are fully ripe when the hulls rub off easily. They should then be picked or knocked to the ground. Remove the hulls within a few hours and dry the nuts in the sun.

WALNUTS—BLACK

Magnificent deciduous trees to 150 ft. with rough nuts that are prized for their rich, oily, distinctively flavored kernels. These are harvested in the fall. All trees tend to bear biennially, but some varieties are worse than others.

Black walnuts grow in Zones 4–8, but do best in their natural range in the eastern half of the country. Self-fruitful, but not reliable because pollen may be shed before pistils are receptive. You should plant two varieties for best nut production.

Varieties

Note. The following are leading varieties which are available from many nurseries and which grow well in many areas. If you live in Zones 4 or 8, however, you will probably do better to buy whatever black walnut varieties a local nursery vouches for.

Myers. Fine nuts with unusually thin shells. Vigorous tree bears regularly and heavily.

Norris. Thin-shelled nuts with large kernels. Tree originated in Tennessee and is better adapted to warmer areas than other varieties listed.

Ohio. An old variety with very large kernels which crack out whole. Resistant to anthracnose, but husks are likely to be infested with maggots.

Thomas. More or less standard variety to which all others are compared. Widely planted, especially in the East. Large nuts of fine flavor and fairly easy to crack. Bears early but is especially inclined to biennial bearing. Very susceptible to anthracnose.

Culture

Like other nuts, black walnuts can be grown from seed but do not come true; so buy grafted varieties.

The trees have deep roots and require a deep soil that is above average in quality, well drained and moisture-retentive. Dig a big hole at least 2 ft. deep and mix in plenty of humus. Also mix in lime to provide a pH of 6.0 to 6.5. Plant the trees at the depth they previously grew. Each needs a space about 60 ft. in diameter, although in a plantation that is grown for timber as well as nuts, trees are often started out 20 ft. apart and gradually thinned.

Do not plant black walnuts near apple trees or the vegetable garden, because the roots contain a toxic substance that damages these plants. In a lawn area, the fallen nuts make mowing difficult.

Water trees regularly during their first year and in dry periods thereafter. Fertilize in the spring with a 10-10-10 mixture at the rate of 1 cup per year of tree age; however, trees that are making strong growth need to be fed only every second or third year. Maintaining a mulch of organic matter around the trees helps to nourish them.

Black walnuts need little pruning except to remove dead and damaged wood and suckers developing below the graft. You must keep an eye on them, however, to see that they develop only a single, straight trunk and main branches with wide crotches. If a tree is grown for timber or as an ornamental specimen in an open area, the lower limbs can be removed gradually as the tree shoots upward. Cut out these limbs before they exceed 1 in. in diameter.

Anthracnose, the most serious disease of black walnuts, is controlled by spraying with zineb when the leaves are about 12 in. long and three times after that at fortnightly intervals. Trees that develop a bushy, broom-like growth called bunch disease should be cut down and burned. Insect pests can be controlled as they appear with malathion or Sevin sprays.

Black walnuts start bearing five or six years after planting. Harvest the nuts as soon as they fall from the trees. At this point they have mild, light-colored kernels. If left on the ground so the husks can decompose, the kernels are dark-colored and more strongly flavored. Remove the husks with a hammer or by rolling them across a rough pavement under a heavy boot. Then wash the nuts and spread them out in a shady, ventilated place to dry for several weeks. They can then be stored in a cool, dry place.

To facilitate cracking of walnuts and other hard-shelled nuts, sprinkle them with water and put them in a tight can with a damp sponge for 12 hours or more. This softens the kernels slightly and allows you to remove them in larger pieces.

WALNUTS—CARPATHIAN

The Carpathian walnut is a Persian walnut similar to the English walnut grown in the Far West but considerably hardier. It grows in Zones 5–8, but does best in 6. Self-fruitful, but like other walnuts you get better nut crops if you plant two different varieties together.

Varieties

Broadview. Very heavy, annual producer of nuts which may be somewhat bitter. Has proved very hardy in New York.

Burtner. Starts growth rather late in the spring and is, therefore, more likely to escape frosts than some other varieties. Fine nuts and plenty of them every year.

Hansen. One of the best. Small, thin-shelled nuts with large kernels. Tree is small and bears regularly. Hardy, but growth starts rather early in the spring and may be killed by late freezes. Reliably self-fruitful.

Lake. Large nuts of very good flavor and excellent cracking quality. Prolific. Does well in the Middle West.

Somers. Medium-size nuts with meaty kernels. Very early. Has done well in central Michigan.

Culture

Carpathian walnuts are grown much like English walnuts. Plant on a north slope so the sun will be slow to force them into growth in the spring. Avoid frosty locations. The soil should be deep, fertile, and well drained.

Give each tree a space 50 ft. across. The Hansen variety, however, needs only 40 ft.

Fertilize with ammonium nitrate or a high-nitrogen balanced fertilizer such as 20-10-10. Minor elements may also be needed.

Prune to a modified leader.

Common insects include huskflies and curculios. Good sanitation practices in the garden help to discourage these to some extent. Application of malathion sprays at three-week intervals from July 1 to about the end of August gives further control.

Trees start to bear in four or five years. Harvest nuts when they drop.

WALNUTS—PERSIAN

Popularly known as English walnuts. Deciduous trees to 60 ft. with large, light brown nuts and delicious light brown kernels differing from black walnuts in that they are milder and less oily. Grow in Zones 8–10 on the Pacific Coast, but most widely grown in the San Joaquin and Sacramento Valleys of California where the summers are long, warm, and dry and the winters cool enough to satisfy the trees' need for chilling. Self-fruitful; however, pollen is not always shed at the time when the pistil is receptive, so for good production you should plant two varieties.

Varieties

Ashley. New variety with large, meaty, light-colored nuts. Early. Very heavy producer and is likely to overbear unless pruned regularly and severely. Susceptible to frost because of early leafing out.

Eureka. An old and still very good and popular variety in California. Large, high quality nuts.

Franquette. Moderate yields of nuts with excellent, light-colored kernels. Late. Tree leafs out very late and is less susceptible to frost damage than other varieties. Most widely planted.

Hartley. Second most popular variety in California but not too reliable farther north. Medium-large nuts of good flavor. Midseason. Consistent producer. Leafs out fairly late. Susceptible to a canker disease.

Payne. Excellent nuts very early in the fall. Bears early and heavily. Susceptible to spring frosts and other problems. Does best in California near the coast where summer temperatures are not high.

Placentia. Most widely planted variety in southern California, but an uneven producer of below-average nuts.

Spurgeon. Big, excellent nuts. Late. Tree resistant to cold injury. Variety was originated in Washington and is popular there and in Oregon.

Culture

Persian walnuts are grown from grafted trees with one-year-old tops and three-year-old roots. But unfortunately, a disease called blackline, which sometimes develops in the graft union between the scion and the stock, has been killing many trees. The problem is particularly acute in Oregon, and if you live there, you should make sure that the trees you buy are grafted on Manregian rootstocks. In California, where the disease generally has not reached alarming proportions, the favorite rootstocks are the northern California black walnut and the Paradox, although plants on these roots are affected by the disease.

Plant Persian walnuts in a place where they will escape late spring freezes and are not exposed to cold winter winds. The soil should be a well-drained, deep, humusy loam. Set trees 1 in. deeper than they previously grew. Tie them to sturdy stakes and keep them staked until the trunks are 5 in. across.

Give each tree a space 60 ft. in diameter.

Water young trees regularly. Mature trees should be irrigated deeply during the growing season. In California's interior valleys trees are watered enough to raise their total annual supply to as much as 60 in.

Mulching with organic material is highly recommended, at least while the trees are reasonably small.

Young trees need little fertilizer for three or four years if they are planted in good soil and mulched; but it does no harm to give them a handful or two of ammonium nitrate. From the fifth to the tenth year, however, give each tree 3 cups of ammonium nitrate in early spring. Then increase to 6 cups until the tree is 15 years old; to 12 cups until the tree is 22 years old; and finally to 18 cups.

In California the only other element that is commonly called for is zinc. This is supplied by driving glazier's points or large triangles of galvanized iron through the bark and into the sapwood about ¼ in. The wedges are installed 1 to 2 in. apart in spirals up the tree. In small trees use ten glazier points per inch of trunk circumference.

In Oregon and parts of California boron is, after nitrogen, the element most often in short supply. To correct this, apply agricultural-grade borax at one-third the rate recommended for ammonium nitrate.

Pruning consists of cutting newly planted trees back one-third to one-half and then training them to a modified leader with four or five scaffold branches. If these and other branches grow unusually long in any year before the trees start to bear, they should be headed back one-third to one-half to keep them from bending down to the ground under the weight of the nuts. Although regular pruning of mature trees was once considered unnecessary, it is now recommended—especially for the very fruitful new varieties. The main aim should be to keep the tops thinned out to allow light to penetrate and to encourage more vigorous branch growth.

To control walnut blight, which is a common disease, spray with Bordeaux mixture when the leaves start to appear and again after pollination. Additional applications may be required in wet weather. Spray with malathion or Sevin to control insect pests as they appear.

Persian walnuts start to bear in about five years. Harvest the nuts soon after they drop, remove the husks (if they remain around the nuts), wash the nuts, and spread them out to dry in a warm, shady place.

11

Growing a Few
Unclassified Food Plants

When I say these are unclassified plants, I mean only that they do not fit into any of the plant groups described in the preceding chapters.

This a small, varied and interesting non-group. Except for the sugar maple, the plants are not important food plants in this country. On the other hand, they are no less important than a few of the plants covered earlier. The chances are that if you raise them, you will do so as much for their ornamental or conversation value as for their food value. But I hardly think there is anything very wrong with that.

CAROB

Also called St. John's bread, the carob is a beautiful evergreen tree to 40 ft. producing foot-long, bean-filled pods in the fall. The pods, which are rich in sugar and protein, are usually used as livestock feed, but are also made into chocolate-flavored meal and syrup for human consumption.

The trees grow in Zones 8b–10, but require protection in the colder areas for the first two or three years.

Although there are some self-fruitful hermaphrodite carobs, it is generally best to plant male and female trees for certain fruit production. There are a number of varieties, but they are not easy to find. Take what you can get.

Culture

The sex of the carob cannot be determined until it starts to flower at several years of age; so when you buy trees, you take a chance. In any case, buy grafted plants which are growing in containers and which have not developed very deep tap roots.

Grow in a sunny spot away from the house (because the flowers of the male tree have an unpleasant odor). For full development, the trees need a space 30 ft. in diameter; but they may be planted much closer together to form a dense hedge. Stake young trees and enclose the trunks in wire mesh for a year or two in order to thwart rabbits. Gophers must also be eliminated, since they have a liking for young carob roots.

The soil need be of only average quality, but must be deep and well drained. During the growing season, irrigate the trees once or twice and mulch the soil around them to conserve moisture. Feed in the spring with a balanced fertilizer. Start with 1 cup for new plants and increase the amount every year till you reach about ten.

The trees are pruned only enough to remove broken and diseased branches and the suckers that may be thrown up from the ground. Seal all cuts with paint to protect trees against verticillium wilt. If wilt does attack a tree (the foliage looks scorched and branches die), cut back the branches to live wood.

Carobs start to bear at six years of age. The pods are ready to harvest when they turn dark brown and fall to the ground. Pods remaining on the tree are knocked down. Allow the pods to dry on the ground under the tree for several days before bagging them. They can be stored in a dry place almost indefinitely.

FIDDLEHEADS

Fiddleheads are the young shoots sent up in the spring by various deciduous ferns. They get their name from their resemblance to the handle of a violin. Two ferns that are especially prized for their fiddleheads— which are boiled and served as greens—are brakes *(Pteridium a quilinum)* and male ferns *(Dryopteris filix-mas)*. Both grow to about 3 ft. in Zones 4–7.

Culture

You may be able to buy the ferns named above, but it is just as easy to dig them up from the wild in early spring and transplant them to the garden. Very large clumps should be divided. Each mature plant takes up a space about 2 ft. in diameter, but the plants can be set closer together if you will divide them more frequently.

Brakes grow in sun or light shade in average soil containing some humus. Male ferns grow in light to moderate shade in very humusy soil. When planting, make sure the crowns are not covered. Keep watered until the ferns start making growth. Thereafter the plants need to be watered only in long dry spells. Do not fertilize or cultivate deeply; but keep weeds pulled out. Leave the fronds that die down in the fall around the plants as a mulch.

Ferns are bothered by few pests; but if they are growing in an area through which dogs and children travel, they should be protected with a low wire fence, because they are easily broken. Do not get alarmed about the small specks that develop in definite patterns on the undersides of the fronds: They are the spore cases.

Don't collect fiddleheads the first year after planting ferns. From then on you can collect about a third to a half of those put up by each plant. Cut off the shoots when they are 4 to 6 in. tall, before they start to unfold.

ROSES

Many of the species roses produce berry-like, red fruits—called hips —which are made into tasty jam or soup with a very high Vitamin C content. Probably the best of these is *Rosa rugosa* and its hybrids. The plants are very prickly, dense, erect, and reach a height of about 6 ft. The flowers are single and delightfully fragrant. The hips—about 1 in. across —ripen in late summer. Plants are self-fruitful. They grow in Zones 4–7, but do especially well in the Northeast near the sea.

Rose petals are also made into jam and syrup and are candied. For these you can use any rose species or variety with a rich fragrance. Products made from petals, however, are inferior to those made from hips.

Culture

If you cannot find plants to buy, you can propagate your own from greenwood stem cuttings taken in late spring and summer. Plant the cuttings in the garden in the fall when they have a good root system. It is generally better, however, to plant roses in the spring.

They require full sun and excellent drainage. The soil can be of average quality, but it is a very good idea to mix in a couple of spadefuls of humus and 1 cup of balanced fertilizer. Keep plants watered well for a couple of weeks. Thereafter they need almost no attention, but it helps to water them deeply in long dry spells and to apply 1 cup of fertilizer every spring. Keep dead and broken canes cut out.

Plants spaced 3 ft. apart will form a tough hedge.

Harvest the rose hips as soon as they are fully grown, firm, and red. Cut off the ends before using. For jam, you should also remove the seeds.

SUGAR MAPLE

The sugar maple is the principal source of maple syrup and maple sugar. It is a handsome, 110-ft., deciduous tree growing mainly east of the Mississippi in Zones 3–7; however, it does best in the Northeast. Secondary sources of syrup are the black, silver, and red maples.

Culture

Buy trees or dig them from the wild in the spring. Plant in the sun in average soil that is well drained. Give each tree a space at least 40 ft. across. Keep them watered until they are established, and fertilize annually for the first three years with 2 or 3 cups of balanced fertilizer.

Established trees need little care, although you should water them occasionally in times of drought. Trees that are not doing as well as they might can be fed every two or three years with about 20 cups of fertilizer. Cut out dead and broken branches in the winter before the sap runs.

You can start tapping maples when the trunks attain a diameter of 8 inches. Thereafter you can tap a tree every year without hurting it.

Easy way to tap a sugar maple.

The tapping is done in late winter when the sap begins to run. In Vermont, this is about March 1; further south you can start a bit earlier. If you want to go into the syrup-making business in a big way, you can buy special equipment for tapping, collecting, and boiling down the sap. Otherwise, to tap a tree, all you have to do is drill a slightly slanting hole about 1½ in. deep in a sunny side of the trunk at a height of about 3½ ft.; then drive in a short length of tight-fitting pipe which is cut open at the tree end to form a trough to catch the sap. I use rigid ½-in. copper tube in 8-in. lengths. The trough is about 1½ in. long and two-thirds of the pipe diameter. A notch is cut in the other end of the pipe and a bucket hung from it. A lightweight, 5-qt. paint pail is about the right size except for very large trees. Ideally the pail should be covered to keep out debris, rain, insects, and sometimes mice. But a cover is a nuisance to keep in place, and since the sap is later boiled and strained, it is not essential. You can also tie a large, plastic freezer bag to the pipe to catch the sap; but it's a nuisance, too.

Maple sap runs most freely on warm days following nights when the temperature drops below freezing. The amount of sap given off varies between trees and also from day to day. On good days, my trees—with a trunk diameter of 15 to 18 in.—average about 2 qts. in 24 hours. But several of them have at times produced over 5 qts. Huge trees may have several taps and will, of course, produce even more sap.

The sap may run for as long as a month, but don't count on it. At the beginning of the run it looks like water; at the end it is quite viscous. If you weary of collecting the sap, you can let it drip on the ground or you can shut it off with a cork. In any event, remove the pipe or cork from the trunk when the sap finally stops running. The hole in the tree need not be treated.

The process of boiling down the sap produces a great deal of steam, so the job should be done outdoors. One quart of sap yields only about one ounce of thin syrup and an even smaller amount of sugar. Sealed in sterilized bottles, the syrup will keep at normal house temperatures for a good many months.

SUNFLOWERS

Sunflowers grown for their seeds, which are eaten like nuts or fed to the birds, are giant annuals to 10 ft. with yellow and brown flowers 1 to 2 ft. across. Zones 3–10. 1 packet produces 30 plants. Sow seeds ½ in. deep. Germination: 10 days. Seeds mature in 90 days.

Varieties

Plant any giant variety; but the biggest of all are mammoth Russian varieties such as Peredovik and Armavirec.

Culture

Sow seeds where they are to grow after danger of frost is past or start them earlier under glass. Since wide-spaced plants have larger flowers, sow the seeds in rows 2 to 3 ft. apart, and thin the plants to stand at least 18 in. apart. Sidedress with a balanced fertilizer such as 10-10-10 when the plants are well up, and give them a second dose six weeks later. Although sunflowers are remarkably drought-resistant, they will do better if watered in dry spells. When the plants are up a foot or two, provide each one with a tall, sturdy stake; otherwise they will droop badly, look sad and perhaps buckle after storms.

Seeds develop from the center of the flower outward. As they mature, keep your eye out for hungry birds: you may have to cover the flowers with a light netting. When seeds begin to dry and fall from the heads, cut the heads and dry them face up in the sun.

VIOLETS

Perennials to 1 ft. The flowers and leaves appearing in the spring are unusually rich in Vitamin C; and the leaves also have an extraordinarily high Vitamin A content. The flowers are used to make jam, jelly, syrup, and they are sometimes candied. The leaves can be used as cooked greens. Violets grow in Zones 3–8, depending on the species.

Varieties

Any of the species violets which grow wild can be used for food, but the best are those with the richest fragrance. The common blue violet is especially good.

Culture

Dig up plants from the wild in the early spring or after the tops die down in the summer. Divide the roots and plant just beneath the soil surface in light shade (however, violets that grow naturally in open fields demand full sun). Give each plant a space about 8 in. across. The soil should be well drained; and for best results, you should mix in a quantity of humus.

Water in dry weather. The plants generally need little fertilizer, but a light sprinkling in the spring stimulates growth and flowering. If plants are attacked by insects or diseases, spray with an all-purpose insecticide-fungicide; but don't use flowers or leaves after that.

Harvest the flowers when they open. Just pull off the heads: the stems are not used. The leaves are best for eating when young.

Index

Index